THE LOS ANGELES TIMES
CALIFORNIA
COOKBOOK

THE LOS ANGELES TIMES
CALIFORNIA
COOKBOOK

Compiled and Edited by Betsy Balsley, *Food Editor*

and the Food Staff of the Los Angeles Times

Rose Dosti, Barbara Hansen, Daniel P. Puzo, *Staff Writers*

Minnie Bernardino, *Test Kitchen Director,* Marge Powers, *Copy Editor*

Nancy Brashear, *Editorial Aide,* Helen Stefanac, *Recipe Tester*

HARRY N. ABRAMS, INC., PUBLISHERS, NEW YORK

Editor: Darlene Geis
Designer: Linda Schifano

Library of Congress Cataloging in Publication Data
Main entry under title:

The Los Angeles Times California Cookbook.

  Includes index.
  1. Cookery, American—California. I. Title:
California cookbook.
TX715.L867   641.5   81-1322
ISBN 0-8109-1277-5   AACR2

Illustrations © Harry N. Abrams, Inc.

CONTENTS

INTRODUCTION

THIS first official *Los Angeles Times* cookbook is not a textbook on cooking but a record of how people in the West like to cook. It is the first volume of recipes compiled by the food staff of *The Times*. But in actuality, the staff all but publishes a widely disseminated cookbook each week in the form of one of the largest newspaper food sections in the United States. Food articles from *The Times* appear not only in Los Angeles but in newspapers elsewhere in this country and abroad that subscribe to the Los Angeles Times–Washington Post News Service.

In Los Angeles, cooking is a serious pursuit and recipes must be accurate, detailed, and, above all, delicious. Food writers gather recipes not only from Los Angeles but from all over the world to please the wide-ranging tastes of *Times* readers. Home economists keep *The Times*'s large test kitchen busy throughout the week testing recipes—discarding some, altering and improving others—developing new dishes, and preparing food for photography.

The Times Food Section offers food ideas as varied as the demographic makeup of the city. Mexican, Chinese, Japanese, Middle Eastern, and other ethnic recipes, regional American dishes, vegetarian favorites, elaborate French presentations, homemade Italian pastas, as well as simple casseroles based on convenience foods illustrate the rich diversity of California tastes.

Recipe sources are many. Contributors include chefs, celebrities, members of the food and beverage industry, local and visiting cooking authorities, winery and agricultural representatives, readers, cooking teachers, and church and social groups.

Weekly columns reflect readers' broad interests: restaurant specialties appear in the reader-request column called "Culinary SOS"; Mexican dishes are featured in "Border Line," an exploration of authentic Mexican cuisine and California-style variations. Ingredients and cooking procedures are discussed in "You Asked About . . ." while still another column reviews wines. And readers submit their favorite dishes to the "My Best Recipe" column, which has produced many of *The Times*'s most memorable offerings.

The Times Food Section has expanded from a few pages to the large section that now averages well over 40 pages, usually in two parts, that is published today. In addition to recipes, the Food Section presents the latest developments in nutrition, food technology, and consumer issues, educating its readers to shop and cook more wisely.

Choosing the recipes for this book from the thousands that have been printed was a challenge. It was easy to select the best, the most popular, and typical dishes, but even in a 408-page book it was impossible to include them all. The final selection testifies to the fact that California is an exciting place in which to cook. Its wide range of ingredients, fine fresh produce, superb wines, and an innovative approach contribute to a lively cuisine.

This recipe collection makes it possible to cook California-style in any part of the country.

How to Use Our Recipes

THE success of our recipes lies in using the correct key ingredients in the proper amounts and package sizes. Unless alternate choices are given, do not substitute ingredients. In some cases, such as seasonings, herbs and spices may be altered to taste as indicated.

- Most recipes describe preparation of ingredients in the ingredient list or directions. Do as much advance preparation of all ingredients as well as of cooking utensils (greasing, lining with wax paper, etc.) as possible before assembling the dish.

- When blending, mixing, cutting, or grinding, use your judgment in substituting available home equipment (following manufacturer's directions) for the tool specified in the recipe. For example, you may wish to use a food processor or electric mixer with a dough hook instead of kneading dough by hand.

- All measures are standard and should be level.

- Baking or cooking temperatures are expressed in Fahrenheit.

- *The Times* has a specific style for the wording of recipe ingredients. For example, 1 cup rice, cooked is different from 1 cup cooked rice: the first will yield more than the second measure as rice triples in volume when cooked.

Special Preparation Techniques

To CARAMELIZE SUGAR—place sugar in skillet over low heat, stirring occasionally, until it melts and turns golden brown.

To CREAM BUTTER, shortening, etc.—beat with spoon or electric mixer at medium speed until mixture is soft and smooth.

To CHOP—use knife with quick cutting strokes to cut into small free-form pieces.

To CUBE—cut into squares 1/2 to 1 inch on all sides.

To DICE—cut into 1/4-inch cubes.

To MINCE—cut or chop pieces very finely, about 1/8 inch across or finer.

To SLICE DIAGONALLY—cut food at an angle into thin or thick slices.

To CUT IN (pastry making)—using two knives, scissors-fashion, or a pastry blender, mix solid fat into flour mixture until crumbly or mealy.

To FOLD IN (whipping cream, beaten egg whites)—slowly blend one mixture into another using a circular motion: with rubber spatula or large metal spoon, cut down into one mixture, bring some of the mixture up and over the other mixture on the surface, repeating this process until blended.

To GREASE—brush or rub shortening on surface of pan as indicated in recipe.

To MELT CHOCOLATE—place chocolate in top of double boiler or in custard cup. Melt over hot or gently simmering, not boiling, water. Or use the microwave oven, following manufacturer's directions.

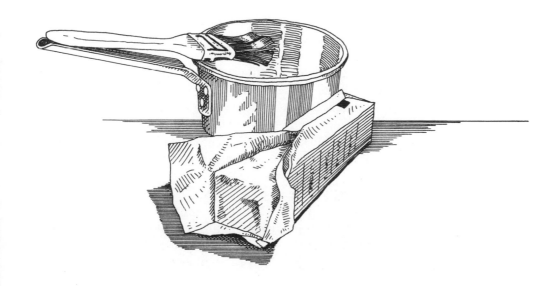

Guide to Ingredients

Almonds, blanched—peeled, boiled almonds. To prepare, cover shelled, unskinned almonds with cold water in saucepan. Bring to boil, then drain. Cool in cold water, then press each almond between fingers to remove skin.

Baking powder—refers to double-acting baking powder.

Bread crumbs, fine dry—available packaged, plain or seasoned. To prepare at home, dry white bread slice in 250-degree oven until crisp but not browned, then break up and crush in blender container or with rolling pin. One ($5/8$-inch-thick) slice of untrimmed white bread makes $1/3$ cup crumbs.

Bread crumbs, soft—coarse to fine crumbs made from day-old white bread slices. To prepare, crumble bread in blender container or between fingers. One ($5/8$-inch-thick) slice of untrimmed white bread makes 1 cup crumbs.

Bulgur—also known as cracked wheat, popular throughout the eastern Mediterranean and the Middle East.

Butter or margarine—when unspecified, refers to salted butter or margarine. Do not use the whipped or soft types, or diet or imitation margarine. Many wrappers have a printed measuring guide; if not available, bring the fat to room temperature and press firmly into a cup or spoon measure, leveling off with spatula.

Chicken—when size is unspecified, refers to medium fryers, $2^1/2$ to $3^1/2$ pounds.

Chiles, green—available canned in diced or whole form; also available fresh in some parts of the country.

Chiles, crushed dried—flake form with seeds; spicy hot.

Chinese chile oil—a Chinese ingredient made with oil that is cooked with dried hot red chiles. Available packaged or may be made at home.

Chocolate—

    unsweetened—bitter chocolate that comes packaged as bars or squares; 8 (1-ounce) squares to a package.

    semisweet—comes in bars or packages of squares.

    semisweet pieces—also known as chocolate chips.

    sweet cooking—a combination of chocolate, sugar, and cocoa butter; comes in bars.

    milk—eating chocolate, made with sugar, milk, and vanilla.

    cocoa—powdered form of chocolate with part of the cocoa butter removed. Do not use instant cocoa, which is a mixture of cocoa, sugar, milk solids, flavorings, and some emulsifiers.

Coconut—1 pound packaged coconut equals 5 to 6 cups flake or shredded.

    flake—flatter and more moist than the shredded type. Available in cans or bags.

    shredded—dry sweetened type. Available in bags.

Coconut milk—to prepare, grate chunks of fresh coconut meat in blender container or food processor bowl with 1 cup of fresh coconut water. Squeeze through a damp cheesecloth to obtain rich coconut milk. For a less rich coconut milk, add 1 to 3 cups boiling water to grated fresh coconut and let stand 1 hour. Press through cheesecloth.

Coconut cream—prepare as above, allow coconut milk to stand until cream rises to top, then spoon off cream carefully.

Eggs—use large eggs for the recipes; if you have smaller or jumbo eggs, measure. One large egg equals 1/4 cup.

Five-spice powder—reddish-brown spice combination of star anise, anise pepper, fennel, cloves, and cinnamon.

Flour—when unspecified, refers to all-purpose flour, unsifted.
    sifted flour—sift all-purpose flour before measuring; do not pack flour down or shake cup.

Green onions—also known as scallions.

Herbs—preferably fresh. When substituting dried herbs for fresh, use 1/3 to 1/2 of the fresh amount called for.

Hoisin sauce—a sweetish thick sauce made of soybeans and Chinese seasonings. Available canned or bottled.

Jicama—large white fleshy root vegetable from a Mexican or tropical vine. Crisp juicy flesh may be eaten raw or cooked.

Lychee fruit—the canned variety of this oval-shaped fruit with a milky white pulp is peeled, pitted, and preserved in light syrup.

Mai fun—rice sticks. Thin brittle noodles made from rice flour. When deep-fried (as for Chinese chicken salad) they become puffy, white, and crisp.

Milk—when unspecified, refers to homogenized pasteurized whole milk.
    skim—liquid form, with less than 0.5 percent milk fat.
    instant nonfat powder—refers to the nonfat powdered form, not the dry whole milk available in health-food stores.
    evaporated—always use undiluted in the recipes unless otherwise specified.

Mirin—Japanese sweet rice wine used for cooking.

MSG—monosodium glutamate; usage is optional. Tasteless in itself, it is used to enhance other foods.

Oil—any oil of vegetable origin (unless specified as olive oil or sesame oil, which have distinctive flavors).

Pastry shell—pie crust made from standard pastry recipes using flour, salt, shortening, and water.

Phyllo—also known as filo. Very thin sheets of dough used in pastries and savory dishes in Middle Eastern cookery.

Pie shell—when unspecified, refers to any kind of crust, usually pastry crust, but cracker, chocolate, or nut crust may be used.

Plum sauce—a chutney-like sauce made from plums, apricots, vinegar, chile, and sugar, used as a condiment with roast duck and other meats and also in cooking. Available bottled or canned.

Raisins—refers to dark seedless type unless golden is specified.

Red pepper—also known as cayenne.

Rice—use regular long-grain rice unless specified as converted, medium grain, short grain, brown, wild, glutinous, or instant precooked.

Sai fun—bean threads or cellophane noodles. Hard, fine noodles made from mung beans.

Salt—plain iodized salt.

Shortening—hydrogenated solid fat made from vegetable oils or a combination of vegetable and animal oils. Do not substitute butter or oil. Sold in 1- or 3-pound cans.

Soda—baking soda. Mixtures containing soda should be baked as soon as mixed, as the soda starts reacting once combined with any liquid.

Star anise—dried brown seed cluster shaped like a star, with licorice-like or anise flavor. May be used ground or tied in cheesecloth bag.

Sugar—when unspecified, refers to granulated white sugar.

   brown—refers to light brown sugar (dark brown contains more molasses). Always pack down to measure.

   powdered—same as confectioners'. If recipe does not call for it to be sifted, first measure without sifting, then sift if desired, particularly if lumpy.

Tahini—sesame seed paste, available in Middle Eastern groceries.

Tofu—soybean curd, packed in water. Bland, custard-like, white precooked cakes that are made from pureed soybeans.

Vinegar—when unspecified, cider or white may be used for general cooking. Distilled white vinegar is usually preferred for pickling or canning as it is clear and colorless.

APPETIZERS

PPETIZERS rise and wane in popularity in California even more speedily than do trends in fashions. Some, such as the heaps of crisp raw vegetables served with an infinite variety of dips, made it to the top during the peak of the health-food movement. Unlike other snacks, they have remained favorites as nibble foods probably because of their low calories, fresh taste, and colorful visual appeal. Jicama has joined other fresh vegetables as a dipper in recent years, as have zucchini and daikon, or Japanese white radish. Dips are served frequently because they are easy to handle and lend themselves to tasty innovations using curry, refried beans, cheese, wines, mustard, and even peanut butter.

Many Southern California appetizer favorites reflect the international character that is typical of California cooking. A single cocktail buffet may feature an array of hors d'oeuvres inspired by the cuisines of Mexico, Italy, China, Japan, France, Scandinavia, and Indonesia. Mexican-style appetizers probably take first place in popularity as there is little doubt that our near neighbor has exerted a heavy influence on Southern California cuisine.

Some appetizers, such as pumpernickel toast, Chinese shrimp toast, ceviche, chile con queso, guacamole, and teriyaki shrimp or beef, are classics and go on forever. Still other appetizers, such as spiced nuts and crocked cheeses, seem to be holiday favorites, possibly because they are easy to make and are wonderful kitchen gifts.

Guacamole, page 16

Guacamole

Guacamole can be used as a topping for tostadas and other Mexican dishes as well as for a dip.

2 medium avocados, peeled and seeded
2 medium tomatoes, peeled and coarsely chopped
1/4 cup chopped onion

2 tablespoons lemon juice
1/4 cup chopped green chiles
Salt, pepper

MASH avocados with a fork. Add tomatoes, onion, and lemon juice and blend well. Add green chiles and season to taste with salt and pepper. Serve at once with crackers and chips.

Makes about 3 cups.

California Guacamole Dip

The addition of mayonnaise makes this version of guacamole typically Californian.

1 avocado, peeled and seeded
1 tablespoon lemon juice
2 tablespoons chopped canned green chiles
1/2 cup chopped tomato

2 tablespoons mayonnaise
1 teaspoon salt
1/8 teaspoon garlic powder
4 drops hot pepper sauce

PUREE avocado with lemon juice in blender container. In small bowl combine avocado mixture, green chiles, tomato, mayonnaise, salt, garlic powder, and hot pepper sauce. Cover and chill 1 hour. Serve with chilled artichokes.

Makes about 1 1/2 cups.

Refried Bean Dip

The addition of a liberal amount of taco sauce turns refried beans into a lively dip.

1 (29-ounce) can refried beans
1 (4-ounce) can chopped ripe olives
1/2 cup minced onion

1/4 cup bottled taco sauce
1 teaspoon garlic salt
1 1/4 cups shredded cheddar cheese
Tortilla chips

COMBINE refried beans, olives, onion, taco sauce, garlic salt, and 1 cup cheese. Spoon into 1-quart baking dish and sprinkle with remaining 1/4 cup cheese. Bake at 350 degrees 30 minutes. Serve with tortilla chips.

Makes 3 cups.

Deluxe Nachos

1 dozen corn tortillas
   Lard for deep frying
   Salt
1 cup shredded Monterey Jack
   cheese
1 cup shredded cheddar
   cheese

2 or 3 jalapeño chiles, finely
   chopped
   Refried Beans
1 cup finely diced toma-
   toes
1 cup finely chopped
   cilantro

Nachos are basically corn chips topped with cheese and a chile slice. This version from the Red Onion chain of restaurants is much more elaborate than most and quite good.

CUT tortillas in quarters and fry in deep hot lard until crisp. Drain and season lightly with salt. Arrange tortillas in single layer on large ovenproof platter. Sprinkle half the Jack and cheddar cheeses over tortilla chips. Sprinkle chiles over cheeses. Top with dollops of Refried Beans and gently spread over mixture. (Reserve any extra beans for another use.) Sprinkle with half the remaining cheeses. Top with tomatoes and cilantro, then with remaining cheeses. Bake at 375 degrees until cheese is melted and bubbly, about 15 minutes. Serve at once.

Makes 48.

Refried Beans

2 cups dry pinto beans
1 large onion
1 ham hock

Water
1/2 cup lard
Salt

Place beans, whole onion, and ham hock in saucepan. Add enough water to cover. Bring to boil, cover, and simmer about 1¹/₂ hours, or until beans are tender. Remove onion and ham hock. Drain beans. Heat lard until very hot. Add to beans and mash with potato masher. Season to taste with salt.

Spicy Tuna Dip

1 (13-ounce) can tuna
1 (6.5-ounce) jar or can jalapeño chiles, chopped

1 onion, minced
1/2 cup mayonnaise
   Chopped cilantro

This dip from Carlos 'n Charlie's, a popular Mexican restaurant on Sunset Boulevard, combines jalapeño chiles and tuna.

MIX tuna with chopped jalapeño chiles and jalapeño liquid. Add onion to tuna mixture. Stir in mayonnaise until consistency is mushy. Sprinkle cilantro on top and serve with tortilla chips, if desired.

Makes 1¹/₂ cups.

Empanadas

The spiced meat mixture called picadillo fills these pastry turnovers, which are a Latin American specialty.

3 onions, minced
2 tablespoons shortening
1 pound ground beef or leftover chopped beef or lamb roast
1/2 cup bouillon
1 cup raisins
1 teaspoon cumin seeds, crushed
1 teaspoon crushed oregano
20 pitted green olives, chopped
Salt, red pepper
2 hard-cooked eggs, chopped
Pastry for 2-crust 9-inch pie

COOK onions in shortening until tender but not browned. Add beef and brown lightly, stirring to break into small pieces. Add bouillon, raisins, cumin seeds, oregano, and olives. Simmer 30 minutes. Season to taste with salt and red pepper. Remove from heat and stir in eggs. Cool. Roll pastry on floured surface to about 1/4-inch thickness. Cut into 2-inch rounds. Place 1 tablespoon filling on each, fold over, and seal edges. Pierce tops with fork. Bake at 375 degrees 15 minutes, or until browned. Serve hot or cold.

Makes about 3 1/2 dozen.

Soft Cheese Dip

Many Southern California restaurants serve dips to go with cocktails. This spicy cheese dip is a favorite at Jungry José's in Long Beach.

1/4 cup butter or margarine, softened
1/2 pound mild cheddar cheese, shredded
2 tablespoons minced parsley
1 1/2 tablespoons minced jalapeño chile
1/2 teaspoon hot pepper sauce
1 tablespoon Worcestershire sauce

CREAM butter until light and fluffy. Add cheese, parsley, jalapeño, chile, hot pepper sauce, and Worcestershire and beat until smooth.

Makes 1 1/2 cups.

Malibu Chile con Queso

1 pound sharp cheddar
  cheese or pasteurized
  process cheese
1 (7-ounce) can green chile
  salsa
1 (7-ounce) can diced green
  chiles
1/3 cup chopped red onion
1 green pepper, finely diced

1 tablespoon garlic powder
  or to taste
  Garlic salt
1/2 teaspoon oregano
1/4 teaspoon paprika
1 teaspoon chili powder
  (optional)
  Fried corn tortilla wedges
  or chips

Zesty Mexican seasonings give lots of flavor to this hot cheese dip.

CUT cheddar cheese in small chunks (or process cheese in large chunks) and place in top of double boiler. Cook over hot water, stirring, until cheese is half melted. Add chile salsa, green chiles, onion, green pepper, garlic powder, garlic salt, oregano, paprika, and chili powder. Cook slowly, stirring constantly, until cheese is completely melted and mixture is well blended. Serve at once, keeping mixture hot in a chafing dish or other warming device. Mixture will be quite runny. Let cool slightly if a thicker dip is desired. Serve with fried tortilla wedges as dippers.

Makes 4 to 5 cups.

Ceviche

1 cup scallops, cut in halves
1 cup halibut, cut in 1/4-inch
  cubes
  Lime juice
1 cup chopped peeled tomato
1/4 cup chopped green onions
1/4 cup olive oil
1 tablespoon dry white wine
1 tablespoon wine vinegar
1 tablespoon chili sauce

1 cup tomato juice
  (optional)
1/4 teaspoon oregano
8 pitted green olives
  Salt, pepper
1/2 cup cooked small shrimp
  (optional)
1 1/2 tablespoons minced
  parsley

Marinating seafood in lime juice is a novel method of "cooking" familiar to anyone who visits the beach resorts of Mexico.

PLACE scallops and halibut in shallow porcelain or glass dish. Add 1 cup of lime juice. If juice does not cover fish add more. Cover and let stand at room temperature for 3 hours. Mix tomato, green onions, oil, wine, vinegar, chili sauce, tomato juice, oregano, and olives. Season to taste with salt and pepper. Drain fish and rinse in water, then drain well. Add fish to sauce along with shrimp. Chill. Serve in individual glass bowls topped with a sprinkling of parsley.

Makes 8 to 10 servings.

Fried Won Tons

1/2 pound ground pork,
  chicken, or beef
1/2 pound shrimp, shelled,
  deveined, and minced
1/2 cup minced mushrooms
1/2 cup diced water chestnuts
2 green onions, finely
  chopped

3 egg yolks
2 tablespoons soy sauce
3/4 pound won ton wrappers
  Oil for deep frying
  Won Ton Sauce

MIX pork, shrimp, mushrooms, water chestnuts, green onions, egg yolks, and soy sauce in skillet. Cook, stirring often, until meat and egg yolks are cooked. Cool. Place about 1 tablespoon of meat mixture in each wrapper. Fold squares in halves diagonally and press edges together with a fork. Fry triangles in deep oil heated to 375 degrees until golden. Serve with Won Ton Sauce.

Makes 50.

Won Ton Sauce

1/4 cup cornstarch
1/3 cup brown sugar, packed
1/2 cup soy sauce

1 1/2 cups water
2 cloves garlic, sliced
2 tablespoons oil

Mix cornstarch, brown sugar, soy sauce, and water until smooth. Fry garlic in hot oil until lightly browned. Skim out garlic and set aside. Slowly pour cornstarch mixture into hot oil and cook, stirring, until thickened. Top with fried garlic.

Oriental Meatballs

2 eggs
1 tablespoon soy sauce
1 tablespoon sugar
1 pound lean pork, ground
2/3 cup minced green onions

1/3 cup minced Chinese
  cabbage
1 teaspoon salt
1/4 cup flour
  Oil

BEAT eggs lightly. Add soy sauce and sugar and mix well. Add pork, green onions, and cabbage and mix thoroughly. Add salt and flour. Blend well. Form into 1-inch balls. Fry in very hot oil that is at least 1-inch deep. Drain on paper towels. Serve on wood picks. Meatballs may be prepared in advance and refrigerated or frozen. Reheat just before serving.

Makes about 5 dozen.

Oriental Spareribs

2 cups water
$^1/_2$ cup soy sauce
1 clove garlic, minced
3 pounds spareribs, cut in
    2-inch pieces
2 tablespoons brown sugar

1 tablespoon cornstarch
1 tablespoon sesame seeds
2 tablespoons chopped green
    onion
$^1/_4$ teaspoon ginger

COMBINE water, $^1/_4$ cup soy sauce, and garlic in large saucepan. Place ribs in liquid and bring to boil. Reduce heat, cover, and simmer over low heat 1 hour. Remove cover, bring to boil, and cook 20 minutes longer. Drain, reserving $^1/_4$ cup cooking liquid. Mix remaining $^1/_4$ cup soy sauce, brown sugar, cornstarch, sesame seeds, green onion, and ginger. Place spareribs and reserved $^1/_4$ cup cooking liquid in skillet over medium heat. Pour seasoned soy mixture over ribs and cook, turning ribs often and spooning sauce over until sauce is thickened and adheres to ribs, about 10 minutes. Keep warm in chafing dish.

Makes about 2 dozen.

Shrimp Toast

$1^1/_2$ pounds fresh or frozen
    shrimp, shelled and
    deveined
    Salt water
6 ounces ground pork
1 tablespoon sherry
1 tablespoon soy sauce
1 teaspoon salt
$^1/_4$ teaspoon MSG (optional)
$^1/_2$ teaspoon black pepper

$^1/_2$ cup finely chopped
    green onions
    Cornstarch
1 teaspoon sesame oil
3 eggs
14 to 16 thin slices white
    bread
$^1/_3$ cup fine dry bread
    crumbs
1 cup oil

SOAK shrimp in salt water and drain well. Chop finely and mix with pork, sherry, soy sauce, salt, MSG, pepper, green onions, $^1/_2$ tablespoon cornstarch, sesame oil, and 1 egg. Mix well. Dredge each slice of bread in cornstarch. Shake off excess. Spread shrimp-pork mixture generously over one side of each bread slice. Beat remaining eggs in bowl. Brush eggs over bread and filling. Sprinkle bread crumbs over filling. Cut bread slices into quarters diagonally. Heat oil in deep fryer to 375 degrees. Slide bread, filling side down, into hot oil. Fry until golden, then turn to brown other side lightly. Drain on paper towels. Serve hot.

Makes 56 to 64.

Shrimp, Teriyaki-Style

1/2 cup soy sauce
1/2 cup olive oil
1/2 cup sherry
2 tablespoons lemon juice or
* vinegar*
1/2 teaspoon garlic salt
1/2 teaspoon ginger

1/4 teaspoon rosemary
1/4 teaspoon thyme
1/4 teaspoon oregano
1/4 teaspoon marjoram
2 pounds shrimp, shelled and
* deveined*

MIX soy sauce, oil, sherry, lemon juice, garlic salt, ginger, rosemary, thyme, oregano, and marjoram. Pour over shrimp. Let stand 1 to 2 hours. Remove shrimp from marinade and broil 5 to 7 minutes.

Makes 12 to 14 servings.

Wined Teriyaki Strips

A hibachi or barbecue of some type is almost always to be found on a western patio. The first bite of these easy appetizers will show why outdoor cooking is so popular.

2 large flank steaks
1 cup dry white wine
1/2 cup soy sauce
1 1/2 tablespoons minced onion
1/4 teaspoon minced garlic
2 tablespoons lemon juice

2 tablespoons brown sugar or
2 tablespoons honey
1 (10 1/2-ounce) can beef broth
1 (1-inch) piece gingerroot,
* crushed*

SLICE steaks diagonally across grain into 1/4 × 1-inch strips and place in large bowl. Mix wine, soy sauce, onion, garlic, lemon juice, brown sugar, broth, and gingerroot. Pour over meat and let marinate 1 hour, turning 3 or 4 times. Thread on skewers and grill over coals until meat reaches desired degree of doneness.

Makes 30 to 40.

Stuffed Chinese Pea Pods

We first sampled these unusual appetizers at Narsai's in Berkeley. They're a bit tricky to prepare, but don't forget it's the cook's privilege to eat the rejects. Serve them when you have plenty of preparation time and want to offer guests something different.

1/2 pound Chinese pea pods
1 (3-ounce) package cream
* cheese, softened*

1 (5-ounce) jar blue cheese
* spread*
Milk

WASH Chinese pea pods, but do not stem. Blanch in boiling water for 30 to 60 seconds. Drain and chill. Combine and beat cream cheese, blue cheese spread, and enough milk to make a medium-stiff filling. When ready to serve, cut a tiny slit in each pea pod near the stem end. Place cheese filling mixture in a pastry tube fitted with a

No. 2 (fine writing) tip. Ease tip into the slit and fill the pea with cheese mixture. Do not overfill or pods will split. Serve chilled.

Makes 3 to 4 dozen.

Chinese Tacos

1 pound minced cooked pork, chicken, or beef
1/2 cup minced celery
1/4 cup minced onion
2 tablespoons minced and soaked dried Oriental mushrooms
Dash white pepper

1 tablespoon light soy sauce
1/2 to 1 tablespoon curry powder
3/4 pound won ton wrappers
Oil for deep frying

COMBINE pork, celery, onion, mushrooms, white pepper, soy sauce, and curry powder and mix well. Place 1 teaspoon filling just off center of each won ton wrapper. Fold wrapper over filling, forming a rectangle. Pleat open edges and press to seal. Fry in deep oil heated to 375 degrees until golden brown.

Makes 50.

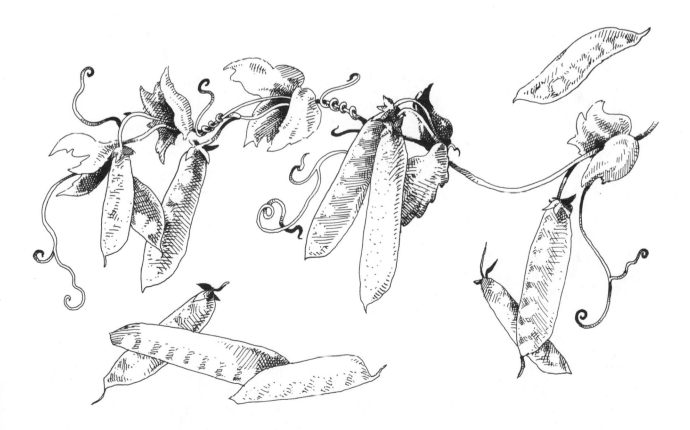

Honolulu Potstickers

Snacking on dim sum, the Chinese answer to hors d'oeuvres, is a favorite pastime of westerners who dote on Chinese cuisine. Readers who had enjoyed these at the Honolulu Mandarin restaurant on Hawaiian vacations asked for the recipe.

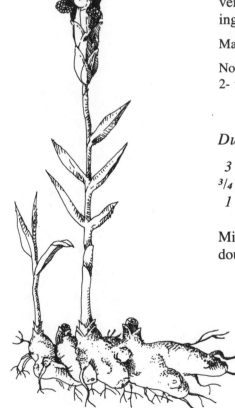

³/₄ pound lean pork, ground
2 teaspoons MSG (optional)
1¹/₂ teaspoons salt
6 tablespoons soy sauce
6 tablespoons sesame oil
1¹/₂ cups chopped green
  onions
2 to 3 ¹/₂-inch pieces gingerroot, minced
2¹/₂ cups chopped Chinese
  cabbage
Dumpling Dough
Oil

MIX pork with a small amount of water to make a paste. Add MSG, salt, soy sauce, sesame oil, green onions, gingerroot, and cabbage. Roll Dumpling Dough into a long roll about 1 inch in diameter and cut into 50 pieces. Flatten each piece with palm of hand and roll into a thin, round pancake about 3 to 4 inches in diameter. Place about 2 tablespoons cabbage filling in center of each dough round. Fold over to form a semicircle. Pinch edges together to form a crimped edge. Heat large skillet until a drop of water sizzles in it. Add 2 teaspoons oil and heat. Place batch of dumplings without overlapping in skillet. Cook over medium heat until bottoms are golden. Reduce heat and add ²/₃ cup water. Cover and cook until water has evaporated. Drain any remaining liquid from pan. Place serving plate over pan and invert so dumplings are served fried side up. Repeat frying and steaming until all potstickers are cooked. Serve at once.

Makes 50.

Note: For miniature hors d'oeuvres, cut dough into 60 to 70 pieces to form 2- to 3-inch circles.

Dumpling Dough

3 cups flour
³/₄ cup warm water
1 egg, beaten

Mix flour with water and egg. Stir to mix well and knead until a soft dough is formed. Let stand 30 minutes before using.

Satay

1 pound beef sirloin
1 cup Indonesian kecap
2 tablespoons vinegar
2 tablespoons sugar
1 clove garlic, minced

1 teaspoon ground coriander
1/2 teaspoon salt
1/4 teaspoon white pepper
    Peanut Sauce

Indonesian-style kebabs, called satay, make excellent appetizers. Grilling them over charcoal adds to their flavor.

SLICE beef in 1/4-inch-thick strips, then cut in 1-inch triangles. Blend kecap, vinegar, sugar, garlic, coriander, salt, and white pepper in bowl. Add beef and marinate at least 24 hours, turning occasionally. Place beef triangles close together on skewers, using 4 to a skewer. Cook over hot coals, turning and basting frequently with marinade. Spoon Peanut Sauce over satays or serve as dip.

Makes 6 servings.

Note: Indonesian kecap is a sweetened soy sauce available in Oriental markets.

Peanut Sauce

1/2 onion, grated
1/2 teaspoon ground coriander
1 tablespoon oil
1 cup water

1/4 cup peanut butter
1 tablespoon Indonesian kecap
Salt

Sauté onion and coriander in oil until onion is tender. Add water and bring to boil. Stir in peanut butter and kecap until smooth. Season to taste with salt.

Makes about 1 1/2 cups.

Indonesian Meatballs

1 pound ground beef
1 teaspoon salt
1/4 teaspoon pepper
1/2 teaspoon ground cumin
1/2 teaspoon ground coriander

1/4 cup flake coconut
1/2 small clove garlic, crushed
1 egg
Oil

COMBINE meat, salt, pepper, cumin, coriander, coconut, garlic, and egg, mixing only until blended. Form into 1/2-inch balls. Heat 1 or 2 tablespoons oil in skillet and brown meatballs, about 1/3 at a time, shaking pan occasionally to retain round shapes. Add more oil if needed to brown remaining meatballs. Serve on wood picks.

Makes 6 to 7 dozen.

Sujata's Curried Chicken Wings

Sujata, half of the Indian dance team of Sujata and Asoka, made these delightful curried tidbits as part of the tiffin menu in Pasadena's Pacificulture-Asia Museum. Her curry paste can easily be adapted to other foods that would be enhanced by a spicy touch.

16 chicken wings   4 to 6 teaspoons Curry Paste
  Salt   1/4 cup oil

RINSE chicken wings, cut off wing tips, and reserve for another use. Separate remaining 2 joints, making 32 chicken pieces. Season chicken to taste with salt. Add Curry Paste and mix. Add oil, mix, and marinate overnight in refrigerator. Place chicken pieces on broiling pan and broil until well browned on each side, turning once, about 20 to 25 minutes.

Makes 8 servings.

Note: For spicier wings add more of the Curry Paste to marinade.

Curry Paste

1/4 cup ground coriander
 1 tablespoon ground cumin
 1 tablespoon turmeric
1/2 teaspoon chili powder
 2 teaspoons ground black
   mustard seeds (optional)
1/2 teaspoon ground cloves

1/2 teaspoon ground
   cardamom
1/2 teaspoon cinnamon
 3 tablespoons cider
   vinegar
2 to 3 tablespoons water

Combine coriander, cumin, turmeric, chili powder, mustard seeds, cloves, cardamom, and cinnamon. Mix with vinegar, then little by little add water until mixture has a paste consistency.

Makes 1/2 cup.

Bacon-Wrapped Wafer I
(Mrs. Franklin Gindick's Version)

These deceptively simple hors d'oeuvres made the local party circuit because, it was said, the Duchess of Windsor served them. Which, if any, of the three versions offered was hers is anyone's guess.

Bacon slices
Waverly wafers

CUT bacon slices in halves. Separate crackers at perforations. Wrap bacon strip around center of each individual cracker (bacon will adhere when overlapped). Place on broiler rack, seam side down, over a drip pan. Bake (do not broil) at 350 degrees 20 to 25 minutes, or until bacon is crisp.

Bacon-Wrapped Wafer II
(Bill Fry's Version)

Brush bacon-wrapped crackers lightly with honey before baking.

Bacon-Wrapped Wafer III
(Mrs. Jules Stein's and Mrs. Alfred Bloomingdale's Version)

Sprinkle bacon-wrapped crackers lightly with brown sugar before baking.

Deep-Fried Squid

2 pounds squid
2 tablespoons lemon juice
1 teaspoon salt
1/8 teaspoon white pepper
2 tablespoons milk

1 egg, beaten
1 cup flour
Oil for deep frying
Lemon wedges

Italian fishermen from San Pedro to San Francisco introduced deep-fried squid and now the natives are hooked.

HAVE squid cleaned, skinned, and ink sacs removed. Cut into 1/2-inch rings. Sprinkle lemon juice, salt, and white pepper on squid. Combine milk and egg. Dip squid into milk mixture and roll in flour. Place squid in single layer in hot oil heated to 350 degrees and cook 3 to 5 minutes until squid is lightly browned. Drain on paper towels. Serve with lemon wedges.

Makes 6 servings.

Marinated Squid

2 pounds squid
Salt, pepper
1/4 cup oil, preferably olive
1/3 cup lemon juice
1 teaspoon chopped mint

1 tablespoon chopped parsley
1 clove garlic, minced
Lettuce
2 tomatoes, sliced
Lemon wedges

HAVE squid cleaned, skinned, and ink sacs removed. Rinse and dry on paper towels and cut into 2-inch rings. Drop squid into boiling salted water, reduce heat, and simmer 30 minutes, or until squid is tender. Drain squid and season to taste with salt and pepper. Combine oil, lemon juice, mint, parsley, and garlic and pour over squid. Marinate in refrigerator several hours. Serve on bed of lettuce and garnish with tomato slices and lemon wedges.

Makes 6 to 8 servings.

Caponata
(Eggplant Appetizer)

Caponata, the Italian antipasto, is gaining popularity here as a topping on burgers and hot dogs.

$^1/_4$ cup oil, preferably olive
1 small eggplant, peeled and cut in 1-inch cubes
4 stalks celery, cut in $^1/_2$-inch slices
$^1/_2$ cup pitted green olives, chopped
1 large onion, minced

1 clove garlic, crushed
1 tablespoon capers
$^1/_4$ cup tomato paste
1 cup water
$^1/_4$ cup vinegar
1 tablespoon sugar
1 teaspoon salt

HEAT oil in large skillet and fry eggplant cubes until lightly browned. Add celery, olives, onion, and garlic. Cook until vegetables are crisp-tender. Combine capers, tomato paste, water, vinegar, sugar, and salt. Pour over vegetables in skillet, stir lightly, and simmer 1 minute. Remove from heat. Cool and place in covered container in refrigerator until thoroughly chilled. Serve on lettuce leaves, if desired.

Makes 3 to 4 cups.

Stuffed Mushrooms, Italian-Style

Italian seasonings make these stuffed mushrooms popular Southern California cocktail fare.

16 medium mushrooms
  Olive oil
  Italian seasoning, crushed
1 large clove garlic, minced
$^1/_2$ pound hot Italian sausage, casings removed

5 green onions, chopped
1 teaspoon Worcestershire sauce (optional)
$^1/_2$ cup shredded Monterey Jack cheese

REMOVE stems from cleaned mushrooms by gently twisting base to snap off. Chop stems and set aside. Generously coat inside and outside of each mushroom cap with oil. Place in baking dish, open side up. Sprinkle insides with Italian seasoning to taste. Heat 1 tablespoon oil in skillet and sauté garlic. Add sausage, crushing with spoon into smaller pieces. Cook thoroughly, then add chopped mushroom stems. Stir-fry 1 minute. Add green onions and stir-fry another minute. Add Worcestershire. Stuff each mushroom cap generously with sausage filling and sprinkle with cheese. Broil 10 to 12 inches from heat for 2 minutes, or until cheese is melted.

Makes 16 servings.

Flaming Greek Cheese

Casseri or Kefalotere cheese
Ice water
Flour

Butter or margarine
Lemon juice
Cognac

Ann Pappas, a Los Angeles hostess and restaurateur, developed this recipe some years ago for one of her restaurants.

CUT Casseri cheese into ¹/₂-inch slices, allowing about 4 ounces for each serving. Chill slices in ice water. Pat dry and dust with flour. For each serving, melt 3 tablespoons butter until it sizzles but does not brown. Add cheese slices and sauté quickly on both sides. Do not overcook or cheese will melt and stick to pan. For each serving, squeeze juice of ¹/₂ lemon into skillet and sprinkle with a few drops of cognac. Ignite. Serve cheese when flames die down.

Note: Casseri and Kefalotere are hard Greek cheeses which can be found at most Greek or Middle Eastern grocery stores or gourmet food shops.

Cheese Triangles

1 cup shredded Monterey
   Jack cheese or cottage
   cheese
2 eggs, well beaten
¹/₂ cup chopped parsley

1 teaspoon salt
10 sheets phyllo pastry
1 cup unsalted butter, melted

Phyllo pastry forms a delicate, flaky package for an American cheese in this western version of an Armenian appetizer.

COMBINE cheese, eggs, parsley, and salt and mix well. Cut each sheet of phyllo dough in halves, working with one sheet at a time. Keep rest of pastry sheets covered with a damp towel until ready to use. Brush with butter and fold each half twice vertically to form a narrow strip. Place about 1 tablespoon of cheese mixture at one end of each strip. Fold one corner across filling to form a triangle. Brush with more butter. Continue folding in triangles, flag-style, and brushing layers with butter. Place triangles on baking sheets and bake at 350 degrees until pastry is golden, about 15 to 20 minutes.

Makes 20.

Scandinavian Meatballs

At Scandia these meatballs are served in a copper chafing dish at the bar while one enjoys cocktails.

½ cup soft bread crumbs
Milk
½ pound twice-ground beef or veal
½ pound twice-ground pork
1 egg
1 teaspoon salt

¼ teaspoon black pepper
Dash allspice
½ cup chopped onion
2 tablespoons butter or margarine
Clarified butter
Flour

SOAK bread crumbs in ½ cup milk. Combine moistened crumbs with beef, pork, egg, salt, pepper, and allspice. Cook onion in 2 tablespoons butter until tender and add to meat mixture. Beat mixture while slowly adding ½ cup lukewarm milk. Chill until mixture is firm enough to roll into 50 to 60 meatballs. Heat clarified butter in skillet. Add meatballs and fry. When cooked through, drain off fat. Dust meatballs lightly with flour. Add sufficient milk to make a thin gravy and simmer a few minutes. Adjust seasonings.

Makes 50 to 60.

Gravad Lax
(Scandinavian Salmon)

Gravad lax, lox, or gravlox, as cured salmon is called, is especially famous at Scandia restaurant, where this recipe originated.

1 (2-pound) piece salmon
3 tablespoons salt
3 tablespoons sugar
1 tablespoon crushed peppercorns

½ bunch dill
Mustard Dill Sauce

THAW salmon, if frozen. Cut salmon in halves lengthwise. Remove bones. Combine salt, sugar, and peppercorns. Rub half the spice mixture over one salmon half and place fish, skin side down, in baking dish. Spread dill over. Rub other half of salmon with remaining spice mixture and place, skin side up, on first salmon half. Cover with foil. Place a plate on top of fish and a weight on top of plate. Refrigerate 48 hours. Turn fish over every 12 hours, separating fillets slightly to baste with pan liquid. When ready to serve, scrape away dill and seasonings. Place fillets, skin side down, on cutting board. Cut salmon diagonally in thin slices away from skin. Serve cold with Mustard Dill Sauce.

Makes 24 servings.

Note: At Scandia, once the flesh is sliced from the salmon skin, the skin is cut in narrow strips and dropped into very hot deep oil to cook until crisp. A piece of crisped skin is served with each serving of gravad lax.

Mustard Dill Sauce

1/4 cup Dijon-style mustard
3 tablespoons sugar
2 tablespoons vinegar

1 teaspoon dry mustard
1/3 cup oil
3 tablespoons chopped dill

Combine mustard, sugar, vinegar, and dry mustard. Slowly beat in oil until thick. Stir in dill. Chill.

Makes 3/4 cup.

Batter-Fried Zucchini Sticks

1 cup sifted flour
1 teaspoon baking powder
1/2 teaspoon salt
1 egg, lightly beaten
1 cup milk

2 tablespoons oil
1 pound zucchini, cut into
    3- or 4-inch sticks
Oil for deep frying
Hollandaise Sauce

Deep-fried zucchini sticks are on the list of popular West Coast appetizers—with or without a Hollandaise dip.

SIFT flour with baking powder and salt. Combine egg, milk, and 2 tablespoons oil. Slowly add to dry ingredients, beating until smooth. Pat zucchini sticks very dry and if desired dredge lightly in flour. Dip pieces, one at a time, in batter. Fry in deep oil heated to 375 degrees until golden brown, about 1 to 2 minutes. Drain on paper towels. Sprinkle with more salt, if desired. Serve with Hollandaise Sauce.

Makes 2 dozen.

Hollandaise Sauce

4 egg yolks
1 tablespoon water or dry
    white wine
1/2 cup butter or margarine,
    softened

1/4 teaspoon salt
    Dash black pepper
1 tablespoon lemon juice

Beat egg yolks until thick and light-colored. Mix in water and transfer to top of a double boiler set over barely simmering water. Heat and stir 2 to 3 minutes until warm, not hot, and eggs have begun to thicken. Add butter, 2 tablespoons at a time, beating continuously until well blended. Cook, beating, 2 to 3 minutes until sauce thickens enough to coat back of spoon. Remove from heat and stir in salt, pepper, and lemon juice.

Makes about 3/4 cup.

Note: Vegetables that may be substituted for zucchini include artichoke hearts, carrot sticks, cauliflowerets, parsley sprigs, sliced parsnips, sweet potato sticks, and rutabaga cubes.

Marinated Zucchini

Zucchini is one vegetable Californians like as well raw as cooked. This spicy appetizer from the Pasadena Hilton Hotel is a fine example of a creative way to marinate the fresh vegetable.

1 cup bottled chili sauce
2 teaspoons grated Parmesan cheese
2 tablespoons red wine vinegar
2 tablespoons olive oil

Dash oregano
Dash garlic powder
Juice of 1/2 lemon
Salt, pepper
4 large zucchini

COMBINE chili sauce, cheese, vinegar, oil, oregano, garlic powder, and lemon juice and beat with whisk. Season to taste with salt and pepper. Wash zucchini and slice crosswise about 1/8-inch thick. Add to dressing and chill 4 hours or longer, turning several times.

Makes 6 to 8 servings.

French-Fried Potato Skins

Introduced during the peak of the natural-food craze, protein-packed potato skins make healthful snacks.

Potatoes
Oil for deep frying
Salt

Garlic salt, celery salt, or grated Parmesan cheese (optional)

SCRUB potatoes thoroughly with a brush. Using potato peeler, cut off long thin spirals of skin from potatoes. (Use potatoes for another dish.) Cover skins with very cold water and let stand 30 minutes to 1 hour. Drain and carefully pat curls dry with paper towels. Drop curls into deep oil heated to 390 degrees and fry until golden brown and crisp, about 1 minute. Drain on paper towels and sprinkle with salt or garlic salt, celery salt, or Parmesan cheese. Serve hot.

Spicy Marinated Mushrooms

Tiny, tangy appetizers like these disappear rapidly when calorie-counters find them at cocktail parties.

1 pound small mushrooms
3/4 cup red wine vinegar
1/4 cup water
1/2 cup oil
1 bay leaf, crumbled

1 teaspoon tarragon
1/4 teaspoon salt
1 clove garlic, crushed
1 tablespoon chopped chives

RINSE mushrooms quickly or wipe with damp towels. Trim ends of stems. Combine vinegar, water, oil, bay leaf, tarragon, salt, garlic, and chives. Mix well. Pour marinade over mushrooms, cover, and marinate in refrigerator at least 12 hours. Stir or turn occasionally.

Makes 6 to 8 servings.

Caviar Mold

1 envelope unflavored gelatin	Dash hot pepper sauce
1/4 cup water	4 ounces caviar (lumpfish or
Sour cream	white fish)
2 tablespoons mayonnaise	Salt, white pepper
2 tablespoons lemon juice	Parsley sprigs
2 teaspoons grated onion	Toast rounds or unsalted
1/4 teaspoon sugar	crackers

SPRINKLE gelatin over water and let stand until softened. Warm 1 cup sour cream over low heat, add gelatin, and stir constantly until gelatin melts, 1 to 2 minutes. Remove from heat and add mayonnaise, lemon juice, onion, sugar, and hot pepper sauce, blending well. Place caviar in a strainer and rinse carefully with cold water. Shake strainer to remove excess water. Reserve 1 tablespoon caviar. Add remaining caviar to sour cream mixture, stirring gently. Season to taste with salt and white pepper. Turn into greased 2-cup mold or into 8 to 10 small individual molds and chill until firm, about 3 to 4 hours. Unmold on serving plate. Place about 6 tablespoons of sour cream on top of large mold or 1 tablespoon on each individual mold. Place some of reserved caviar on top of sour cream. Surround with parsley and accompany with toast rounds.

Makes 8 to 10 servings.

Shrimp Puffs

1 pound shrimp, peeled, deveined, and minced	1/2 teaspoon salt
12 water chestnuts, diced	1 egg, lightly beaten
2 tablespoons flour	Oil for deep frying
1 teaspoon sherry	Mustard-Soy Dip

MIX shrimp, water chestnuts, flour, sherry, salt, and egg together well. Shape mixture into 1-inch balls, drop into deep oil heated to 350 degrees, and fry until golden brown. Drain on paper towels and serve hot with Mustard-Soy Dip.

Makes 36.

(continued on overleaf)

Mustard-Soy Dip

$^1/_2$ teaspoon vinegar
1 teaspoon sugar
2 teaspoons dry mustard

$^1/_2$ teaspoon water
$^1/_2$ cup soy sauce

Mix vinegar, sugar, and mustard until smooth. Add water to make a thick paste. Gradually stir in soy sauce and mix well.

Makes about $^1/_2$ cup.

Lamb Appetizer

15 slices white bread
   Butter or margarine, melted
   Celery seeds
1 cup ground cooked lamb
$^1/_4$ cup mayonnaise
1 small onion, minced

$^1/_4$ teaspoon paprika
1 teaspoon lemon juice
2 tablespoons chopped chives
   Pimiento strips or parsley
   sprigs

TRIM crusts from bread. Brush one side of each slice with melted butter and sprinkle with celery seeds. Cut each slice in 3 strips and place on baking sheet. Bake at 425 degrees 8 to 10 minutes. Blend lamb, mayonnaise, onion, paprika, lemon juice, and chives. Spread each toast strip with about $1^1/_2$ teaspoons meat mixture and garnish with pimiento strips.

Makes 45.

Lamb-Stuffed Mushrooms

1 pound ground lamb
2 teaspoons prepared
   horseradish
1 teaspoon chopped chives
$^1/_2$ teaspoon garlic salt

   Pepper
18 large mushrooms
$^2/_3$ cup dry sauterne
$^1/_4$ cup butter or margarine,
   melted

MIX together lamb, horseradish, chives, and garlic salt. Season to taste with pepper. Remove stems from mushrooms and stuff caps with lamb mixture. Place in shallow baking dish. Combine sauterne and butter and pour over mushrooms. Bake at 350 degrees 20 minutes, or until meat is browned.

Makes 18.

Picnic Pâté

3/4 cup butter or margarine
1 pound chicken livers
1/2 pound mushrooms, chopped
1/3 cup finely sliced green
    onions
1 teaspoon salt

2/3 cup Riesling or sauterne
1 clove garlic, minced
1/2 teaspoon dry mustard
1/8 teaspoon rosemary
    Dash dill weed
    Melba toast

MELT 1/4 cup butter in skillet. Add chicken livers, mushrooms, green onions, and salt. Cook 5 minutes. Add wine, garlic, mustard, rosemary, and dill weed and simmer 5 minutes more, or until chicken livers and mushrooms are very tender and liquid is almost completely absorbed. Cool slightly. Blend in blender container or food processor bowl until almost smooth. Blend in remaining butter. Add additional salt if needed. Pack into a crock. Chill 8 hours or longer. Serve with melba toast.

Makes 3 cups.

Rumaki Pâté

1/2 pound chicken livers,
    cooked
3 tablespoons soy sauce
1/2 cup butter or margarine,
    softened
1/2 teaspoon onion salt
1/2 teaspoon dry mustard
1/4 teaspoon nutmeg
    Dash hot pepper sauce

1 (8-ounce) can water
    chestnuts, drained and
    coarsely chopped
6 slices bacon, cooked and
    crumbled
2 tablespoons chopped green
    onion
    Melba toast or crackers

IN blender container or food processor bowl, finely chop chicken livers, a few at a time. When all are chopped, return to blender container and add soy sauce, butter, onion salt, mustard, nutmeg, and hot pepper sauce. Blend until smooth and well mixed, scraping down sides frequently. Add water chestnuts and bacon. Mix in thoroughly by hand. Spoon into 1 large or 5 small molds, pressing firmly so all air pockets are removed. Chill. Unmold by dipping quickly into hot water up to rim and allow to soften to room temperature before serving. Garnish with green onion. Serve with melba toast.

Makes about 1 1/2 cups.

Chicken Wings Pacifica

This, one of the most popular appetizers ever printed in The Times, *was sent to us by D. J. McClary of Placentia, California.*

12 to 15 chicken wings
1 cup soy sauce
1 cup brown sugar, packed

*1/2 cup butter or margarine
1 teaspoon dry mustard
3/4 cup water*

DISJOINT chicken wings, discarding bony tips. Arrange meatier wing parts in shallow baking pan. Combine soy sauce, brown sugar, butter, mustard, and water and heat until sugar and butter dissolve. Cool and pour over wings. Marinate in refrigerator 2 hours, turning occasionally. Bake, in marinade, at 350 degrees 45 minutes, turning once and spooning marinade over chicken occasionally. Drain on paper towels and serve hot or cold.

Makes 24 to 30.

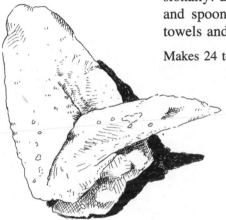

Napa Valley Chicken Wings

These messy but utterly delicious chicken wing appetizers were served at a special party at Napa Valley's Domaine Chandon Winery restaurant.

8 chicken wings
1/4 cup cornstarch
2 teaspoons salt
1/2 teaspoon white pepper
Oil
1 small tomato, peeled, seeded, and thinly sliced crosswise

*1/2 medium green pepper, thinly sliced crosswise
1/2 small onion, thinly sliced in rings*
Wine Dressing

DISJOINT chicken wings, discarding bony tips. Push flesh to one end of bone on remaining parts. With sharp knife, remove smaller bone in wing portion containing 2 bones. Press fleshy ends of chicken pieces to flatten so they will stand upright. Dredge chicken in cornstarch mixed with salt and white pepper. Set aside to dry for 30 minutes. Heat oil to depth of 1/2 inch in heavy skillet and fry chicken until golden brown and tender, about 7 minutes on each side. Drain on paper towels and freeze or refrigerate if not to be used at once. Combine tomato slices, green pepper, and onion slices with Wine Dressing and mix well. To serve, bring chicken wings to room temperature and arrange upright in Wine Dressing mixture in a shallow casserole.

Makes 16.

Wine Dressing

1 cup olive oil
1 cup tarragon wine vinegar
3/4 cup dry white wine
1 clove garlic, mashed
1/2 teaspoon dry mustard

1/2 teaspoon sugar
1/2 teaspoon basil, crushed
1/2 teaspoon oregano, crushed
1/2 teaspoon tarragon, crushed
Salt, pepper

Combine oil, vinegar, wine, garlic, mustard, sugar, basil, oregano, and tarragon. Season to taste with salt and pepper. Blend well.

Makes about 2³/₄ cups.

Pumpernickel Toast

1 loaf unsliced pumpernickel
  bread
1/2 cup butter or margarine

1 to 2 cloves garlic, crushed
1/2 cup grated Parmesan
  cheese

Pumpernickel toast is a specialty at several of Los Angeles's finest restaurants, where it is served in baskets with cocktails.

FREEZE bread. With a sharp knife, slice bread paper thin. Melt butter over low heat. Add garlic and cheese and stir for a few seconds to blend well. With pastry brush, spread one side of each bread slice with butter mixture. Arrange slices in single layers on ungreased baking sheets. Bake at 275 degrees until crisp, about 15 to 20 minutes. Bread will curl slightly at edges. Cool, then store in airtight container until ready to use. Serve as an appetizer or with soups or salads.

Makes 30 to 40.

Chipped Beef Dip

1 (8-ounce) package cream
  cheese, softened
2 tablespoons milk
1 (2¹/₂-ounce) jar chipped
  beef, finely snipped
2 tablespoons instant minced
  onion

2 tablespoons finely chopped
  green pepper
1/8 teaspoon pepper
1/2 cup sour cream
1/4 cup ground or finely
  chopped walnuts
Potato chips

BLEND cream cheese and milk. Stir in chipped beef, onion, green pepper, and pepper. Mix well. Stir in sour cream. Spoon into shallow baking dish and sprinkle walnuts over top. Bake, uncovered, at 350 degrees 15 minutes. Serve hot with potato chips.

Makes about 1¹/₂ cups.

Curry Dip

A popular Burbank restaurant, The Castaway, was our source for this easy dip that is especially good with crisp, raw vegetables.

1 cup mayonnaise
1¹/₂ teaspoons curry powder
¹/₂ teaspoon dry mustard

2 teaspoons lemon juice
¹/₈ teaspoon salt

BLEND together mayonnaise, curry powder, mustard, lemon juice, and salt. Chill and serve as dip for fresh cut vegetables or seafood, if desired.

Makes about 1 cup.

Camembert aux Noix

Serve a wheel of Camembert this way next time you want to make an impression on cocktail guests.

¹/₄ cup butter, softened
¹/₄ cup ground pecans
   Hot pepper sauce
2 tablespoons lemon juice

1 (8-ounce) wheel Camembert
   or Brie, chilled
   Toast points

CREAM softened butter until light and fluffy. Blend in pecans, a few drops of hot pepper sauce, and lemon juice. Cut Camembert in halves horizontally while still firm. Spread bottom layer with butter mixture. Replace top of cheese. Chill until filling is firm. Slice in thin wedges ¹/₂ hour before serving. Serve on toast points.

Makes about 8 servings.

Roquefort Mousse Spread

4 eggs, separated
1 tablespoon unflavored
   gelatin
¹/₄ cup cold water
¹/₂ pound Roquefort cheese,
   crumbled

¹/₂ cup whipping cream,
   whipped
¹/₂ cup finely chopped walnuts
   Crackers

BEAT egg yolks until creamy yellow and thick. Soften gelatin in water and dissolve over low heat. Add to egg yolks, mixing well. Beat egg whites until very soft peaks form. Fold into yolk mixture. Stir in cheese. Blend thoroughly but gently. Fold in whipped cream and nuts. Spoon into 4-cup mold and chill several hours. Unmold to serve. Serve with crackers.

Makes 3¹/₂ cups.

Delices au Gruyère

1/4 cup butter or margarine
Flour
1 1/2 cups hot milk
Salt, pepper
1/2 pound Gruyère cheese, grated
3 egg yolks

1 egg
1/4 cup milk
1 tablespoon oil
Fine dry bread crumbs
Oil for deep frying

Delices au Gruyère is a French version of the Italian mozzarella marinara (fried cheese in tomato sauce). It's one of our most requested recipes.

MELT butter in saucepan over low heat. Blend in 5 tablespoons flour and cook, stirring, until mixture is golden. Add hot milk and cook, stirring, until sauce is smooth and thick. Cook over low heat 8 to 10 minutes longer. Season to taste with salt and pepper. Add cheese and stir until melted. Beat egg yolks, stir into sauce, and cook and stir 3 minutes, being careful not to let sauce boil. Spread mixture in a well-greased, shallow 12 x 7-inch pan and cool. Cover with wax paper and chill. Cut mixture into 10 or more equal portions and form each into a ball or cone. Roll in flour, then in egg beaten with milk and 1 tablespoon oil. Drain on paper towels, then roll in crumbs. Fry in deep oil heated to 370 degrees 1 to 1 1/2 minutes, or until golden. Drain on paper towels. Serve plain as appetizers or with tomato sauce as a luncheon dish.

Makes 6 to 8 servings.

Cheese Crock Blend

1 (3-ounce) package cream cheese, softened
1/4 pound sharp cheddar cheese, shredded
1/4 pound blue cheese, crumbled

2 to 4 tablespoons brandy, sherry, or port
1/8 teaspoon red pepper
1/2 cup finely chopped walnuts
Bread or crackers

BEAT cream cheese until smooth. Beat in cheddar and blue cheeses. Gradually beat in enough brandy to make the spread creamy. Add red pepper and stir in walnuts. Pack into crocks or jars, cover tightly with plastic wrap or foil, and refrigerate until serving time. This spread is best if aged 4 or 5 days. Let stand at room temperature 1/2 hour or so before serving. Serve with small thin slices of rye or French bread, crackers, toasted water biscuits, or Scandinavian flatbread. If a hot canapé is desired, spread cheese mixture on melba toast or crackers and broil until cheese is melted and bubbly. Decorate with walnut half, if desired.

Makes about 2 cups.

Cheese Coins

1/2 cup butter or margarine,
 softened
2 cups shredded cheddar or
 Monterey Jack cheese
1/2 teaspoon dry mustard
1/2 teaspoon seasoned salt

2 teaspoons finely chopped
 canned green chiles
2 teaspoons minced pimiento
1/2 teaspoon Worcestershire
 sauce
1 1/4 cups flour

BEAT butter, cheese, mustard, seasoned salt, green chiles, pimiento, and Worcestershire until blended. Add flour to make a stiff dough. Form into small balls (about 1/2 inch in diameter). Place on ungreased baking sheets, press lightly with tines of fork, and bake at 350 degrees 15 minutes, or until lightly browned. Serve hot or cold. These will keep for 1 to 2 weeks in an airtight container.

Makes about 2 1/2 dozen.

Cheese-Chile Appetizer

Similar to a quiche without a crust, these chile-spiced appetizers are a California specialty.

1/2 cup butter or margarine
10 eggs
1/2 cup flour
1 teaspoon baking powder
 Dash salt

1 (7-ounce) can diced green
 chiles
2 cups cottage cheese
1 pound Monterey Jack
 cheese, shredded

MELT butter in 13 x 9-inch pan. Beat eggs lightly in large bowl. Add flour, baking powder, and salt and blend. Add melted butter, green chiles, cottage cheese, and Jack cheese and mix until just blended. Turn batter into pan and bake at 400 degrees 15 minutes. Reduce heat to 350 degrees and bake 35 to 40 minutes longer. Cut into small squares and serve hot.

Makes about 24.

Curried Almonds

2 tablespoons salt
1 1/2 teaspoons curry powder

3 tablespoons olive oil
2 cups blanched almonds

PLACE salt and curry powder in paper bag. Heat oil in skillet and add almonds. Toast lightly, being careful not to scorch or burn. Drain and place almonds in paper bag and shake well.

Makes 2 cups.

Hot Brie with Toasted Almonds

1 cup slivered blanched
  almonds, toasted
1 (8-inch) wheel Brie

SPRINKLE toasted almonds evenly over Brie. When ready to serve, place on wooden plank or board with handle and bake at 350 degrees until Brie begins to bulge around sides and is hot. Serve with sesame crackers, if desired.

Makes 20 servings.

Sheila Ricci chose a delightful way to pamper customers when she ran a tearoom in Beverly Hills and served them Brie cheese prepared this way.

Spiced Almonds

¹/₂ cup blanched whole al-
  monds
Butter or margarine
Dash garlic salt

Dash onion salt
Dash ginger
Dash nutmeg
1 tablespoon soy sauce

TOAST almonds in butter over low heat. Sprinkle with salts, ginger, nutmeg, and soy sauce. Shake pan to distribute spices. Cook and stir until nuts are dry.

Makes ¹/₂ cup.

Fried Walnuts, Chinese-Style

The Hunan restaurant in Los Angeles's Chinatown shared their recipe for these crisp, sweet snacks that are equally good as a light dessert or as an appetizer.

1 pound walnut halves
1 cup water

³/₄ cup sugar
Oil for deep frying

WASH walnuts to remove excess flaky coating. Combine water and sugar in saucepan and cook 5 minutes to make a syrup. Place walnuts in jar with cover. Pour sugar syrup over walnuts. Cool, cover, and let stand overnight. Heat oil to 350 degrees and add drained nuts. Deep-fry 2 to 3 minutes. Drain on paper towels and serve at once.

Makes about 4 cups.

Curried Nuts

3 cups mixed shelled nuts
1 teaspoon butter or
   margarine, melted

¹/₂ teaspoon curry powder
¹/₂ teaspoon salt

SPREAD nuts in shallow pan and toast in oven at 275 degrees 20 minutes, shaking pan once or twice. Drizzle nuts with melted butter. Combine curry powder and salt and sprinkle over nut mixture. Stir well.

Makes 3 cups.

Oaxacan Nuts

Packaged in attractive containers, these spicy nuts make delightful small gifts.

2 tablespoons olive oil
2 teaspoons garlic salt
2 pounds canned mixed nuts
1 (5/8-ounce) package chili
   seasoning mix

2 teaspoons extra-hot chili
   powder

HEAT oil with garlic salt. Add nuts, reduce heat, and toss, using 2 spoons, until nuts are well coated. Transfer to large bowl. Blend chili seasoning and chili powder and add to nuts. Toss mixture until nuts are well coated. Store in airtight container and refrigerate for at least 2 days to blend flavors. Nuts may be frozen. If frozen, reheat at 350 degrees 5 minutes.

Makes 2 pounds.

A steady stream of requests throughout the years has kept this illustrious collection of soups front-page classics.

A high preference for sturdy hot soups is perhaps a paradox in a place where the temperature often exceeds eighty degrees even in winter. But they are toted in vacuum bottles to Hollywood Bowl pre-concert repasts or tailgate picnics at the beach, or they are left to simmer away in slow cookers by clever modern-day menu planners who want to come home to a meal already prepared.

Light and elegant chilled soups are often associated with more formal living, but they are versatile enough to go to the beach as refreshing pick-me-ups or appear as the first course at a formal dinner party. The western shopper's easy access to a broad array of dewy fresh vegetables and fruits is readily apparent when one peruses our most popular cold soup recipes. Tomatoes, cucumbers, zucchini, carrots, avocados, berries, and other fruits all are used as basic ingredients in these well-seasoned, chilled soups.

The recipes come from far and near: chefs at sea, home cooks, a bevy of restaurant chefs, church groups, and great hosts and hostesses, among others. Yet they all fit nicely into the Southern California food scene.

Chilled Cream of Vegetable Soup, page 46

Chilled Cream of Vegetable Soup

1 cup chopped celery leaves
1 medium carrot, diced
1 small green pepper, diced
1 cup chopped spinach leaves
1/2 cup chopped parsley
1 large onion, chopped
4 cups chicken broth
3 sprigs parsley
1 bay leaf
1/2 teaspoon thyme
2 whole cloves

1 clove garlic
1/4 cup uncooked rice
  Salt, pepper
2 egg yolks
2 cups half and half
  Sour cream
  Minced parsley
  Minced chives
2 medium tomatoes, peeled
  and chopped

COMBINE celery leaves, carrot, green pepper, spinach, chopped parsley, onion, and chicken broth in kettle. Tie parsley sprigs, bay leaf, thyme, cloves, and garlic in a small square of cheesecloth. Add to broth mixture along with rice. Season to taste with salt and pepper. Bring to boil, cover, and simmer 40 minutes. Discard seasonings in cheesecloth bag. Press soup through fine sieve or puree in blender. Return soup to kettle and bring to boil. Beat egg yolks and stir a few tablespoons of soup into the yolks. Stir yolk mixture into hot soup and cook, stirring, until smooth. Do not boil. Stir in half and half and simmer 2 or 3 minutes, stirring constantly. Remove from heat and chill thoroughly. If soup separates, stir before serving. Spoon into chilled soup bowls, add a dollop of sour cream, and sprinkle with parsley, chives, and tomatoes.

Makes 4 to 6 servings.

Avocado Soup

A creamy, chilled avocado soup was introduced to us at Bernard's, the elegant French restaurant in the Biltmore Hotel in downtown Los Angeles. There it is served in icy avocado-shell cups, but it's just as good in a pretty glass bowl.

2 large avocados
2 cups chicken broth
  Salt, pepper

2 cups whipping cream
2 tablespoons cognac
2 tablespoons sherry

PEEL avocados and dice pulp. Puree pulp in blender container with chicken broth. Season to taste with salt and pepper. Gradually stir in whipping cream. Chill. Add cognac and sherry just before serving.

Makes about 4 cups.

Note: To make frozen avocado-shell cups for soup, cut a slice from stem end of avocado. Scoop out pulp and discard seed. Reserve cap. Use pulp for soup or puree with small amount of lemon juice and freeze for future use. Place shell upright in cup or egg carton. Freeze until firm. To serve, embed avocado shell in crushed ice in a dessert dish or soup icer. Carefully spoon in soup and lean cap against side of avocado.

Gazpacho de Los Angeles

1 (46-ounce) can tomato juice
1 medium green pepper,
  minced
1 small onion, minced
1 cucumber, peeled and
  minced
2 small canned green chiles,
  minced
1 tablespoon Worcestershire
  sauce

1 teaspoon seasoning blend
1/2 teaspoon minced garlic
1 tablespoon olive oil
1 tablespoon chopped chives
2 drops hot pepper sauce
  MSG (optional)
  Salt, white pepper
  Lemon wedges

If there is such a thing as a Los Angeles-style gazpacho, the Velvet Turtle, a popular restaurant chain in the Los Angeles area, turns out one of the best.

COMBINE tomato juice, green pepper, onion, cucumber, chiles, Worcestershire, seasoning blend, garlic, olive oil, chives, and hot pepper sauce. Season to taste with MSG, salt, and white pepper. Chill thoroughly. Serve with lemon wedges.

Makes 6 to 8 servings.

Note: For a smooth gazpacho served with vegetable garnishes, blend tomato mixture in blender container until smooth. Serve with additional diced cucumber, green pepper, and croutons on the side.

Curried Cold Asparagus Soup

1 pound asparagus
5 cups chicken broth
  Salt
1/4 cup unsalted butter
1/4 cup flour

3 egg yolks
1 to 2 teaspoons curry powder
3/4 cup whipping cream
  Dash lemon juice
  Freshly ground pepper

SNAP off woody ends from asparagus stalks. Clean stalks with vegetable peeler, cut off tips, and reserve. Combine chicken broth and asparagus stalks in large kettle. Heat to boiling, cover, reduce heat, and simmer 40 to 45 minutes. Drop asparagus tips into boiling, lightly salted water and cook 3 to 5 minutes or until tender. Drain and reserve. Puree broth and asparagus stalk mixture in blender container. Melt butter in heavy saucepan, add flour, and cook, stirring, for 2 minutes without browning. Add puree all at once and bring soup to boil. Cook over low heat until thickened and mixture lightly coats a spoon. Stir a small amount of soup into egg yolks. Add egg mixture to soup. Stir in curry powder, cream, and lemon juice. Season to taste with salt and pepper. Stir asparagus tips in gently. Serve chilled.

Makes 4 to 6 servings.

Consommé Madrilène

This attractive, yet very simple, consommé is the creation of Udo Nechutnys, chef and co-owner of the Miramonte Restaurant and Country Inn in St. Helena, located in the heart of Napa Valley's wine district.

6 large tomatoes
2 large green peppers, cored, seeded, and quartered
1 leek, trimmed and cut in chunks
4 egg whites, lightly beaten

8 cups rich chicken stock
Salt, pepper
1 small bunch chives, finely chopped
1 (2-ounce) jar chopped pimiento

PEEL, core, and dice 4 tomatoes. Place in large saucepan and add green peppers, leek, and egg whites, mixing well. Add chicken stock and season to taste with salt and pepper. Place over medium low heat and slowly bring to boil. Boil 5 to 10 minutes. Strain through a sieve or strainer lined with linen towel or cheesecloth. Discard vegetables and refrigerate consommé until serving time. Just before serving, peel, core, and seed remaining 2 tomatoes and dice fine. Mix with chives and pimiento and place 1 or 2 tablespoons of mixture in bottom of each soup bowl. Pour chilled consommé over vegetables and serve at once. Consommé should be thick and syrupy but not set.

Makes 8 servings.

Minted Berry Soup

4 cups strawberries, boysenberries, or raspberries
1/4 cup brown sugar, packed
1/4 teaspoon salt
1/2 teaspoon cinnamon
1/4 teaspoon cloves
1 (4/5-quart) bottle California sauterne

1 tablespoon chopped fresh mint or 1 teaspoon dried mint
1 envelope unflavored gelatin
1/3 cup cold water
Mint sprigs

WASH berries and, if necessary, hull. Crush berries lightly with a potato masher or fork. Place in saucepan and stir in brown sugar, salt, cinnamon, and cloves. Add sauterne and bring to boil. Add chopped mint and simmer 2 or 3 minutes. Meanwhile, soften gelatin in cold water. Stir in boiling soup until dissolved. Pour into shallow pan and chill until thickened, about 3 hours. Pile jellied soup into chilled cups. Garnish each serving with a sprig of mint.

Makes 6 to 8 servings.

Chilled Zucchini Carrot Soup

3 tablespoons butter or
   margarine
1/2 cup chopped leeks
1 pound zucchini, diced
2 tablespoons flour
3 1/4 cups chicken broth
1 1/2 cups buttermilk

1/8 teaspoon oregano or thyme
1 tablespoon lemon juice
1/8 teaspoon white pepper
   Salt
   Thin zucchini slices
1/2 cup finely shredded carrot

Southern Californians grow zucchini in their backyards with great abandon. Then they try to decide what to do with a burgeoning crop. One popular solution is this soup. Crisp, raw carrots are shredded and sprinkled over the top to add both color and texture.

MELT butter in saucepan, add leeks and zucchini, and sauté until tender. Stir in flour and cook 1 minute. Gradually add chicken broth, stirring until mixture thickens slightly and comes to a boil. Puree mixture in blender container. Stir in buttermilk, oregano, lemon juice, white pepper, and season to taste with salt. Chill. Serve in mugs. Garnish with zucchini slices and shredded carrot.

Makes 6 servings.

Cold Cucumber Soup

3 medium cucumbers
2 tablespoons butter
1 leek, chopped
2 bay leaves
1 tablespoon flour
3 cups chicken broth

1 teaspoon salt
1 cup half and half
   Juice of 1/2 lemon
   Chopped dill
   Sour cream

This cold cucumber soup from Hollywood's Scandia restaurant makes a delightful addition to a summer luncheon menu.

PEEL and thinly slice 2 cucumbers. Melt butter, add sliced cucumbers, leek, and bay leaves, and cook slowly until tender but not brown. Discard bay leaves. Add flour and mix well. Add chicken broth and salt and bring to boil, then reduce heat and simmer 20 to 30 minutes, stirring occasionally. Puree through a sieve or in blender container and chill soup in refrigerator several hours. Peel, halve, and remove seeds from remaining cucumber, then grate. Add to soup with half and half, lemon juice, and chopped dill to taste. Serve in cold soup cups and top each serving with a dollop of sour cream.

Makes 6 servings.

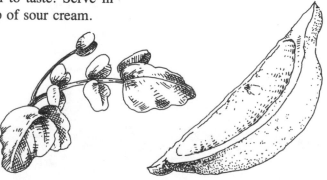

Vichyssoise

The Victor Hugo Inn in Laguna Beach is no more, but its classic vichyssoise recipe continues to be a reader favorite.

4 tablespoons butter or margarine
4 leeks, mostly white part, chopped
1 onion, chopped
4 cups water
4 cups chicken broth

2¹/₂ tablespoons flour
Salt, white pepper
4 potatoes, peeled and cubed
1 cup whipping cream
2 cups half and half
Chopped chives

MELT 1 tablespoon butter in large kettle, add leeks and onion, and cook until tender but not browned. Add water and broth and bring to boil. Knead flour into remaining 3 tablespoons butter to form a paste and stir into boiling mixture with wire whisk to blend well. Season to taste with salt and white pepper. Add potatoes, reduce heat, and simmer until potatoes are soft. Press through sieve. Cool. Add cream and half and half to soup, then chill. Top each serving with sprinkling of chopped chives.

Makes 10 to 12 servings.

Carrot Vichyssoise

An inspired cook, singer Larry Kert added carrots to a vichyssoise recipe and came up with a delicately sweet chilled soup that makes a beautiful starter for a meal. Serve this in clear glass bowls or cups to make the most of its lovely pale peach color.

2 cups chopped, peeled white potatoes
1¹/₂ cups sliced carrots
3 leeks, white part only, sliced
5 cups chicken broth

1 teaspoon salt
Dash white pepper
1 cup half and half
Sour cream
Chopped chives

COMBINE potatoes, carrots, leeks, and broth in large saucepan. Bring to boil, then simmer, uncovered, for 25 minutes or until vegetables are tender. Puree vegetables and liquid, half at a time, in blender. Empty into mixing bowl. Stir in salt, white pepper, and half and half. Chill well. Serve in cups or mugs, garnished with a dollop of sour cream and a sprinkling of chopped chives.

Makes 6 servings.

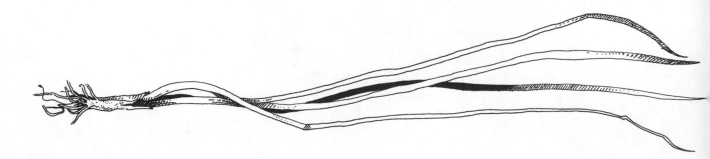

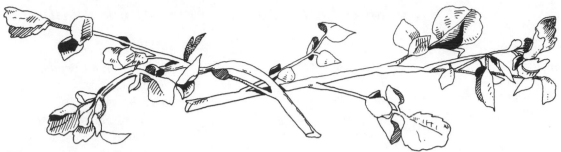

Watercress Soup

2 tablespoons butter
1 onion, coarsely chopped
Stems from 2 bunches watercress, chopped
4 russet potatoes, peeled and quartered

Chicken broth
Salt, pepper
1 cup whipping cream

Les Frères Taix, one of the oldest French restaurants in Los Angeles, uses watercress stems to enhance the flavor of this potato-based soup.

MELT 1 tablespoon butter in large saucepan over medium heat. Add onion and sauté until tender. Add chopped watercress stems and cook until tender. Add potatoes and enough broth to cover. Season to taste with salt and pepper and cook 45 minutes, or until potatoes are soft. Puree mixture in blender container. Return to pan and boil briskly a few minutes, stirring constantly. Add remaining 1 tablespoon butter and whipping cream, and heat through. Remove from heat, check for desired consistency, and season to taste with salt and pepper.

Makes 6 servings.

Clam Chowder

6 to 8 slices bacon, cut in ¹/₄-inch strips
3 large white onions, sliced and quartered
4 potatoes, peeled and diced
1 (6¹/₂-ounce) can minced clams
1 (6¹/₂-ounce) can chopped clams

2 quarts milk
2 teaspoons Worcestershire sauce
1 tablespoon butter or margarine
Salt, pepper
Chopped parsley

The late Art Ryon, a former restaurant critic for the Los Angeles Times, *made this rendition of clam chowder famous with our readers.*

FRY bacon and onions in large kettle until just brown. Add potatoes, clams with their liquid, and milk. Add Worcestershire and butter and season to taste with salt and pepper. Cook, uncovered, over very low heat, about 30 minutes, or until potatoes are tender. Do not allow to boil. Sprinkle with parsley.

Makes 8 to 10 servings.

Mahalia Jackson's New Orleans Okra Gumbo

This gumbo is one of our most frequently requested soup recipes. The singer Mahalia Jackson shared it with us in an interview some years before her death in 1972.

4 large blue crabs
4 pounds shrimp
   Oil
1½ pounds beef stew meat,
   cut in 1-inch cubes
1 pound cooked ham, cut in
   1-inch cubes
1 pound link sausage, sliced
½ pound chicken gizzards,
   sliced
1 pound salt pork, cut in
   ½-inch cubes
2 (1-pound 12-ounce) cans
   whole tomatoes
4 bay leaves, crumbled

2 large onions, diced
2 large green peppers,
   diced
4 to 6 stalks celery, diced
4 cloves garlic, crushed
2 pounds chicken wings
   and backs
2 (10-ounce) packages
   frozen okra, thawed, or
   1½ pounds fresh okra
¼ cup sugar
¼ cup parsley flakes
   Salt, pepper
   Hot cooked rice

CLEAN crabs, discarding spongy substance in main shell. Reserve claws and other meaty portions. Clean shrimp, reserving shells. Place shrimp shells in deep saucepan with water to cover generously and simmer 30 minutes or longer to make a broth. Pour oil into heavy skillet to a depth of ⅛ inch. Heat and add beef, ham, sausage, gizzards, and salt pork. Sauté until lightly browned, stirring occasionally. Pour meat mixture into large kettle and add 1 can tomatoes and enough broth drained from shrimp shells to cover generously. Add bay leaves, cover, and simmer about 30 minutes. Heat 2 tablespoons more oil in skillet and add onions, green peppers, celery, and garlic. Sauté until lightly browned, stirring now and then. Add vegetable mixture and chicken parts to kettle and simmer 30 minutes longer. Heat 2 tablespoons oil in another heavy skillet, add okra and cook, stirring often, until it is lightly browned and loses its stickiness, about 30 minutes. Add shrimp to okra and sauté 3 or 4 minutes longer, or until shrimp turns pink. Stir in 2 tablespoons sugar. Add okra mixture to kettle. Drain second can of tomatoes, reserving liquid. Add tomatoes, crab, and enough of the tomato liquid and water from shrimp shells to keep mixture in kettle soupy. Simmer about 30 minutes. Add parsley flakes and remaining 2 tablespoons sugar. Season to taste with salt and pepper. Serve at once or refrigerate and reheat at a later time. Serve over hot rice in deep soup bowls. Pass hot pepper sauce and crackers with gumbo, if desired.

Makes 10 to 12 servings.

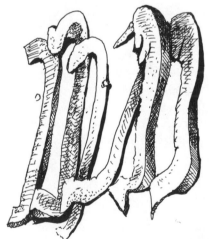

Lala's Gumbo

1/4 pound bacon, cut in 1-inch
squares
2 pounds okra, cut in 1/2-inch
pieces
2 medium onions, diced
2 stalks celery, diced
(optional)
4 cloves garlic, minced
1 (1-pound) can whole
tomatoes

4 cups boiling water
2 bouillon cubes
3 tablespoons flour
1 cup cold water
Salt, pepper
1 1/2 pounds shrimp, shelled,
deveined, and cut in
1-inch pieces
Hot cooked rice

Lala's gumbo is quite different
from Mahalia Jackson's, but
it's equally popular with Los
Angeles Times readers.

FRY bacon until crisp in large kettle. Reserve bacon drippings. Sauté okra in half of reserved drippings, stirring constantly, about 10 minutes. Place okra in kettle with bacon. Add rest of drippings to skillet and sauté onions and celery until onions are tender but not browned. Add garlic, mix well, then add half of tomatoes. Cook, stirring occasionally, until tomatoes darken in color somewhat. Add remaining half tomatoes and simmer 5 minutes. Pour into kettle with okra. Add 1 cup boiling water and mix well. Add second cup of boiling water and 1 bouillon cube. Stir over medium heat until gumbo comes to boil. Add a third cup of boiling water and remaining bouillon cube, reduce heat, and simmer 20 minutes. Add last cup boiling water and cook 10 minutes. Blend flour with cold water until smooth. Add to boiling gumbo and let come to boil again, stirring constantly. Season to taste with salt and pepper. Add shrimp and simmer 5 minutes. Let stand 20 minutes before serving or refrigerate overnight and reheat. Serve hot gumbo over hot rice in soup plates.

Makes 6 to 8 servings.

Peanut Butter Soup

2 tablespoons minced onion
3 tablespoons butter
1 tablespoon flour
1 cup peanut butter

4 cups chicken broth
Salt, pepper
1 cup whipping cream
1 tablespoon Madeira

This delicious soup, made from
the all-time favorite school
lunch sandwich spread, is
served at the Velvet Turtle in
Los Angeles. It is versatile
enough to be served as an
appetizer soup or as a main
dish.

COOK onion in butter until soft in 2-quart saucepan. Add flour and cook, stirring, until smooth. Stir in peanut butter, add chicken broth. Season to taste with salt and pepper. Cook, stirring, over low heat until thickened and smooth. Add cream. Just before serving, add Madeira.

Makes 6 servings.

Won Ton Soup

The extra won tons made for this practical soup from General Lee's restaurant in Chinatown, Los Angeles, will freeze well. Use them in later editions of the same soup or fry them in deep, hot oil to serve as hors d'oeuvres.

1 dried Oriental mushroom
1 egg, beaten
1/4 pound ground pork
1/4 pound coarsely chopped raw shrimp
2 teaspoons minced green onion
1/2 teaspoon MSG (optional)

2 tablespoons soy sauce
1/2 teaspoon salt
1 tablespoon sesame oil
Dash white pepper
1 pound won ton wrappers
1 egg white
Chicken broth

SOAK mushroom in warm water until soft, remove and discard stem, and mince cap. Combine mushroom, egg, pork, shrimp, green onion, MSG, soy sauce, salt, sesame oil, and white pepper and mix well. Place 1/2 teaspoon filling in center of each wrapper. Moisten wrapper edges with egg white and fold into triangle, pressing edges to seal. Moisten two farthest points of triangle with water and press together firmly. Drop filled won tons into large pot of boiling water. Cook 10 minutes, drain, and place 2 or 3 in each bowl. Pour hot chicken broth into each bowl and garnish with finely sliced green onions, if desired.

Makes 50 won tons.

Note: Use only as many won tons as needed for soup. Remaining uncooked won tons may be frozen for future use. Thaw frozen won tons before cooking.

Mushroom Barley Soup

Les Bresnik, a fine amateur chef in Los Angeles, added buttermilk to an old Jewish recipe for barley soup and got this rib-sticking, heartwarming soup meant for a chilly night.

3 quarts water
2 cups dried Oriental mushrooms
1 1/2 to 2 pounds flanken
Salt, pepper
1 cup pearl barley

4 green onions, sliced
2 tablespoons oil
2 tablespoons beef or chicken stock base
4 cups buttermilk

COMBINE water, mushrooms, and flanken in large kettle. Season to taste with salt and pepper. Bring to boil, reduce heat, and simmer 45 minutes. Meanwhile, rinse and drain barley. Sauté barley and green onions in oil until barley is lightly toasted. Add to soup and stir in stock base. Simmer 45 minutes longer, or until barley is tender. Adjust seasonings, if needed. Gradually add buttermilk. Bring to boil, remove and slice flanken, and serve soup at once with flanken on the side.

Makes 8 servings.

Noodles in Broth

1 (1-pound) package udon (thick noodles)
2 quarts chicken broth
2 cups cubed cooked chicken, turkey, pork, or ham
1 carrot, grated

2 green onions, sliced in 1-inch pieces
1/4 cup diagonally sliced celery
1/2 cup thinly sliced bok choy
Salt, pepper

Udon, thick Japanese noodles, are wonderful in an Oriental-style chicken soup.

COOK udon according to package directions. Drain and rinse under cold water. Heat chicken broth. Add chicken, carrot, green onions, celery, and bok choy, then season to taste with salt and pepper. Simmer 5 to 10 minutes to barely cook vegetables. Divide noodles among 6 bowls. Ladle in soup.

Makes 6 servings.

Onion Soup Fondue

3/4 cup unsalted butter
4 to 6 large onions, thinly sliced
8 cups beef broth
1 teaspoon chicken stock base

White pepper
12 ounces Monterey Jack cheese
French or sourdough bread, sliced 1-inch thick
Garlic Toast

One of the most popular onion soups in Los Angeles comes from a restaurant chain, Hamburger Hamlet. Loaded with onions and cheese, this is one of those meal-in-one soups.

MELT butter in large kettle, add onions, and sauté until transparent but not browned. Add beef broth and chicken stock base. Cover and simmer 2 to 3 hours. Remove from heat and refrigerate overnight or several hours. Discard chilled surface fat. Reheat and season to taste with white pepper. Slice cheese into 12 slices. Lightly toast 12 bread slices and top each with 1 slice Jack cheese. Pour soup into individual ovenproof serving bowls and top with slice of bread and cheese. Run bowls under broiler just until cheese bubbles and is soft but not browned. Serve with Garlic Toast on the side.

Makes 12 servings.

Garlic Toast

Spread bread slices with garlic-flavored butter and grated Parmesan cheese and toast lightly.

Broccoli Cheese Soup

Although hospital food seldom rates raves, a former patient tipped us off to this ever-popular soup created by the cafeteria chefs at UCLA Medical Center.

$^1/_2$ pound broccoli, chopped
$1^3/_4$ cups boiling water
  Salt
2 tablespoons minced onion
$^1/_4$ cup melted butter or margarine

3 tablespoons flour
$3^1/_2$ cups evaporated milk
4 cups skim milk
$3^1/_4$ cups shredded cheddar cheese
  Pepper

COOK broccoli until tender in lightly salted boiling water. Drain. Cook onion in butter until tender but not brown. Blend in flour. Add milks and cook and stir until smooth and thickened. Add cheese and broccoli and season to taste with salt and pepper. Stir until cheese is melted. Heat soup through but do not boil.

Makes 8 servings.

Split Pea Soup

Andersen's restaurant in Buellton, near the Danish community of Solvang in Southern California, is so famous for its split pea soup they finally began to can the soup. Andersen's willingly shared the recipe with Times *readers anyway.*

8 cups water
2 cups green split peas
1 stalk celery, coarsely chopped
1 large carrot, chopped

1 small onion, chopped
$^1/_4$ teaspoon thyme
  Dash red pepper
1 bay leaf
  Salt, pepper

COMBINE water, peas, celery, carrot, onion, thyme, red pepper, and bay leaf in large kettle. Season to taste with salt and pepper. Boil vigorously for 20 minutes, then reduce heat, cover, and simmer until split peas are tender. Press soup through a fine sieve and reheat to boiling point.

Makes 8 servings.

Split Pea Soup with Spareribs

3 pounds spareribs
8 cups water
1 pound yellow or green split peas
2 stalks celery, cut in chunks
3 carrots, cut in chunks
4 leeks, trimmed and diced

1 teaspoon hickory smoked salt
1 teaspoon salt
$^1/_4$ teaspoon thyme
2 bay leaves
10 sprigs parsley
10 black peppercorns

COMBINE spareribs and water in large kettle. Bring to boil. Wash and drain peas and add to ribs along with celery, carrots, leeks, smoked salt, salt, and thyme. Tie bay leaves, parsley, and peppercorns in a small square of cheesecloth and drop into soup. Cover, reduce heat, and simmer 3 to 4 hours, or until the soup is the consistency of thin porridge. Add hot water from time to time if needed. Remove ribs from soup, strip meat off bones, and return meat to soup. Adjust seasonings, if needed. Reheat, remove bundle of herbs, and ladle soup into hot bowls.

Makes 6 to 8 servings.

Bean Soup

1½ cups dry navy beans
6½ cups water
  ¼ pound link sausage, diced
  3 tablespoons shredded carrot
  3 tablespoons chopped green onions

1 beef bouillon cube
½ cup canned condensed tomato soup
1½ teaspoons salt
  Dash pepper
1 tablespoon instant mashed potato granules

COMBINE beans, 5½ cups water, sausage, carrot, green onions, and bouillon cube. Bring to boil, cover, and reduce heat. Simmer 2 hours. Let cool 1 hour then drain, saving liquid. Grind or mash bean mixture and add to bean liquid. Combine undiluted tomato soup, salt, pepper, and potato granules with 1 cup water. Add to bean mixture. Cook over low heat 30 minutes, stirring occasionally.

Makes 8 to 10 servings.

An interview with the galley crew of the former destroyer-escort U.S.S. McGinty elicited this recipe for a hearty bean soup thickened with—of all things—mashed potato granules. It captured the hearts of our readers the moment it appeared.

Lentil Soup Borracho

1 pound lentils, rinsed
4 cups beer
3 cups chicken broth
1 pound lean ground beef
1 cup cooked ham pieces
1 pound smoked sausage or kielbasa, thinly sliced

1 cup coarsely chopped celery
1 cup chopped red onion
1 teaspoon chopped garlic
½ teaspoon rosemary
½ teaspoon basil
1 cup sliced mushrooms
  Salt, pepper

COMBINE lentils, beer, and broth in large kettle or Dutch oven. Bring to boil, reduce heat, and simmer. Brown ground beef in skillet. Drain off fat. Add beef with ham, sausage, celery, onion, garlic, rosemary, basil, and mushrooms to kettle and cook 1 hour, or until tender. Season to taste with salt and pepper.

Makes 10 to 12 servings.

Father John Wishard of Our Lady of Malibu Church was only kidding when he called this robust main dish soup "borracho," which means drunkard in Spanish. The alcohol in the four cups of beer cooks away, leaving only the yeasty flavor of the hops.

Lentil Soup

The lentil soup from the Sportsmen's Lodge, a family restaurant in Studio City, is a reader favorite.

2 cups lentils, rinsed
9 cups water
1 ham bone
¹/₂ pound bacon, diced
³/₄ cup chopped onion
³/₄ cup chopped celery
¹/₂ cup chopped carrots
¹/₂ cup chopped leeks

1 clove garlic, minced
1 bay leaf
¹/₂ teaspoon thyme
2 teaspoons salt
¹/₄ teaspoon pepper
2 tablespoons vinegar
6 frankfurters, sliced

COMBINE lentils with water and ham bone in large kettle. Bring to boil, reduce heat, and simmer 45 minutes, stirring occasionally. Sauté bacon in skillet until it is transparent but has not changed color. Add onion, celery, carrots, leeks, garlic, bay leaf, thyme, salt, and pepper to bacon. Cook and stir 4 minutes. Add to lentils and simmer 45 minutes longer, stirring occasionally. Add vinegar and frankfurters. Bring again to simmer and remove from heat.

Makes 6 to 8 servings.

Minestrone

It would be difficult to find a lustier minestrone than this one from Valentino, a fine Italian restaurant in Santa Monica.

3 cloves garlic, minced
1 cup chopped celery
1 cup chopped onions
1 cup chopped carrots
2 tablespoons oil (not olive)
¹/₂ teaspoon thyme
¹/₂ teaspoon oregano
2 to 3 bay leaves
1 (1-pound) can tomato puree

5 puree cans water
2 bunches spinach, chopped, or 1 (10-ounce) package frozen chopped spinach
1 (1-pound) can green beans
1 (1-pound) can or 1 (10-ounce) package frozen peas
1 (1-pound) can red kidney beans
8 ounces shell macaroni
Salt, pepper

SAUTÉ garlic, celery, onions, and carrots in oil until vegetables are crisp-tender. Add thyme, oregano, bay leaves, tomato puree, and water. Bring to boil and add spinach, green beans, peas, and kidney beans. Bring again to boil and add macaroni. Reduce heat and simmer until macaroni is cooked *al dente*. Do not overcook. Season to taste with salt and pepper.

Makes 6 to 8 servings.

Green Chile Yogurt Soup

2 tablespoons butter or
  margarine
1 tablespoon oil
4 to 5 cloves garlic, minced
1 medium onion, chopped
2 teaspoons paprika
4 cups chicken broth
1½ pounds tomatoes,
  chopped
1 (4-ounce) can diced
  green chiles

¼ teaspoon chili powder
  Salt, pepper
2 cups plain low-fat
  yogurt
2 to 4 ounces Monterey Jack
  or cheddar cheese,
  shredded
1 tablespoon chopped
  cilantro

Typical of the blend of cultures in Los Angeles is this spicy combination of yogurt, a European and Middle Eastern food, and Mexican seasonings.

MELT butter in large kettle and add oil. Add garlic and sauté until lightly browned. Remove garlic and set aside. Add onion to butter and sauté until tender. Add paprika and sauté 1 minute. Add chicken broth, tomatoes, chiles, and chili powder. Season to taste with salt and pepper. Bring to boil, reduce heat, and simmer about 20 minutes. Stir in yogurt slowly and cook over low heat just until heated through. Do not boil or yogurt will curdle. Add reserved garlic. Ladle into soup bowls and sprinkle with cheese and cilantro.

Makes 6 servings.

Menudo

4 pounds veal knuckles or beef
  shins
3 pounds tripe, cut into
  ½-inch pieces
4 cloves garlic, minced
2 cups chopped onions
1 tablespoon crushed dried red
  chiles

2 teaspoons salt
2 teaspoons oregano
2 teaspoons chili powder
1 teaspoon coriander
4 quarts water
2 (1-pound) cans hominy
  Chopped cilantro or green
  onions

According to Mexican tradition, menudo is a terrific cure for hangovers.

HAVE veal knuckles cracked or beef shins cut into short lengths. Place in large kettle with tripe. Add garlic, onions, crushed chiles, salt, oregano, chili powder, coriander, and water. Cover, bring to boil, reduce heat, and simmer 6 hours, or until tripe is very tender. Add drained hominy and simmer 30 minutes longer. Remove bones and adjust seasonings. Sprinkle with chopped cilantro.

Makes 8 to 10 servings.

Sopa de Albóndigas

The spicy Mexican sausage called chorizo flavors the meatballs (albóndigas) in this version of a typical Mexican soup.

1 cup soft bread cubes
1/4 cup milk
1/2 pound lean ground beef
1/2 pound chorizo, casings removed
1 egg
  Seasoned salt
1 cup diced celery

1/3 to 1/2 cup coarsely chopped cilantro
1 large onion, minced
1/2 cup sliced carrots
2 cups cubed zucchini
2 1/2 cups beef broth
1 (1-pound 12-ounce) can whole tomatoes

COMBINE bread cubes and milk and mix with ground beef, chorizo, egg, and 1/2 teaspoon seasoned salt. Chill 30 minutes. Combine celery, cilantro, onion, carrots, zucchini, broth, and tomatoes in large kettle. Bring to boil, cover, reduce heat to simmer, and cook 15 minutes. Shape meat mixture into 16 or more meatballs. Add to soup, cover, and simmer 45 minutes, or until meat is done. Adjust seasonings. Serve immediately.

Makes 8 servings.

Bulgarian Meatball Soup

The women of St. George's Bulgarian Eastern Orthodox Church in Los Angeles introduced this outstanding main dish soup to our readers in 1968 and the recipe is still frequently requested.

1 pound ground beef
6 tablespoons rice
1 teaspoon paprika
1 teaspoon savory
  Salt, pepper
  Flour
6 cups water
2 beef bouillon cubes
1/2 bunch green onions, sliced
1 large green pepper, chopped

2 medium carrots, peeled and thinly sliced
3 to 4 tomatoes, peeled and chopped
1 or 2 small yellow chiles, split and most seeds removed
1/2 bunch parsley, minced
1 egg
  Juice of 1 lemon

COMBINE beef, rice, paprika, and savory. Season to taste with salt and pepper. Mix lightly but thoroughly. Form into 1-inch balls, then roll in flour. Combine water, bouillon cubes, 1 tablespoon salt, 1 teaspoon pepper, green onions, green pepper, carrots, and tomatoes in large kettle. Cover, bring to boil, reduce heat, and simmer 30 minutes. Add meatballs, cover, and bring to boil again. Reduce heat and simmer 20 minutes. Add chiles and simmer, covered, 40 minutes, or until rice is cooked. Add parsley during last 5 minutes of cooking time. Taste and add more salt and pepper, if needed. Just before serving, beat egg with lemon juice. Stir 1 to 2 tablespoons hot soup into egg mixture, then stir egg mixture into soup. Heat and stir until soup is thickened slightly, but do not allow to boil.

Makes 8 to 10 servings.

SALADS

THE abundant selection of fresh fruits and vegetables in California markets all year round has been an inspiration to salad chefs. Long before the rest of the country became aware of the gastronomic possibilities and beneficial effects of raw fruits and vegetables, salads were the stars of California menus.

The burgeoning interest in health foods and natural-food restaurants all across the country began here on the West Coast. Do-it-yourself salad bars are a popular feature of many steak houses and other restaurants, while for those who entertain at home, the ingredients for a pile-it-on, make-your-own salad create an attractive display at the buffet table.

The health-food salad, with its obligatory alfalfa sprouts and sunflower seeds, the spinach and mushroom salad, the various stuffed avocado and Cobb salads all originated in California and took the country by storm. On the other hand, ethnic salads such as the tostada, Chinese chicken salad, and Middle Eastern tabbouleh are adopted favorites.

Californians have a choice of five or six different varieties of lettuce almost all year long. This easy availability is so much a part of California life that in preparing this book the customary tossed green salad was almost overlooked.

Fruits, too, are important ingredients of California salads. The infinitely varied kinds that come on the market throughout the year make it possible to enjoy natural sweets often, without fear of monotony.

But salads are in no way restricted to those based on fresh fruits and vegetables. Meats, fish and seafood, eggs, pastas, and a host of other ingredients are merrily tossed together in interesting combinations of pleasing flavors and textures. There probably is little that is edible raw that some imaginative California cook hasn't found a place for in a tantalizingly attractive salad bowl.

Tossed Mixed Greens, page 64

Tossed Mixed Greens

A tossed green salad is such a basic component of California menus we rarely are asked for a recipe. There are two important rules to remember in preparing one, however: the greens must be crisp and there should be just enough dressing to coat them.

2 small heads romaine
2 small heads butter lettuce
2 cups torn spinach leaves
1 cup coarsely chopped watercress leaves
1 cup oil
1/2 cup vinegar

1/4 cup sugar
2 tablespoons chili sauce
2 tablespoons minced onion
1/8 teaspoon black pepper
1/2 teaspoon salt
1/4 teaspoon paprika

TEAR romaine and butter lettuce into pieces and combine in a bowl with spinach and watercress. Chill until ready to serve. Mix oil, vinegar, sugar, chili sauce, onion, pepper, salt, and paprika in jar with a tight-fitting lid. Shake dressing vigorously to blend well. Chill dressing. Shake again before tossing with greens. Add only enough dressing to coat greens.

Makes 12 servings.

California Chef Salad

No two chef's salads are alike, but if there is such a thing as a California version, this one probably fills the bill.

2 tomatoes, cut in wedges
8 cups torn salad greens
1/4 cup sliced green onions
2 cucumbers, sliced
4 thin slices salami or cooked ham, cut in strips

1/2 cup cubed cooked turkey or chicken
Thousand Island Dressing

TOSS tomatoes, greens, green onions, and cucumbers together. Place in deep salad bowl and top with salami and turkey. Serve dressing separately.

Makes 6 to 8 servings.

Thousand Island Dressing

1 1/2 cups mayonnaise
1/2 teaspoon salt
1/4 teaspoon black pepper
   Dash red pepper
1 tablespoon lemon juice

1 tablespoon catsup
1 teaspoon Worcestershire sauce
1/2 cup chili sauce
Minced parsley

Combine mayonnaise, salt, black pepper, red pepper, lemon juice, catsup, Worcestershire, and chili sauce. Chill. Serve in sauce boat. Garnish with minced parsley.

Makes 2 cups.

Salad Niçoise

1 head butter lettuce	$^1/_2$ cup pitted black olives
French Dressing I	2 or 3 hard-cooked eggs,
3 cups sliced cold cooked	peeled and quartered
potatoes	6 to 12 anchovy fillets
3 cups cold cooked cut green	2 to 3 tablespoons minced
beans	fresh tarragon, chives,
4 tomatoes, quartered	basil, or chervil
2 cups large chunks canned	
tuna, chilled	

Salad Niçoise is turning up on more and more restaurant menus. It has quite a following among the salad-loving lunch bunch.

LINE shallow bowl or dish with large outer leaves of lettuce. Break remaining lettuce into bowl and toss with 2 tablespoons French Dressing I. Separately season potatoes, beans, tomatoes, and tuna with dressing and arrange over lettuce. Garnish with olives, eggs, and anchovies. Pour $^1/_2$ to $^3/_4$ cup dressing over all and sprinkle with herbs.

Makes 6 servings.

French Dressing I

$^1/_4$ cup wine or cider vinegar	$^1/_8$ teaspoon black pepper
1 tablespoon water	$^1/_4$ teaspoon dry mustard
$^1/_2$ teaspoon salt	$^1/_4$ teaspoon crushed basil
$^1/_4$ teaspoon garlic salt	$^3/_4$ cup oil

Blend vinegar, water, salt, garlic salt, pepper, mustard, and basil thoroughly. Beat in oil or shake mixture in jar with tight-fitting cover until thoroughly mixed. Shake or beat again before using.

Makes about 1 cup.

Chicken Salad

$2^1/_4$ cups diced, cooked	$^3/_4$ teaspoon prepared mustard
chicken	$^3/_4$ cup mayonnaise
$^1/_4$ cup chopped sweet pickle	Salt, pepper
$^1/_4$ cup diced celery	

Simple home-style dishes like this easy chicken salad are specialties at the Knott's Berry Farm amusement park in Buena Park.

COMBINE chicken, sweet pickle, and celery in large bowl. Blend mustard with mayonnaise and stir into chicken mixture until well-coated. Season to taste with salt and pepper.

Makes about $2^1/_2$ cups.

Avocado Filled with Crabmeat

This idea of using an herbed mayonnaise dressing with crab and avocado came from the Huntington Sheraton Hotel in Pasadena.

2 avocados
1/2 pound crabmeat
Dash hot pepper sauce (optional)
1/4 cup minced celery
Mayonnaise
Lemon juice
MSG (optional)
Salt, pepper
Shredded lettuce

4 hard-cooked eggs, chopped
4 anchovy fillets
4 strips pimiento
1 lemon, cut in 4 wedges
1 tomato, cut in 4 wedges
Black olives
Parsley sprigs
Herbed Mayonnaise Dressing

CUT avocados in halves and remove seeds. Flake crabmeat and combine with hot pepper sauce, celery, and enough mayonnaise to moisten. Season to taste with lemon juice, MSG, salt, and pepper. Place avocado halves on shredded lettuce, fill with crab mixture, and sprinkle generously with chopped eggs. Garnish with anchovies, pimiento strips, lemon and tomato wedges, olives, and parsley. Serve Herbed Mayonnaise Dressing on side.

Makes 4 servings.

Herbed Mayonnaise Dressing

1 cup mayonnaise
Dash tarragon
Dash chervil
2 tablespoons chopped chives

2 to 3 tablespoons tomato puree

Combine mayonnaise, tarragon, chervil, and chives. Add just enough tomato puree to give dressing a pourable consistency and delicate color.

Makes 1 1/4 cups.

California Shrimp Bowl

Shrimp of any size will do in this salad, but medium shrimp are really the best.

1 1/2 pounds unshelled shrimp
1 tablespoon pickling spice
2 or 3 celery tops
Salad greens

2 tomatoes, cut in wedges
2 tablespoons capers
2 hard-cooked eggs, sliced
3 tablespoons bottled oil and vinegar dressing

DROP shrimp into boiling salted water to cover and add pickling spice and celery tops. Bring again to boil and cook, uncovered, 2 to 3 minutes. Drain, peel, and devein shrimp. Place in bowl, cover tightly, and chill several hours. Line serving bowl with greens. Arrange shrimp and tomato wedges in bowl. Sprinkle with capers and garnish with sliced eggs. Sprinkle with dressing and serve at once. Pass more dressing, if desired.

Makes 6 servings.

Curried Crab and Rice Salad

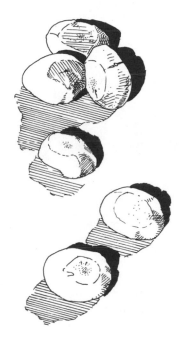

<table>
<tr><td>1/2 pound crabmeat</td><td>1/2 teaspoon soy sauce</td></tr>
<tr><td>1 1/4 cups cooked rice, chilled</td><td>Salt, pepper</td></tr>
<tr><td>1/3 cup chopped celery</td><td>1/2 teaspoon curry powder</td></tr>
<tr><td>2 green onions, chopped</td><td>1/2 cup mayonnaise</td></tr>
<tr><td>1/4 cup sliced water chestnuts</td><td>6 medium tomatoes</td></tr>
<tr><td>1 tablespoon lemon juice</td><td>Lettuce</td></tr>
</table>

RESERVE some crabmeat for garnish and combine the rest with rice, celery, green onions, and water chestnuts. Mix lemon juice, soy sauce, 1/4 teaspoon salt, dash pepper, curry powder, and mayonnaise. Add to crab mixture and toss to coat lightly, then chill well. With stem end down, cut tomatoes into 6 wedges, cutting to, but not through, base of tomatoes. Spread sections apart and season to taste with salt and pepper. Place tomatoes on lettuce-lined plates. Fill with crab-rice mixture. Garnish with reserved crab.

Makes 6 servings.

Tropical Fruit Salad

<table>
<tr><td>1 pineapple, peeled, cored, and cut into sticks</td><td>1/4 cup pineapple juice</td></tr>
<tr><td></td><td>1 tablespoon lemon juice</td></tr>
<tr><td>1 mango, peeled and sliced</td><td>1/2 teaspoon salt</td></tr>
<tr><td>1 papaya, peeled and sliced lengthwise</td><td>1/2 teaspoon curry powder</td></tr>
<tr><td></td><td>1/8 teaspoon ginger</td></tr>
<tr><td>1 orange, peeled and sectioned</td><td>1 tablespoon honey</td></tr>
<tr><td>Salad greens</td><td>1/2 cup oil</td></tr>
</table>

ARRANGE pineapple sticks, mango and papaya slices, and orange sections in rows on greens on platter. Combine pineapple and lemon juices, salt, curry powder, and ginger. Blend thoroughly. Stir in honey and oil and mix well. Blend again just before using. Sprinkle fruit with just enough dressing to give a glossy appearance. Serve salad at once.

Makes 6 to 8 servings.

Tabbouleh
(Bulgur Salad)

Tabbouleh, a bulgur or cracked wheat salad of Middle Eastern origin, is wonderful with barbecued lamb, steaks, or other meats. Fresh mint is a must.

$^1/_2$ cup bulgur
$^1/_2$ cup minced green onions
 1 cup minced parsley
$^1/_2$ cup minced fresh mint
 2 cups coarsely chopped, peeled tomatoes

$^1/_3$ cup lemon juice
$^1/_2$ teaspoon salt
$^1/_4$ teaspoon black pepper
$^1/_3$ cup olive oil
 Romaine leaves

SOAK bulgur in cold water to cover for 10 minutes. Drain and squeeze as dry as possible in clean tea towel or by pressing with back of spoon against a sieve. Place drained bulgur in a bowl and add green onions, parsley, mint, and tomatoes. Stir in lemon juice, salt, and pepper. Let stand about 30 minutes to allow flavors to blend. Stir in oil. Pile mixture in a bowl and surround with inside leaves of romaine to use for scooping.

Makes 6 to 8 servings.

International Salad

This international salad combines French dressing, Oriental soy sauce, and jicama, a Mexican vegetable that is becoming better known across the country. Jicama can't be called pretty, but its tough, brown skin hides a wonderfully crisp apple-like texture and flavor that is exceptionally good in salads.

$^1/_2$ pound spinach, torn in bite-size pieces
 1 cup stemmed watercress
$^1/_2$ small jicama, peeled and thinly sliced

 1 red onion, thinly sliced in rings
$^1/_2$ cup French Dressing II
$^1/_2$ teaspoon soy sauce

TOSS spinach and watercress together in large bowl. Add jicama and onion rings. Blend French Dressing II and soy sauce. Pour over salad and toss. Serve at once.

Makes 4 servings.

French Dressing II

$^2/_3$ cup red wine vinegar
 1 tablespoon dry mustard
 1 teaspoon garlic powder
$^1/_2$ teaspoon white pepper

 1 teaspoon salt
 Dash tarragon
 2 cups oil

Blend vinegar, mustard, garlic powder, white pepper, salt, and tarragon. Stir in oil. Let dressing stand 2 hours, then refrigerate. Use as much as is needed, refrigerating remainder for use as needed up to 2 weeks.

Makes $2^2/_3$ cups.

Greek Salad

1 large head iceberg lettuce
1 cup chopped green onions
1 cucumber, sliced
2 large tomatoes, cut in
   wedges
1 green pepper, diced
1 cup red radish halves

2 tablespoons minced parsley
1 cup cubed feta cheese
$1/2$ cup Greek-style olives
$3/4$ cup olive oil
$1/2$ cup vinegar
1 small clove garlic, minced
   Salt, pepper

It may not be authentic, but it's delicious and it's what Angelenos call Greek salad.

TEAR lettuce into bite-size pieces and place in large bowl. Add green onions, cucumber, tomatoes, green pepper, radishes, parsley, cheese, and olives. Combine oil, vinegar, and garlic, and season to taste with salt and pepper, blending well. Pour dressing over salad just before serving and toss lightly but thoroughly.

Makes 6 to 8 servings.

Curried Chicken Salad

1 ($3^1/2$-pound) chicken
$1/2$ cup chopped green pepper
$1/2$ cup chopped onion
$1/2$ cup chopped celery
$1/2$ cup coarsely cut prunes
$1/2$ cup golden raisins

$1/2$ cup seedless grapes
$1/2$ cup diced cantaloupe
   Curry Dressing I
4 papayas
   Lettuce leaves
   Tomato slices

The Egg & Eye restaurant on Wilshire Boulevard in Los Angeles combines the tastes and textures of several different fruits with chicken in this spicy curry-flavored salad.

COOK chicken in boiling salted water until tender, about 35 to 40 minutes. Drain, reserving broth for other use. Cool chicken, then remove bones and skin and cut meat into chunks. Combine chicken with green pepper, onion, celery, prunes, raisins, grapes, cantaloupe, and Curry Dressing I and toss to mix well. Chill. Cut papayas in halves and remove seeds. Spoon chicken salad into papaya cavities and serve on lettuce leaves garnished with tomato slices.

Makes 8 servings.

Curry Dressing I

1 cup whipping cream
$1/3$ cup mayonnaise

1 teaspoon curry powder
   Salt, pepper

Combine cream, mayonnaise, and curry powder in blender container and blend until smooth. Season to taste with salt and pepper.

Makes about $1^1/2$ cups.

Curried Egg Salad

1 envelope unflavored gelatin
2 cups chicken broth
1 tablespoon curry powder
4 hard-cooked eggs, sliced

Sliced pitted black olives
Crisp salad greens
Tomato wedges

SOFTEN gelatin in ¼ cup chicken broth. Bring remaining broth to boil and stir in softened gelatin and curry powder until dissolved. Chill gelatin mixture until syrupy. Arrange some of the egg slices in bottom of greased 3-cup ring mold and pour enough gelatin around eggs to anchor in place. Gently push some sliced olives into gelatin in mold in a decorative pattern. Chill until firm. Stir remaining eggs into remaining gelatin and pour over firm layer. Chill until firm. Unmold onto plate and garnish with crisp greens, tomato wedges, and additional hard-cooked eggs, quartered, if desired.

Makes 4 servings.

Salad Surprise

This may seem an odd combination of ingredients, but visitors to Hawaii's beautiful Mauna Kea Beach Hotel, where this salad is served, often request the recipe.

1 pineapple, peeled, cored, and diced
2 cups cherry tomatoes, cut in halves
2 medium avocados, peeled, seeded, and diced

1 cup red wine vinegar
1 small clove garlic, mashed (optional)
½ cup oil
Salt, pepper
Lettuce cups

COMBINE pineapple, tomatoes, and avocados in large bowl. Combine vinegar, garlic, and oil and season to taste with salt and pepper. Pour dressing over pineapple mixture and toss to mix. Let stand, refrigerated, for several hours. Drain and serve in lettuce cups.

Makes 4 to 6 servings.

Caesar Salad

3 cloves garlic, peeled
1/2 cup olive or corn oil
2 eggs
1 medium head crisp chilled romaine lettuce, torn in bite-size pieces
2 tablespoons wine vinegar
Juice of 2 lemons

Salt, pepper
Dash Worcestershire sauce
6 to 8 tablespoons grated Romano or Parmesan cheese
1 1/2 cups toasted croutons

The Hotel Caesar in Tijuana, a short hop over the border in Mexico, lays claim to having originated this famous salad.

PLACE garlic cloves in oil in jar and let stand at least 4 hours before preparing salad. When ready to serve, coddle eggs by placing them in simmering, not boiling, water 2 minutes. Remove garlic from oil and add seasoned oil to lettuce in deep salad bowl. Add vinegar, lemon juice, and eggs and season to taste with salt and pepper. Add Worcestershire, cheese, and croutons. Roll (do not toss) salad until ingredients are well mixed.

Makes 6 to 8 servings.

Mystery Tomato Mold

3 (3-ounce) packages raspberry gelatin
1 1/4 cups boiling water
3 (1-pound) cans stewed tomatoes

6 drops hot pepper sauce
Salad greens
Stuffed green olives
Cheese-flavored crackers
Sour Cream Dressing

This unusual aspic is a real oldie that never loses favor with our readers.

DISSOLVE gelatin in hot water. Break up tomatoes and stir into gelatin along with hot pepper sauce. Pour mixture into lightly greased 9 x 5-inch loaf pan. Chill until firm. Unmold on bed of greens. Garnish with stuffed green olives and cheese crackers. Serve with Sour Cream Dressing.

Makes 12 servings.

Sour Cream Dressing

2 tablespoons prepared horseradish
1 pint sour cream
Salt

Stir horseradish into sour cream. Season to taste with salt.

Makes 2 cups.

Cracker Tomato Salad

This old-time recipe with its unusual combination of ingredients never fails to surprise those trying it for the first time.

16 saltine crackers, broken
    into quarters
 1 (1-pound) can whole toma-
    toes, cut up
¹/₃ cup chopped dill pickle

¹/₃ cup mayonnaise
    Salt, pepper
 1 hard-cooked egg, diced
    Lettuce cups

PLACE half the crackers in a shallow salad bowl. Top with half the tomatoes with their juice and sprinkle with half the pickles. Spread with half the mayonnaise and season to taste with salt and pepper. Repeat layers. Sprinkle with diced egg and chill 2 hours before serving. Serve in lettuce cups.

Makes 4 to 6 servings.

Nutty Coleslaw

At Gulliver's restaurant, the specialty of the house is prime ribs, but the coleslaw often steals the show.

6 cups shredded cabbage
¹/₄ cup chopped green onions
¹/₃ cup chopped celery
¹/₃ cup unsalted, roasted
    peanuts
2 tablespoons sugar

1¹/₂ teaspoons seasoned salt
 2 tablespoons red wine
    vinegar
²/₃ cup bottled Italian
    dressing

COMBINE cabbage, green onions, celery, and peanuts in a large bowl. Blend sugar, salt, vinegar, and dressing. Pour over cabbage mixture and toss well.

Makes 8 to 10 servings.

24-Hour Slaw

This old-fashioned oil-and-vinegar slaw is a wonderful do-ahead salad. Although the dressing is boiling when added to the cabbage, the chilled slaw is deliciously crisp.

³/₄ cup sugar
 1 large head cabbage,
    shredded

2 large red onions, thinly
    sliced
    Hot Dressing

STIR sugar into cabbage. Place half of cabbage in large bowl. Cover with onion slices. Top with remaining cabbage. Pour boiling Hot Dressing over slowly. Do not stir. Cover and refrigerate at once. Chill 24 hours. Stir well before serving.

Makes 8 to 10 servings.

Hot Dressing

1 teaspoon celery seeds
1 teaspoon sugar
1 teaspoon dry mustard

1¹/₂ teaspoons salt
1 cup cider vinegar
1 cup oil

Combine celery seeds, sugar, mustard, salt, and vinegar in saucepan. Bring to a rolling boil. Add oil, stirring, and return to rolling boil.

Makes about 2 cups.

Jicama Salad

1 medium jicama, peeled
2 navel oranges, peeled
   Salt
1 teaspoon chili powder
2 tablespoons chopped
   unsalted peanuts (optional)

¹/₈ teaspoon crushed dried red
   chiles (optional)
   Lettuce

This spicy salad comes from Mexico, where jicamas, oranges, and other fruits and vegetables often are served with a sprinkling of chili powder.

CUT jicama into bite-size pieces and place in large bowl. Section oranges and cut into bite-size pieces, holding sections over bowl so juice will fall into it. Season to taste with salt. Add chili powder, peanuts, and crushed chiles. Mix well, chill, and serve on lettuce.

Makes 6 to 8 servings.

Beer Potato Salad

3 pounds potatoes
2 cups diced celery
1 small onion, chopped
   Salt
1 cup mayonnaise
2 tablespoons prepared
   mustard

¹/₄ teaspoon hot pepper sauce
¹/₂ cup beer
2 tablespoons chopped
   parsley

Beer added to the dressing makes this potato salad a standout.

COOK potatoes in skins until tender. When cool, peel and dice. Add celery and onion and season to taste with salt. Blend together mayonnaise, mustard, and hot pepper sauce. Gradually stir in beer. Add parsley. Pour over potato mixture. Mix lightly with fork, being careful not to break potatoes. Chill.

Makes 8 servings.

Marinated Mushroom Salad

Some mushroom salads call for the dressing to be added at the last moment. At Le St. Germain in Los Angeles, the mushrooms are marinated in the dressing for awhile before the salad is served.

1 pound large white
  mushrooms
  Juice of ¹/₂ lemon
2 tablespoons chopped parsley

2 tablespoons chopped chives
  Vinaigrette Dressing
2 tomatoes, sliced

SLICE mushrooms and toss with lemon juice. Add parsley, chives, and Vinaigrette Dressing. Toss, chill, then toss again before serving. Garnish with a few tomato slices.

Makes 4 servings.

Vinaigrette Dressing

3 tablespoons vinegar
2 tablespoons Dijon-style
  mustard

1 cup oil
  Dash white wine
  Salt, pepper

Blend together vinegar and mustard. Gradually add oil, pouring in a thin stream and beating until mixture thickens slightly. Add wine and season to taste with salt and pepper.

Makes about 1¹/₂ cups.

Chicken Fruit Salad in Pineapple Boats

When you want a chicken salad that's out of the ordinary, try this extravagant mixture of chicken and fruit tossed with macadamia nuts and a sweet poppy-seed dressing.

2 large pineapples
2 cups diced cooked chicken
1 large papaya, peeled,
  seeded, and cubed
1 cup sliced celery
2 oranges, peeled and cut in
  segments

1 cup watermelon balls
1 to 2 bananas, peeled and
  sliced
3 kiwi, peeled and sliced
  Poppy-Seed Dressing
  Coarsely chopped
  macadamia nuts

CUT a horizontal slice in each pineapple to make a boat, leaving top leaves intact. Remove meat of pineapple and cut into chunks (2 to 3 cups). In large bowl, combine drained pineapple chunks, chicken, papaya, celery, oranges, watermelon, bananas, and kiwi. Toss at once with Poppy-Seed Dressing to taste. Chill until ready to serve. Before serving, toss with ¹/₂ cup chopped nuts. Serve in pineapple shells and sprinkle with more nuts, if desired.

Makes about 8 servings.

Note: If desired, the salad may be served in a watermelon shell instead of in pineapple boat.

Poppy-Seed Dressing

3/4 cup sugar
1 teaspoon dry mustard
1 teaspoon salt
1/3 cup vinegar

4 1/2 teaspoons onion juice
1 cup oil
4 1/2 teaspoons poppy seeds

Combine sugar, mustard, salt, and vinegar. Stir in onion juice. Slowly add oil, beating constantly until thick. Add poppy seeds and beat a few minutes. Store in refrigerator but avoid putting in a very cold spot as dressing may separate. If dressing separates, pour off clear part. Beat clear portion, then slowly beat in poppy-seed mixture.

Makes about 2 cups.

Chicken Cantonese Salad

1 head iceberg lettuce, chopped
1 (6 3/4-ounce) package rice sticks
Oil for deep frying
3 cups diced or shredded cooked chicken

6 tablespoons toasted sliced almonds
Mustard Mayonnaise Dressing

Chinese chicken salads turn up on menus from Chinatown to department store tearooms. This one is from Bullock's Del Amo branch.

PLACE chopped lettuce in bowl. Deep fry rice sticks in oil heated to 370 degrees 1 to 2 minutes, until puffed. Drain on paper towels. Add rice sticks to lettuce and toss. Add chicken and almonds and toss with Mustard Mayonnaise Dressing to taste.

Makes 6 servings.

Note: Rice sticks, sometimes called rice noodles or mai fun, can be found in Chinese markets and Oriental food sections of some supermarkets.

Mustard Mayonnaise Dressing

2 cups mayonnaise
1 1/4 teaspoons Worcestershire sauce
2 teaspoons soy sauce

2 teaspoons oil
4 teaspoons prepared mustard
1/8 teaspoon lemon juice

Combine mayonnaise, Worcestershire, soy sauce, oil, mustard, and lemon juice. Mix until smooth. Store in covered jar in refrigerator.

Makes about 2 cups.

Chicken Salad Kon-Tiki

Scandia's chicken salad is mixed with a curry dressing and served in cantaloupe halves.

2 cups diced, cooked chicken breast
³/4 cup diced celery
¹/2 cup freshly grated coconut

1 tablespoon chutney
Curry Dressing II
2 cantaloupes

COMBINE chicken, celery, coconut, and chutney and mix well. Toss with Curry Dressing II. Cut cantaloupes in halves, remove seeds, and fill cavities with chicken mixture.

Makes 4 servings.

Curry Dressing II

¹/2 cup mayonnaise
¹/2 cup sour cream
1 teaspoon curry powder

1 teaspoon lime juice
Dash sugar
Salt, pepper

Blend together mayonnaise, sour cream, curry powder, lime juice, and sugar. Season to taste with salt and pepper.

Makes about 1 cup.

Flaming Spinach Salad

A light but impressive meal, this sweet-and-sour spinach salad is flamed with cognac just before serving.

3 pounds spinach, washed and stemmed
12 ounces bacon, diced
1 small onion, chopped
¹/3 cup red wine vinegar
Juice of 1¹/2 lemons

4 teaspoons prepared mustard
¹/2 cup sugar
¹/4 teaspoon Worcestershire sauce
1¹/2 ounces cognac

DRY spinach leaves and place in flameproof bowl. Cook bacon in skillet until crisp. Remove bacon from skillet and set aside. Add onion to drippings in pan and cook until transparent. Add vinegar, lemon juice, mustard, sugar, and Worcestershire and blend well. Quickly pour over spinach. Return skillet to fire, add cognac, and flame. Pour over spinach and toss lightly. Sprinkle with reserved bacon.

Makes 6 to 8 servings.

Spanish Rice Salad

2 cups chilled, cooked rice
1/2 cup chilled, thinly sliced cooked carrots
1/2 cup chilled, cooked cauliflowerets
1/2 cup chopped tomato
1/3 cup minced green onions Oil-and-Vinegar Dressing
2 tablespoons chopped pimiento or black olives

Serve this salad with cold meats or poultry for a light supper or lunch.

COMBINE rice, carrots, cauliflowerets, tomato, and green onions. Add just enough Oil-and-Vinegar Dressing to moisten salad. Garnish with pimiento or olives.

Makes 4 servings.

Oil-and-Vinegar Dressing

1/4 cup oil
1 tablespoon lemon juice
1 teaspoon onion juice
2 teaspoons wine vinegar
1 teaspoon celery seeds
1 teaspoon dry mustard
1 teaspoon sugar
Salt, pepper

Combine oil, lemon juice, onion juice, vinegar, celery seeds, mustard, and sugar. Season to taste with salt and pepper.

Makes about 1/3 cup.

Bombay Salad

8 apples, thinly sliced
4 cups mayonnaise
1/2 (1-pound) bottle chutney
1/4 cup sugar
1 tablespoon curry powder
1/2 cup lime juice
1/2 cup toasted shredded coconut
1/2 cup toasted slivered almonds

We first tasted this curry-flavored apple salad while watching the horses run at Santa Anita Racetrack. The salad was a winner.

COMBINE apples, mayonnaise, chutney, sugar, curry powder, lime juice, coconut, and almonds in chilled bowl. Toss gently to mix well without breaking apples. Chill thoroughly.

Makes 10 to 12 servings.

Offbeat Chicken Salad

This chicken salad was so appetizing and so unusual it won a "My Best Recipe" prize in 1977.

1½ cups diced, cooked chicken
1 cup diced celery
1 medium green pepper, diced
4 green onions, thinly sliced
2 to 3 sprigs parsley, chopped
¼ cup slivered toasted almonds or 10 Greek-style olives, pitted and cut in fine pieces
6 large leaves lettuce (romaine, escarole, or salad bowl), torn in bite-size pieces
¼ teaspoon black pepper
Yogurt-Horseradish Dressing

COMBINE chicken, celery, green pepper, green onions, parsley, almonds, lettuce, and pepper in medium bowl. Add Yogurt-Horseradish Dressing and toss gently but thoroughly.

Makes 4 to 6 servings.

Yogurt-Horseradish Dressing

¼ cup plain low-fat yogurt
2 tablespoons prepared horseradish
2 tablespoons oil
1 small clove garlic, crushed (optional)

Combine yogurt, horseradish, oil, and garlic. Chill until ready to use.

Makes about ½ cup.

Chinese Chicken Salad

The crisp texture of the julienne-cut Chinese pea pods makes this chicken salad from a Beverly Hills French deli, Le Grand Buffet, special.

4 whole chicken breasts
1½ cups chicken broth
1 cup diagonally sliced green onions
1 cup water chestnuts, sliced
1 cup sesame seeds, lightly toasted
1 pound Chinese pea pods, trimmed and cut julienne
Dijon-Sherry Dressing
Salt, pepper

POACH chicken breasts in chicken broth over medium heat 20 minutes, or until done. Let cool in broth. Remove from broth, remove skin and bones from breasts, and cut meat into ¼-inch strips. Crisp green onions in bowl of ice water. Mix chicken, water chestnuts, sesame seeds, pea pods, and green onions in large bowl. Toss with as much Dijon-Sherry Dressing as desired. Season to taste with salt and pepper.

Makes 8 servings.

Dijon-Sherry Dressing

1 (¹/₂-inch) piece gingerroot,
   peeled
¹/₄ cup dry sherry
2 egg yolks
2 tablespoons Dijon-style
   mustard

2 teaspoons sugar
   Juice of 1 lemon
¹/₂ cup olive oil
¹/₂ cup peanut or sesame oil
2 tablespoons soy sauce
   Salt, pepper

Marinate gingerroot in sherry several hours or overnight. Beat egg yolks with mustard. Add sugar and lemon juice and stir to dissolve. Combine oils. Add oils in thin stream to yolk mixture, whisking constantly until thickened and smooth. Remove gingerroot from sherry and add sherry to yolk mixture with soy sauce. Season to taste with salt and pepper.

Makes 2 cups.

Best Macaroni Salad

2 cups warm cooked
   macaroni
3 tablespoons oil
1 tablespoon vinegar
1 teaspoon salt
¹/₈ teaspoon black pepper
2 frankfurters (optional)

¹/₃ cup pitted black olives
³/₄ cup diced cucumber
³/₄ cup diced celery
2 green onions, thinly sliced
¹/₄ cup diced sweet pickle
¹/₄ cup diced pimiento
¹/₂ cup mayonnaise

Put the "franks" in this macaroni salad and you'll have a true one-dish meal.

BLEND macaroni with oil, vinegar, salt, and pepper and toss lightly. Allow to cool thoroughly. Steam frankfurters 5 to 10 minutes. Cool and dice. Cut olives in halves. Combine macaroni, frankfurters, olives, cucumber, celery, green onions, pickle, and pimiento. Add mayonnaise and mix lightly. Chill thoroughly.

Makes 4 to 6 servings.

Ensalada Chalupa Compuesta
(Mexican Composed Salad)

In California parlance a chalupa is the same as a tostada—a crisp corn tortilla—in this instance with salad piled atop it. Señor Pico & Mama Gruber, a restaurant specializing in Mexican food, provided this tasty combination.

Lettuce
6 cups shredded lettuce
6 corn tortillas, fried until crisp
3 cups refried beans
3/4 cup shredded cheddar cheese
1 1/2 cups shredded cooked chicken breast or 1 1/2 cups cooked, peeled, and deveined shrimp

1 1/2 cups guacamole
6 green pepper rings
18 thinly sliced onion rings
6 pitted black olives
6 small ripe tomatoes, quartered

COVER each of 6 dinner plates with lettuce leaves. Top each with 1/2 cup shredded lettuce. Place fried tortillas on baking sheet. Spread each with 1/2 cup refried beans. Sprinkle 2 tablespoons cheese over beans on each tortilla. Place tortillas under broiler until cheese melts, then place 1 tortilla on top of shredded lettuce on each plate. Sprinkle each with another 1/2 cup shredded lettuce, then add 1/4 cup chicken. Top each salad with 1/4 cup guacamole. Garnish with 1 green pepper ring and 3 onion rings. Top with olive. Arrange 4 tomato quarters around base of each salad.

Makes 6 servings.

Note: To make guacamole, see recipe on page 16.

Tunisian Eggplant Salad

1 (12½-ounce) can chunk-
   style tuna
1 pound eggplant
½ cup boiling water
1 large green pepper,
   chopped
1 clove garlic, crushed
½ cup olive oil

⅓ cup red wine vinegar
1 teaspoon oregano
1 teaspoon salt
1 large tomato, seeded and
   chopped
Crisp salad greens
¼ cup crumbled feta cheese

DRAIN tuna. Cut eggplant in 1-inch cubes. Steam over boiling water 2 to 5 minutes until eggplant is tender. Drain. Arrange with green pepper in a 2-quart shallow casserole. Combine garlic, oil, vinegar, oregano, and salt in covered jar. Shake well. Pour over eggplant mixture. Cover and refrigerate 1 hour. Drain marinade and reserve for other use. Toss marinated vegetables with tomato and tuna. Spoon into salad bowl lined with crisp greens. Top with crumbled cheese.

Makes 4 servings.

Chef's Salad

6 strips bacon
8 cups torn salad greens
2 tomatoes, cut in wedges
2 hard-cooked eggs, sliced
4 ounces sliced Swiss cheese,
   cut in strips

4 ounces sliced cooked ham,
   cut in strips
1 cup toasted croutons
Creamy Mustard Dressing

COOK bacon until crisp and drain, reserving 2 tablespoons drippings for dressing. Crumble bacon and combine with greens, tomatoes, eggs, cheese, ham, and croutons. Toss at table with Creamy Mustard Dressing.

Makes 8 servings.

Creamy Mustard Dressing

2 tablespoons bacon
   drippings
¼ cup prepared mustard

¼ cup sour cream
2 tablespoons vinegar
2 teaspoons sugar

Blend drippings, mustard, sour cream, vinegar, and sugar until smooth.

Makes about ¾ cup.

Molded Egg Salad

This makes an attractive buffet or brunch dish.

2 envelopes unflavored gelatin
1/2 cup cold water
1/2 cup boiling water
1 1/2 cups mayonnaise
1/4 cup lemon juice
1/2 teaspoon salt
1/8 teaspoon hot pepper sauce
1 tablespoon grated onion
12 hard-cooked eggs
1/4 cup minced parsley
1/2 cup chopped green pepper
Green pepper strips

SOFTEN gelatin in cold water. Add boiling water and stir until dissolved. Add mayonnaise, lemon juice, salt, hot pepper sauce, and onion. Blend well. Cut several center slices from eggs for garnish. Separate remaining yolks and whites. Mash yolks and chop whites fine. Pack mashed yolks in greased 8 x 4-inch glass loaf pan. Pour half the gelatin mixture over yolks. Arrange egg slices flat against sides of pan, anchoring in gelatin. Chill until partially set. Sprinkle parsley and chopped green pepper over gelatin layer. Cover with chopped whites, then remaining gelatin. Chill until firm. Unmold and garnish with green pepper strips.

Makes 12 servings.

Seafood Salad Lorenzo

A crowd-pleasing salad from The Times's executive dining room, this seafood offering is flexible in preparation. In place of the langostinos, for instance, you could easily substitute crabmeat.

1/2 cup finely chopped celery
4 ounces cooked bay shrimp
6 ounces cooked langostinos
1/2 pound halibut steak, poached, boned, and flaked
1 tablespoon chopped chives
Lorenzo Dressing
Lemon juice
Curly endive
2 tomatoes, peeled and sliced
3 hard-cooked eggs, sliced
Lemon wedges
Pitted black olives, halved
Canned white asparagus
Belgian endive

COMBINE celery, shrimp, langostinos, halibut, and chives in large bowl. Add enough Lorenzo Dressing to moisten, season to taste with lemon juice, and gently toss. Let stand 1 hour in refrigerator. Mound seafood mixture on large platter lined with curly endive. Surround edges with alternate slices of tomatoes and inverted lemon wedges. Top each tomato slice with slice of hard-cooked egg and half an olive. Garnish with asparagus and Belgian endive. If desired, garnish top of seafood mound with Belgian endive centered with tomato rose made from end slices of tomatoes. Serve with remaining dressing.

Makes 4 to 6 servings.

Note: This recipe can easily be multiplied to serve larger groups.

Lorenzo Dressing

1½ cups mayonnaise	4 anchovy fillets, minced
4½ tablespoons catsup	1½ teaspoons lemon juice
4½ tablespoons chili sauce	Salt, pepper
1½ teaspoons horseradish	Worcestershire sauce

Combine mayonnaise, catsup, chili sauce, horseradish, anchovies, and lemon juice and season to taste with salt, pepper, and Worcestershire. Blend well.

Makes about 2¼ cups.

Cobb Salad

½ head iceberg lettuce	6 strips bacon, cooked and diced
½ bunch watercress	1 avocado, peeled and diced
1 small bunch curly endive	3 hard-cooked eggs, diced
½ head romaine	½ cup Roquefort cheese, crumbled
2 tablespoons minced chives	Special French Dressing
2 medium tomatoes, peeled, seeded, and diced	
1 whole chicken breast, cooked, boned, skinned, and diced	

The Cobb salad, a creation of the Original Hollywood Brown Derby restaurant, is a stunning mosaic of ingredients which are tossed together at the table. It's an excellent main dish for a luncheon or warm weather supper.

CHOP lettuce, watercress, endive, and romaine in very fine pieces using knife or food processor. Mix together in 1 large wide bowl or individual wide shallow bowls. Add chives. Arrange tomatoes, chicken, bacon, avocado, and eggs in narrow strips or wedges across top of greens. Sprinkle with cheese. Chill. At serving time toss with ½ cup Special French Dressing. Pass remaining dressing.

Makes 6 servings.

Special French Dressing

¼ cup water	½ teaspoon Worcestershire sauce
¼ cup red wine vinegar	¾ teaspoon dry mustard
¼ teaspoon sugar	½ clove garlic, minced
1½ teaspoons lemon juice	¼ cup olive oil
½ teaspoon salt	¾ cup vegetable oil
½ teaspoon black pepper	

Combine water, vinegar, sugar, lemon juice, salt, pepper, Worcestershire, mustard, garlic, and oils. Chill. Shake well before using.

Makes about 1½ cups.

Leon Salad

Movie stars flock to the La Scala Boutique in Beverly Hills to lunch on Leon salad and a bottle of white wine.

1 head iceberg lettuce, finely chopped
1 head romaine, finely chopped
1/4 pound Italian salami, cut julienne
4 ounces mozzarella cheese, shredded
1 (15 1/2-ounce) can garbanzo beans, drained
Leon Dressing

COMBINE iceberg lettuce, romaine, salami, cheese, and beans in a bowl. Toss with Leon Dressing and serve.

Makes 6 servings.

Leon Dressing

1/4 cup oil
2 tablespoons wine vinegar
1 teaspoon dry mustard
1/2 teaspoon salt
1/2 teaspoon black pepper
1/4 cup grated Parmesan cheese

Combine oil, vinegar, mustard, salt, pepper, and Parmesan cheese.

Makes about 1/2 cup.

Taco Salad

The taco salad appears on California tables in many variations, but all include crunchy corn chips.

1 1/2 pounds ground beef
Bottled French dressing
1/4 cup chopped onion
1/2 teaspoon salt
1/4 teaspoon black pepper
1/2 teaspoon oregano
1/2 head iceberg lettuce, finely shredded
2 tomatoes, cut in wedges
1 (8-ounce) can whole kernel corn, drained
1 (8-ounce) can garbanzo beans, drained
1/2 cup radish slices
1 (6 1/4-ounce) package tortilla or corn chips
1 avocado, peeled and sliced
4 ounces sharp cheddar cheese, shredded
Pitted black olives, sliced
Sour cream

BROWN meat and drain off fat. Add 1/3 cup French dressing, onion, salt, pepper, and oregano. Simmer 5 minutes. Combine lettuce, tomatoes, corn, beans, radishes and enough dressing to moisten. Toss lightly. For each salad, serve meat mixture over tortilla chips. Top with lettuce mixture, avocado, cheese, olives, and sour cream, as desired.

Makes 4 to 6 servings.

Three Bean Salad

2 cups cooked or canned green
  beans, drained
1 cup canned garbanzo beans,
  drained
1 cup canned red kidney
  beans, drained

1 medium onion, sliced
  Herbed Dressing
  Lettuce
  Bacon, cooked and crumbled

Bean salads are picnic favorites in Southern California. From three beans you can go on to four, five, or six.

COMBINE green, garbanzo, and kidney beans with onion in large bowl. Pour Herbed Dressing over vegetables and refrigerate at least 1 hour. To serve, scoop beans onto lettuce leaves. Garnish with crumbled bacon.

Makes 6 servings.

Herbed Dressing

1/2 cup oil
1/4 cup wine vinegar
 1 clove garlic, minced
1/2 teaspoon dry mustard
1/2 teaspoon basil

1/2 teaspoon oregano
1/4 teaspoon rosemary
 1 tablespoon minced parsley
 1 tablespoon capers

Combine oil, vinegar, garlic, mustard, basil, oregano, rosemary, parsley, and capers in covered jar. Mix and set aside until needed.

Makes about 1 cup.

Creamy Coleslaw

3/4 cup mayonnaise
 3 tablespoons sugar
1 1/2 tablespoons white wine
  vinegar
1/3 cup oil
1/8 teaspoon garlic powder
1/8 teaspoon onion powder
1/8 teaspoon dry mustard

1/8 teaspoon celery salt
  Dash black pepper
 1 tablespoon lemon juice
1/2 cup half and half
1/4 teaspoon salt
 1 large head cabbage, very
  finely shredded

The Original Pantry is a landmark in downtown Los Angeles. This coleslaw is a good example of what keeps diners coming back.

BLEND together mayonnaise, sugar, vinegar, and oil. Add garlic and onion powders, mustard, celery salt, pepper, lemon juice, half and half, and salt. Stir until smooth. Pour over cabbage in large bowl and toss until cabbage is well coated.

Makes 8 to 10 servings.

Watermelon Salad Boat

You can't have a patio party in Southern California without a scooped-out watermelon filled with fruit. If the avocado dressing is not to your liking, toss the fruit with the poppy-seed dressing on page 95 instead.

1 large long watermelon, well chilled
1 honeydew melon, scooped into balls
   Seedless grapes
   Diced mangoes or peaches

   Strawberries, halved
   Sliced bananas, sprinkled with lemon juice
   Coarsely chopped nuts (optional)
   Avocado Dressing

USING a sawtooth pattern, trace a zigzag horizontally around top third of watermelon. Cut through melon with sharp knife, removing top. Cut flesh of melon into balls or chunks, leaving shell 1-inch thick. Combine watermelon with honeydew balls, grapes, mangoes, strawberries, bananas, and nuts. Toss gently. Pile fruits into watermelon boat. Serve with Avocado Dressing.

Makes 10 to 12 servings.

Avocado Dressing

1 cup whipping cream
2 tablespoons powdered sugar
1/2 teaspoon salt
2 avocados, halved, seeded, peeled, and mashed

1/2 cup pineapple juice or 1/4 cup lemon juice
1 tablespoon finely chopped candied ginger

Whip cream with powdered sugar and salt. Mix avocados and pineapple juice thoroughly. Fold into whipped cream with ginger.

Makes about 2 1/2 cups.

Beef Salad

1/4 cup red wine vinegar
1/4 cup water
2 tablespoons lemon juice
2 tablespoons sugar
1/4 teaspoon dill weed
1/2 teaspoon salt

   Dash white pepper
3 cups julienne-cut cold roast beef
1 small onion, thinly sliced
8 cups torn salad greens
1 cup sour cream

SIMMER vinegar, water, lemon juice, sugar, dill weed, salt, and white pepper together 10 to 15 minutes. Cool and toss with beef and onion. Chill. Drain, reserving marinade. Place greens in bowl. Top with beef and onion. Combine sour cream with reserved marinade. Toss with greens and beef.

Makes 6 to 8 servings.

Seafood Salad with Avocado Hollandaise Dressing

Lettuce leaves
1 (10-ounce) package frozen
    asparagus spears, cooked
1 pound large shrimp, cooked,
    shelled, and deveined
1/2 pound scallops or cubed
    white fish, cooked in butter

2 hard-cooked eggs, sliced
1/3 cup pitted black olives
    Avocado Hollandaise
    Dressing

This rich avocado dressing enhances almost any kind of seafood salad. It's pretty, too.

ARRANGE lettuce leaves on large platter. Top with asparagus, shrimp, scallops, and eggs arranged in any fashion desired. Garnish with olives. Serve with dressing.

Makes 6 servings.

Avocado Hollandaise Dressing

 2 eggs
1/4 cup lemon juice
1/2 cup butter or margarine,
    melted
 1 avocado, peeled, seeded,
    and chopped

1 teaspoon salt
    Dash red pepper
    Onion salt

Blend eggs with lemon juice in blender container until lemon colored. Slowly add bubbly hot butter at low speed. Add avocado and blend into butter mixture until smooth. Add salt, red pepper, and onion salt to taste. Chill at least 30 minutes.

Makes 1¹/₄ cups.

Crab Louis

Louis dressing, and this salad, originated in San Francisco many years ago.

4 large butter lettuce
  leaves
1 large head iceberg
  lettuce, shredded
2 to 3 cups cooked crabmeat
  or 2 (7½-ounce) cans
  crabmeat, chilled and
  drained

4 hard-cooked eggs
4 tomatoes, cut in wedges
2 tablespoons chopped chives
  Salt
  Louis Dressing
  Large pitted black olives

LINE salad bowl or 4 serving plates with butter lettuce leaves. Place shredded lettuce on top of leaves. Mound crab on top of lettuce. Slice 2 hard-cooked eggs and arrange with tomato wedges around crab. Rice 2 remaining hard-cooked eggs or put through a sieve and sprinkle over crab with chopped chives. Season to taste with salt. Pour dressing over salad. Garnish with olives.

Makes 4 servings.

Louis Dressing

2 cups mayonnaise
1 cup chili sauce
½ teaspoon tarragon vinegar
½ teaspoon prepared
  horseradish

1 teaspoon Worcestershire
  sauce
¼ cup chopped green pepper
¼ cup chopped pimiento
  Salt, pepper

Combine mayonnaise, chili sauce, vinegar, horseradish, Worcestershire, green pepper, and pimiento. Season to taste with salt and pepper. Stir well. Chill, covered.

Makes about 3½ cups.

Grapefruit and Spinach Salad

1½ pounds spinach, washed
  and stemmed
2 tablespoons crumbled blue
  cheese

½ cup Sherry Dressing
4 grapefruit, peeled and
  sectioned
  Salt, pepper

DRY spinach leaves on paper towels. Refrigerate in plastic bag to crisp. Combine cheese and Sherry Dressing and toss with spinach leaves and grapefruit sections in large bowl. Season to taste with salt and pepper.

Makes 6 to 8 servings.

Sherry Dressing

1 egg
1 teaspoon sugar
1/4 teaspoon salt
2 cups olive oil

2 cups vegetable oil
1/2 cup vinegar
1/2 cup sherry
1 clove garlic, barely crushed

Mix egg, sugar, and salt together. Add olive oil, vegetable oil, and vinegar alternately, beating well, until all the oil is added. Slowly add sherry and garlic and blend.

Makes 5 cups.

Rice Salad Tropicale

1 cup uncooked rice
2 cups orange juice
1/4 teaspoon salt
1 teaspoon grated lemon peel
1/4 cup mayonnaise
1/2 cup sour cream
2 cups fresh pineapple chunks
1/2 cup raisins

1 cup miniature
  marshmallows
2 tablespoons sugar
1/4 cup pineapple juice
1/3 cup thinly sliced green
  pepper
1/3 cup toasted slivered
  almonds (optional)

This attractive salad is a good choice for a summer luncheon.

COMBINE rice, orange juice, and salt in saucepan. Bring to a boil and stir lightly with a fork. Reduce heat and simmer, covered, about 20 minutes, or until rice is tender and liquid has been absorbed. Cool thoroughly. Place rice in bowl and add lemon peel, mayonnaise, sour cream, pineapple, raisins, marshmallows, sugar, pineapple juice, green pepper, and almonds. Mix lightly but well. Chill until ready to serve.

Makes 6 to 8 servings.

Creamy Waldorf Salad

1 cup sour cream
1 tablespoon sugar
1/2 teaspoon salt
1 tablespoon lemon juice

2 large red apples, chopped
1 cup chopped celery
1/3 cup chopped walnuts

COMBINE sour cream, sugar, salt, and lemon juice. Combine apples, celery, and walnuts and fold in dressing mixture. Serve immediately.

Makes 6 servings.

Chinese-Style Buffet Salad

Oil for deep frying
1 (6¾-ounce) package rice sticks
2 whole chicken breasts, cooked, skinned, boned, and shredded
½ pound medium shrimp, cooked
1 cup thinly sliced celery
1 cup slivered almonds
1 large zucchini or cucumber, cut in 2-inch-long julienne strips

1 (1-pound) package won ton wrappers, cut in strips and deep-fried (optional)
1 (8-ounce) can water chestnuts, thinly sliced (optional)
1 large head iceberg lettuce, shredded
1 cup thinly sliced red radishes
1 cup chopped green onions
Soy Dressing

HEAT 2 to 3 cups oil to about 370 degrees in deep fryer or wok. Drop rice sticks, about 1 ounce at a time, into oil. They will puff up immediately upon contact with hot oil. Remove at once, before they brown, and drain on paper towels. Cool and store in airtight container until ready to use. To serve salad, arrange rice sticks, chicken, shrimp, celery, almonds, zucchini, won ton wrappers, and water chestnuts in separate serving bowls. Combine and toss together shredded lettuce, radishes, and green onions. Let guests build their own Chinese-style salads, beginning with lettuce mixture as base. Serve Soy Dressing separately.

Makes about 6 servings.

Soy Dressing

2 tablespoons sesame oil
¼ cup vegetable oil
½ cup cider vinegar
¼ cup soy sauce
6 tablespoons sugar

1 teaspoon 5-spice powder
1 clove garlic, minced (optional)
2 tablespoons toasted sesame seeds

Combine sesame oil, vegetable oil, vinegar, soy sauce, sugar, 5-spice powder, garlic, and sesame seeds in jar with a tight-fitting cover. Let stand at room temperature at least 1 hour to blend flavors. Shake before serving.

Makes about 1¼ cups.

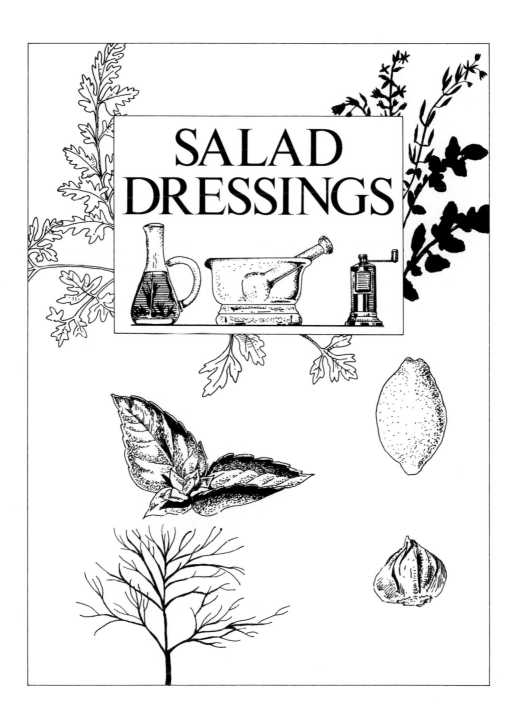

SALAD
DRESSINGS

E can always tell when the restaurant business is doing well in Southern California. Requests pour in for salad dressing recipes from restaurants of every description, from tiny neighborhood eateries to those with international reputations.

Salad dressing preferences are as varied as the salad ingredients. Simple herb-flavored oil-and-vinegar varieties are always popular, particularly when a good wine vinegar is used and a touch of mustard is added. Honey-flavored, tart-sweet dressings and the ever-popular poppy-seed dressing are leading choices for fruit salads, while pourable creamy dressings made with yogurt or sour cream are more popular than the heavier mayonnaise-type dressings for mixed vegetable salads. Of course anything with blue cheese receives much attention, as do the low-calorie dressings which Californians have elevated to an art in both variety and flavor.

Thousand Island dressings seem to turn up on hamburgers more often than on salads, and it should be mentioned that Californians often marinate less tender cuts of meat in their favorite oil-and-vinegar dressings before barbecuing them.

In restaurants and homes the house dressing can be as distinctive as a signature. We are delighted that so many friends and readers have shared their prized recipes.

Oil and Vinegar for Vinaigrette Dressing, page 94

Vinaigrette Dressing

Oil-and-vinegar dressings rank high in popularity with salad fans. This one, from Hollywood's Scandia restaurant, is particularly good sprinkled over thick slices of beefsteak tomatoes or thinly sliced mushrooms.

1 cup oil
1/2 cup white wine vinegar
2 tablespoons crushed ice
   Whites of 2 hard-cooked
   eggs, diced
2 tablespoons chopped chives

1 tablespoon chopped parsley
1/2 cup minced onion
1 tablespoon sugar
   Dash salt
   Dash MSG (optional)
   Dash black pepper

MIX oil and vinegar in bowl with ice. Add eggs, chives, parsley, onion, sugar salt, MSG, and pepper. Blend with whisk.

Makes about 2 cups.

Creamy Mustard Dressing

This unusual yet versatile dressing from the Gingerhouse restaurant in Tarzana is terrific with tossed greens. The recipe makes a large amount, but it keeps well in the refrigerator.

2 eggs
10 tablespoons Dijon-style
   mustard
1 1/2 teaspoons salt
1 1/2 teaspoons black pepper
2 teaspoons tarragon
1 teaspoon anchovy paste

1 tablespoon sherry
   Juice of 1/2 lemon
1/2 cup red wine vinegar
2 teaspoons caraway seeds
1 small clove garlic, crushed
5 cups oil

COMBINE eggs, mustard, salt, pepper, tarragon, anchovy paste, sherry, lemon juice, vinegar, caraway seeds, and garlic in bowl. Whisk until well blended. Gradually add oil until desired consistency is achieved.

Makes about 5 3/4 cups.

Basic Blender Mayonnaise

1 egg
2 tablespoons lemon juice
1 teaspoon dry mustard

3/4 teaspoon salt
1/4 teaspoon white pepper
1 cup oil

COMBINE egg, lemon juice, mustard, salt, and white pepper in blender container or food processor bowl. Cover and blend at low speed until mixed. Increase speed to high, uncover, and remove center cap. Add oil in a thin, slow, steady stream. Blend until all oil is added and mayonnaise is smooth and creamy. If necessary, turn motor off and stir occasionally. Replace cover before turning motor back on. Keep mayonnaise refrigerated and use within 7 to 10 days.

Makes 1 cup.

Anchovy Mayonnaise

3 egg yolks
1 tablespoon vinegar
  Salt
1 tablespoon Dijon-style
  mustard
2 cups oil

1 teaspoon lemon juice
1¹/₂ teaspoons mild English-
  style mustard (optional)
1¹/₂ teaspoons anchovy paste
  Pepper

A local artist served this mayonnaise with cold roast pork, but it also enhances vegetable salads.

ALLOW egg yolks to come to room temperature. Place them in bowl and beat with vinegar, salt to taste, and mustard, using a wire whisk. Add oil in a thin stream, beating vigorously while pouring until sauce becomes very thick. Thin sauce with lemon juice. Add any remaining oil in a fine stream, beating vigorously. Add English-style mustard and anchovy paste. Season to taste with pepper. Chill.

Makes about 2¹/₄ cups.

Thousand Island Dressing

1 hard-cooked egg, chopped
¹/₂ cup catsup
¹/₂ cup tomato puree
2 cups mayonnaise
¹/₄ cup dill pickle relish
1 tablespoon chopped green
  olives
2 teaspoons minced chives

2 tablespoons minced pi-
  miento
¹/₂ teaspoon salt
¹/₄ teaspoon black pepper
1 teaspoon dry mustard
¹/₂ teaspoon MSG
  (optional)
³/₄ to 1 cup buttermilk

Fiasco, a popular Marina del Rey restaurant, makes a wonderfully rich Thousand Island dressing that is excellent on hamburgers as well as salads.

COMBINE egg, catsup, tomato puree, mayonnaise, relish, olives, chives, pimiento, salt, pepper, mustard, and MSG and beat. Gradually beat in buttermilk until desired consistency is reached.

Makes about 4¹/₂ cups.

Poppy-Seed Dressing

1¹/₂ cups sugar
2 teaspoons dry mustard
²/₃ cup vinegar

3 tablespoons onion juice
2 cups oil
3 tablespoons poppy seeds

Fruit salads and poppy-seed dressings have had a longtime affinity for each other. This dressing recipe is the classic saltless version.

COMBINE sugar, mustard, vinegar, and onion juice. Gradually add oil and beat until smooth. Add poppy seeds and blend well. Chill, covered, in refrigerator.

Makes about 1 quart.

Dill Dressing

This dill dressing from the Hollywood tearoom of the Assistance League of Southern California complements chilled cooked seafood beautifully.

2 cups mayonnaise
4 teaspoons dill weed or ¼ cup chopped fresh dill
¼ cup white vinegar

2½ tablespoons prepared mustard
2½ tablespoons sugar

PLACE mayonnaise in bowl and stir in dill, vinegar, mustard, and sugar. Beat until fluffy. Chill.

Makes about 2½ cups.

Basic French Dressing

The French dressing served at Scandia restaurant is made more interesting by the addition of Hungarian paprika. It takes kindly to the addition of crumbled blue cheese if you feel the need.

1 cup oil
¼ cup wine vinegar
3 tablespoons water
2½ teaspoons sugar
1 teaspoon dry mustard
½ teaspoon MSG (optional)
1 teaspoon black pepper

2½ teaspoons salt
1¼ teaspoons Worcestershire sauce
1¼ teaspoons Hungarian paprika
1 teaspoon grated onion

COMBINE oil, vinegar, and water and beat until blended. Add sugar, mustard, MSG, pepper, salt, Worcestershire, and paprika and beat until blended. Add onion and beat well.

Makes 1¾ cups.

Blue Cheese Dressing Variation

Add 2 ounces crumbled blue cheese to prepared Basic French Dressing.

French Dressing

The house dressing at Le St. Germain, a fine French restaurant in Hollywood, brings out the best in greens and thinly sliced mushrooms or other vegetables.

½ teaspoon salt
½ teaspoon black pepper
¼ teaspoon white pepper
1 tablespoon Dijon-style mustard

1 teaspoon hot dry mustard
2 tablespoons red wine vinegar
3 tablespoons red wine
10 tablespoons peanut oil

COMBINE salt, black pepper, white pepper, and mustards and mix well. Add vinegar and wine and beat until smooth. Gradually add oil and beat until dressing coats a metal spoon. (The consistency should not be too thin or too thick.) Serve with cold vegetables or salad greens.

Makes 1 cup.

Honey French Dressing

2/3 cup sugar
1 teaspoon dry mustard
1 teaspoon paprika
1/4 teaspoon salt
1 teaspoon celery seeds

1/3 cup honey
5 tablespoons vinegar
1 tablespoon lemon juice
1 teaspoon grated onion
1 cup oil

MIX sugar, mustard, paprika, salt, and celery seeds. Add honey, vinegar, lemon juice, and onion. Slowly beat oil into dressing with rotary beater.

Makes 2 cups.

Honey Dressing

1/4 cup vinegar
1 cup mayonnaise
1 teaspoon prepared mustard
1 teaspoon sugar
1 teaspoon minced onion

1/2 cup honey
1/4 teaspoon minced parsley
    Salt, pepper
1/2 cup oil

This rich, smooth dressing sweetened with honey from the Odyssey restaurant in Mission Hills is delightful on fruit salads.

MIX vinegar, mayonnaise, and mustard until smooth. Add sugar, onion, honey, and parsley and season to taste with salt and pepper. Slowly beat in oil until well blended.

Makes 2 cups.

Green Goddess Dressing

1 cup sour cream
1 cup mayonnaise
1 tablespoon lemon juice
1 tablespoon white wine
    vinegar

1 tablespoon anchovy paste
1 teaspoon minced parsley
1/3 cup diced onion
    Salt, pepper

Green goddess dressing originated in San Francisco, but we like this Southern California version from the former Stuft Shirt restaurant in Pasadena.

BLEND together sour cream, mayonnaise, lemon juice, vinegar, anchovy paste, parsley, and onion and season to taste with salt and pepper. Mix well. Dressing may be refrigerated in covered container up to 2 weeks.

Makes about 2 cups.

97

Papaya-Seed Dressing

Residents of Hawaii claim that papaya seeds aid digestion. Maybe that's why Southern Californians visiting the islands found this recipe for papaya-seed dressing from the Shera-ton Kauai Hotel so appealing.

1 cup sugar
1 teaspoon dry mustard
1 cup white or tarragon
  vinegar
Dash MSG (optional)

1 tablespoon salt
1 cup oil
1 small onion, minced
3 tablespoons papaya seeds

PLACE sugar, mustard, vinegar, MSG, and salt in blender container. Blend and gradually add oil and onion. When thoroughly blended, stir in papaya seeds.

Makes 3 cups.

Mock Blue Cheese Dressing

The Times's "My Best Recipe" column is the source of many of our most unusual recipes. This one was sent by a reader who uses it in place of a real blue cheese dressing. It will appeal to those who love the flavor of blue cheese but not its high price.

2 cups mayonnaise
1 cup buttermilk
1 cup sour cream
1/2 teaspoon salt
1/2 teaspoon coarsely ground
  black pepper

1/2 teaspoon garlic powder
1 teaspoon Worcestershire
  sauce
1 teaspoon white wine
  vinegar

COMBINE mayonnaise, buttermilk, sour cream, salt, pepper, garlic powder, Worcestershire, and vinegar. Beat until well blended. Dressing may be stored in covered jar in the refrigerator 3 to 4 weeks.

Makes about 1 quart.

Low-Calorie Tomato Dressing

Calorie-counters who are hungry for flavor will find this a very satisfactory salad dressing.

1/2 teaspoon dry mustard
1 teaspoon water
1/2 cup tomato juice
3 tablespoons oil
2 tablespoons lemon juice
1/2 teaspoon salt

Dash black pepper
1 tablespoon chopped green
  onion
1 tablespoon Worcestershire
  sauce

BLEND mustard with water in bowl and let stand 5 minutes. Add tomato juice, oil, lemon juice, salt, pepper, green onion, and Worcestershire and beat well. Store in covered jar and chill. Shake well before using. Serve with greens.

Makes about 1 cup, 26 calories per tablespoon.

Spinach Salad Dressing

1/2 cup red wine vinegar
    Dash tarragon
1 teaspoon Dijon-style
    mustard

2 cups peanut oil
    Salt, pepper

A charming Santa Monica restaurant with the unlikely name of the Bicycle Shop serves this simple, well-flavored dressing over crisp, fresh spinach leaves.

BRING vinegar and tarragon to boil. Cool. Blend mustard and cooled vinegar-tarragon mixture in deep bowl. Stir well. Gradually add oil, beating constantly until well blended. Season to taste with salt and pepper.

Makes 2¹/₂ cups.

Caesar Dressing

1 egg
2¹/₂ teaspoons salt
5 teaspoons coarsely ground
    black pepper
1 tablespoon garlic powder
1¹/₂ (2-ounce) cans anchovy
    fillets, drained and
    chopped
1 tablespoon MSG (optional)
4 cups oil

2¹/₂ teaspoons dry English-
    style mustard
3 tablespoons lemon juice
2 teaspoons steak sauce
    Few dashes hot pepper
    sauce
3 tablespoons
    Worcestershire sauce
3 tablespoons wine vinegar
3 tablespoons catsup

Still another popular Scandia restaurant dressing is this one that utilizes the classic Caesar salad ingredients.

COMBINE egg, salt, pepper, garlic powder, anchovies, MSG, oil, and mustard and mix with 1¹/₂ tablespoons lemon juice. Add steak sauce, hot pepper sauce, Worcestershire, vinegar, catsup, and remaining 1¹/₂ tablespoons lemon juice. Beat until blended and thick.

Makes 5¹/₂ cups.

Yogurt Dressing

1 (8-ounce) carton plain
    yogurt
1/3 cup finely chopped onion
1/2 clove garlic, minced

1/4 cup minced celery leaves
1/4 cup minced parsley
1/2 teaspoon salt

This is a low-calorie salad dressing so thick and rich that it can easily double as a dip for crisp, raw vegetables.

BLEND together yogurt, onion, garlic, celery, parsley, and salt. Chill to blend flavors. Stir well just before serving.

Makes 1¹/₄ cups, 9 calories per tablespoon.

Special Garlic Dressing

Californians have a special fondness for garlic dressings. The Smoke House restaurant in Toluca Lake serves a fine one.

1 cup mayonnaise
1 teaspoon dry mustard
1 teaspoon sugar
1 teaspoon MSG (optional)
1 tablespoon lemon juice
1 tablespoon red wine vinegar

1 teaspoon coarsely ground black pepper
1 teaspoon garlic powder
1 egg yolk
Salt

COMBINE mayonnaise, mustard, sugar, MSG, lemon juice, vinegar, pepper, garlic powder, and egg yolk and season to taste with salt. Whip well. Chill dressing thoroughly. Serve over green salads.

Makes about 1½ cups.

Creamy Garlic Dressing

Another good oil-and-vinegar dressing with a garlicky flavor is this one from Robaire's, a French bistro in Los Angeles.

1 cup cottonseed oil
¼ cup white wine vinegar
2 tablespoons mayonnaise
1 teaspoon dry mustard

½ teaspoon crushed garlic
1 teaspoon salt
½ teaspoon white pepper

COMBINE oil, vinegar, mayonnaise, mustard, garlic, salt, and white pepper in jar. Cover and shake well.

Makes about 1½ cups.

Oriental Salad Dressing

As a delightful accommodation to the western penchant for salads, the Benihana of Tokyo restaurant in Los Angeles serves this interesting dressing over greens.

½ cup soy oil
2 tablespoons white vinegar
1 tablespoon tomato paste
1 tablespoon soy sauce
1 tablespoon MSG (optional)

½ teaspoon salt
½ teaspoon ginger
½ cup sliced celery
¼ cup coarsely chopped onion

COMBINE oil, vinegar, tomato paste, soy sauce, MSG, salt, ginger, celery, and onion in blender container and blend at medium speed 3 to 4 seconds until celery is finely grated.

Makes 1¼ cups.

FISH &
SHELLFISH

THE popularity of fish and shellfish is on the rise in Southern California, probably because of the trend to lighter, healthier meals. Broiled fish, whether prepared on the backyard barbecue or the kitchen range, is always popular, particularly when laced—and served—with a good California wine. Other preparations for fish and shellfish reflect the influence of international travel and the abundance of interesting ethnic restaurants to be found on the local scene. Shrimp is fried to a golden hue in an airy batter for Japanese tempura. Cilantro, chiles, and tomatoes are combined in a zesty Mexican-style sauce in which a whole fish is baked. And commercial fishermen of Portuguese and Italian ancestry have adapted traditional fish stew recipes to Pacific fish and shellfish to create California's unique cioppinos.

The wide variety of fish and shellfish indigenous to West Coast waters has quite a following. Sand dabs, with their sweet and tender flesh, are coated lightly with flour or cornmeal and quickly sautéed. And when Dungeness crabs or abalone are available, westerners are quick to make the most of their very special flavors.

Fish is fast and easy to prepare, low in calories, and as versatile as chicken. This selection of fish specialties reflects the growing awareness and diversity of fish and shellfish available at home, the local pier, or the finest restaurant.

Marinated Cracked Dungeness Crab, page 104

Marinated Cracked Dungeness Crab

2 large Dungeness crabs,
  cooked, disjointed, and
  cracked
1 cup olive oil
3/4 cup wine vinegar
2 cloves garlic, minced

1/2 cup chopped parsley
1 lemon, sliced and squeezed
1 teaspoon oregano
1 teaspoon black pepper
  Salt

PLACE crabs in shallow bowl and add oil, vinegar, garlic, parsley, lemon, oregano, and pepper. Season to taste with salt. Cover and refrigerate 1 hour.

Makes 2 to 4 servings.

Bouillabaisse

Although bouillabaisse is more likely to appear on menus in the coastal areas of Oregon and Washington, this version from the old Ted's Grill in Santa Monica developed quite a following in Southern California.

2 to 3 quarts fish stock
4 cups clam juice
3/4 cup flat beer
2 carrots, sliced
  diagonally
4 stalks celery, sliced
  diagonally
1 clove garlic, crushed
1 leek, cut in 1/4-inch
  slices
4 to 8 saffron threads
1 tablespoon cornstarch

2 cups dry white wine
  Salt, white pepper
  Hot pepper sauce
  MSG (optional)
4 (8-ounce) lobster tails
8 to 12 medium unshelled
  shrimp
12 to 16 scallops
8 to 12 clams, well scrubbed
4 (4- to 5-ounce)
  halibut fillets, 1/2-inch
  thick

MAKE fish stock by simmering 1 to 2 pounds heads and bones of white-fleshed fish only in 2 to 3 quarts of water for about 2 hours. Add water as needed. Strain stock into large kettle. Add clam juice, beer, carrots, celery, garlic, leek, and saffron. Bring to boil, reduce heat, and simmer until carrots are crisp-tender. Combine cornstarch with 1/2 cup wine and stir into simmering sauce. Simmer 5 minutes, then season to taste with salt, white pepper, hot pepper sauce, and MSG. Add lobster tails, shrimp (that have been split down back and sand vein removed), scallops, clams, and halibut. Add 1 1/2 cups wine. Bring to boil and boil 8 to 10 minutes, or until lobster is done and clams open. Serve in large bowls with generous amounts of liquid. Serve garlic toast or hot crisp sourdough French bread slices with Bouillabaisse, if desired.

Makes 6 servings.

Grilled Swordfish with Barbecue Sauce

2 pounds swordfish fillets
1 cup catsup
1/3 cup lemon juice
1/4 cup oil
2 teaspoons Worcestershire sauce

1 clove garlic, minced
1/2 cup chopped onion
1/4 cup water
1 teaspoon sugar
1/4 teaspoon hot pepper sauce
1 small bay leaf

A barbecue grill is used for far more than just hot dogs and hamburgers in Southern California. In this case swordfish fillets are marinated in a tomatoey sauce before grilling, and the same sauce is used as a baste while they cook.

CUT fillets into serving-size portions. Place fish in single layer in shallow baking dish. Combine 1/2 cup catsup, lemon juice, oil, Worcestershire, and garlic. Pour sauce over fish. Cover and refrigerate about 1 hour, turning fish once. Remove fish, reserving sauce. Use half of reserved sauce for brushing fish while grilling. Combine remaining half of sauce with remaining catsup, onion, water, sugar, hot pepper sauce, and bay leaf. Simmer about 20 minutes to blend flavors and thicken. Place fish on well-greased, hinged wire grills. (If barbecuing fish on standard grill, then brush fish with oil before cooking.) Cook about 5 inches from moderately hot coals 8 minutes. Baste with sauce. Turn and cook 7 to 8 minutes longer, or until fish flakes easily when tested with a fork. Brush fish with sauce as needed during cooking. To serve, spoon barbecue sauce over fish.

Makes 6 servings.

Stuffed Fillets of Sole

1 tablespoon minced shallots
1/4 cup chopped onion
6 ounces mushrooms, sliced
2 tablespoons butter or margarine
6 ounces crabmeat
Salt, pepper

Garlic, crushed
Dash hot pepper sauce
1 tablespoon minced parsley
Dash ground cumin
Dash sherry
12 fillets of sole
Caper Sauce

Crabmeat-and-mushroom stuffing enhances the delicate sole fillets called for in this recipe, and a creamy caper sauce makes the dish special.

SAUTÉ shallots, onion, and mushrooms in butter until tender. Add crabmeat and season to taste with salt, pepper, and garlic. Add hot pepper sauce, parsley, cumin, and sherry. Cook, stirring, until blended and somewhat dry. Place 6 fillets in buttered baking dish. Cover fish fillets with crabmeat stuffing. Place remaining 6 fillets over stuffing and bake at 325 degrees 10 to 15 minutes, or until done. Transfer to warm serving platter and top with Caper Sauce. Garnish with sprigs of parsley, if desired.

Makes 6 servings.

(continued on overleaf)

Caper Sauce

3 tablespoons flour
5 tablespoons melted butter or margarine
2 cups seasoned fish stock
2 egg yolks

1/2 cup whipping cream
2 tablespoons lemon juice
Salt, pepper
5 tablespoons capers

Blend flour and 3 tablespoons butter in saucepan over medium heat. Gradually add fish stock. Beat egg yolks and mix with cream and lemon juice. Season to taste with salt and pepper. Stir into stock mixture. Do not let boil. Strain, then add 2 tablespoons butter and capers.

Makes about 2³/₄ cups.

Sole in White Wine Sauce

Another elegant way to serve sole is to lace it lightly with a mushroom- and shrimp-flavored white wine sauce.

2 tablespoons butter or margarine
1/2 pound mushrooms, sliced
Juice of 1/2 lemon
Salt
6 (6- to 8-ounce) fillets of sole

White pepper
1/2 cup dry white wine
1/2 pound small cooked shrimp
1¹/₂ cups White Wine Sauce

MELT butter in skillet and add mushrooms, lemon juice, and dash salt. Brown mushrooms lightly. Skim out mushrooms and set aside. Season fish to taste with salt and white pepper and fold each fillet in half. Arrange in one layer in skillet. Add wine, cover, and poach gently until fish flakes easily, about 10 minutes. Carefully lift fish from broth to hot platter. Boil broth rapidly, uncovered, until reduced to 1/3 the original volume. Stir reduced broth, mushrooms, and shrimp into White Wine Sauce. Heat thoroughly and pour over hot fish.

Makes 6 servings.

White Wine Sauce

3 tablespoons butter or margarine
2 shallots, minced
2 teaspoons flour

1/2 cup dry white wine
1/2 cup milk
1/2 cup whipping cream
Salt, white pepper

Melt butter, add shallots, and cook until lightly browned. Stir in flour. Add wine, milk, and cream. Cook, stirring, until thickened. Season to taste with salt and white pepper. Simmer 10 minutes to blend flavors. Serve with fish.

Makes 1¹/₂ cups.

Abalone Stuffed with Crabmeat

Butter or margarine
2 shallots, minced
1 cup cooked crabmeat
Cream Sauce
Salt, white pepper
Dash red pepper
1/2 teaspoon dry mustard

1/2 teaspoon Worcestershire
  sauce
  Juice of 1/2 lemon
4 large abalone steaks
2 eggs, beaten
  Flour

Scuba divers eagerly await abalone season. Most of the time their catch doesn't make it beyond a campfire on the beach, but when it does, this is a wonderful way to prepare it.

MELT 1 tablespoon butter in small saucepan, add shallots, and cook until tender but not browned. Add crabmeat and heat thoroughly. Add enough Cream Sauce to bind, about 1/2 cup. Season to taste with salt and white pepper and add red pepper, mustard, Worcestershire, and lemon juice. Carefully pound abalone steaks between 2 sheets of wax paper until very thin (unless purchased already pounded). Dip abalone in eggs seasoned to taste with salt and white pepper. Coat with flour and set aside. Melt 2 tablespoons butter in heavy skillet. Add abalone and brown quickly on one side. Turn and brown other side. Do not overcook as abalone will toughen. Place abalone steaks on platter and spoon crabmeat stuffing on each. Roll and arrange on serving platter, seam side down.

Makes 4 servings.

Cream Sauce

2 tablespoons butter or
  margarine
2 tablespoons flour

Salt, pepper
1 cup warm milk

Melt butter in skillet and stir in flour. Season to taste with salt and pepper. Cook, stirring, over medium heat about 1 minute but do not allow flour to brown. Add milk and cook and stir 1 or 2 minutes until mixture comes to boil and thickens.

Makes about 1 cup.

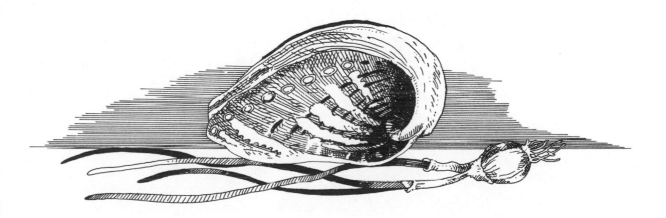

Abalone Steaks

12 abalone slices	Flour
2 eggs, beaten	2 tablespoons butter or
Salt, pepper	margarine
Dash red pepper	2 tablespoons oil

PREPARE abalone slices for cooking by pounding each between sheets of wax paper until almost lacy. Season eggs to taste with salt and pepper and add red pepper. Dip abalone slices, one at a time, in egg mixture, then coat with flour. Heat butter with oil in skillet until butter melts and mixture is hot. Add abalone slices and cook a few at a time until golden on both sides. Remove to heated platter and keep hot while cooking remaining abalone.

Makes 6 servings.

Whitefish Italienne

Perino's, an old and elegant restaurant that has remained a favorite of Los Angelenos over the years, serves this excellent fish dish which features a memorable tomato sauce.

4 pounds whole whitefish, dressed	5 drops lemon juice
1 tablespoon clarified unsalted butter	Dash salt
	$1/2$ cup dry white wine
2 teaspoons diced shallots	Sauce Italienne
4 ounces mushroom caps, sliced	Chopped parsley

HAVE whole fish filleted, trimming off any skin. Heat butter in skillet. Add shallots and fish. Place mushrooms over fish and add lemon juice, salt, and wine. Cover with wax paper or lid so that steam can escape while cooking. Cook slowly over medium heat 10 minutes, making sure steam escapes. Remove from heat and with spatula transfer fish and mushrooms to warmed platter. Reduce liquid in pan by half over medium heat, keeping lid or wax paper on skillet to prevent too much steam from escaping. Add Sauce Italienne to pan liquid and cook 2 to 3 minutes. Pour sauce over fish and serve with boiled potatoes or a green vegetable, if desired. Garnish with chopped parsley.

Makes 6 servings.

Note: To clarify butter, place over low heat in small saucepan until melted and milky solids separate from fat. Pour off clear fat and discard solids. Do not allow to boil.

Sauce Italienne

⅓ cup clarified unsalted butter
½ medium onion, diced
 4 beefsteak tomatoes, peeled
 2 tablespoons tomato paste
¼ teaspoon black pepper

2 teaspoons sugar
1 teaspoon salt
 Dash nutmeg

Heat clarified butter in skillet and add onion. Cook until tender but not brown. Cut tomatoes in halves horizontally, squeeze out and discard seeds and juice, then dice remaining pulp. Add to skillet and stir. Add tomato paste and stir again. Add pepper, sugar, salt, and nutmeg. Simmer 15 minutes. Add additional seasoning if desired.

Makes about 2 cups.

Baked Fish with Vegetables

 1 (2-pound) whole red
   snapper or whole sea bass
   or fillets
   Salt, pepper
2½ lemons, halved
 1 bunch fresh fennel leaves
   or 2 teaspoons dried
   fennel seeds
½ cup butter or margarine

1 onion, thinly sliced
2 medium potatoes, peeled
  and very thinly sliced
2 tomatoes, peeled and
  quartered
½ cup white wine
3 tablespoons Pernod
  Chopped parsley

This often-requested recipe is a popular menu item at Hawaii's Kahala Hilton Hotel. The fish and vegetables are baked together, picking up additional flavor from wine, fennel, and Pernod seasonings.

SEASON fish inside and out with salt and pepper to taste and juice of ½ lemon. If fillets are used, sprinkle both sides with salt, pepper, and lemon juice. Place fennel leaves or seeds inside fish or sprinkle over fillets. Melt butter in large skillet. Brown fish on both sides. Transfer fish and juices to 13 x 9-inch baking pan. Arrange onion and potato slices around fish and bake at 375 degrees 30 minutes. Add tomatoes, pour wine over fish, and sprinkle with Pernod. Bake 10 minutes longer, or until fish flakes easily with fork and potatoes are done. Serve from baking dish or arrange fish on large platter with tomatoes, potatoes, and onions. Pour juices over fish and sprinkle with parsley. Garnish with remaining lemon halves.

Makes 6 servings.

Mexican-Style Snapper

Fish topped with a mild chile-flavored tomato sauce is a recipe from Veracruz that is very popular in Southern California.

2 tablespoons oil
1 clove garlic, minced
1 cup sliced onion
3 cups peeled, seeded, and chopped tomatoes
2 long green chiles, peeled, seeded, and cut in strips

1¼ teaspoons salt
1 tablespoon lime juice
Coarsely ground black pepper
1¾ pounds red snapper fillets
Flour

HEAT oil in large skillet, add garlic and onion, and sauté 5 minutes. Stir in tomatoes, chiles, salt, and lime juice. Season to taste with pepper and mix thoroughly. Dredge fish fillets in flour, shaking to remove any excess. Add fish fillets to skillet. Simmer until fish flakes easily. Remove fillets to serving plate and keep warm. Cook sauce about 2 minutes longer, or until slightly thickened, then spoon sauce over fish and serve.

Makes 6 to 8 servings.

Lemon-Rice Stuffed Snapper

1 (3- to 4-pound) whole red snapper, dressed
1½ teaspoons salt

Lemon-Rice Stuffing
Butter or margarine, melted

CLEAN fish thoroughly and dry. Sprinkle inside and out with salt. Stuff fish loosely with Lemon-Rice Stuffing. Close opening with small skewers or wood picks. Place fish on well-greased 15 x 9-inch, bake-and-serve platter. Bake at 350 degrees 40 to 60 minutes, or until fish flakes easily when tested with a fork. Baste occasionally with butter. Remove skewers.

Makes 6 servings.

Lemon-Rice Stuffing

¾ cup chopped celery
½ cup chopped onion
¼ cup butter or margarine, melted
3 cups cooked rice
⅓ cup sour cream

¼ cup diced, peeled lemon
2 tablespoons grated lemon peel
1 teaspoon paprika
1 teaspoon salt
⅛ teaspoon ground thyme

Cook celery and onion in butter until tender. Combine with rice, sour cream, lemon, lemon peel, paprika, salt, and thyme in large mixing bowl.

Makes about 4 cups.

Halibut in Wine Sauce

2 pounds halibut steaks
¹/₄ cup flour
¹/₂ teaspoon salt
   Dash white pepper
1 tablespoon chopped parsley
¹/₄ cup olive oil
1 clove garlic, crushed

1 large onion, chopped
1 carrot, grated
2 stalks celery, chopped
1 large tomato, chopped
¹/₄ cup water
³/₄ cup dry white wine

THAW fish if frozen. Combine flour, salt, white pepper, and parsley. Dredge fish in flour mixture. Heat oil in skillet. Add fish and fry until golden brown on each side. Remove from skillet. Add garlic, onion, carrot, and celery to skillet. Cook 10 to 15 minutes, or until tender. Add tomato and water. Simmer 10 minutes. Puree sauce in blender container or food processor bowl. Stir in wine. Return to skillet. Place halibut in sauce, cover, and simmer 5 minutes.

Makes 4 to 6 servings.

Poached Salmon with Pink Mayonnaise

1 (7- to 8-pound) whole salmon, dressed
¹/₂ cup butter or margarine,
   melted
2 cups champagne or white
   wine
1 large carrot, thinly sliced
1 large onion, thinly sliced
1 stalk celery, diced

2 teaspoons salt
3 sprigs parsley
10 black peppercorns
1 bay leaf
¹/₄ teaspoon crushed thyme
   Cucumber slices
   Lemon slices
   Green onion tops
   Pink Mayonnaise

This delicious poached salmon keeps turning up on buffets, partly because it tastes so good and partly because it looks so pretty.

PLACE salmon in generously greased baking pan large enough to fit fish. Combine butter, champagne, carrot, onion, celery, and salt and pour over fish. Tie parsley, peppercorns, bay leaf, and thyme in cheesecloth bag and place in pan liquid. Cover fish pan with foil, but do not allow foil to touch surface of fish. Bake at 350 degrees 60 minutes or longer, depending on size of fish, basting every 15 minutes. Salmon should be fork-tender when done. Cool slightly in pan, then carefully remove, using 2 spatulas, to large serving platter. (Protect sides of platter with wax paper while decorating fish.) Remove skin from center of salmon, making slits with knife along skin for an even edge. Arrange cucumber and lemon slices in a floral design along sides of salmon, using split tops of green onions as stems. If desired, spoon Pink Mayonnaise around fish, or serve it separately.

Makes 10 to 12 servings.

(continued on overleaf)

Pink Mayonnaise

2 cups mayonnaise	Dash paprika
¼ teaspoon salt	2 teaspoons lemon juice
⅛ teaspoon white pepper	Red food color

Blend together mayonnaise, salt, white pepper, paprika, and lemon juice. Stir in a drop or two of food color to tint mixture pale pink.

Makes 2 cups.

Dill Broiled Salmon

1 teaspoon dill weed	6 salmon steaks
2 tablespoons white vinegar	1 teaspoon salt
3 tablespoons oil	Dash black pepper

COMBINE dill weed, vinegar, and oil and beat to mix thoroughly. Let stand at room temperature at least 1 hour. Sprinkle both sides of salmon steaks with salt and pepper. Beat oil mixture again to mix. Dip fish in oil mixture and place on preheated greased broiler rack. Broil about 2 inches from source of heat 5 to 8 minutes, or until lightly browned. Baste with oil mixture and turn carefully. Brush other side with oil mixture and broil 5 to 8 minutes longer, or until fish flakes easily when tested with a fork. Serve hot and garnish each serving with a sprinkling of chopped parsley or paprika and lemon slice or wedge, if desired.

Makes 6 servings.

Grilled Salmon

The garlicky topping on these buttery salmon steaks adds a wonderful flavor fillip.

6 medium salmon steaks, about 1-inch thick	¼ teaspoon dill weed
⅓ cup olive oil	1 teaspoon salt
4 cloves garlic, crushed	1 cup fine dry bread crumbs
½ cup chopped parsley	¼ cup butter or margarine, softened

PLACE salmon on well-greased broiler pan. Combine and blend oil, garlic, parsley, dill weed, and salt in blender container. Stir in bread crumbs and set aside. Brush steaks with butter. Broil about 4 inches from heat 8 minutes, or until fish flakes easily when tested with a fork. Spread about 2 tablespoons garlic mixture on each salmon steak. Return to broiler and broil 1 or 2 minutes, or until lightly browned.

Makes 6 servings.

Sand Dabs Meunière

6 to 8 sand dabs
   1 teaspoon salt
  1/8 teaspoon black pepper
     Flour

6 to 8 tablespoons butter or
      margarine
  1/4 cup minced parsley

This delicate fish is found only in the Pacific coastal waters from Alaska to Mexico. Westerners particularly like it cooked in a simple parsley-butter sauce.

HAVE sand dabs cleaned, removing heads and tails. Large sand dabs may be filleted. Sprinkle with salt and pepper and dredge lightly in flour. Heat 4 tablespoons butter until almost sizzling. Add fish, a few at a time, and cook quickly until lightly browned, turning to brown other side. Remove to warm platter and cook remaining fish, adding more butter if needed. When all fish are cooked, add 2 tablespoons butter to drippings in pan and heat until lightly browned. Pour over fish and sprinkle with parsley. Garnish with lemon wedges, if desired.

Makes 6 to 8 servings.

Crispy Corn-Coated Sand Dabs

1/2 cup cornmeal
1/2 teaspoon salt
1/4 teaspoon black pepper

4 sand dabs
1 cup buttermilk
  Oil for deep frying

MIX cornmeal with salt and pepper. Dip fish in buttermilk, then coat with cornmeal mixture. Pour oil to a depth of 1 1/2 inches in skillet. Heat until hot and add fish. Cook until golden, turning once. Garnish with sprigs of watercress or parsley and lemon slices, if desired.

Makes 4 servings.

Shark Steaks

2 pounds shark fillets or steaks
  Salt, pepper
  Dash paprika

1/2 cup butter or margarine
  Juice of 1/2 lemon

Shark is gaining favor as a food fish. When it was served this way at a Universal Studios screening of Jaws II, *we were hooked.*

SEASON fish fillets to taste with salt, pepper, and paprika. Melt butter in saucepan. Add lemon juice. Place fish on broiler rack. Gently pour lemon-butter over fish. Broil on both sides until fish flakes easily when tested with a fork.

Makes 6 servings.

Filet de Truite en Chemise
(Fillet of Trout in a Jacket)

Wolfgang Puck, the versatile chef-partner at Ma Maison, a favorite dining spot for celebrities, serves this elegant trout frequently. If the thought of making puff paste is too forbidding, check local bakeries. Many of them sell it by the pound and it freezes well.

6 (10-ounce) trout, boned
1 cup fresh scallops
2 eggs
1 cup whipping cream
1 teaspoon minced chives
1 teaspoon minced parsley
1 teaspoon minced tarragon

Kosher salt
Pepper
Red pepper
2 pounds Puff Pastry
1 egg yolk
2 teaspoons water
Beurre Blanc

FILLET trout and set aside. Place scallops in food processor bowl with steel knife blade in position. Add 1 egg. Blend until pureed evenly. With processor on, slowly add whipping cream through feeder tube. Add chives, parsley, and tarragon. Blend well. Season to taste with kosher salt, pepper, and red pepper. Test seasoning by poaching a small amount of mixture in boiling, salted water. Season trout fillets to taste with salt and pepper. Spread 1/6 of scallop mixture on one fillet and cover with a second fillet. Using 1/3 pound of Puff Pastry per trout, roll out 6 1/8-inch-thick rectangles 2 inches longer than the trout and twice as wide plus 1 inch. Beat remaining egg. Place each stuffed trout fillet on half of pastry rectangle, leaving about 1 1/2 inches of pastry at end for tail. Brush pastry edges with beaten egg, fold second half over, and press close to trout with tines of fork to seal. With sharp knife, trim excess pastry away from sides and head of fish. Cut pastry at end of fish in a triangle to indicate tail. Being careful not to pierce pastry, mark head, gill line, eye, and mouth of fish with knife. Bend a large pastry tube tip into an oval shape and use to mark scales, again being careful not to pierce pastry. Mark ribs in tail with knife. Brush pastry with egg yolk beaten with water. Bake at 375 degrees for about 20 minutes, or until golden brown. Serve with Beurre Blanc.

Makes 6 servings.

Puff Pastry

1 pound flour
1 teaspoon salt
1 cup ice water

1 pound unsalted butter,
  slightly softened

Sift flour and salt together into a large bowl. Add water and blend, working mixture as little as possible in order to make a stiff ball. Wrap dough in plastic wrap and refrigerate 20 minutes. Shape butter into a square 1/2-inch thick, wrap in plastic wrap, and chill. Place dough on floured board and roll into a rectangle about 1/2-inch thick. Place chilled butter in center of dough. Fold both ends of rectangle over center, one on top of the other, covering the butter. Wrap in plastic wrap and refrigerate 20 minutes. Roll out dough from center to edge into a rectangle 15 x 8 inches and 1/2-inch thick. Fold in thirds. Position dough so shorter edge faces you. Roll out and fold dough again in same manner. Wrap in plastic wrap and refrigerate 20 minutes. Repeat last process twice more, refrigerating dough for 20 minutes between each turn. After last turn, refrigerate 20 minutes, or until ready to use.

Makes about 2 pounds puff pastry.

Note: Because puff pastry can be tricky to handle, it is better to measure the flour by weight than by volume. Excess pastry can be frozen if wrapped tightly.

Beurre Blanc

1 cup dry white wine	3/4 pound unsalted butter
2 large shallots, chopped	Juice of 1/2 lemon
1 tablespoon chopped tarragon	Salt, white pepper
1 cup whipping cream	Chopped chives

Combine wine, shallots, and tarragon in saucepan and bring to boil. Boil until mixture is reduced to 1/3 the original volume. Add cream and boil until mixture is reduced to half. Reduce heat, add butter by small pats, but do not let boil. Add lemon juice and season to taste with salt and white pepper. Strain, sprinkle with chives, and serve with trout.

Makes about 2 1/2 cups.

Soy-Grilled Fish

1/4 cup soy sauce	1 clove garlic, crushed
2 tablespoons sherry, sake, or bouillon	4 to 6 small whole panfish, dressed
2 teaspoons sugar	2 tablespoons oil
1/4 teaspoon ground ginger	

A teriyaki-style marinade adds a distinctive flavor to fish grilled over hot coals.

COMBINE soy sauce, sherry, sugar, ginger, and garlic. Brush marinade over fish and let stand about 30 minutes. Grease grill or place fish in hinged basket. Brush with remaining marinade and cook over hot coals about 5 minutes. Brush with oil, turn, and grill about 10 minutes longer, basting with marinade and oil and turning once or twice. Cook only until fish flakes easily with a fork. Serve with additional soy sauce and seasoned cooked rice, if desired.

Makes 4 to 6 servings.

Campfire Squid

Using a big rock as a chopping block and cooking in a heavy skillet over a wood campfire, Jean-Michel Cousteau prepared squid this way on the beach in Catalina.

8 squid
1/4 cup olive oil
1/2 cup chopped onion
2 cloves garlic, chopped
1/2 lemon, chopped
4 bay leaves

1/4 teaspoon thyme
Dash paprika
Salt, pepper
1 tablespoon flour
4 cups cooked rice

CLEAN squid. Separate head from body, reserving legs and ink sac. Chop legs and reserve. Squeeze ink from sac over a small bowl and reserve ink. Remove quill from body and peel off outer skin of squid. Set squid aside. Heat half the oil in large skillet over medium coals or on range. Add onion, garlic, lemon, bay leaves, thyme, and paprika and season to taste with salt and pepper. Cook until onion is translucent. Mix ink with flour to make a paste. Add chopped legs, half the onion mixture from pan, and half the rice. Season to taste with salt and pepper. Stuff squid with rice mixture and secure opening with wood picks. Heat remaining oil with remaining onion mixture in skillet. Place stuffed squid in pan and cook, turning often, until golden on all sides, about 10 minutes. Remove squid and bay leaves and spread remaining rice in a layer in pan. Arrange squid over rice, cover, and cook 10 minutes longer. Serve squid over rice and garnish with parsley sprigs and lemon wedges, if desired.

Makes 4 servings.

Lobster Cantonese

For the best results in preparing this attractive Chinese dish cook the lobster pieces as quickly as possible. The beaten egg added to the sauce makes it richer and creamier.

2 pounds lobster tails
1 clove garlic, minced
1 teaspoon fermented black beans, washed and drained
2 tablespoons oil
1/4 pound ground pork
1 1/2 cups hot water
1 1/2 tablespoons soy sauce

1 teaspoon MSG (optional)
2 tablespoons cornstarch
3 tablespoons dry sherry
1 egg
3 tablespoons water
Cilantro sprigs
Green onion curls
Hot cooked rice

THAW lobster if frozen. With sharp knife, pry lobster meat from shell and slice into medallions. Mince garlic and black beans together. Heat oil in wok or skillet and add garlic mixture. Cook and stir a few seconds. Add pork and cook about 10 minutes, stirring to break up meat. Add hot water, soy sauce, and MSG. Add lobster medallions and cook 2 minutes. Mix cornstarch and sherry and stir into sauce. Beat egg with 3 tablespoons water and blend into sauce. Cook over low heat 30 seconds, stirring constantly. Sauce should be creamy but not heavy. Spoon sauce into center of platter. Arrange medallions in the sauce in a decorative pattern. Garnish with cilantro and green onion curls. For each serving, place a few lobster medallions over rice in bowl. Spoon sauce over lobster.

Makes 4 to 6 servings.

Shrimp Tempura

3 cups cake flour
2 eggs, beaten
2 cups ice water
1 pound large shrimp
6 large mushrooms, sliced
3 slices eggplant, cut in strips
6 strips celery, 3 inches long

3 carrots, cut in 3-inch-long strips
6 slices sweet potatoes, cut in 3-inch-long strips
6 green beans
Oil for deep frying
All-purpose flour
Tempura Sauce

The Mikado, a Japanese restaurant in North Hollywood, is known for its lacy, golden shrimp tempura. Be sure to use ice water and don't overmix if you want a lovely crisp batter on the shrimp.

Mix cake flour with eggs and ice water until batter is slightly lumpy. Chill. Shell and devein shrimp, leaving tail intact. Flatten slightly with sturdy whack of a cleaver or flat side of a heavy knife so shrimp will not curl while cooking. Arrange shrimp, mushrooms, eggplant, celery, carrots, sweet potatoes, and green beans attractively on large tray or platter. Heat oil in deep kettle to 350 degrees. Beat batter. Dip shrimp into all-purpose flour, then into chilled batter, shaking to remove excess batter. Slip into deep fat and fry until shrimp rise to surface. While shrimp are bobbing on surface of oil, dollop a bit of batter on top of each shrimp and cook until batter is crisp and slightly golden. Turn once and remove with slotted spoon or fork and drain on wire rack. Keep hot. Dip vegetables in flour and batter and cook same way. Continue to cook and drain shrimp and vegetables, a few at a time, adjusting heat during cooking to maintain 350 degree temperature. Keep batter cool. To serve, place an equal amount of the various foods on each plate. Serve with Tempura Sauce as a dip.

Makes 6 servings.

Tempura Sauce

1 cup soy sauce, preferably Japanese-style
1/2 cup mirin
3 cups water

1 teaspoon MSG (optional)
1 Japanese radish (daikon), grated

Combine soy sauce, mirin, water, and MSG in saucepan and bring to boil. Place small amount of sauce in tiny saucers with 1 teaspoon of the grated radish. Dip cooked vegetables and shrimp into sauce, scooping up a bit of radish as food is dipped.

Makes about 4½ cups.

Hot Buttered Scampi

Tracton's in Los Angeles serves scampi absolutely swimming in garlic-flavored butter. If the amount horrifies you, you can cut down on it, but we like it their way.

1 pound butter, clarified
1 tablespoon minced garlic
1 teaspoon salt

1 teaspoon pepper
1 1/2 pounds large shrimp, shelled and deveined

HEAT 3 tablespoons butter in large skillet. Add garlic and sauté. Add salt and pepper and the shrimp, which can be butterflied, if desired. Sauté until shrimp change color and are tender. Add remaining butter and heat through. Place shrimp on plates and spoon hot butter over.

Makes 4 to 6 servings.

Note: To clarify butter, see recipe on page 108.

Breaded Scampi

Although Gulliver's restaurant chain specializes in prime ribs, their scampi have also developed a following.

2 cups soft bread crumbs
3/4 cup butter or margarine
1 pound shrimp, shelled and deveined
2 cloves garlic, crushed

Salt
MSG (optional)
Juice of 1/2 lemon
2 teaspoons chopped parsley

SAUTÉ bread crumbs in butter until golden and crisp. Add shrimp and continue to toss and cook until shrimp are firm and have turned red. Add garlic and season to taste with salt and MSG. Add lemon juice and parsley. Serve in small heated individual casseroles.

Makes 4 to 6 servings.

Garlic Prawns

A wok is an ideal utensil for cooking these large shrimp quickly.

2 tablespoons oil
2 or 3 cloves garlic, crushed or minced
1 pound large prawns, shelled, deveined, and butterflied

2 green onions, cut in diagonal strips
4 1/2 teaspoons cornstarch
2 tablespoons soy sauce
2 tablespoons rice wine or dry sherry

HEAT wok. Add oil and heat. Add garlic and stir-fry briefly. Do not brown. Add prawns. Stir-fry just until prawns turn pink. Stir in green onions. Combine cornstarch, soy sauce, and rice wine and add to wok. Toss and cook until sauce thickens and clears. Do not overcook. Serve at once.

Makes 4 servings.

Shrimp Boiled in Beer

2 (12-ounce) cans beer
1 small onion, peeled
1/2 cup lemon juice
1 teaspoon celery salt
1 sprig parsley
1 teaspoon salt
1 bay leaf

1/2 teaspoon thyme
1/2 teaspoon basil
3 whole cloves
2 black peppercorns
Dash ground cumin
1 pound shrimp, unshelled

COMBINE beer, onion, lemon juice, celery salt, parsley, salt, bay leaf, thyme, basil, cloves, peppercorns, and cumin. Bring to boil. Reduce heat and simmer, covered, 10 minutes. Drop shrimp into stock and bring to boil. Reduce heat again and simmer 3 to 5 minutes, or until shrimp are pink. Remove shrimp from stock and allow to cool briefly. To eat shrimp, hot or cool, simply shell and dip in cocktail sauce or melted butter as desired.

Makes 3 to 4 servings.

Shangyi Shrimp
(Spicy Shrimp)

1 pound shrimp, shelled and
   deveined
1 teaspoon rice wine
1 egg white
2 1/2 teaspoons cornstarch
1 cup oil
1 small hot red dried chile,
   seeded and sliced
3/4 cup diagonally sliced
   celery

3 wood ears (black fungus),
   softened in hot water and
   cut into strips
1/2 teaspoon soy sauce
1/2 teaspoon sugar
1/2 teaspoon ground coriander
1/2 cup chicken broth
1 tablespoon grated orange
   peel

A spicy shrimp dish of the type served in Shangyi, a city in China's Hebei province, is popular at the Mandarin Shanghai in Los Angeles's Chinatown.

BUTTERFLY shrimp and press as much liquid from shrimp as possible, using palms of hands to prevent breaking. Place shrimp in bowl. Mix wine with egg white and add to shrimp. Mix to coat well. Sprinkle with 1 1/2 teaspoons cornstarch and toss to coat. Heat oil in wok or skillet to 350 degrees and add shrimp. Cook until shrimp turns pink in color. Drain shrimp on paper towels. Remove all but 1 teaspoon oil from wok and heat. Add chile and stir-fry until dark, but not scorched. Add celery and wood ears and stir-fry until well-mixed and glistening. Combine soy sauce, sugar, coriander, and chicken broth and add to wok. Cook until simmering. Mix remaining 1 teaspoon cornstarch with a few drops of water to make a paste and stir into liquid in pan. Add shrimp and orange peel and stir to heat through and coat well with sauce.

Makes 6 to 8 servings.

Shrimp Provençale

The Hungry Tiger chain of restaurants serves shrimp with an herb-flavored tomato sauce that complements the shellfish very nicely.

2 pounds shrimp, shelled and deveined
Butter or margarine

$^1/_2$ cup dry white wine
Sauce Provençale

SAUTÉ shrimp in only as much butter as needed until barely tender. Add wine and cook over high heat until wine is almost absorbed. Arrange shrimp on platter and serve topped with Sauce Provençale.

Sauce Provençale

$^1/_2$ cup diced onion
2 tablespoons olive oil
4 cups crushed, canned plum tomatoes
$^3/_4$ cup tomato puree
$1^1/_2$ cups water

1 teaspoon black pepper
1 teaspoon basil, crushed
$^1/_2$ teaspoon oregano, crushed
2 teaspoons salt
1 teaspoon garlic powder

Sauté onion in oil until tender but not browned. Add tomatoes, tomato puree, water, pepper, basil, oregano, salt, and garlic powder and simmer $1^1/_2$ hours.

Makes about 6 cups.

Crab Tostadas

A crisp tortilla topped with lettuce, cheese, and crabmeat makes a delicious Mexican-style luncheon dish.

1 ($7^1/_2$-ounce) can crabmeat
1 tomato, diced
$^1/_2$ avocado, peeled and diced
3 green onions, sliced
1 tablespoon lemon juice
$^1/_4$ teaspoon salt

$^1/_4$ teaspoon hot pepper sauce
1 tablespoon oil
4 corn tortillas
1 cup shredded lettuce
1 cup shredded sharp cheddar cheese

DRAIN crabmeat and shred, reserving 4 larger pieces for garnish. Combine crabmeat, tomato, avocado, green onions, lemon juice, salt, and hot pepper sauce. Chill. Heat oil in skillet. Quickly turn tortillas one at a time in hot oil until softened. Press into 4 ($4^1/_2$-inch) tart pans or custard cups and heat at 350 degrees 5 to 8 minutes, or until crisped. To serve, divide lettuce among tortilla shells. Top with a layer of shredded cheese and then crab salad. Garnish with reserved crab pieces.

Makes 4 servings.

Skewered Scallops

1 pound scallops
2 large green peppers, halved and seeded
2 cups cherry tomatoes
1/3 cup lemon juice
3 tablespoons honey

3 tablespoons prepared mustard
2 tablespoons melted butter or oil
1 1/2 teaspoons curry powder

The curried honey mixture brushed on these broiled scallops gives them a nice golden color and a delightful flavor. Be careful not to overcook them.

THAW scallops if frozen. Rinse with cold water to remove any shell particles. Cut large scallops in halves. Cut green peppers into 1-inch squares. Alternate scallops, tomatoes, and green pepper squares on skewers. Place skewered scallops on a well-greased broiler pan. Combine lemon juice, honey, mustard, butter, and curry powder. Brush scallops and vegetables with mixture. Broil about 4 inches from heat 5 to 7 minutes. Turn carefully and brush again with curry mixture. Broil 5 to 7 minutes longer, basting once.

Makes 6 servings.

Joe's Cioppino

1 rock lobster
6 Alaskan king crab legs
6 large shrimp
1 onion, sliced
1 clove garlic, minced
2 tablespoons oil
1 tablespoon chopped parsley
3 tablespoons pine nuts

2 (8-ounce) cans tomato sauce
1 (10 1/2-ounce) can tomato puree
2 cups water
Salt, pepper
2 tablespoons raisins
1 pound spaghetti

No collection of California recipes could possibly be complete without at least one cioppino recipe. A San Pedro tuna fisherman of Italian ancestry prepared this one for us.

CLEAN lobster, remove tomalley, and set aside. Do not shell tail. Cut lobster tail through shell in halves lengthwise, then crosswise. Rinse. Clean and crack crab legs. Shell and devein shrimp. Cook onion and garlic in oil until golden brown. Add lobster tomalley, parsley, and pine nuts. Cook, stirring now and then, until nuts are lightly browned. Place lobster, meat side down, in onion mixture and cook 3 minutes. Add crab legs, shrimp, tomato sauce, tomato puree, and water and season to taste with salt and pepper. Bring to boil. Add raisins and simmer 1 hour. Just before serving, cook spaghetti *al dente* and drain. Strain sauce and serve with spaghetti. Serve shellfish separately.

Makes 6 to 8 servings.

Note: Whole lobster must be used to obtain tomalley, the grayish-green substance located in the body portion of the lobster.

Linguine with White Clam Sauce

When the Bel-Air Hotel serves a white clam sauce, it's a true, rich white sauce lightly flavored with lemon juice.

1¹/₂ cups thoroughly degreased fresh or canned chicken stock
1¹/₂ cups dry white wine
3 shallots, sliced
3 celery tops with leaves, cut in 2-inch pieces
4 sprigs parsley
1 bay leaf
10 black peppercorns
3 dozen clams, shelled
White Sauce
2 pounds linguine or fettuccine noodles, cooked and drained
¹/₂ cup butter or margarine
Salt
White pepper
¹/₄ cup grated Parmesan cheese

COMBINE stock, white wine, shallots, celery, parsley, bay leaf, and peppercorns in 2-quart saucepan. Bring to a boil over high heat. Reduce heat and simmer, uncovered, 20 minutes. Strain into 12-inch skillet. Add clams. Cover and simmer 3 minutes. Transfer clams to large mixing bowl and quickly reduce remaining stock to 2 cups. Reserve for White Sauce. Prepare White Sauce. When sauce is finished, discard any juices that have accumulated under clams in bowl and stir clams into ²/₃ cup sauce. Return to remaining sauce and blend well. Lightly sauté cooked linguine in butter and season to taste with salt and white pepper. Spoon into well-greased individual baking dishes. Top with clam sauce mixture. Sprinkle with grated Parmesan cheese and place under broiler 30 seconds to brown.

Makes 6 servings.

White Sauce

¹/₄ cup butter or margarine
5 tablespoons flour
2 cups reserved reduced clam stock
³/₄ cup milk
2 egg yolks
¹/₄ to ¹/₂ cup whipping cream
Few drops lemon juice
Salt
White pepper
Garlic powder

MELT butter in 2-quart saucepan. Stir in flour. Cook over low heat 1 minute, stirring constantly. Remove pan from heat and gradually stir in reduced stock and milk, whisking constantly. Cook until sauce comes to boil and thickens, then reduce heat and simmer 1 minute. Mix egg yolks and ¹/₄ cup cream in small bowl and stir in 2 tablespoons of the heated sauce. Whisk heated egg mixture back into remaining sauce in pan. Bring sauce to boil, constantly whisking, and boil 30 seconds. Remove from heat and season to taste with lemon juice, salt, white pepper, and garlic powder. Sauce should coat a metal spoon fairly thickly. If too thick, thin with remaining cream.

Makes about 2³/₄ cups.

PASTA & RICE

PASTA means Italian food to most people. But in Los Angeles pasta is just as likely to be Chinese, Japanese, or Thai—all cuisines in which noodles and rice play an important part.

Italian restaurants are well-patronized, however, and Los Angeles can boast its own versions of fettuccine, mostaccioli, spaghetti, linguine, lasagna, and other pasta classics. Sauces may be elaborate or so simple it takes only the time required to cook the spaghetti to prepare them.

Home cooks often make their own pasta, but markets offer ample varieties, including the bean and rice noodles used in Oriental cuisines.

Rice similarly reflects the ethnic richness of Los Angeles. Fried rice and fluffy steamed rice go with Chinese meals while stickier steamed rice accompanies Japanese dishes. And many Californians like zesty rice casseroles spiked with chiles, cheese, and tomatoes. Then there are the rice pilafs of the Middle East, the risottos of Italy, and the very different rice dishes of Southeast Asia such as Indonesian nasi goreng, a spicy fried rice.

Both rice and pasta also appear in soups and salads, attesting to the versatility of these foods that have been the mainstay of many of the world's oldest civilizations.

Fettuccine Alfredo, page 126

Fettuccine Alfredo

The chef at Ristorante Alfredo alla Scrofa in Rome revealed the secret of his "true" version of fettuccine Alfredo. No cream. Just butter and soft, moist grated Parmesan cheese.

Homemade Fettuccine
Noodles
1 cup butter or margarine,
softened

Grated Parmesan cheese
Freshly ground black pepper

DROP fettuccine in boiling salted water and cook until fettuccine rises to surface, about 2 minutes. Quickly drain and place in warm bowl containing half the softened butter. Top with lumps of remaining butter and 1/3 to 1/2 cup cheese. Toss lightly, using fork and spoon, about 2 minutes, until fettuccine is well coated and a creamy sauce is formed. Serve sprinkled with pepper and additional grated cheese.

Makes 4 to 6 servings.

Homemade Fettuccine Noodles

1 cup semolina flour
1 cup all-purpose unbleached
   flour

2 eggs
1 tablespoon olive oil, about
Dash salt

Combine flours in large bowl. Mix well. Make a well in center of flour and drop in eggs, oil, and salt. Using a fork, beat mixture into flour, working up to the rim gradually and incorporating wet ingredients with flour thoroughly. If too dry, add a few drops of water. When combined, moisten hands with oil and work dough, kneading and folding about 10 minutes until smooth and pliable. Keep on kneading 5 minutes longer until dough is completely smooth. (Kneading, because of the toughness of the semolina flour, will be difficult, but keep going. Keep hands moistened with oil during kneading process to help stretch the dough and make it pliable.) Form into a ball, cover, and let stand 10 minutes to rest. Process through pasta machine according to manufacturer's directions or roll very thin. Cut for fettuccine noodles. Use at once or allow to dry and store for future use.

Makes enough pasta for 6 servings.

Sour Cream Fettuccine

Sour cream is the hidden flavoring in this fettuccine recipe from the Marina del Rey restaurant, Fiasco.

1 pound fettuccine noodles
1 cup sour cream
1 cup whipping cream
2 tablespoons butter or
   margarine

Grated Parmesan cheese
Salt
Freshly ground black pepper

COOK fettuccine until tender and drain. Meanwhile, combine sour cream, whipping cream, and butter in saucepan. Heat but do not boil.

Add Parmesan cheese and season to taste with salt and pepper. Pour sauce over hot fettuccine and toss. Sprinkle with additional Parmesan cheese and chopped parsley, if desired. Serve at once.

Makes 8 servings.

Fettuccine with Ham and Turkey

12 ounces fettuccine noodles
1/2 cup unsalted butter
8 large mushrooms, sliced
1/2 cup chopped cooked ham
1/2 cup chopped cooked turkey
  breast
1 teaspoon chicken stock base

2 1/2 cups half and half
1 tablespoon flour
3/4 teaspoon salt
1/4 teaspoon white pepper
1/2 cup grated Parmesan
  cheese
Chopped parsley

Ham and turkey are combined with mushrooms in this main dish fettuccine recipe from Little Joe's, an Italian restaurant in the heart of Los Angeles's Chinatown.

COOK fettuccine in 4 quarts boiling salted water about 7 minutes. Drain and return to pan. Add 1/4 cup butter and toss until melted. Meanwhile, melt remaining butter in skillet, add mushrooms, and sauté lightly. Add ham and turkey and sauté 5 minutes. Combine stock base, 1/2 cup half and half, and flour in saucepan and cook, stirring, until mixture comes to boil and thickens. Stir in remaining half and half, salt, and white pepper and cook, stirring, until mixture comes to boil. Add mushroom mixture to sauce and stir until well mixed. Add sauce to noodles and toss, then add cheese and toss again. Sprinkle each serving with chopped parsley.

Makes 6 to 8 servings.

Fettuccine with Walnut Pesto Sauce

3 cups coarsely chopped
  parsley
1 cup walnuts
3 large cloves garlic
2 tablespoons grated
  Parmesan cheese

1 teaspoon salt
1 teaspoon basil
1 cup olive oil
1 pound fettuccine noodles

The Park Ritz in Arcadia serves fettuccine with an interesting walnut-flavored pesto sauce.

COMBINE parsley, walnuts, garlic, Parmesan cheese, salt, basil, and oil in food processor container and process until well blended and mixture is thick. Keep at room temperature. Meanwhile, cook fettuccine in plenty of boiling salted water until just tender, but firm to the bite, and drain. Turn onto warm platter and top with walnut pesto sauce. Toss until fettuccine is well coated with sauce. Serve with additional Parmesan cheese, if desired.

Makes 8 servings.

Sicilian Mostaccioli

Members of St. Peter's Italian Catholic Church in downtown Los Angeles prepare this Sicilian-style pasta dish for special functions at the church.

2 tablespoons oil
1 pound coarsely ground beef
1/4 cup chopped onion
2 to 3 cloves garlic, minced
1/2 pound mushrooms, sliced
1 (1-pound 12-ounce) can Italian-style tomatoes

1 (8-ounce) can tomato sauce
1/4 cup chopped parsley
1 tablespoon chopped fresh basil or 2 teaspoons dried basil
1 pound mostaccioli or other large pasta
Grated Parmesan cheese

HEAT oil and add ground beef, onion, and garlic. Cook until beef is crumbly and onion is tender. Add mushrooms and cook until tender. Crush tomatoes with liquid and add to meat mixture with tomato sauce, parsley, and basil. Bring to boil, reduce heat, and simmer over low heat 1 hour, stirring occasionally to prevent sticking. When ready to serve, cook mostaccioli in boiling salted water until tender. Drain. Toss mostaccioli with enough sauce to coat lightly. Serve topped with more sauce and sprinkle with Parmesan cheese to taste.

Makes 6 servings.

Mostaccioli

Young gymnasts may look trim and slim but their appetites could put farm hands to the blush. We acquired the recipe for this hearty pasta dish from members of the Southern California Acro Team (SCAT) in 1972 and it, like them, has held up well.

2 pounds Italian sausage (1 pound hot and 1 pound mild)
1 pound ground beef
1 large onion, chopped
1 large green pepper, chopped
1 (1-pound 12-ounce) can Italian-style tomatoes
1 (1-pound 12-ounce) can tomato puree
2 (6-ounce) cans tomato paste

2 cups water
2 tablespoons vinegar
Salt, pepper
Oregano
2 pounds mostaccioli
1 pound shredded mozzarella cheese
2/3 cup grated Parmesan cheese

REMOVE sausage from casing, brown in skillet, and drain. Add beef and brown, stirring to keep crumbly. Add onion and green pepper and cook until tender. Add undrained tomatoes, tomato puree, tomato paste, water, and vinegar. Season to taste with salt, pepper, and oregano. Simmer 1 hour, stirring occasionally. Cook mostaccioli in boiling salted water until just tender. Drain and rinse. Layer mostaccioli, then meat sauce, then mozzarella and Parmesan cheeses in 2 (4-quart) casseroles. Bake at 350 degrees 45 minutes to 1 hour, or until bubbly.

Makes about 16 servings.

Pake Noodles

1 cup hot cooked noodles
3 tablespoons butter or
   margarine
1 tablespoon fine dry bread
   crumbs

1 tablespoon sesame seeds,
   toasted
¼ teaspoon MSG (optional)
   Salt, pepper

Trader Vic's in Beverly Hills added a soupçon of sesame seeds to noodles for a definitely different flavor.

MIX together hot noodles, butter, bread crumbs, sesame seeds, and MSG and season to taste with salt and pepper.

Makes 1 to 2 servings.

Fideo

3 tablespoons oil
4 coils fideo (coil vermicelli)
2 tablespoons minced onion
1 clove garlic, minced

½ cup canned tomato sauce
3 cups water
   Salt, pepper

HEAT oil, add fideo, and cook until lightly browned. Add onion and cook until tender. Add garlic, tomato sauce, and water and season to taste with salt and pepper. Bring to boil. Lower heat, cover, and simmer for 10 minutes.

Makes 6 servings.

Peasant-Style Spaghetti

1 tablespoon minced garlic
1 pound tomatoes, peeled and
   chopped
1 tablespoon oil
5 ounces prosciutto, minced
½ teaspoon black pepper

¼ teaspoon oregano
12 ounces spaghetti, cooked
   and drained
   Chopped parsley
   Grated Parmesan cheese

Prosciutto and fresh tomatoes are the main ingredients in the peasant-style sauce served over spaghetti at Santa Monica's Valentino.

SAUTÉ garlic and tomatoes in hot oil in skillet until tender, about 5 minutes. Add prosciutto, pepper, and oregano. Reduce heat and simmer until ingredients are blended, about 2 to 3 minutes. Toss with spaghetti and sprinkle with parsley. Serve with Parmesan cheese.

Makes 4 servings.

Spaghetti Mizithra
(Greek-Style Spaghetti)

A popular family spaghetti restaurant in Hollywood, The Spaghetti Factory, is the source of this unusual Greek-style spaghetti dish made with Kasseri and Romano cheeses.

1 pound spaghetti
1 cup butter or margarine
1/2 pound Kasseri cheese, grated

1/4 pound Romano cheese, grated
1/4 cup chopped parsley

COOK spaghetti until tender but firm to the bite and drain. Melt butter in large skillet and cook just until it turns brown. Meanwhile, combine cheeses. Place spaghetti on warm platter, sprinkle with mixed cheeses, then drizzle with browned butter. Sprinkle with parsley.

Makes 6 servings.

Spaghetti Gorgonzola

The Sunday Home Magazine feature, ''Guys and Galleys,'' led us to Sergio Gentilli and his blue-cheese-flavored spaghetti.

6 ounces Gorgonzola or blue cheese, crumbled
1 cup whipping cream
12 ounces spaghetti, cooked and drained

Salt
Freshly ground black pepper

COMBINE cheese with whipping cream in saucepan. Cook over low heat just until cheese melts, stirring constantly. Combine spaghetti with hot cheese mixture. Season to taste with salt and freshly ground pepper.

Makes 4 servings.

Spaghetti Casserole

This spaghetti casserole is often served by prominent local hostess Mrs. Lee de Laittre, known for her hearty buffets.

1 (10 3/4-ounce) can condensed cream of mushroom soup
1 1/2 soup cans milk
1/2 teaspoon black pepper
Seasoned salt
Sugar
1 (12-ounce) package thin spaghetti

1 pint sour cream
1 1/2 pounds sharp American cheese, shredded
1 onion, minced
1 cup round butter cracker crumbs
1/2 cup butter or margarine

BLEND together soup, milk, and pepper. Season to taste with seasoned salt and sugar. Set aside. Bring 4 quarts water to boil. Add spaghetti, remove from heat, and let stand until spaghetti becomes pliable, about 10 minutes. Drain. Place a layer of spaghetti in 13 x 9-inch greased baking pan, spread with a thin layer of sour cream, sprinkle with a thick layer of cheese, and top with a layer of onion. Repeat layers until ingredients are used. Pour soup mixture over spaghetti mixture. Sauté crumbs in butter until golden. Sprinkle over casserole and bake at 325 degrees 1 hour or until casserole is bubbly and spaghetti is done.

Makes 10 servings.

Cappellacci
(Stuffed Pasta Squares)

1¹/₂ pounds ricotta cheese	Salt, pepper
³/₄ pound spinach, cooked and chopped	1 tablespoon oil
	Pasta Squares
1 teaspoon nutmeg	Tomato Sauce
4 eggs	
Grated Parmesan or sharp pecorino cheese	

Another favorite from Valentino in Santa Monica, this one takes a bit more time. Cappellacci, ravioli-like stuffed pasta squares, are filled with a ricotta and spinach mixture and baked in a tomato sauce.

COMBINE ricotta, drained spinach, nutmeg, eggs, and cheese in bowl and mix well. Season to taste with salt and pepper. Bring large pot of generously salted water to boil. Add oil. Drop each piece of pasta into boiling water and cook 3 to 4 minutes, or just until pasta floats to surface. Remove at once and plunge into bowl filled with ice water 1 minute. Drain pasta on clean cloth to prevent sticking. Place 1 tablespoon stuffing in center of each pasta square. Fold square into triangle, then again into smaller triangle. Press edges to seal. Pour a layer of Tomato Sauce in large baking pan. Arrange cappellacci in rows, slightly overlapping. Cover with sauce and sprinkle with additional Parmesan cheese. Bake at 400 degrees 5 to 7 minutes.

Pasta Squares

4 eggs	¹/₂ teaspoon salt
2 teaspoons oil	2 cups flour

Combine eggs, oil, and salt in bowl and whisk until well blended. Add flour, a little at a time, beating after each addition. Turn out onto well-floured board and knead several minutes until dough is firm and smooth but not dry. Add more flour if necessary to prevent sticking. Cover and let stand at slightly warm temperature about 30 minutes to ripen. Cut dough in 2-inch portions and roll out slightly to flatten enough to fit into pasta machine. Roll in machine starting with thickest setting and progressing to next to the finest setting until pasta is very thin (expansion takes place during cooking). Continue until all dough is rolled into strips. Place strips on floured board and lightly flour. Cut in 4-inch squares and let rest 10 minutes before cooking.

(continued on overleaf)

Tomato Sauce

1 medium onion, finely
chopped
5 cloves garlic, crushed
10 tablespoons olive oil
2 (14 ½-ounce) cans Italian-
style tomatoes, cut in small
pieces

6 to 8 sprigs fresh or 2
teaspoons dried basil
2 teaspoons salt
Pepper
1 tablespoon sugar

Sauté onion and garlic in oil until golden. Add undrained tomatoes and basil and season to taste with salt and pepper. Bring to boil and simmer 15 minutes. Add sugar at the last minute.

Makes about 4½ cups.

Conchiglie con Zucchine
(Pasta Shells with Zucchini)

A Times food staffer had this dish at El Toula in Milan and immediately acquired the recipe.

½ cup butter or margarine
1 clove garlic, minced
3 or 4 zucchini, sliced
1 teaspoon dried
rosemary leaves,
crushed
Salt, pepper

1 pound large pasta shells
2 tablespoons chopped
parsley, optional
⅓ cup grated Parmesan
cheese

MELT butter in large skillet or shallow saucepan. Add garlic and zucchini and cook until crisp-tender. Add rosemary and season to taste with salt and pepper. Increase heat and cook a few minutes to blend flavors. Remove from heat. Meanwhile, cook pasta in boiling salted water until tender but still firm to the bite. Drain thoroughly and add to zucchini mixture. Heat and toss until shells are well coated with sauce, about 2 to 3 minutes. Add parsley and cheese. Toss again and serve at once.

Makes 6 to 8 servings.

Lasagna

8 ounces lasagna noodles
1 pound cube steaks, pounded tender
2 tablespoons oil
1¹/₂ cups sliced mushrooms
1 cup chopped onions
¹/₄ cup chopped green pepper
2 (6-ounce) cans tomato paste
3 cups water

1 clove garlic, crushed
1 teaspoon salt
¹/₈ teaspoon black pepper
¹/₂ teaspoon oregano
¹/₂ teaspoon basil
2 cups ricotta cheese
2 cups shredded mozzarella cheese
¹/₂ cup grated Parmesan cheese

COOK lasagna noodles in boiling salted water until tender. Drain. Rinse well. Cut steaks into 1¹/₂ x ¹/₂-inch strips. Brown well in oil in large skillet. Add mushrooms, onions, and green pepper. Cook, stirring, until tender. Stir in tomato paste, water, garlic, salt, pepper, oregano, and basil. Boil gently, uncovered, 20 minutes. Stir occasionally. Place ¹/₃ of sauce in bottom of 13 x 9-inch baking dish. Arrange half of noodles on top of sauce. Spread 1 cup ricotta cheese over noodles. Top with half of remaining sauce, 1 cup mozzarella cheese, and ¹/₄ cup Parmesan cheese. Add additional layers of remaining noodles, ricotta cheese, sauce, and mozzarella and Parmesan cheeses. Bake at 350 degrees 25 to 30 minutes. Let stand 5 to 10 minutes before serving.

Makes 6 to 8 servings.

La Scala, one of the outstanding restaurants in Beverly Hills, has been pleasing the palates of Italian cuisine aficionados for a long time with this meaty lasagna.

Pasta Pomodoro
(Tomato Pasta)

1 cup butter or margarine
1 onion, minced
6 cloves garlic
4 (28-ounce) cans Italian-style tomatoes
2 to 3 beef bouillon cubes
2 teaspoons salt

4 or 5 small dried red hot chiles (optional)
2 tablespoons olive oil
2 pounds macaroni
1¹/₂ cups grated Parmesan cheese

MELT butter and add onion and whole garlic cloves. Sauté until onion is golden. Add tomatoes with liquid and simmer over low heat 1¹/₂ hours, or until sauce is thick. Add bouillon cubes, season to taste with salt, and heat until cubes dissolve. Add chiles and simmer 30 minutes longer. When ready to serve, remove garlic cloves and chiles. Stir in oil. Meanwhile, cook macaroni until tender but firm and drain. Pour tomato sauce over macaroni and add cheese. Toss with fork and spoon until sauce and cheese are well distributed.

Makes 8 to 10 servings.

Gianpiero Moretti, an Italian race-car driver and industrialist, loves to cook this tomato-sauced pasta for his crew and fellow drivers after a race.

(continued on overleaf)

Pasta Amatriciana
(Smoked Macaroni)

Add 1 cup chopped bacon to sauce along with chiles and simmer 30 minutes.

Pasta Aubergine Salad

Cold pasta salads make wonderful light meals. This one with eggplant was developed in The Times *test kitchen.*

1 medium eggplant
Salt
Dressing
6 ounces vermicelli, cooked and well drained
1 (9-ounce) package frozen artichoke hearts, cooked and drained

1 large tomato, peeled and diced
1/2 cup chopped chives or green onions
2 tablespoons minced cilantro (optional)
Lettuce

CUT eggplant (unpeeled) in 3-inch-long strips. Rinse and sprinkle generously with salt. Toss and let stand 15 minutes, then drain on paper towels. Steam, covered, over 1 inch boiling water 15 minutes, or until eggplant is tender. Drain well. Combine eggplant with Dressing, vermicelli, artichoke hearts, tomato, chives, and cilantro. Toss well to blend. Cover and chill well. Mound salad in lettuce-lined platter or bowl.

Makes 6 to 8 servings.

Dressing

1 1/2 to 2 cloves garlic, minced
1/2 cup oil
2 tablespoons champagne vinegar
2 tablespoons lemon juice
1 teaspoon sugar
3/4 teaspoon dry mustard

1/8 teaspoon white pepper
Dash red pepper
1 teaspoon crushed oregano
2 tablespoons minced parsley (optional)
1/8 teaspoon paprika
Salt

Combine garlic, oil, vinegar, lemon juice, sugar, mustard, white pepper, red pepper, oregano, parsley, and paprika in covered jar. Shake until well blended. Season to taste with salt and shake again.

Makes about 3/4 cup.

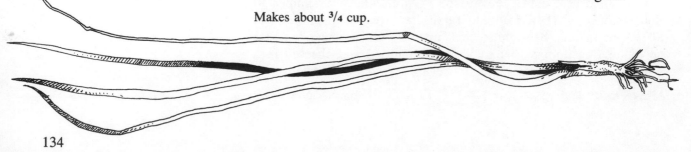

Vegetable Macaroni and Cheese Casserole

1 1/2 cups shredded process
    cheese food
1/2 cup mayonnaise
1 cup milk
1 (10 3/4-ounce) can
    condensed cream of onion
    soup
4 tablespoons butter or
    margarine

3 cups diced broccoli
2 medium tomatoes, diced
1/2 pound elbow macaroni,
    cooked and drained
1/2 cup seasoned dry bread
    crumbs
1/4 cup grated Parmesan
    cheese

This vegetable-laden macaroni and cheese dish was developed in The Times *test kitchen. It's a wonderful choice for a meatless meal or potluck dinner.*

COMBINE cheese, mayonnaise, milk, and cream of onion soup and mix well. Melt 2 tablespoons butter in small skillet and sauté broccoli about 3 minutes. Remove from heat. Add tomatoes, then mix with cheese mixture. Add macaroni. Turn into 2 1/2-quart baking dish. Melt remaining 2 tablespoons butter and stir in bread crumbs and Parmesan cheese. Sprinkle over casserole. Bake 35 to 45 minutes, or until heated through.

Makes about 8 servings.

Macaroni and Cheese with Chiles

2 cups medium elbow
    macaroni
1/4 cup butter or
    margarine
3 tablespoons flour or
    masa harina
1 teaspoon salt
1/4 to 1/2 teaspoon garlic
    powder
1/8 teaspoon black pepper

3 cups milk
1/4 cup grated onion
1 (4-ounce) can diced green
    chiles
1 (2-ounce) jar pimiento,
    chopped
3 cups shredded Monterey
    Jack cheese
1/2 cup crushed tortilla chips
    Paprika

Chiles and tortilla chips give this macaroni and cheese casserole a Mexican flavor.

COOK macaroni in boiling salted water until tender but firm and drain. Melt butter in large saucepan. Blend in flour, salt, garlic powder, and pepper. Cook, stirring constantly, 2 minutes. Slowly add milk, stirring until smooth. Add onion, chiles, and pimiento. Cook until thickened. Stir in cheese and cook until melted. Combine macaroni and cheese sauce. Pour into 2 1/2-quart casserole. Top with tortilla crumbs and sprinkle with paprika. Bake at 350 degrees 25 minutes. Serve at once.

Makes 6 servings.

One Pot Pasta Dinner

Ideal for the lazy or busy cook, this easy supper dish cooks beef, pasta, and sauce together in the same pot at once.

1¹/₂ pounds ground beef
1 tablespoon oil
1¹/₂ cups chopped onion
1¹/₂ cups chopped celery
1¹/₂ cups catsup
3 cups water
1 tablespoon Worcestershire sauce
2 teaspoons salt
¹/₈ teaspoon black pepper

¹/₂ teaspoon dry mustard
1 teaspoon oregano
8 ounces curly macaroni
1 cup shredded American cheese
¹/₂ cup grated Parmesan cheese
2 tablespoons chopped parsley

LIGHTLY brown beef in oil in 5-quart Dutch oven. Add onion and celery and cook until onion is tender. Add catsup, water, Worcestershire, salt, pepper, mustard, and oregano. Mix well. Stir in macaroni. Cover and simmer 25 to 35 minutes, or until pasta is tender. Just before serving, fold in American cheese and sprinkle with Parmesan cheese and parsley.

Makes 8 servings.

Pork Fried Rice

Chinese-style fried rice is an excellent dish when one wants to use up odd bits and pieces of leftovers.

Oil
¹/₂ pound lean pork, cut in thin strips, or 2 cups diced roast pork or Chinese barbecued pork
¹/₂ teaspoon sugar
¹/₂ teaspoon salt
¹/₂ cup sliced green onions with tops

¹/₂ cup sliced celery
3 cups cold cooked rice
1 cup bean sprouts
3 tablespoons soy sauce
2 eggs, beaten
Chopped cooked pork, Egg Pancake, and Green Onion Brushes for garnish

HEAT 3 tablespoons oil in wok or large skillet. Add pork, season with sugar and salt, and stir-fry over high heat until browned and cooked. Add green onions and celery and cook until crisp-tender. Add rice and bean sprouts and cook until rice is heated through, stirring to mix with meat and vegetables. Add soy sauce and stir to mix. Make a well in center of rice, pour in beaten eggs, allow to set, and scramble with chopsticks, then stir into rice. Or heat 1 tablespoon oil in separate pan, pour in eggs and allow to set, pushing set portion aside to allow uncooked egg to run underneath. Cut into strips and stir into rice. Turn rice out onto platter and top with chopped cooked pork and shredded Egg Pancake. Make a border of Green Onion Brushes around rice.

Makes 6 servings.

Egg Pancake

1 egg
1 tablespoon water
1/8 teaspoon salt
2 teaspoons oil

Combine egg, water, and salt and beat. Heat wok or large skillet over medium high heat. Add oil and pour in egg mixture. Tilt pan to coat surface. Cook until pancake is set and bottom is slightly golden. Turn and cool, then roll up tightly and slice crosswise into slivers.

Green Onion Brushes

Select large green onions. Cut off root ends, leaving as much white part as possible. Cut onions in 3-inch lengths. Place on board and using sharp knife, make slashes lengthwise from each end, cutting 1/2 inch toward center. Place in bowl of cold water and onions will open up and curl back. Chill in water 1 hour or overnight. Drain well before using.

Nasi Goreng
(Indonesian Fried Rice)

1/4 cup oil or rendered pork fat
1 pound cubed pork butt
2 small onions, sliced
2 green onions, chopped
1 Chinese sausage, finely sliced
4 eggs
Salt, pepper
1 jalapeño chile, sliced
6 cups cold cooked rice
1 chicken or beef bouillon cube (optional)
1 tablespoon butter
1 cucumber, peeled
Oil for deep frying

Danny Ungerer, born in Sumatra and a teacher of Indonesian cooking in Pasadena, makes delectable fried rice this way.

HEAT oil or render pork fat in wok or large skillet. Add pork and sauté until browned. Add half of sliced onions and cook until tender. Add green onions and sausage. Break 2 eggs into center of ingredients and mix lightly. Season to taste with salt and pepper and add jalapeño chile. Before eggs are set, add rice and stir. Crumble bouillon cube over rice. Cook about 10 minutes or until rice is heated through, stirring constantly. Heat butter in medium skillet. Beat remaining eggs in separate bowls and season to taste with salt and pepper. Add one egg at a time to skillet and cook each into a flat pancake. Remove from skillet, roll up, and cut crosswise into strips. Cut ridges in cucumber by running a fork down sides. Cut in thin slices. Deep fry remaining onion in oil until crisp. Drain. Arrange rice on large platter. Surround with cucumber slices. Garnish rice with egg strips and sprinkle with fried onions.

Makes 6 servings.

Rice Sticks with Vegetables

Rice-flour noodles, called mai fun or rice sticks, are mixed with vegetables and bean sprouts in this dish from the Golden Dragon, a Cantonese restaurant in Chinatown.

3 quarts water
1 (13 ³/₄-ounce) package rice sticks
2 stalks celery
4 ounces Chinese pea pods
1 ounce Oriental dried mushrooms, softened in water

¹/₄ cup oil
1 pound bean sprouts
1 tablespoon curry powder
1 cup chicken broth
Salt
Soy sauce

BRING water to boil and add rice sticks. Cook 2 minutes, then drain. Rinse with cold water and drain. Cut celery, pea pods, and mushrooms into thin slices. Heat oil until hot and add rice sticks. Cook, stirring, until brown. Remove rice sticks from pan and drain. Add celery, pea pods, mushrooms, and bean sprouts and cook over high heat 2 minutes, stirring constantly. Combine curry powder and chicken broth and add to pan. Season to taste with salt. Pour over rice sticks and toss to serve. Serve with soy sauce.

Makes 6 to 8 servings.

Chile Rice Casserole

¹/₄ cup chopped green onions
2 cups chicken broth
1 teaspoon salt
2 cups uncooked instant rice
1 (4-ounce) can diced green chiles

1 pint sour cream
1¹/₂ cups shredded cheddar cheese
¹/₂ cup cherry tomatoes, cut in halves

COMBINE green onions, broth, and ¹/₂ teaspoon salt and heat to boiling. Stir in rice, cover, and let stand in warm place 5 minutes. Stir chiles into sour cream with remaining ¹/₂ teaspoon salt. Layer rice, cheese, and sour cream mixture in a 1¹/₂-quart baking dish, dotting rice with tomatoes and ending with sour cream mixture. Bake at 350 degrees 20 minutes or until heated through.

Makes 8 to 10 servings.

Mexican Rice

1 small onion, chopped
2 tablespoons oil
1 clove garlic, minced
1 cup uncooked rice

1 tomato, peeled and chopped
2 cups consommé
1/2 teaspoon ground cumin
   Salt

SAUTÉ onion in oil until tender but not browned. Add garlic and rice and cook, stirring often, until rice is pale golden. Add tomato, consommé, and cumin, and season to taste with salt. Bring to boil, cover, and simmer over very low heat until liquid is absorbed and rice is tender, about 15 to 20 minutes.

Makes 4 to 6 servings.

Risotto

1 medium onion, diced
1/2 cup butter or margarine
1 cup uncooked long-grain
   rice

1 3/4 cups consommé
1/2 cup sherry
1/2 cup grated Parmesan
   cheese

SAUTÉ onion in 1/4 cup butter in large skillet until golden brown. Add rice and stir until rice turns yellow. Add consommé and sherry. Bring to boil, then reduce heat. Cover and let simmer 15 to 20 minutes until liquid is absorbed. Add remaining 1/4 cup butter and stir in cheese.

Makes 6 servings.

Armenian Rice Pilaf

1/4 pound butter or margarine
1/2 cup vermicelli
2 cups uncooked long-grain
   rice

4 cups chicken broth
1 teaspoon MSG (optional)
   Salt

This classic Armenian pilaf mixes rice with vermicelli, providing an interesting texture as well as flavor combination.

MELT butter in heavy pan or Dutch oven. Break vermicelli in small pieces, add to pan, and cook until golden brown, stirring constantly. Add rice and stir until rice is well coated with butter. Add boiling broth and MSG and season to taste with salt. Cook, covered, over low heat until liquid is absorbed, about 25 minutes. Stir lightly with fork. Let stand in warm place 15 to 20 minutes before serving.

Makes 8 servings.

Dirty Rice

This rice dish, transplanted to the West from the deep South, is a popular accompaniment to poultry.

2 tablespoons oil
2 tablespoons flour
1 cup chopped onions
1 cup chopped celery
$^1/_2$ cup chopped green pepper
2 cloves garlic, minced
$^1/_2$ pound ground beef
$^1/_2$ pound ground pork

$^1/_2$ pound chicken giblets, chopped
2 teaspoons salt
$^3/_4$ teaspoon black pepper
$^3/_4$ teaspoon red pepper
1 cup chicken broth or water
3 cups hot cooked rice
1 cup sliced green onion tops

HEAT oil in Dutch oven. Add flour and cook until flour is a deep red-brown. Stir constantly to prevent burning. Add onions, celery, green pepper, and garlic and cook until tender. Stir in beef, pork, giblets, salt, and black and red peppers. Cook until meat is browned. Blend in broth. Cover and simmer 25 minutes. Stir in rice and green onions and cook 5 minutes longer.

Makes 6 servings.

Lemon Rice

Maldonado's, a Pasadena restaurant, uses lemon to add flavor to this creamy rice side dish.

1 cup uncooked rice
$1^1/_2$ cups boiling water
Salt
Peel and juice of $^1/_2$ lemon

$^1/_4$ cup butter
$^3/_4$ cup whipping cream, warmed
Chopped parsley

ADD rice to boiling water. Season to taste with salt. Cook, covered, over medium heat until rice is tender, stirring occasionally, about 20 minutes. Do not overcook. Sauté lemon peel in butter about 3 minutes. Remove peel. Add butter to cooked rice. Add lemon juice gradually, tossing, until seasoned to taste. Add half of warmed cream, folding gently. Add enough additional cream to coat all grains of rice. Place in ovenproof serving dish and keep warm until serving time. Garnish with chopped parsley.

Makes 6 servings.

CHOLESTEROL-CONSCIOUS though we all may be, who can resist sampling savory omelets, gossamer soufflés, or any number of other delectable egg dishes on occasion? Quiches are probably the most frequently found egg dishes on local menus, and there are so many variations one need never fear monotony. Vegetables, meats, seafood, cheeses, and chiles are just a few of the ingredients likely to turn up in a California quiche.

Eggs, not unexpectedly, play a prominent role in the informal menus served at the leisurely brunch, a weekend institution in Southern California. Quiches appear often, as do omelets and soufflés. Angelenos are also fond of offering guests a choice of foods, such as the popular brunch menu centered around do-it-yourself omelets. Whoever has mastered the knack of turning out perfect omelets is drafted to prepare them on the spot, adding fillings of the guests' choices from an assortment provided.

Still other egg dishes that have wide appeal in the West are those that reflect Mexico's strong influence on our cuisine. Chiles, cheeses, corn, and tomatoes are combined with eggs in many delightful breakfast, lunch, and supper offerings. The strong, often spicy, flavors that prevail in Mexican cooking and the delicately bland taste and texture of eggs make them excellent companions.

Eggs and Flour for Spinach Quiche, page 144

Spinach Quiche

Color, texture, and taste make fresh spinach a natural complement to eggs, as demonstrated by this quiche and the omelet and soufflé recipes that follow it.

4 ounces Gruyère cheese, shredded
1 (9-inch) unbaked pastry shell
1 medium onion, chopped
1 tablespoon butter or margarine
4 eggs

2 cups whipping cream
3/4 pound spinach, cooked, drained, and chopped
1/2 teaspoon salt
Dash nutmeg
Dash white pepper

SPRINKLE cheese in pastry shell. Cook onion in butter in small skillet until tender. Mix eggs, cream, spinach, onion, salt, nutmeg, and white pepper. Pour over cheese. Bake at 425 degrees until knife inserted 1 inch from edge comes out clean, about 30 to 35 minutes. Let stand 10 minutes before serving.

Makes 6 servings.

Rolled Spinach Omelet

Here's a real show-off dish—a puffy omelet in the shape of a jelly roll, with a creamy spinach filling for flavor and color contrast.

3/4 pound spinach
1/4 cup butter or margarine
1 1/2 tablespoons fine dry bread crumbs
6 eggs, separated
1/2 teaspoon cream of tartar

1 1/4 teaspoons salt
3 tablespoons flour
1 cup milk
3/4 cup shredded Muenster cheese

WASH spinach and remove stems. Cook spinach in water clinging to leaves until just tender. Drain well, pressing out excess water, then chop fine. Lightly grease jelly-roll pan and line bottom with wax paper to fit pan. Grease paper with 1 tablespoon butter, then sprinkle with crumbs. Beat egg whites with cream of tartar and 1/2 teaspoon salt until stiff. With same beater, beat yolks well. Slowly pour yolks over egg whites while gently folding in. Turn egg mixture into prepared pan and spread evenly with spatula. Bake at 350 degrees about 12 minutes until lightly puffed and very lightly browned on top. Meanwhile, melt remaining 3 tablespoons butter in saucepan, then blend in flour. Stir in milk and remaining 3/4 teaspoon salt. Cook and stir until sauce boils and thickens. Add spinach and 1/2 cup cheese and stir over medium heat until cheese melts. Turn omelet out onto cloth towel. Carefully peel paper from omelet and spread with hot spinach mixture. Roll up as for jelly roll and place on serving platter. Sprinkle top with remaining 1/4 cup cheese. Cut into slices to serve.

Makes 6 servings.

Spinach Soufflé

3 tablespoons butter or
  margarine
1/4 cup flour
1 teaspoon salt
1/4 teaspoon black pepper
  Dash nutmeg

1 cup milk
4 egg yolks
1 cup drained, chopped,
  cooked spinach
2 teaspoons minced onion
5 egg whites

MELT butter and blend in flour, salt, pepper, and nutmeg. Gradually stir in milk and cook, stirring, until smooth and thickened. Cool slightly. Beat egg yolks until light and stir into cream sauce, blending well. Stir in spinach and onion. Beat egg whites until stiff. Stir 1/4 of egg whites into spinach mixture, blending well. Fold rest of whites into sauce lightly but thoroughly. Turn into 1-quart soufflé dish and bake at 375 degrees 35 to 45 minutes, or until golden. Serve at once.

Makes 4 servings.

Never-Fail Cheese Soufflé

  Butter or margarine,
    softened
10 slices white bread
12 ounces sharp cheddar
    cheese, shredded
12 ounces mozzarella cheese,
    shredded
 8 eggs, lightly beaten

3 1/2 cups half and half
1/4 teaspoon paprika
1 teaspoon minced onion
1/2 teaspoon curry powder
1/8 teaspoon red pepper
1 teaspoon Worcestershire
  sauce
1 teaspoon dry mustard

Every host or hostess needs a soufflé that can be counted on never to fail. This one with its bread base is it.

BUTTER sides and bottom of a 13 x 9-inch baking dish or 2 (9-inch) square baking dishes. Remove crusts from bread, butter each slice, and cut in cubes. Place half the buttered cubes in baking dish and sprinkle with half the cheddar and mozzarella cheeses, then add the remaining bread in another layer and top with the remaining cheeses. Combine eggs, half and half, paprika, onion, curry powder, red pepper, Worcestershire, and mustard. Pour over bread and cheese mixture. Cover and refrigerate overnight. Bake at 325 degrees 1 hour, or until knife inserted in center comes out clean and top is lightly browned.

Makes 8 to 10 servings.

Cold-Start Cheese Soufflé

A cold-start soufflé is an energy saver as there is no need to preheat the oven. It will work well in any gas oven and in electric ovens that don't use both top and bottom elements to bring the oven to the proper temperature.

Grated Parmesan cheese
Butter or margarine
6 tablespoons flour
$^1/_2$ teaspoon salt
Dash black pepper or red pepper

$1^1/_4$ cups milk
6 eggs (at room temperature), separated
$^1/_2$ cup coarsely shredded Swiss cheese
$^1/_4$ teaspoon cream of tartar

GREASE a 2-quart straight-sided soufflé dish, about $7^1/_2$ inches in diameter. Dust lightly with 1 tablespoon Parmesan cheese. Tear off sheet of wax paper 2 inches longer than circumference of dish. Fold lengthwise into thirds. Lightly grease one side. Wrap wax paper around soufflé dish, greased side against dish, letting 2-inch rim extend above top edge. Secure with metal paper clips or string. Melt 5 tablespoons butter in medium saucepan. Remove from heat. Stir in flour, salt, and pepper until smooth. Gradually stir in milk. Bring to boil, stirring. Reduce heat and simmer, stirring constantly, until mixture becomes very thick and begins to leave bottom and sides of pan. Beat egg yolks. Gradually beat into cooked mixture. Add $^1/_2$ cup Parmesan cheese and the Swiss cheese. Beat until well combined. Add cream of tartar to egg whites. Using an electric mixer, beat at high speed until stiff peaks form. Carefully fold beaten egg whites into warm cheese mixture until well blended. Turn into prepared dish. Place soufflé in cold oven. Turn oven temperature to 350 degrees. Bake 40 to 50 minutes or until soufflé is puffed and golden. Remove from oven and discard collar. Serve immediately.

Makes 4 to 6 servings.

Make-Ahead Sausage Soufflé

Here is a quick and easy dish that can be prepared the night before and served with little fuss for a company brunch the next day.

$^1/_2$ pound hot bulk pork sausage
4 eggs
3 slices white bread, crumbed

$1^1/_2$ cups milk
$^1/_2$ teaspoon salt
$^1/_2$ teaspoon dry mustard
1 cup shredded cheddar cheese

BROWN sausage in skillet, stirring to crumble. Drain off fat and set sausage aside. Beat eggs until light colored. Add bread crumbs, milk, salt, dry mustard, and sausage. Stir in cheese. Spoon into 1-quart soufflé dish. Cover and refrigerate overnight. The next day bake at 325 degrees 1 hour and 15 minutes, or until knife inserted in center comes out clean. Serve immediately.

Makes 4 servings.

Chile-Corn Soufflé

¹/₄ cup butter or margarine	4 eggs, separated
¹/₄ cup flour	¹/₂ (4-ounce) can diced green
1 teaspoon salt	chiles, drained
¹/₄ teaspoon black pepper	1 cup ground fresh corn
¹/₂ teaspoon paprika	kernels
1 cup milk	

MELT butter and blend in flour, salt, pepper, and paprika. Add milk and cook and stir until thickened. Beat egg yolks lightly, add small amount of hot sauce, blend, and return mixture to hot sauce. Cook, stirring, a few minutes. Add chiles to sauce. Stir in corn. Beat egg whites until stiff but still moist. Fold ¹/₃ of the egg whites into corn mixture, mixing well. Fold in remaining egg whites lightly. Turn into ungreased 1-quart soufflé dish or straight-sided casserole. Place in pan of hot water and bake at 350 degrees about 50 minutes.

Makes 6 servings.

Chiles and corn, the most basic ingredients of Mexican cookery, combine here in an American-style soufflé. Serve it as a meatless main dish or as a side dish.

Blue Cheese Yogurt Soufflé

¹/₃ cup shredded Gruyère	1 cup plain low-fat yogurt
cheese	1 cup crumbled blue cheese
Butter or margarine	Dash red pepper
¹/₂ cup flour	4 eggs, separated
³/₄ cup milk	

LIGHTLY grease a 7- or 8-inch soufflé dish. Sprinkle bottom of dish with Gruyère cheese. Tear off sheet of wax paper 2 inches longer than circumference of dish. Fold lengthwise into thirds. Lightly grease one side. Wrap wax paper around soufflé dish, greased side against dish, letting 2-inch rim extend above top edge. Secure with metal paper clips or string. Melt ¹/₃ cup butter in small saucepan and stir in flour. Slowly add milk and half the yogurt, stirring constantly until thickened. Stir in blue cheese, remaining yogurt, and red pepper. Beat egg yolks lightly. Pour a small amount of yogurt mixture into yolks. Stir well and return to rest of yogurt mixture. Cook 1 minute, stirring. Beat egg whites until they form soft peaks. Fold into yolk mixture gently. Do not overmix. Pour into prepared soufflé dish. Bake at 350 degrees 40 to 50 minutes, or until done. Serve immediately.

Makes 6 servings.

Note: For a taller soufflé, use 5 egg whites and 4 egg yolks.

Herbed Blue Cheese Soufflé

¹/4 cup butter or margarine
¹/4 cup flour
1 cup milk
¹/2 teaspoon salt
¹/4 teaspoon black pepper
¹/4 cup crumbled blue cheese,
*   packed*

4 eggs, separated
1 tablespoon chopped chives
*   or green onion*
2 tablespoons chopped parsley
1 cup soft bread crumbs

MELT butter in small saucepan. Blend in flour, then gradually stir in milk. Cook over low heat, stirring constantly, until sauce bubbles and thickens. Stir in salt, pepper, and cheese. Beat in egg yolks, one at a time. Fold in chives, parsley, and bread crumbs. Beat egg whites until stiff but not dry. Fold in ¹/3 of egg whites until well blended, then fold in remaining egg whites. Pour mixture into greased 1-quart casserole. Bake at 450 degrees 15 minutes, reduce heat to 400 degrees, and bake 25 to 30 minutes longer, or until puffed and brown. Serve at once.

Makes 4 servings.

Soufflé au Roquefort

A reader won a "My Best Recipe" award for this Roquefort cheese soufflé. Served with fresh fruit and a green salad, it makes a wonderful brunch or luncheon party dish.

Butter or margarine
¹/3 cup shredded Gruyère
*   cheese*
¹/2 cup flour
1³/4 cups milk

1 cup crumbled Roquefort
*   cheese*
*   Pepper*
4 eggs, separated

LIGHTLY grease a 7- or 8-inch soufflé dish. Sprinkle Gruyère cheese over bottom of dish. Tear off strip of wax paper 2 inches longer than circumference of dish. Fold lengthwise into thirds. Lightly grease one side. Wrap wax paper around soufflé dish, greased side against dish, letting 2-inch rim extend above top of edge. Secure with metal paper clips or string. Melt ¹/3 cup butter in saucepan. Blend in flour, then slowly add milk, stirring constantly, until smooth and thickened. Stir in Roquefort cheese and season to taste with pepper. Pour small amount of sauce into lightly beaten egg yolks, stir well, and return to mixture. Cook, stirring, 1 minute. Beat egg whites until stiff but not dry. Fold into yolk mixture gently. Do not overmix. Pour into prepared soufflé dish. Bake at 350 degrees 40 to 50 minutes, or until done. Serve immediately.

Makes 6 servings.

Cheese and Watercress Pie

1 pound feta cheese, crumbled
1 (8-ounce) package cream
    cheese, softened
2 eggs
1 bunch watercress, minced

Dash nutmeg
Dash black pepper
Dash sugar
Egg Pastry

Feta cheese and fresh watercress give this pie from the Greenhouse restaurant a distinct Mediterranean flavor.

COMBINE cheeses, eggs, watercress, nutmeg, pepper, and sugar in mixer bowl and mix thoroughly. Divide Egg Pastry in halves. Roll half of pastry almost paper-thin and fit into 9-inch pie plate. Spread filling into shell. Roll other half of pastry very thin and place over filling. Trim and crimp edges. Brush with beaten egg white, if desired, and bake at 325 degrees 45 to 55 minutes, or until pastry is golden. Cut in wedges to serve.

Makes 6 servings.

Egg Pastry

 2 cups flour
$^1/_4$ cup butter or margarine,
    softened

 1 egg
    Dash salt
$^1/_3$ to $^1/_2$ cup cold water

Combine flour, butter, egg, and salt in bowl and work with fingers until mixture resembles coarse crumbs. Add enough cold water to make a soft dough. Wrap in wax paper and chill 2 hours.

Crustless Cheese Pie

 2 tablespoons butter or
    margarine
 1 onion, chopped
1$^1/_2$ cups shredded sharp
    cheddar cheese
 1 tablespoon flour
 4 eggs, well beaten

 1 cup milk
 1 teaspoon salt
$^1/_4$ teaspoon black pepper
 4 slices bacon, cooked crisp
    and crumbled
$^1/_2$ cup finely crushed potato
    chips

A crustless cheese pie, with crisp bacon and potato chip topping, was popular some years back when calorie counting became a widespread concern.

HEAT butter in small skillet. Add onion and cook until golden, about 5 minutes. Mix cheese with flour and sprinkle into greased 9-inch pie plate. Spoon onion and drippings evenly over cheese. Beat eggs with milk, salt, and pepper until smooth. Pour mixture into pie plate. Sprinkle with bacon and potato chips. Bake at 350 degrees 40 to 45 minutes, or until puffed and brown. Cut in wedges to serve.

Makes 6 to 8 servings.

Spanish Omelet

The Spanish sauce served over the omelet at Little Joe's in downtown Los Angeles is also great on fish and chicken.

6 eggs, separated
1/8 teaspoon black pepper
1/4 teaspoon salt
1/4 cup water

1 tablespoon butter or
 margarine
Spanish Sauce

BEAT egg yolks with pepper until thick and lemon-colored. Add salt and water to whites and beat until stiff but not dry. Fold yolks into whites. Heat butter in large skillet with ovenproof handle until just hot enough for drop of water to sizzle. Pour in omelet mixture. Level surface gently, reduce heat, and cook on top of stove until puffy and slightly browned on bottom, about 5 minutes. Lift omelet at edge to judge color. Place in oven and bake at 325 degrees 12 to 15 minutes, or until knife inserted in center comes out clean. To serve, fold omelet in half and top with Spanish Sauce.

Makes 2 to 3 servings.

Spanish Sauce

1 cup sliced onions
1 clove garlic, minced
1 cup diced green pepper
1/4 cup oil
1/2 cup mushrooms, sliced

1/2 cup tomato puree
1 (1-pound 12-ounce) can
 Italian-style tomatoes
Salt, pepper

Sauté onions, garlic, and green pepper in oil until tender. Add mushrooms and cook until tender. Add tomato puree and tomatoes with liquid and season to taste with salt and pepper. Cook, breaking up tomatoes, 15 to 20 minutes.

Makes about 6 cups.

Guacamole Omelet

2 eggs
1 tablespoon water
 Salt, pepper
1/2 avocado, peeled

1/2 teaspoon lemon juice
 Dash seasoned salt
3 or 4 drops hot pepper sauce
1 small tomato, chopped

MIX eggs, water, and a dash of salt and pepper. Beat briskly. Pour into hot nonstick skillet or omelet pan. Stir with circular motion while shaking the pan vigorously over heat. Stir until eggs begin to set. Let stand 2 to 3 seconds and shake pan. Omelet should move freely. In a small bowl mash avocado until chunky. Add lemon juice, seasoned salt, hot pepper sauce, and tomato. Mix well. Spoon mixture over half of omelet. Slip broad spatula under omelet and fold in half carefully.

Makes 1 serving.

Zucchini Omelet

1 tablespoon butter or
  margarine
1 medium zucchini, sliced
  Salt, pepper
1/4 teaspoon minced garlic
4 eggs, beaten

1 tablespoon dry sherry
1/2 cup grated Parmesan
  cheese
  Hollandaise Sauce*
  Minced parsley

MELT butter in omelet pan. Add zucchini and cook until tender. Season to taste with salt and pepper. Combine garlic, beaten eggs, and sherry and pour over zucchini. Cook, lifting gently at sides to allow uncooked egg to flow underneath. When eggs are set, sprinkle with Parmesan cheese and fold omelet in half. Slide onto a warm platter, top with Hollandaise Sauce, and sprinkle with parsley.

Makes 2 servings.   *See recipe on page 31.

Apple-Bacon Quiches

  Quiche Pastry Tart Shells
5 eggs
1 tablespoon butter or
  margarine
1 cup diced Canadian bacon
2 cups thinly sliced, unpeeled
  red Delicious apples

1 tablespoon flour
1 3/4 cups half and half
1/2 teaspoon salt
1/8 teaspoon nutmeg
1/4 teaspoon caraway seeds
1/2 teaspoon dry mustard
1 cup shredded Swiss cheese

PREPARE tart shells. Pierce all over with fork tines. Separate 1 egg. Beat egg white lightly and brush over bottom and sides of shells. Bake below center of oven at 425 degrees 15 minutes. Meanwhile, melt butter and sauté bacon 1 minute. Add apple slices, cover, and cook about 10 minutes, until apples are almost translucent. Beat remaining whole eggs with the remaining egg yolk. Add flour, half and half, salt, nutmeg, caraway seeds, and dry mustard and mix well. Sprinkle the cheese evenly among the tart shells, top with apples and bacon. Pour egg mixture into shells. Bake at 375 degrees about 30 minutes, or until set in center. Cool to lukewarm before cutting.

Makes 6 servings.   (continued on overleaf)

Quiche Pastry Tart Shells

2¹/₄ cups sifted flour   ³/₄ cup shortening
  1 teaspoon salt   5 tablespoons cold milk

Combine flour and salt. Cut in shortening until particles are size of peas. Sprinkle with about 5 tablespoons cold milk, adding just enough to make a stiff dough. Shape into 6 balls. Roll out on lightly floured board to 6-inch circles and fit into 6 (5-inch) tart pans. Fold edges under and build up a high fluted rim.

Mushroom Crêpe Quiches

  Crêpes   4 eggs
¹/₄ cup butter or margarine   1 cup whipping cream
¹/₂ cup chopped onion   ¹/₂ teaspoon salt
¹/₂ pound mushrooms, sliced   Dash red pepper
¹/₂ cup shredded Swiss cheese

LINE 12 (3-inch) custard or muffin cups with 1 crêpe each, being careful not to puncture them. Melt butter in skillet and sauté onion until tender. Add mushrooms and cook 5 minutes longer. Place about 2 tablespoons mushroom mixture in each crêpe-lined cup. Sprinkle each with 2 teaspoons cheese. Beat together eggs, whipping cream, salt, and red pepper. Pour about 3 tablespoons of mixture into each cup over cheese. Bake at 375 degrees 25 to 30 minutes, or until knife inserted near center comes out clean. Let stand 5 minutes before serving.

Makes 12 crêpe quiches.

Crêpes

  2 eggs   ¹/₂ cup flour
²/₃ cup milk   ¹/₄ teaspoon salt
  1 tablespoon oil

Lightly beat eggs in medium bowl. Stir in milk and oil. Gradually stir in flour and salt and beat until smooth. Cover and refrigerate 2 hours. Lightly brush a 6- or 7-inch crêpe pan with oil and heat until hot. Stir batter. Add a scant 2 tablespoons of batter to hot pan and quickly tilt so that entire bottom of pan is completely covered. Cook crêpe, turning once, until lightly browned on both sides. Repeat until all batter is used, brushing pan with oil as needed.

Makes 12.

Liz's Tomato Quiche

1/2 pound Gruyère cheese,
  shredded
1 (9-inch) unbaked pastry
  shell
3 tomatoes, peeled, chopped,
  and drained
3 tablespoons instant minced
  onion
3 tablespoons hot water
  Salt, pepper
1 teaspoon basil
2 eggs
3/4 cup milk
2 tablespoons grated Parmesan cheese

Tomatoes and basil give this quiche Italian flair, although it was created in Los Angeles by a food staff member's sister. Two kinds of cheese add to the rich flavor.

SCATTER Gruyère cheese over pastry shell. Spread a layer of tomatoes over cheese. Add onion, which has been soaked in hot water until softened. Season to taste with salt and pepper and add basil. Beat eggs and milk together and pour over tomatoes. Sprinkle on Parmesan cheese. Bake at 350 degrees 45 minutes, or until done.

Makes 6 to 8 servings.

Pizza Quiche

8 ounces thinly sliced
  pepperoni
1 (9-inch) unbaked pastry
  shell
2/3 cup shredded Swiss cheese
1/2 cup sliced black olives
1 cup chopped green pepper
3 eggs
2 tablespoons flour
1 cup milk
  Grated Parmesan cheese
1 (8-ounce) can tomato sauce
  with mushrooms
1/2 teaspoon salt
1/4 teaspoon basil
1/4 teaspoon oregano
6 thin rings green pepper

SAUTÉ pepperoni, covered, 2 or 3 minutes, or until warmed through. Set aside. Bake pastry shell at 400 degrees 5 minutes. Remove from oven and sprinkle 1/3 cup Swiss cheese over bottom evenly. Sprinkle on half the pepperoni and top with olives, chopped green pepper, remaining Swiss cheese, and rest of pepperoni. Beat eggs and flour until smooth. Blend in milk, 1/4 cup grated Parmesan cheese, tomato sauce, salt, basil, and oregano. Pour into pastry shell. Sprinkle with 2 tablespoons grated Parmesan cheese and top with green pepper rings. Bake at 400 degrees 15 minutes. Reduce heat to 325 degrees and bake about 40 to 45 minutes longer, or until knife inserted near center comes out clean. Remove from oven and garnish outer edge of pie with prebaked pastry cutouts, if desired. Let stand 10 minutes before cutting in wedges.

Makes 4 to 6 servings.

Chorizo Quiche in Cornmeal Crust

If spicy Mexican-style chorizo sausage isn't available in your market, make your own, using the recipe on page 225.

6 slices Monterey Jack cheese
    Cornmeal Crust
1/2 pound chorizo, casings
    removed
1/4 cup sliced green onions

4 eggs
2 cups whipping cream or half
    and half
    Salt, pepper

PLACE cheese slices on bottom of unbaked Cornmeal Crust. Fry sausage until cooked and crumbly. Drain off fat. Sprinkle sausage on top of cheese, then top with green onions. Lightly beat eggs in bowl, stir in whipping cream, and season to taste with salt and pepper. Pour over cheese and chorizo mixture. Place on bottom rack of oven and bake at 450 degrees 15 minutes. Reduce heat to 350 degrees and bake an additional 25 to 30 minutes. Let stand 10 minutes before cutting.

Makes 6 servings.

Cornmeal Crust

1/2 cup cornmeal
3/4 cup sifted flour
1/2 teaspoon salt

1/8 teaspoon black pepper
1/3 cup shortening
4 to 5 tablespoons cold water

Sift together cornmeal, flour, salt, and pepper. Cut in shortening until mixture resembles coarse crumbs. Add water, 1 tablespoon at a time, stirring lightly until mixture forms a ball. Turn out onto lightly floured board or canvas and roll dough to 13-inch circle. Fit loosely into 9-inch pie plate or quiche pan. Fold edge under and flute.

Elegant Quiche

This superior—and very rich—quiche recipe came to us from Stratton's restaurant in Los Angeles's Westwood district.

1 onion, chopped
1 tablespoon butter or
    margarine
    Dash thyme
1 bay leaf
5 ounces bacon, chopped
5 eggs

2 egg yolks
1 cup half and half
    Dash nutmeg
1/3 pound Swiss cheese,
    shredded
    Pastry Shell

SAUTÉ onion in butter. Add thyme and bay leaf. Remove bay leaf. Cook bacon until crisp, then drain. Blend together eggs, yolks, half and half, and nutmeg. Place bacon, onion, and cheese in Pastry Shell. Cover with egg mixture. Bake at 350 degrees 35 to 40 minutes, or until knife inserted near center comes out clean.

Makes 6 servings.

Pastry Shell

2 cups flour	*1 tablespoon oil*
Dash salt	*2 to 4 tablespoons cold water*
1 cup butter or margarine	

Mix flour and salt together in bowl. Cut in butter and oil until mixture resembles coarse meal. Sprinkle with water, tossing with fork until dough holds together. Gather into a ball and chill a few minutes if dough is too soft to handle. Roll out pastry on floured board and fit into 10-inch quiche pan or pie plate.

Quiche Dauphine

¹/₄ cup flour	*¹/₄ cup white wine*
1 teaspoon salt	*¹/₂ cup sliced water chestnuts*
¹/₄ teaspoon white pepper	*4 eggs*
¹/₄ teaspoon rosemary	*2 cups whipping cream or milk*
¹/₂ teaspoon garlic powder	*1 (10-inch) baked pastry shell*
¹/₂ pound chicken livers	*1 cup shredded Gruyère cheese*
¹/₄ cup diced onion	
2 tablespoons oil	

Chicken livers and water chestnuts are used in the filling of this quiche from one of the Salmagundi restaurants in San Francisco.

Combine flour, salt, white pepper, rosemary, and garlic powder. Dredge chicken livers in flour mixture. Sauté onion in oil until tender, add and gently stir-fry livers. Stir in wine and cook until liquid is absorbed, stirring constantly. Remove from heat. Add water chestnuts. Beat eggs and whipping cream together. Fill pie shell with chicken liver mixture. Pour egg mixture over livers. Sprinkle top with cheese. Bake at 300 degrees 1 hour and 15 minutes.

Makes 6 servings.

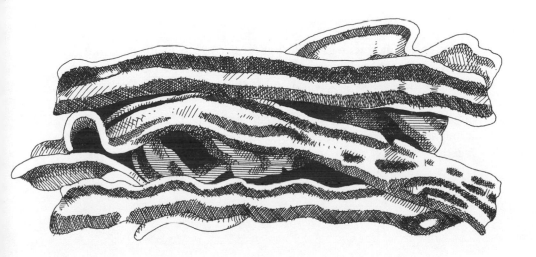

Huevos en Rabo de Mestiza
(Poached Eggs in Tomato-Chile Sauce)

Chile strips, tomatoes, and cheese add color to a brunch dish you can serve right from the skillet.

$^1/_3$ cup oil
2 medium onions, thinly sliced
2 (1-pound) cans whole tomatoes
1 (7-ounce) can whole green chiles, cut into strips
2 cups chicken broth or water

1 teaspoon salt
$^1/_2$ teaspoon sugar
$^1/_8$ teaspoon black pepper
8 eggs
2 to 3 ounces Monterey Jack cheese, cut into 8 slices

HEAT oil in large, deep skillet. Add onions and cook until tender but not browned. Place tomatoes in blender container or food processor bowl and blend until chopped but not pureed. Add tomatoes and chiles to onion and cook 5 minutes. Add broth, salt, sugar, and pepper and cook 5 minutes longer. Break each egg onto small plate and slide into hot broth mixture carefully so as not to break yolk. Arrange a cheese slice on top of each egg. Cover and cook gently 5 to 8 minutes, or until eggs are set and cheese is melted.

Makes 8 servings.

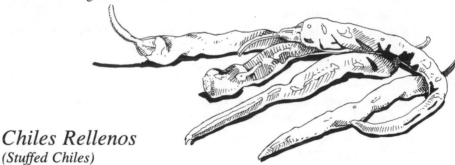

Chiles Rellenos
(Stuffed Chiles)

A rich tomato sauce tops the chiles rellenos from El Cholo, one of the oldest Mexican restaurants in Los Angeles.

6 eggs, separated
Dash salt
6 canned whole green chiles
9 ounces shredded cheddar cheese

Melted shortening for deep frying
Relleno Sauce

BEAT egg whites with salt until stiff. Fold in beaten yolks and mix well. Stuff each chile with 3 tablespoons cheese. Heat shortening in large skillet. Drop a heaping tablespoon of egg mixture into hot shortening and spread with back of spoon. Place a stuffed chile on egg mixture and cover with another spoonful of egg, sealing batter around chile. Fry until puffy and browned on each side, turning gently. Drain on paper towels and keep hot while frying remaining chiles. Serve with Relleno Sauce.

Makes 6 servings.

Relleno Sauce

1 cup chopped onions
1/2 cup chopped green pepper
   Dash minced garlic
2 tablespoons oil
2 (1-pound) cans whole
   tomatoes, cut up

1/2 teaspoon salt
1/8 teaspoon black pepper
1/4 teaspoon oregano

Sauté onions, green pepper, and garlic in oil until onions are tender. Add tomatoes, salt, pepper, and oregano. Cover and simmer 15 minutes.

Makes 4 cups.

Huevos Rancheros
(Ranch-Style Eggs)

Oil
1 cup minced onions
1 large clove garlic, crushed
1 (1-pound 12-ounce) can
   Italian-style tomatoes,
   sieved
1 (4-ounce) can green chiles,
   drained, seeded, and
   minced

1 teaspoon salt
1/2 teaspoon sugar
1/8 teaspoon black pepper
1/8 teaspoon ground coriander
12 corn tortillas
12 eggs
1 ripe avocado, peeled and
   thinly sliced

Breakfast eggs take on new life when served the Mexican way atop crisp corn tortillas and bathed with spicy tomato sauce. Refried beans are a traditional accompaniment.

HEAT 3 tablespoons oil in large saucepan. Add onion and garlic and cook over low heat until transparent, about 5 minutes. Stir in tomatoes, chiles, salt, sugar, and pepper. Bring to boil, reduce heat to low, and simmer, uncovered, 1 hour. Stir occasionally. Stir in coriander. Keep sauce hot. Pour oil to a depth of 1/8 inch in small heavy skillet and heat over medium-high heat. Fry tortillas one at a time about 1 minute on each side, or until lightly browned. Add more oil as needed. Overlap two tortillas on each of six heated plates. Heat 3 tablespoons oil in 10- to 12-inch skillet. Carefully break 6 eggs into hot oil and fry over medium heat until whites are set but yolks are still soft. Separate eggs with a spatula and place each egg on a tortilla. Repeat with remaining eggs and oil. Spoon a ring of sauce around each egg and garnish with avocado slices. Serve extra sauce on the side. Accompany with Spicy Refried Beans (see recipe on page 240).

Makes 6 servings.

Scotch Eggs

*Scotch eggs make wonderful
picnic snacks, with or without
the sauce.*

1/3 cup milk
2/3 cup dry bread crumbs
1 1/2 cups minced cooked ham
2 eggs, beaten

1/4 teaspoon celery salt
1/8 teaspoon white pepper
6 hard-cooked eggs
Mustard Sauce

COMBINE milk and crumbs in saucepan and cook to a thick paste, about 2 minutes over medium heat, stirring constantly. Add minced ham, beaten eggs, celery salt, and pepper. Mix well and cool. Roll shelled eggs in the ham mixture, patting to coat, and place in shallow baking dish. Bake at 350 degrees 20 minutes. Serve with Mustard Sauce on side.

Makes 6 servings.

Mustard Sauce

2/3 cup mayonnaise
4 teaspoons prepared mustard
2 teaspoons sugar

Blend mayonnaise, mustard, and sugar.

Makes about 3/4 cup.

Mustard Eggs

*The Capistrano Depot
restaurant in San Juan
Capistrano, California, gave us
their recipe for mustard eggs, a
wonderful brunch dish.*

1/4 cup butter or margarine
1/4 cup flour
2 cups milk
1 bay leaf
1 small onion, halved
2 egg yolks
1/4 cup whipping cream
1 tablespoon dry mustard

1/4 cup grated Parmesan
  cheese
1/2 teaspoon salt
  Dash red pepper
8 hard-cooked eggs
16 slices bacon, cooked crisp
8 toast triangles

MELT butter over low heat. Add flour and cook, stirring, over low heat 3 to 5 minutes. Let cool. In double boiler, heat milk, bay leaf, and onion until hot, not boiling. Add butter and flour mixture and cook, stirring, until sauce is thickened and smooth. Strain sauce. Beat egg yolks with whipping cream until blended. Add small amount of sauce to egg mixture, stirring constantly, then return mixture to remaining sauce in pan. Cook until well blended and smooth. Mix dry mustard to a paste with a small amount of water. Combine with cheese, salt, and red pepper and add to sauce. Whip with wire whisk until smooth and creamy, about 1 to 2 minutes. Thin sauce with additional milk if sauce is too thick. Slice hard-cooked eggs and arrange in a large casserole or 4 individual casseroles. Cover with mustard sauce and place bacon slices on top. Bake at 350 degrees 5 minutes to heat through. Serve with toast triangles.

Makes 4 servings.

Joe's Special

1/2 pound spinach, chopped, or 1 (10-ounce) package frozen chopped spinach, thawed	1 small onion, diced	
	1/2 teaspoon basil	
	1/4 teaspoon marjoram	
1 tablespoon olive oil	1/4 teaspoon oregano	
1 tablespoon butter or margarine	1 teaspoon salt	
	1/4 teaspoon black pepper	
1 pound ground beef	4 eggs	

Southern Californians have adopted this San Francisco specialty partially because of its low cost, nutritional value, and simply because it tastes so good.

IF using frozen spinach, place in strainer and drain well. Heat oil and butter in large, heavy skillet. Add ground beef and cook, stirring, until browned and crumbly. Add onion and cook until tender but not browned. Stir in basil, marjoram, oregano, salt, and pepper. Stir in drained spinach and cook until liquid in spinach has evaporated. Beat eggs, add to meat mixture and cook, stirring, until eggs are set.

Makes 4 to 6 servings.

Bacon-Stuffed Eggs

12 hard-cooked eggs	1 tablespoon capers
1 (3-ounce) package cream cheese, softened	10 slices bacon, diced and cooked crisp
1/2 cup sour cream	
1/2 teaspoon dill weed	

SHELL eggs and cut in halves lengthwise. Remove egg yolks, place in bowl, mash with a fork, and set aside. Beat cream cheese until fluffy, then blend in mashed egg yolks, sour cream, dill, capers, and bacon. Fill egg whites generously with yolk mixture, cover, and chill overnight. Garnish each with sprig of watercress, if desired.

Makes 24.

Blue-Cheese-Stuffed Eggs

6 hard-cooked eggs
$1/4$ cup crumbled blue cheese
2 tablespoons mayonnaise
2 tablespoons whipping
cream
1 tablespoon minced parsley

$1/4$ teaspoon salt
$1/8$ teaspoon black pepper
$1/4$ teaspoon celery salt
1 tablespoon tarragon
vinegar

CUT eggs in halves and remove yolks. Mash yolks with cheese, mayonnaise, whipping cream, parsley, salt, pepper, celery salt, and vinegar until thick and smooth. Fill egg whites with mixture. Chill until ready to serve.

Makes 3 to 4 servings.

Favorite Cheese Casserole

Californians delight in casseroles combining green chiles and cheese. This is one of many versions. Try it as a side dish with barbecued steak or ribs.

1 pound Monterey Jack
cheese, shredded
1 pound cheddar cheese,
shredded
2 (4-ounce) cans diced green
chiles
4 eggs, separated

$2/3$ cup evaporated milk
1 tablespoon flour
$1/2$ teaspoon salt
$1/8$ teaspoon black pepper
2 medium tomatoes, sliced

COMBINE cheeses and chiles and spoon into well-greased 12 x 7-inch baking dish. Beat egg whites until stiff peaks form. Combine egg yolks, evaporated milk, flour, salt, and pepper in another bowl and mix until well blended. Fold beaten whites into yolk mixture. Pour egg mixture over cheese in baking dish. Using a fork, swirl egg mixture through cheese. Bake at 325 degrees 30 minutes. Remove from oven and decorate with sliced tomatoes. Bake 30 minutes longer, or until knife inserted in the center comes out clean.

Makes 6 to 8 servings.

Cottage Cheese Delight

1 pound Monterey Jack
   cheese, shredded
1 cup milk
1 cup flour

1 pint cottage cheese
6 eggs, lightly beaten
1/2 cup butter or margarine,
   melted

Super-rich and delicious, this can be cut in squares and served with a tossed green salad and crusty bread for luncheon or a light supper.

COMBINE Monterey Jack cheese, milk, flour, cottage cheese, eggs, and 1/2 the melted butter in bowl. Brush remaining half of melted butter over bottom and sides of 12 x 7-inch baking dish. Pour cheese mixture into dish and bake at 375 degrees 40 minutes or until golden and set.

Makes 12 to 15 servings.

Cheese Strata

5 slices white bread
4 eggs, beaten
2 cups milk
3/4 teaspoon brown sugar
3/4 teaspoon Worcestershire
   sauce

3/4 teaspoon seasoned salt
3/4 teaspoon dry mustard
   Dash white pepper
2 1/2 cups shredded cheddar
   cheese
   Cheese Sauce (optional)

Cheese stratas make excellent meatless main dishes. This do-ahead recipe came from Bullock's Pasadena store.

THE day before serving, remove crusts and cut bread into cubes. Combine beaten eggs, milk, brown sugar, Worcestershire, seasoned salt, dry mustard, and white pepper in an ovenproof casserole. Stir in bread and cheese and refrigerate overnight. When ready to cook, place casserole in pan of water and bake at 325 degrees 45 minutes. Serve with Cheese Sauce.

Makes 6 servings.

Cheese Sauce

2 tablespoons butter or
   margarine
2 tablespoons flour
1 cup milk

Salt, white pepper
1 cup shredded cheddar
   cheese

Melt butter in saucepan and stir in flour. Cook, stirring, until smooth paste is formed. Do not let brown. Add milk all at once, stirring constantly. Season to taste with salt and white pepper. Add cheese and cook, stirring, until cheese is melted and sauce is smooth.

Makes about 1 1/2 cups.

Monterey Fondue

Monterey in the title indicates that a dish contains Monterey Jack cheese. Often green chiles are included too.

12 slices bread
   Soft butter or margarine
1 (12-ounce) can whole kernel corn, drained
1 (7-ounce) can whole green chiles

2 cups shredded Monterey Jack cheese
4 eggs, lightly beaten
3 cups milk
1 teaspoon salt

TRIM crusts from bread. Spread bread with butter, then cut slices in halves. Arrange half the bread slices in a greased shallow 3-quart baking dish. Cover with half the corn. Seed chiles, cut into strips, and arrange half the chile strips over corn. Sprinkle with half the cheese. Repeat layers. Combine eggs, milk, and salt and pour over ingredients in casserole. Cover and refrigerate 4 hours or longer. Bake at 350 degrees 45 to 50 minutes, or until puffy and brown.

Makes 6 to 8 servings.

Poached Eggs with Asparagus and Wine Sauce

Using wine instead of water as the poaching liquid for these eggs gives this brunch dish a gourmet touch.

2 tablespoons butter or margarine
2 tablespoons flour
2 tablespoons minced parsley
1 teaspoon grated onion
1/2 teaspoon salt
1/4 teaspoon tarragon
1/4 teaspoon hot pepper sauce

1 1/2 cups milk
2 cups dry white wine
4 eggs
2 English muffins, split and toasted
3/4 pound fresh asparagus or 1 (10-ounce) package frozen asparagus spears, cooked and drained

MELT butter in saucepan over medium heat. Blend in flour, parsley, onion, salt, tarragon, and hot pepper sauce. Cook, stirring, 2 to 3 minutes. Gradually stir in milk and cook over medium heat, stirring frequently, until mixture thickens and comes to boil, about 10 minutes. Set aside. Heat wine in 8 1/2-inch omelet pan until it begins to boil. Reduce heat so that wine is simmering. Break eggs one at a time into a saucer, then slip them gently into simmering wine. Let eggs cook until white is firm. Using a slotted spoon, remove eggs, drain well, and place on toasted English muffin halves. Place asparagus alongside egg-topped muffin halves on an ovenproof platter and keep warm in low oven while finishing sauce. Add 1/2 cup of the hot poaching wine to the sauce mixture. Cook, stirring, over medium heat until mixture is smooth. Pour wine sauce over eggs and asparagus to serve.

Makes 2 to 4 servings.

CHICKEN

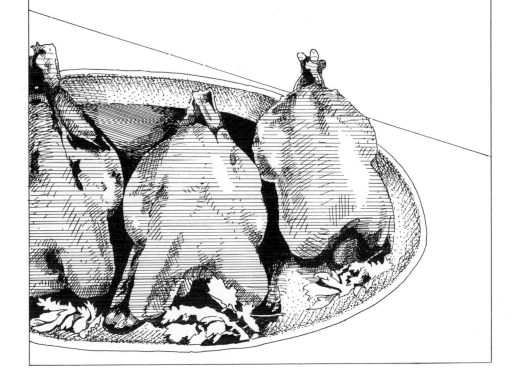

CHICKEN has assumed a more prominent spot on western menus in the last few years because of its virtues of high nutrition and low cost. Chicken contains less total fat as well as less saturated fat than beef and pork and is a lower-cost source of protein than most meats or fish.

Fortunately our community abounds in diverse ethnic cultures which provide an unlimited source of ideas for using this economical bird. Requests pour in for East Indian, Mexican, and Italian recipes, and Chinese restaurants have opened a whole new world of stir-fry chicken dishes. Southern Californians whose palates already were attuned to peppery Mexican foods have taken to spicy Sichuan, Middle Eastern, and Moroccan chicken dishes with alacrity. And French restaurants catering to a calorie-conscious clientele have done their part to introduce exciting preparations. Improvisational restaurants stemming from the health-food era along with creative home cooks have developed recipes for chicken teamed with the bountiful fresh vegetables available here. Fruits, too, combine well with chicken in salads and hot dishes. There is no doubt that chicken's unmatchable versatility will keep it a popular menu item for years to come.

Poularde aux Fines Herbes, page 166

Poularde aux Fines Herbes
(Baked Chicken with Herbs)

A superb example of how a master chef combines herbs, greens, and wine with chicken, this aromatic recipe came from the Miramonte Restaurant and Country Inn located in the heart of California's fine wine-producing area, Napa Valley.

4 large chicken breast halves, boned
1/4 cup butter or margarine, melted
1 1/2 pounds spinach, stems removed
White wine
2 cups chicken stock
2 shallots, finely sliced
2 cups whipping cream
Few leaves fresh sorrel
6 fresh tarragon sprigs
6 to 7 fresh basil leaves
Salt, pepper

PLACE chicken in baking dish with melted butter, turning to coat pieces. Bake at 375 degrees 25 to 30 minutes or until done. Meanwhile wash spinach leaves and pat dry with paper towels. Combine 2 cups white wine, chicken stock, and shallots in wide saucepan or skillet. Bring to boil over medium heat and boil until liquid is reduced to one-fourth original amount. Stir in cream and simmer until sauce thickens to consistency that will coat a wooden spoon, about 10 minutes. Remove chicken from baking dish, discard fat, and deglaze dish with 1 tablespoon white wine, scraping to loosen browned bits. Add to cream sauce and blend. Drop spinach leaves, sorrel, tarragon, and basil into sauce. Bring to boil and boil briefly, stirring gently. Season to taste with salt and pepper. Remove greens from sauce and divide into 4 mounds on serving platter. Remove skin from chicken breasts. Place each piece of chicken on a spinach mound. Spoon sauce over.

Makes 4 servings.

Poulet à l'Ail
(Chicken with Garlic)

A garlicky wine sauce is served over baked chicken at Mon-Arc, a French restaurant on Pico Boulevard in Los Angeles.

2 (2 1/2-pound) chickens, halved or quartered
Salt, pepper
4 cups boiling water
1/4 cup beef broth
3 or 4 bay leaves
1 large onion, chopped
1/2 head garlic (about 4 or 5 cloves), minced
1 tablespoon butter or margarine
1 cup dry white wine
1/2 cup tomato puree
1 tablespoon chopped parsley

SPRINKLE chicken with salt and pepper and bake at 350 degrees 1 hour. Meanwhile, combine water, broth, and bay leaves and bring to boil. Reduce heat and let simmer. Sauté onion and garlic in butter until onion is tender. Add wine and cook over low heat 15 minutes. Stir in broth mixture and tomato puree. Add parsley. Cook over low heat 1 hour. Strain and pour over baked chicken. Garnish with parsley sprigs, if desired.

Makes 8 servings.

Vinegared Chicken

1 (2½- to 3-pound) chicken,
   quartered
¼ cup butter or margarine
1½ teaspoons salt
½ teaspoon black pepper
1 (14½-ounce) can chicken
   broth
⅔ cup dry red wine

½ cup tomato puree
⅓ cup red wine vinegar
1 tablespoon minced shallots
   or green onion
1 clove garlic, mashed
1 teaspoon tarragon, crushed
1 teaspoon sugar
½ bay leaf

Strong as it is, the vinegar in this dish mellows nicely, letting the chicken retain the integrity of its flavor.

BROWN chicken in butter in 12-inch skillet. Remove pieces to roasting pan as they brown. Season with salt and pepper. Drain drippings from skillet. Add broth, wine, tomato puree, vinegar, shallots, garlic, tarragon, sugar, and bay leaf. Heat to boiling and pour over chicken in roasting pan. Bake, uncovered, at 350 degrees until chicken is tender, about 30 minutes. Remove chicken to serving platter and keep warm. Skim fat from pan juices. Pour juices into medium saucepan. Bring to boil and boil until reduced to about 1¼ cups. Pour sauce over chicken.

Makes 4 servings.

Chicken with Tomatillo Sauce

1 (2½- to 3-pound) chicken,
   cut up
3 cups boiling salted water
½ pound tomatillos
½ bunch cilantro
1 stalk celery, cut up
1 cup chopped green onions
1 small bunch leaf lettuce

¼ cup sunflower seeds
3 canned green chiles
¼ teaspoon ground cumin
¼ teaspoon garlic powder
1 teaspoon butter or
   margarine
Salt

This recipe calls for tomatillos, small, green tomatoes with a thin papery husk that is removed before cooking. You'll find them in Mexican markets the year round, but if you can't find them fresh, canned ones can be substituted.

COOK chicken for 45 minutes in boiling salted water to cover. Drain chicken, reserving broth. Keep chicken warm. Remove husks from tomatillos if using fresh. Place half of tomatillos, cilantro, celery, green onions, lettuce, sunflower seeds, and chiles in blender container. Add ¾ cup reserved chicken broth and blend well. Repeat with remaining half of same ingredients plus ¾ cup broth. Combine, then blend in cumin and garlic powder. Heat butter in large skillet, add tomatillo mixture, and simmer 15 minutes over low heat, stirring until thickened. Add more chicken broth if sauce gets too thick. Season to taste with salt. Serve hot over cooked chicken.

Makes about 6 servings.

Chicken Adobo

1 medium chicken, cut up
   Giblets of 1 chicken
6 cloves garlic, crushed
1/2 teaspoon whole
   peppercorns or 1/4 teaspoon
   black pepper
1 small bay leaf

1/4 cup cider vinegar or lemon
   juice
3 tablespoons soy sauce
1/4 teaspoon MSG (optional)
1/2 cup water, about
   Salt
3 cups hot cooked rice

COMBINE chicken and giblets, garlic, peppercorns, bay leaf, vinegar, soy sauce, and MSG in saucepan. Marinate for at least 10 minutes. Add water, cover, and cook over medium heat about 40 minutes, or until chicken is tender. Remove liver and a little of the liquid and puree in blender container. Return to pan. Heat to serving temperature, adjusting salt to taste. If desired, brown cooked chicken pieces in about 3 tablespoons oil, then return to pan and simmer, covered, about 10 minutes. Serve with hot rice.

Makes 4 to 6 servings.

Chicken and Dumplings

2 (2-pound) chickens, halved
1 carrot, chopped
2 stalks celery, chopped
1 medium onion, chopped
1 tablespoon chicken stock
   base or 2 chicken bouillon
   cubes
1/4 cup butter or margarine

1 cup flour
1 ounce sherry
   Juice of 1/2 lemon
   MSG (optional)
   Salt
   Yellow food color (optional)
   Dumplings
1 cup hot cooked peas

PLACE chickens in large saucepan, cover with water, and bring to boil. Simmer until chickens are tender. Remove chickens from pan and set aside. Remove backbones and return them to pan. Add carrot, celery, and onion and simmer 30 minutes. Add chicken stock base for extra flavor. Remove from heat, strain, and reserve stock. Melt butter and stir in flour until smooth. Add to strained reserved chicken stock. Simmer 5 minutes. Add sherry, lemon juice, MSG, salt, and food color. Meanwhile, remove skin from cooked chickens and bone, if desired. Cut in large pieces. Place chicken pieces in casserole. Arrange Dumplings on chicken. Cover with sauce and sprinkle with peas for color.

Makes 4 to 6 servings.

Dumplings

1¹/₂ cups flour
  2 teaspoons baking powder
¹/₄ teaspoon salt

3 tablespoons shortening
³/₄ cup milk

Combine flour, baking powder, and salt in mixing bowl. Cut in short-ening until mixture resembles cornmeal. Stir in milk until just blended. Place about ¹/₂ inch water in saucepan with wire rack that comes 2 to 3 inches above the water line. Cover rack with lightly oiled wax paper, oiled side up. With water gently simmering, drop dumplings by tablespoons onto wax paper, leaving room in between for expansion. Steam 8 minutes, uncovered, then cover and steam 7 minutes longer.

Makes about 10.

Chicken Enchiladas

1¹/₂ chicken breasts
  Oil
¹/₂ cup flour
  1 (28-ounce) can red chile
      sauce
  1 teaspoon sugar
      Salt
      Ground New Mexico or
      California chile (optional)
  1 pint sour cream

      Shredded Monterey Jack
      cheese
      Shredded cheddar cheese
12 corn tortillas
  1 (2¹/₄-ounce) can sliced
      black olives
  1 large onion, finely chopped
      Chopped green onions
      (optional)

A reader sent us the recipe for these enchiladas, which are delicious and easy to make. The seasoning is up to you. If you want them spicy hot, use ground New Mexico chile. If you prefer milder enchiladas, choose ground California chile.

COOK chicken in water to cover until tender. Cool, then discard skin and bones and finely shred meat. Reserve broth. Heat 3 tablespoons oil in large saucepan. Add flour and stir 1 minute. Stir in red chile sauce and half a chile sauce can of reserved chicken broth. Add sugar. Season to taste with salt and ground chile and add sour cream. Blend well, then add ¹/₂ cup each Jack and cheddar cheeses and let melt. To assemble enchiladas, fry each tortilla in oil just until soft-ened. Drain and place on each some of the chicken, sliced olives, chopped onion, a little cheddar cheese, and a tablespoon of sauce. Roll and place seam side down in individual heatproof plates, pie pans, or 13 x 9-inch baking dish. Top with sauce, using at least 2 cups, more if desired. (Remaining sauce can be frozen for another batch of enchiladas.) Sprinkle thickly with shredded Jack and cheddar cheeses. Broil or bake at 350 degrees until cheese is melted and sauce is bubbly. Top with chopped green onions.

Makes 6 servings.

Almond Chicken with Button Mushrooms

When the local Chinese Arts Council planned a Han Dynasty dinner a few years back, local restaurateur David Lee helped them work out this appetizing almond chicken dish.

1/4 cup halved almonds
   Oil
   Cornstarch
1 tablespoon sherry
1 tablespoon oyster sauce
   Salt
1/2 teaspoon sugar
1 pound boneless chicken breast, cubed

2 teaspoons white wine
1/2 egg white
   Pepper
1/4 pound Chinese pea pods
2 water chestnuts, sliced
1/4 cup thinly sliced bamboo shoots
2 dozen fresh or canned button mushrooms

FRY almonds in oil until golden. Drain and set aside. Blend 1 teaspoon cornstarch with 1 teaspoon water. Add sherry, oyster sauce, 1 tablespoon water, 1/2 teaspoon salt, and sugar. Mix well and set aside. Mix chicken, wine, egg white, and 1 teaspoon cornstarch. Season to taste with salt and pepper. Heat 5 tablespoons oil in wok or skillet. Add chicken and stir-fry until chicken is no longer pink. Add pea pods, water chestnuts, bamboo shoots, and mushrooms. Stir-fry for 3 minutes. Stir sherry mixture and add to wok. Cook, stirring, 1 minute longer. Turn out onto serving platter and top with fried almonds.

Makes 4 servings.

Gypsy Chicken

This version of a chicken stew is marvelous. The recipe came from Pioneer Boulangerie, a Santa Monica bakery/restaurant also noted for its excellent French bread.

1 (2 1/2-pound) chicken
3 medium green peppers, cored, seeded, and diced
1 medium onion, diced
1 clove garlic, crushed
3 tablespoons olive oil
1 (1-pound) can whole tomatoes, diced
1 (8-ounce) can tomato sauce
   Dash ground thyme

1 bay leaf
1 teaspoon gumbo filé
   Dash hot pepper sauce
   Dash Worcestershire sauce
   Salt, pepper
2 cups steamed rice
1 (1-pound) can cut okra, drained
1/2 cup sliced black olives

STEAM or cook chicken in boiling water until tender. Remove from pot, let cool slightly, and dice meat, discarding skin and bones. Sauté green peppers, onion, and garlic in oil 10 minutes. Stir in tomatoes with their liquid and tomato sauce. Add thyme, bay leaf, gumbo filé, hot pepper sauce, and Worcestershire, and season to taste with salt and pepper. Cook 20 minutes. Add chicken and steamed rice and cook 15 minutes longer. Add okra and olives and heat through.

Makes 6 servings.

Cold Sliced Chicken Breasts Tarragon

1/4 cup butter or margarine
1 teaspoon salt
1/4 teaspoon black pepper
1/2 teaspoon paprika
4 whole chicken breasts, boned

1 cup dry white wine
2 teaspoons tarragon, crushed
Cherry tomatoes
Horseradish Whipped Cream

Impress guests at a picnic or patio party with this cold tarragon-flavored chicken.

MELT butter in skillet. Sprinkle salt, pepper, and paprika on chicken breasts. Brown in melted butter, then remove and set aside. Pour wine into skillet and stir to scrape up brown bits in pan. Add tarragon. Return chicken to skillet, turning to coat well. Cover and simmer 30 minutes. Cool thoroughly in cooking liquid, then chill. To serve, slice thinly and arrange on platter. Garnish with cherry tomatoes stuffed with Horseradish Whipped Cream.

Makes 6 to 8 servings.

Horseradish Whipped Cream

1/2 cup whipping cream
1 tablespoon prepared horseradish

Whip cream and fold in horseradish.

Makes 1/2 cup.

Chicken Dijonnaise

2 whole chicken breasts
3 tablespoons butter or margarine
1/4 cup chopped onion
1/2 cup dry white wine
2 tablespoons Dijon-style mustard

1 1/2 cups whipping cream
Dash rosemary
Dash thyme
Dash tarragon
Salt, pepper

White wine and a touch of Dijon-style mustard add a bit of a bite to these lightly sautéed chicken breasts. The recipe came from The Egg & Eye in Los Angeles.

BONE, skin, and split chicken breasts, then flatten into cutlets. Sauté chicken in 2 tablespoons butter until cooked on both sides. Remove from pan and keep warm. Melt remaining butter in skillet. Add onion and cook until tender. Add wine and mustard and simmer until mixture is reduced by half. Add whipping cream and simmer until sauce is thick enough to coat a spoon. Strain, then add rosemary, thyme, and tarragon. Season to taste with salt and pepper. Pour over chicken breasts.

Makes 4 servings.

Chicken à la Jerusalem

Executive chef de cuisine Tony Pope of Santa Anita Racetrack, a well-known personality among racing aficionados in Los Angeles, shared this racetrack recipe for the classic chicken dish using either artichoke hearts or bottoms. Tony prefers the hearts.

2 pounds chicken pieces
  Flour
1/4 pound butter or margarine
  Salt, pepper
  Nutmeg
1/2 pound small mushrooms

6 cooked fresh or frozen
  artichoke hearts
1/2 cup cream sherry
1 cup half and half, about
  Minced parsley
  Minced chives

DREDGE chicken in flour. Melt butter in large skillet, add chicken, and sauté until lightly browned. Season to taste with salt, pepper, and nutmeg. Wash mushrooms and pat dry. Add to chicken along with artichoke hearts. Pour sherry over all, cover, and simmer 15 minutes, or until chicken is tender and most of the wine has evaporated. Stir in cream. Add more cream if needed to thin sauce to desired consistency. Add parsley and chives and serve at once.

Makes 4 to 6 servings.

Honey-Baked Chicken

2 (1½- to 2-pound) chickens,
  cut up
1/2 cup butter or margarine,
  melted

1/2 cup honey
1/4 cup prepared mustard
1 teaspoon salt
1 teaspoon curry powder

PLACE chicken pieces in shallow baking pan, skin side up. Combine butter, honey, mustard, salt, and curry powder and mix well. Pour over chicken and bake at 350 degrees 1¼ hours, basting every 15 minutes until chicken is tender and nicely browned.

Makes 4 to 6 servings.

Chicken Gismonda

Chicken Gismonda, a recipe from the Rangoon Racquet Club in Beverly Hills, calls for a buttery combination of mushrooms and spinach, both great favorites here.

2 whole chicken breasts,
  boned
  Salt, pepper
1/2 cup fine dry bread crumbs

1/2 cup butter or margarine
2 pounds spinach, cleaned
  and stemmed
1 cup minced mushrooms

SPLIT chicken breasts. Season to taste with salt and pepper. Roll in bread crumbs and sauté in 4 tablespoons butter in skillet until golden and cooked through. Meanwhile, blanch spinach in boiling water 1 minute. Drain. Brown half the remaining butter in another skillet and sauté spinach until just tender. Remove chicken from pan and add remaining butter. Add mushrooms and sauté until light brown. When ready to serve, place spinach on platter. Arrange chicken breasts over spinach and cover with mushrooms. Drizzle any butter remaining in pan over chicken. Garnish with whole mushrooms, if desired.

Makes 4 servings.

Grilled Mustard Chicken

1 cup white wine
1/2 cup olive oil
   Salt, pepper
   Thyme

1 (3-pound) chicken, cut in
   serving pieces
2 tablespoons dry mustard
1 tablespoon honey

COMBINE wine and oil in large bowl. Season to taste with salt, pepper, and thyme. Place chicken in mixture for at least 1 hour. Remove chicken from marinade, reserving marinade. Broil chicken on both sides in oven or on barbecue grill for 35 to 40 minutes. Meanwhile, combine 2 tablespoons of reserved marinade, dry mustard, and honey. When chicken is just done, brush with mustard sauce and serve.

Makes 4 to 6 servings.

As an alternative to a tomato-based barbecue sauce, some outdoor cooks prefer to brush a honey-mustard sauce over grilled chicken after it is completely cooked.

Spicy Chicken Barbecue

1 cup tomato juice
1/4 cup vinegar
2 tablespoons brown sugar
1 tablespoon cornstarch
1 tablespoon minced onion
1 tablespoon oil
1 teaspoon salt

1 teaspoon dry mustard
1 clove garlic, minced
1/4 teaspoon red pepper
1 chicken or beef bouillon
   cube
2 chickens, cut in quarters

COMBINE tomato juice, vinegar, brown sugar, cornstarch, onion, oil, salt, mustard, garlic, red pepper, and bouillon cube in small saucepan. Bring to boil. Reduce heat and simmer until mixture thickens, about 3 minutes, stirring constantly. Grill chicken quarters 5 to 6 inches from hot coals, turning every 10 minutes, for about 30 to 40 minutes. Baste with barbecue sauce during last 5 to 8 minutes of cooking. Serve with extra sauce.

Makes 8 servings.

Outdoor cooks are partial to the type of barbecue sauce used in this recipe.

Chicken of the Gods

The water chestnut powder
called for in this recipe from
Bali Hai restaurant on San
Diego's Shelter Island adds a
delicate crispy touch to the
chicken. It's available in most
Chinese markets.

1 (2¹/₂- to 3-pound) chicken,
  cut up and boned
1 egg, beaten
1 tablespoon sherry
1 teaspoon soy sauce
  Salt, pepper
¹/₂ cup water chestnut powder
  Oil
¹/₄ cup butter or margarine,
  softened

¹/₄ cup flour
1 tablespoon cornstarch
2 cups seasoned chicken stock
¹/₂ cup whipping cream or half
  and half
2 teaspoons sesame seeds,
  toasted

MARINATE chicken pieces in mixture of egg, sherry, soy sauce, ¹/₄
teaspoon salt, and dash pepper for 15 to 20 minutes. Coat each piece
of chicken with water chestnut powder. Heat 1 inch oil in pan. Add
chicken pieces and cook until tender and browned on both sides. Melt
butter over medium heat and blend in flour and cornstarch. Bring
chicken stock to boil and stir rapidly while adding butter mixture.
Reduce heat and add whipping cream. Season to taste with salt and
pepper. Neatly slice chicken pieces and arrange on hot platter. Cover
with cream sauce. Sprinkle with sesame seeds.

Makes 4 servings.

Mexican-Style Chicken Kiev

'A reader in Beverly Hills sent
in this marvelous party dish of
spicy cheese-stuffed chicken
that made a hit with all who
tried it in our test kitchen.

8 chicken breast halves,
  skinned and boned
1 (7-ounce) can diced green
  chiles
4 ounces Monterey Jack
  cheese, cut in 8 strips
¹/₂ cup fine dry bread crumbs
¹/₄ cup grated Parmesan
  cheese

1 tablespoon chili powder
¹/₂ teaspoon salt
¹/₄ teaspoon ground cumin
¹/₄ teaspoon black pepper
  Butter, melted
  Tomato Sauce

POUND chicken pieces to about ¹/₄-inch thickness. Put about 2 tablespoons chiles and 1 Jack cheese strip in center of each chicken piece.
Roll up and tuck ends under. Combine bread crumbs, Parmesan
cheese, chili powder, salt, cumin, and pepper. Dip each stuffed
chicken in shallow bowl containing 6 tablespoons melted butter and
roll in crumb mixture. Place chicken rolls, seam side down, in oblong baking dish and drizzle with a little melted butter. Cover and
chill 4 hours or overnight. Bake uncovered at 400 degrees 20 minutes
or until done. Serve with Tomato Sauce.

Makes 8 servings.

Tomato Sauce

1 (1-pound) can tomato sauce
1/2 teaspoon ground cumin
1/3 cup sliced green onions

Salt, pepper
Hot pepper sauce

Combine tomato sauce, cumin, and green onions in small saucepan. Season to taste with salt, pepper, and hot pepper sauce. Heat well.

Makes about 2 cups.

Steamed Chicken and Vegetables

1 (3¹/₂-pound) chicken, cut up
2 unpeeled zucchini, thickly sliced diagonally
2 large carrots, peeled and thickly sliced diagonally
2 potatoes, peeled and sliced diagonally

1 large stalk celery, sliced diagonally
2 sprigs parsley
1 sprig tarragon
1 bay leaf
Salt (optional)
Wine Sauce (optional)

The interest in nouvelle cuisine brought us this delicious steamed chicken and vegetable recipe from the elegant L'Orangerie restaurant in Los Angeles. Added to its other virtues, it's commendably low in fat, cholesterol, and calories.

PLACE chicken pieces on steamer rack. Top with zucchini, carrots, potatoes, celery, parsley, tarragon, and bay leaf. Season to taste with salt. Cover and steam over hot water 45 minutes, or until chicken and vegetables are tender. Serve in soup bowl with pan liquids. Serve Wine Sauce on the side.

Makes 4 servings.

Wine Sauce

1 cup dry white wine
1 shallot, minced
1 tablespoon margarine

1 cup chicken stock
Pepper

Boil wine until reduced by half. In another saucepan, sauté shallot in margarine until tender. Add wine and stock and cook until reduced by one-third. Season to taste with pepper.

Makes about 1 cup.

Kung Pao Chi
(Chicken with Chiles and Nuts)

Kung Pao Chi, chicken with nuts and hot dried chiles, is one of the most popular Sichuan dishes at Chinese restaurants in Los Angeles.

1 pound chicken breast, boned and cut in 1-inch cubes
4 tablespoons soy sauce
1½ tablespoons cold water
  Cornstarch
  ¼ teaspoon garlic salt
4 dried red chiles or more, to taste

1 tablespoon white wine or sherry
1 tablespoon sugar
½ teaspoon salt
1 teaspoon sesame oil
  Oil for deep frying
1 teaspoon chopped peeled gingerroot
½ cup peanuts

COMBINE chicken, 2 tablespoons soy sauce, cold water, 1½ tablespoons cornstarch, and garlic salt in bowl. Stir evenly in one direction and let marinate for 30 minutes. Remove tips and seeds from chiles, then cut in 1-inch pieces. Combine remaining 2 tablespoons soy sauce, wine, sugar, 1 teaspoon cornstarch, salt, and sesame oil in small bowl. Heat 2 to 3 inches oil in wok to 400 degrees. Add chicken and fry 30 seconds. Remove chicken and drain off all but 2 tablespoons oil. Heat oil and fry chiles until black. Add gingerroot and chicken, stirring and tossing together. Add soy-wine mixture and cook, stirring, just until thickened. Remove from heat and sprinkle with nuts.

Makes about 4 servings.

Crispy Chicken with Lemon Sauce

Crispy lemon chicken is a favorite of Chinese restaurant-goers. This one, from The Mandarin restaurant in Beverly Hills, is one of the best in The Times *Food Section files.*

1 (3½-pound) chicken
  Chicken stock or water
  Oil
  Juice of 3 lemons, reserving
  1 squeezed half

½ cup sugar
½ cup boiling water
1 tablespoon soy sauce
2 tablespoons cornstarch

COOK chicken in simmering chicken stock to almost cover until nearly tender, about 20 minutes. Remove and suspend over a bowl to dry at room temperature at least 4 hours, or until chicken is thoroughly cooled. Heat enough oil to 350 degrees in wok to deep-fry whole chicken. Add chicken and fry 20 minutes, turning until golden on all sides. Meanwhile, combine lemon juice with the squeezed lemon half, sugar, and boiling water in saucepan. Bring to boil and simmer 2 to 3 minutes until sugar is dissolved. Add 2 teaspoons oil and the soy sauce. Remove from heat and set aside. Split chicken in halves down the back and cut into serving pieces. Reassemble on serving platter and garnish with triangles of lemon peel which have been cut with a serrated knife, if desired. Bring reserved lemon sauce to boil again. Mix cornstarch with small amount of cold water to make a paste and stir into lemon sauce. Cook, stirring, until thickened slightly. Spoon over the chicken pieces.

Makes 4 servings.

Chicken in Cilantro Sauce

1 (2¹/₂- to 3-pound) chicken, cut up
1 teaspoon oregano
1 tablespoon garlic salt
1 teaspoon black pepper

2 tablespoons red wine vinegar
2 tablespoons oil
1 medium onion, chopped
Paprika
Cilantro Sauce

Cilantro, also called coriander or Chinese parsley, has a most distinct flavor when used in quantity. This recipe from a Times *reader uses it to great advantage.*

MARINATE chicken in mixture of oregano, garlic salt, pepper, and vinegar. Heat oil in skillet, add onion, and season to taste with paprika. Cook until onion is tender and golden. Add Cilantro Sauce and cook 2 minutes. Add chicken pieces and water to cover and cook until chicken is tender, about 45 to 55 minutes.

Makes 4 servings.

Cilantro Sauce

1 bunch cilantro, leaves only
1 medium onion, quartered
2 medium tomatoes, quartered

1 green pepper, seeded and chopped
1 yellow chile, seeded

Combine cilantro, onion, tomatoes, green pepper, and chile in blender container and blend until smooth.

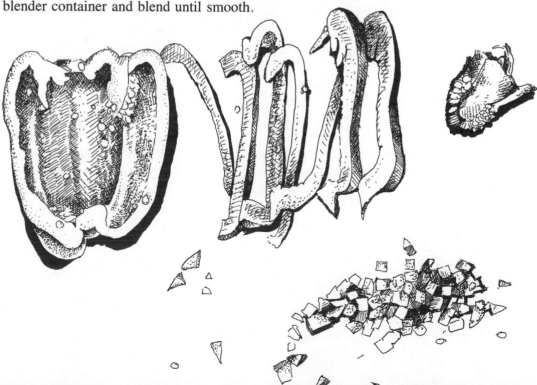

Herb-Baked Chicken

Chicken baked with typical Italian seasonings of rosemary, oregano, and marjoram, like this dish from Scarantino's Italian Inn in Glendale, finds favor locally.

1 (2¹/₂-pound) chicken
3 tablespoons oil
¹/₂ teaspoon salt
¹/₈ teaspoon black pepper

¹/₄ teaspoon MSG (optional)
¹/₄ teaspoon oregano
¹/₄ teaspoon rosemary
¹/₄ teaspoon marjoram

PLACE chicken in baking dish. Brush with oil and sprinkle with salt, pepper, MSG, oregano, rosemary, and marjoram. Bake at 450 degrees 30 to 35 minutes.

Makes 4 to 6 servings.

March of Dimes Bastilla
(Moroccan Chicken Pie)

The emergence of Moroccan restaurants in Los Angeles has heightened interest in Middle Eastern foods. This handsome bastilla, made of phyllo pastry with a chicken filling, won first prize in a March of Dimes cookoff. It's easier to make than it looks once one develops the knack of handling phyllo dough.

1 (2¹/₂- to 3-pound) chicken, cut up
1 whole chicken breast, halved
  Salt, pepper
  Unsalted butter or margarine
4 chicken livers, diced
4 chicken gizzards, diced
4 chicken hearts, diced
1 cup minced onion
2 cloves garlic, minced
2 tablespoons chopped parsley
2 tablespoons chopped mint
1 teaspoon grated gingerroot
¹/₂ teaspoon ground cumin

¹/₂ teaspoon red pepper
¹/₂ teaspoon turmeric
1 teaspoon crumbled saffron threads
3 tablespoons cinnamon
3 cups chicken broth
10 eggs, well beaten
³/₄ cup chopped almonds
2 tablespoons granulated sugar
10 sheets phyllo dough
¹/₂ cup golden raisins, soaked in ¹/₂ cup warm rum
1 tablespoon powdered sugar

PAT chicken pieces dry and season to taste with salt and black pepper. Melt 6 tablespoons butter in skillet and brown chicken well on all sides. Remove from skillet and set aside. Add livers, gizzards, hearts, onion, and garlic to skillet and cook, stirring, until onion is tender. Stir in parsley, mint, ginger, cumin, red pepper, turmeric, saffron, and ¹/₂ teaspoon cinnamon. Stir and cook 1 to 2 minutes longer. Add chicken broth and bring to boil, stirring. Return chicken to skillet and simmer, covered, about 1 hour, or until chicken is very tender. Remove chicken from broth. When cool enough to handle, discard skin and bones and cut meat into chunks. Skim fat from broth. Pour off 2 cups broth and reserve. Reduce remaining broth to about ¹/₂ cup. Scrape bits from bottom of skillet and reserve reduced mixture. Return reserved 2 cups broth to pan and bring to simmer. Pour eggs into simmering broth and whisk until soft creamy curds are formed. Drain off excess liquid, if any. Stir in reserved reduced mixture. Brown almonds in ¹/₄ cup butter, then toss with granulated sugar and 2 tablespoons cinnamon. Melt about 1 cup butter. Overlap 6 sheets phyllo dough in a circle in 12-inch skillet or paella pan, first brushing each sheet with melted butter and letting about half the length of each sheet hang over pan edge. Fold 2 more buttered sheets in half and place in middle of pan. Layer almonds, half the egg mixture, chicken pieces, drained raisins, and remaining egg mixture in pastry-lined pan. Fold sides of dough up and over filling, brushing any dry areas with more butter. Tuck ends in around edges. Place 2 more buttered and folded sheets of phyllo over bastilla, gently tucking in edges to form a smooth surface. Brush generously all over with butter. With sharp knife, score top in a diamond pattern. Bake at 425 degrees 25 to 30 minutes or until deep golden brown. Carefully slide onto serving plate and sprinkle lightly between diamonds with mixture of powdered sugar and remaining cinnamon. Serve warm.

Makes 10 to 12 servings.

Moghlai Chicken

4 whole chicken breasts, split and boned *Seasoned flour*	1¼ teaspoons turmeric	*Nancy Mehta, the wife of the New York Philharmonic Orchestra conductor, shared this fine chicken curry recipe when the couple lived in Los Angeles.*
¼ cup butter or margarine	1 teaspoon red pepper	
2 to 3 large onions, chopped	1 or 2 green chiles, split	
6 large cloves garlic, crushed	1 or 2 large tomatoes, chopped	
1 (½-inch) piece gingerroot, ground	1¼ teaspoons ground cloves	
1¼ teaspoons ground cumin	1¼ teaspoons cardamom	
1¼ teaspoons cumin seeds, crushed	¼ cup brown sugar, packed	
1¼ teaspoons caraway seeds	1 teaspoon saffron	
	2 tablespoons warm milk	
	1 cup sour cream	

DREDGE chicken breasts in seasoned flour and brown in butter. Remove chicken. Add onions, garlic, and ginger and sauté until onions are transparent. Add ground cumin and crushed cumin seeds, caraway seeds, turmeric, red pepper, and chiles. Cook, stirring, 2 to 3 minutes until chiles are browned, spices are mixed, and seeds are lightly fried. Add chicken breasts, tomatoes, and water to cover and simmer about 25 minutes, or until chicken is tender. Remove chicken breasts to a baking dish. Combine cloves, cardamom, brown sugar, and saffron which has been soaked in the warm milk with sour cream and pour over chicken. Heat at 250 degrees to keep warm until serving.

Makes 4 to 8 servings.

Chestnut-Rice Stuffed Game Hens

1 cup rice
1 bouillon cube
1 medium onion, chopped
1/4 pound mushrooms, chopped
1/4 cup chopped celery
   Game hen livers, chopped
   Butter or margarine

1/2 pound chestnuts, shelled
   and crumbled
Salt
Poultry seasoning
1 teaspoon soy sauce
1 egg, beaten
4 (20-ounce) game hens

Game hens are relatively new poultry choices, far less expensive than squab and adaptable to a variety of recipes for small birds. When they first came on the market, they were tiny, weighing only about 16 ounces, but now the 20- to 24-ounce birds can serve two people nicely.

COOK rice in stock made by dissolving bouillon cube in 2 cups hot water. Meanwhile, sauté onion, mushrooms, celery, and livers in 1/4 cup melted butter. Stir in cooked rice and crumbled chestnuts. Season to taste with salt and poultry seasoning. Add soy sauce. Mix in egg. Stuff game hens with mixture. Tie drumsticks to tail and fasten neck skin to back with skewer. Fold wings akimbo with tips turned under back. Place birds breast side up on rack in shallow roasting pan. Brush with melted butter. Roast at 400 degrees 1 hour, or until drumstick twists easily out of thigh joint. Baste during roasting with additional butter and drippings in pan.

Makes 8 servings.

Note: To shell chestnuts, cut an "X" through shell on flat side. Place in pan over high heat with 1 teaspoon oil. Shake until well coated, then roast at 350 degrees until shells and skin can be removed easily.

Bronzed Birds

3 (20-ounce) game hens
1 clove garlic
1 teaspoon salt
1/2 teaspoon black pepper

1/4 cup honey
1/4 cup bourbon
1/2 cup butter or margarine,
   melted

PLACE game hens in shallow baking pan. Crush garlic with salt, then combine with pepper, honey, bourbon, and melted butter. Brush hens with butter mixture and bake at 350 degrees 35 to 40 minutes, basting frequently with remaining butter mixture.

Makes 6 servings.

TURKEY
& DUCK

NCE assigned to holiday meals only, turkey is now a fowl for all seasons. The fact that it provides high-quality protein and is low in fat and cholesterol undoubtedly has something to do with its growing appeal, as does the knowledge that pound for pound it remains a comparatively low-cost meat that is wonderfully easy to prepare.

The ready availability of turkey parts makes it possible to enjoy the bird Benjamin Franklin thought should be our national symbol with no worries about facing endless leftovers. And while turkey wings, thighs, and drumsticks now vie for space over the charcoal with the ever-present hamburger, it is with turkey steaks that local cooks show their culinary creativity and prowess. Sliced turkey breast meat is substituted for veal cutlets in any number of classic dishes or is marinated in delectable Oriental-style sauces and grilled either indoors or over coals on the patio barbecue.

Still another turkey product that has found favor in the West is ground turkey, often used by nutrition-conscious cooks as a replacement for the higher fat red meats.

Roast Turkey with Stuffings, page 184

Roast Turkey with Stuffings

1 whole turkey, fresh or
  thawed
  Dried Fruit-Rice Stuffing
  or
  Apple-Pecan Stuffing
  or
  Sherried Chestnut Stuffing
  or
  Raisin Sausage Stuffing
  Melted butter or margarine

REMOVE turkey neck and giblets from cavities of bird, rinse turkey, and wipe dry. (Cook neck and giblets for broth or to make giblet gravy.) Prepare stuffing of choice. Stuff loosely into neck cavity, then skewer neck skin to back. Stuff body cavity loosely, also. Sew openings shut by lacing a piece of string on wood picks. Fasten down legs either by tying or tucking under skin band. Twist wings akimbo under turkey. Place turkey, breast up, on a rack in shallow roasting pan. Brush with melted butter. If a roast meat thermometer is used, insert into thick part of thigh. Bulb should not touch bone. Roast at 325 degrees. A tent of foil placed loosely over turkey keeps it from browning too fast and may be removed when necessary to baste turkey. Remove foil last half hour for final browning. Turkey is done when thermometer registers 180 to 185 degrees, or when thick part of drumstick feels tender when pressed with thumb and forefinger, or when drumstick and thigh move easily.

Dried Fruit-Rice Stuffing

3/4 cup butter or margarine
1 1/2 cups chopped onions
1 1/2 cups chopped celery with
  leaves
1/3 cup chopped parsley
9 cups cooked brown rice
1 teaspoon marjoram
1/2 teaspoon thyme
1/2 teaspoon sage
  Salt, pepper
3 eggs, lightly beaten
3/4 cup turkey stock or chicken
  bouillon
12 ounces mixed dried fruit

Melt butter in large skillet. Sauté onions, celery, and parsley in butter. Remove from heat and combine with rice in large bowl. Stir in marjoram, thyme, and sage and season to taste with salt and pepper. Add eggs, stock, and fruit. Mix well.

Makes enough stuffing for 12- to 14-pound turkey.

Apple-Pecan Stuffing

Butter or margarine
$2/3$ cup diced onion
$2/3$ cup diced celery
3 cups diced day-old bread
3 cups diced apples
1 teaspoon salt
$1/2$ teaspoon black pepper

$1/8$ teaspoon sage
$1/8$ teaspoon marjoram
$1/8$ teaspoon thyme
$1/2$ teaspoon parsley flakes
$1/2$ cup chopped pecans
$1/2$ cup water

Melt $1/4$ cup butter in skillet. Add onion and celery and cook until tender. Add vegetables to bread cubes. Melt 2 tablespoons butter in skillet. Stir in apples and cook until golden. Add apples to bread mixture. Mix in salt, pepper, sage, marjoram, thyme, parsley, and pecans. Add water and mix thoroughly.

Makes enough stuffing for an 8- to 10-pound turkey.

Sherried Chestnut Stuffing

1 pound fresh or 1 (10-ounce) can chestnuts
2 (6-ounce) packages long-grain and wild rice
4 cups water
$1/2$ cup cream sherry

4 tablespoons butter or margarine
$1/2$ cup sliced onion
$1/2$ cup sliced celery
$1/2$ cup minced parsley

If fresh chestnuts are used, slit shells on one side and cook in boiling water to cover for 20 minutes. Cool, peel off shells and skin, and dice coarsely. Drain and dice canned chestnuts, if used. Cook rice in water according to package directions, using seasonings from package and adding sherry and 1 tablespoon butter. Meanwhile, melt remaining 3 tablespoons butter in skillet. Add onion, celery, and parsley and cook until onion is tender but not browned. Combine rice with vegetables and chestnuts.

Makes enough stuffing for an 8- to 10-pound turkey.

Raisin-Sausage Stuffing

6 cups toasted bread cubes
1 cup raisins
1 pound pork sausage
2 cups chopped celery

1 cup chopped onion
$1/4$ cup brown sugar, packed
1 teaspoon grated lemon peel
2 teaspoons salt

Combine bread and raisins in large bowl. Brown sausage in skillet, stirring to keep crumbly. Pour off most of fat. Add celery and onion and cook until tender. Add brown sugar, lemon peel, and salt. Pour over bread mixture and mix lightly.

Makes enough stuffing for a 12-pound turkey.

Wine-Roasted Turkey

Wine not only serves as a flavorful basting ingredient, it also insures that the meat of this turkey will be moist and tender.

1 (12- to 15-pound) turkey
1 cup rosé wine
1 small onion, halved
2 stalks celery, cut into
   2-inch pieces
1/2 cup butter or margarine,
   melted

1/4 cup orange juice
1 tablespoon lemon juice
1 teaspoon seasoned salt
1/2 teaspoon paprika
1/4 teaspoon onion powder

PREPARE turkey for roasting. Pour 1/2 cup wine inside body cavity of bird. Insert onion and celery. Place turkey on rack in roasting pan and tie legs together. Tuck wings under or skewer against bird. Insert meat thermometer in inner thigh. Brush turkey with melted butter. Roast at 325 degrees 1 hour, uncovered. Combine remaining butter and 1/2 cup wine, orange and lemon juices, seasoned salt, paprika, and onion powder. Use to baste turkey frequently during remainder of cooking time. Total time will be about 3 1/2 hours, or until thermometer registers 180 degrees.

Turkey Teriyaki Kebabs

2 pounds ground turkey
2 eggs
1 cup fine dry bread crumbs
1 cup finely shredded carrot
1/8 teaspoon Chinese 5-spice
   powder
1/2 cup minced onion
   Salt, pepper

Teriyaki Marinade
Cherry tomatoes
Green pepper squares
Onion squares or small
whole onions
Mushrooms
1 pound sliced bacon

COMBINE turkey, eggs, bread crumbs, carrot, 5-spice powder, and onion and season to taste with salt and pepper. Mix lightly but thoroughly. Shape into 1 1/4-inch meatballs. Place in 13 x 9-inch oven-proof dish and pour Teriyaki Marinade over. Turn meatballs in marinade. Let stand in refrigerator, covered, for at least 4 hours. Remove marinade to deep bowl and use to marinate cherry tomatoes, green pepper, onions, and mushrooms. Bake meatballs in dish at 375 degrees 20 to 25 minutes. Cut bacon strips in halves crosswise. Pierce end of bacon strip with skewer, add a meatball, and skewer bacon strip again. Continue weaving bacon strip around meatballs until 3 meatballs have been skewered. Grill about 4 inches from medium hot coals until bacon and meatballs are done, about 20 minutes, brushing with remaining marinade and turning occasionally. Skewer marinated vegetables on tips of skewers and continue grilling 5 to 10 minutes to desired doneness. Serve at once with hot steamed rice, if desired.

Makes about 10 servings.

Teriyaki Marinade

4 cloves garlic, minced
2 teaspoons minced
  gingerroot
$^1/_2$ cup soy sauce
$^2/_3$ cup wine vinegar
$^1/_4$ cup sugar
1 to 2 teaspoons hot chili oil
  or hot pepper sauce to
  taste

Combine garlic, ginger, soy sauce, vinegar, sugar, and chili oil.

Makes about 1$^1/_4$ cups.

Turkey Wrap-Ups

$^1/_4$ cup oil
1 pound ground turkey
2 medium carrots, peeled and
  chopped
1 medium zucchini, chopped
4 green onions, thinly sliced
$^1/_4$ cup soy sauce
$^1/_4$ teaspoon sugar
  Dash garlic powder
  Crisp lettuce

Ground turkey is developing quite a following in the West because it is lower in fat, cholesterol, and total calories than ground lamb, pork, or beef. This Chinese-style recipe makes excellent use of ground turkey.

HEAT 2 tablespoons oil in large skillet. Add turkey and cook about 5 minutes, stirring to break up meat. Remove from skillet. Heat remaining oil in skillet and sauté carrots, zucchini, and green onions 1 minute. Add turkey, soy sauce, sugar, and garlic powder. Cook, stirring, about 1 minute. Turn into serving dish and accompany with lettuce leaves. To eat, wrap filling in a lettuce leaf.

Makes 4 to 5 servings.

Braised Turkey Wings

6 turkey wings
  Paprika
  Salt
  White pepper
  Garlic salt
1 quart chicken broth
$^1/_2$ cup flour
$^1/_2$ cup diced green pepper
1 cup diced onion
1 cup diced peeled tomatoes

Turkey wings may lack glamour but not when the Horseshoe restaurant in Gardena turns them into a wonderful economical entrée.

CUT turkey wings at joints and discard tips. Arrange meatier wing portions in shallow baking dish and season to taste with paprika, salt, white pepper, and garlic salt. Bake at 450 degrees until golden brown, turning as needed to brown evenly, about 20 minutes. Gradually stir chicken broth into flour until smooth. Add green pepper, onion, and tomatoes. Pour sauce over turkey wings and continue baking at 350 degrees 2 hours, or until tender.

Makes 6 servings.

Chinese Turkey Steaks

Steaks cut from a turkey breast cook quickly over hot coals. Chinese-style flavorings used in a marinade basting sauce turn the bland turkey meat into a savory main dish.

1 teaspoon grated gingerroot
1 teaspoon dry mustard
1 teaspoon honey
$1/2$ cup soy sauce
$1/4$ cup oil
3 cloves garlic, minced
1 (3- to 4-pound) boneless
    turkey breast

COMBINE ginger, mustard, honey, soy sauce, oil, and garlic. Let mixture stand 24 hours at room temperature. Cut turkey breast crosswise into 1- to $1^1/2$-inch-thick steaks. (Frozen breasts can be cut also. Thaw before using.) Pour over turkey steaks, cover, and refrigerate for several hours. Drain steaks and cook over hot coals, about 8 minutes on each side. Brush with marinade while cooking, if desired.

Makes about 6 servings.

Turkey Marco Polo

As near as we can figure, we first printed this recipe for Turkey Marco Polo in 1957, and it hasn't lost its appeal for our readers since.

$1^1/2$ pounds fresh or
2 (10-ounce) packages
    frozen broccoli
6 thin slices cooked turkey
6 thin slices cooked ham
Mornay Sauce
Butter or margarine, melted

STEAM broccoli over boiling water until tender, or cook according to package directions. Arrange in 6 individual casseroles or 1 shallow baking dish. Cover with thin slices of turkey and then with ham slices. Spoon Mornay Sauce over ham. Drizzle 1 teaspoon butter over sauce and bake at 450 degrees until golden, about 30 minutes.

Makes 6 servings.

Mornay Sauce

$1/2$ cup butter or margarine
2 egg yolks
1 tablespoon lemon juice
$1/4$ teaspoon salt
Dash red pepper
1 cup White Sauce
3 tablespoons grated
    Parmesan cheese

Divide butter in 3 pieces. Place egg yolks, 1 piece of butter, and lemon juice in top of double boiler. Cook over hot, not boiling, water, stirring constantly with wooden spoon until butter melts. Add second piece of butter, stirring until thick. Add third piece of butter as mixture thickens. Remove from heat and beat until glossy. Add salt, red pepper, and White Sauce and blend well. Stir in Parmesan cheese.

Makes about $1^3/4$ cups.

White Sauce

2 tablespoons butter or
  margarine

2 tablespoons flour
1 cup milk

Melt butter in small saucepan or skillet. Add flour and cook, stirring, for 2 or 3 minutes. Do not allow flour to brown. Add milk all at once and continue to cook, stirring, until sauce becomes smooth and slightly thickened.

Makes 1 cup.

Turkey Scaloppine

1 (1³/₄- to 2-pound) quarter-
  breast of turkey, skinned
  and boned, or 1 (2-pound)
  package turkey breast slices
¹/₄ cup flour
1 teaspoon salt
¹/₄ teaspoon paprika
¹/₈ teaspoon white pepper
2 tablespoons butter or
  margarine

2 tablespoons oil
1¹/₂ cups small mushrooms,
  halved
¹/₄ teaspoon garlic, pressed
³/₄ cup dry white wine
1¹/₂ teaspoons lemon juice
¹/₄ teaspoon Italian
  seasoning, crumbled
1 tablespoon minced parsley

With turkey cutlets readily available in most markets, cost-conscious Californians often substitute them for veal in recipes that call for the more expensive meat.

PLACE turkey breast in freezer 45 minutes to 1 hour until surface of meat is thoroughly chilled and slightly firm. Cut meat crosswise in ¹/₄-inch slices. Mix flour, salt, paprika, and white pepper together. Flour meat slices, shaking off excess. Heat 1 tablespoon each butter and oil in large skillet. Add layer of meat and brown lightly on both sides. As meat is browned, remove and keep warm. Brown remaining turkey, adding remaining butter and oil as needed. When all meat is browned, add mushrooms and garlic to skillet and sauté lightly. Return browned turkey meat to skillet. Combine wine, lemon juice, Italian seasoning, and parsley. Pour over all and simmer rapidly 5 to 10 minutes, or until liquid is reduced and turkey is tender.

Makes 6 servings.

Lychee-Pineapple Duck

Ruby-red roasted ducks are available in Chinese delis and take-out food stands in Los Angeles. Angelenos, who have learned to ask for some of the drippings when they buy the cooked duck, find this a wonderful way to serve it.

1 (3- to 4-pound) Chinese roasted duck	1/4 cup brown sugar, packed
1/3 to 1/2 cup duck drippings	3/4 cup chicken broth, about
1 (20-ounce) can lychees	2 tablespoons cornstarch
1 (13 1/4-ounce) can pineapple chunks	1 medium green pepper, cut in strips
	Salt

CHOP duck in serving pieces. In wok or large pan combine duck drippings, syrups from lychees and pineapple, brown sugar, broth, and cornstarch. Stir until smooth and bring to boil. Lower heat and add duck, lychees, pineapple chunks, and green pepper. Cook gently 3 to 5 minutes. Season to taste with salt. If mixture gets too thick, add more broth.

Makes 6 servings.

Green Peppercorn Duck

Well-known food expert Philip Brown submitted this unusual baked duck recipe with a richly flavored sauce of green peppercorns.

1 (4-pound) duckling	2 teaspoons butter or margarine
2 tablespoons salt	2 teaspoons flour
2 quarts water	1/2 teaspoon star anise
1/2 cup chopped onion	1 tablespoon green peppercorns in wine
1/2 cup chopped celery	Salt
1 bay leaf	
1 clove garlic, minced	

REMOVE backbone from duck and quarter or bone duck, reserving backbone and giblets for broth. Place salt in deep saucepan, add duck pieces, and cook for 20 minutes. Remove duck, place in a shallow casserole, and bake at 350 degrees 45 minutes, increasing heat to 375 degrees during last 10 minutes. Combine giblets, backbone, and water in saucepan, cover, and bring to boil. Reduce heat and simmer 2 hours. Skim off fat. Add onion, celery, bay leaf, and garlic to broth, cover, and simmer 20 minutes. Strain. Melt butter in a saucepan, stir in flour, and cook 1 to 2 minutes. Add broth, and cook until slightly thickened. Add star anise and green peppercorns and season to taste with salt. Serve sauce over duck.

Makes 4 servings.

LAMB & VEAL

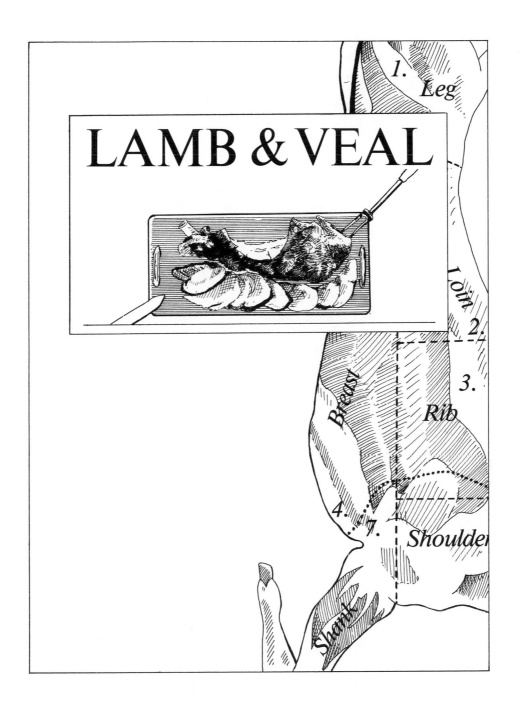

1. Leg

Loin 2.

3. Rib

Breast

4. 7. Shoulder

Shank

I F there is a distinctly western preference for the way lamb is served, it is for the meat to be cooked simply to a medium state with a pink interior. Yet, despite this affinity for the underdone, West Coast denizens also are fond of lamb that has been braised for hours, to the point where the meat barely clings to the bones.

When a barbecue is in order, lamb is not neglected by outdoor cooks. A boneless, butterflied leg of lamb, grilled over coals until it is sizzling crisp and brown on the outside and a delicate pink on the inside, is often the centerpiece at a poolside or patio dinner party.

Many of the lamb recipes that have appeared in *The Times* have obvious ethnic origins, with the influences of the Middle East and Mediterranean predominating. And, fortunately for the budget conscious, many of the most requested recipes call for less expensive cuts such as lamb shoulder and lamb breast.

Butterflied Lamb, page 194

Butterflied Lamb

Boneless leg of lamb is especially suited to the barbecue chef who is less than expert when it comes to carving.

1 (5- to 6-pound) leg of lamb, boned and butterflied
Bruised fresh mint leaves
1 cup olive oil
Coarsely ground black pepper

2 cloves garlic, minced
3/4 cup red wine
Juice of 2 lemons

MARINATE lamb 2 hours or more in a mixture of mint, oil, pepper, garlic, wine, and lemon juice. Broil over hot coals as for steak for 45 minutes, or to desired degree of doneness, turning once or twice. From time to time baste with marinade. Slice on the bias.

Makes 6 to 8 servings.

Kibbee
(Lamb and Bulgur)

A growing interest in Middle Eastern foods has made kibbee, a cracked wheat (bulgur) and ground lamb pie, a popular menu item in Southern California.

1/3 cup bulgur
1 pound ground lean lamb
1/4 cup minced onion
1/8 teaspoon oregano
1 1/2 teaspoons salt

Pepper
Nut Stuffing
2 tablespoons butter or margarine

RINSE bulgur and drain by squeezing handfuls at a time. Combine with lamb, onion, oregano, and salt and season to taste with pepper. Mix well. With wet hands press a layer of lamb mixture into a 9-inch pie plate. Top with Nut Stuffing, then with another layer of meat. Smooth surface of meat with wet hand. Cut into wedges before baking as a crust forms during cooking. Dot with butter. Bake at 350 degrees 25 to 30 minutes, or until meat reaches desired degree of doneness.

Makes 4 to 6 servings.

Nut Stuffing

1/2 cup coarsely ground lamb
1/3 cup pine nuts
1/8 teaspoon salt

Pepper
1 tablespoon butter or margarine

Combine lamb, nuts, and salt and season to taste with pepper. Melt butter, add meat mixture, and cook, stirring to keep crumbly, until light brown.

Makes about 3/4 cup.

Lamb Shanks

4 lamb shanks
1 clove garlic, minced
  Salt, pepper
8 medium carrots, cut in 1-
  inch pieces

8 small white onions
8 button mushrooms (caps only)
8 small slices celery
1 (8-ounce) can tomato sauce
1 cup peas

The Musso & Frank Grill in Hollywood has been serving good hearty food for well over half a century. Their recipe for lamb shanks is simplicity itself.

SPRINKLE lamb shanks with garlic and season to taste with salt and pepper. Bake at 350 degrees 30 minutes, turning frequently to brown on all sides. Add carrots, onions, mushrooms, celery, and tomato sauce. Bake at 375 degrees 45 minutes to 1 hour, or until meat is tender. Add peas after 30 minutes baking time.

Makes 4 servings.

Athenian Lamb Stew

1 medium onion, minced
1 clove garlic, crushed
1 tablespoon basil
2 pounds lean lamb shoulder
  or leg, cubed
3 tablespoons olive oil
  Salt, pepper

1 (1-pound 12-ounce) can
  whole tomatoes, crushed
$1/2$ cup rosé wine
1 cup cut green beans
3 medium potatoes, peeled
  and quartered
1 stick cinnamon

At the Pioneer Boulangerie in Santa Monica, a restaurant known for its freshly baked breads and homemade soups, this stew is a standout.

SAUTÉ onion, garlic, and basil with lamb in oil until onion is tender. Season to taste with salt and pepper. Continue cooking until lamb is lightly browned. Add crushed tomatoes and wine. Cook 10 minutes. Add green beans, potatoes, and cinnamon stick. Cover and cook over low heat 1 to $1^{1}/_{2}$ hours, or until lamb is very tender.

Makes 4 servings.

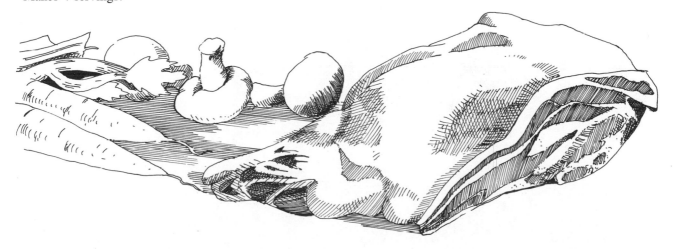

Lamb Satay with Peanut Sauce

Savory Indonesian-style satay makes a wonderful and unusual main dish when served with rice.

¹/₄ cup soy sauce
1 tablespoon lemon juice
2 tablespoons oil
2 tablespoons honey
1 tablespoon grated onion

1 teaspoon coriander
¹/₄ teaspoon black pepper
1 pound boneless lamb, cut in
  ¹/₂-inch cubes
  Peanut Sauce
  Hot cooked rice

COMBINE soy sauce, lemon juice, oil, honey, onion, coriander, and pepper. Pour over lamb and turn to coat meat well. Marinate at least 2 hours. Drain, reserving marinade for basting meat. Thread lamb cubes on 4- to 6-inch skewers. Grill over glowing coals, turning and basting with marinade to brown evenly, about 10 minutes, or until done as desired. Serve hot with warm Peanut Sauce over rice.

Makes 3 to 4 servings.

Peanut Sauce

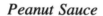

1 tablespoon minced onion
1 clove garlic, minced
  Oil
³/₄ cup chicken broth
¹/₂ cup peanut butter
1 tablespoon molasses

¹/₂ teaspoon lime juice
¹/₂ teaspoon soy sauce
¹/₄ teaspoon ground ginger
  Few drops hot pepper
  sauce

COOK onion and garlic in small amount of oil until tender but not browned. Blend chicken broth with peanut butter in a bowl. Stir in onion mixture, molasses, lime juice, soy sauce, ginger, and hot pepper sauce. Heat, stirring, until slightly thickened. Season to taste with additional hot pepper sauce, if desired.

Makes 1¹/₄ cup.

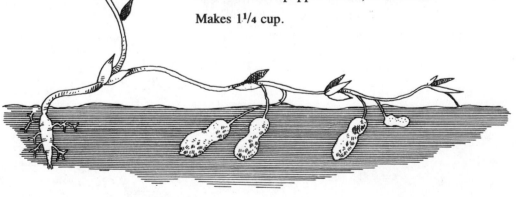

Lamb Casserole

1 onion, chopped
1 1/2 pounds lean lamb, cubed
3 tablespoons oil
3 cups bouillon
1/2 pound prunes, cooked, pitted, and quartered

1 cup uncooked rice
2 sweet red peppers, cut in chunks
1/2 small lemon, thinly sliced
1/2 teaspoon oregano
Salt, pepper

This unlikely sounding combination of lamb, prunes, and sweet red peppers submitted by a Times *reader is surprisingly delicious.*

COOK onion and lamb in oil about 10 minutes until lightly browned. Add bouillon, cover, and simmer 20 minutes. Turn meat mixture into 2-quart casserole. Stir in prunes, rice, red peppers, lemon, and oregano and season to taste with salt and pepper. Cover and bake at 350 degrees 1 hour. Fluff with a fork and serve.

Makes 6 to 8 servings.

Meaty Lamb Bones

3 1/2 to 4 pounds lamb breast or meaty riblets
2 cloves garlic, minced
1 teaspoon salt

1/4 teaspoon black pepper
2 tablespoons lemon juice
1 medium onion, sliced
1 (14 1/2-ounce) can beef broth

At Frank's in Vernon, a café frequented by meat purveyors who supply some of Los Angeles's better known restaurants, chef Pete Milutinovich made this treatment of lamb bones famous. The initial temperature may seem high and the cooking period long, but the end result will allay any doubts.

TRIM any excess fat from meat. Place breast in large open roasting pan, bone side down. Sprinkle with garlic, salt, pepper, and lemon juice. Bake at 450 degrees 40 minutes. Add onion and cook until ribs are browned, about 30 minutes. Reduce heat to 300 or 325 degrees and add broth in bottom of pan. Cook, uncovered, about 1 hour to 1 hour 15 minutes. Cover tightly and steam about 1 hour longer. Add more broth if needed.

Makes about 6 servings.

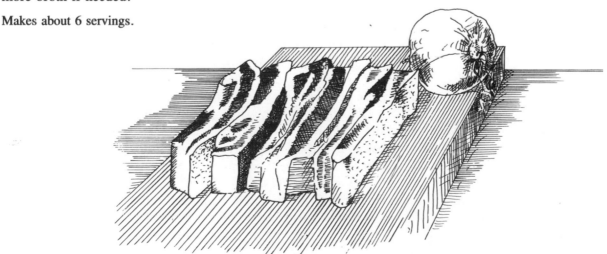

Saltimbocca

Saltimbocca, a delicate veal and prosciutto dish, can be found on the menus of most Italian restaurants in Los Angeles.

8 veal cutlets
1 teaspoon sage
¹/₄ pound prosciutto, cut into 8 slices
3 tablespoons butter or margarine

1 teaspoon chopped parsley
Salt, pepper
Lemon wedges

PLACE cutlets between pieces of wax paper and pound until thin. Sprinkle with sage and place a slice of prosciutto on each cutlet, fastening with wood pick. Melt 2 tablespoons butter in skillet and add cutlets. Cook 2 to 3 minutes on each side. Place cutlets on platter. Melt remaining butter, add parsley, and season to taste with salt and pepper. Scrape brown bits from bottom of pan and pour over cutlets. Serve lemon wedge with each portion.

Makes 4 to 8 servings.

Osso Buco alla Milanese
(Braised Veal Shanks, Milan-Style)

When it comes to flavor, it's hard to beat this Milanese veal dish. It looks beautiful, is easy to serve, and doesn't depend on split-second timing for perfect results.

1 cup finely chopped onion
²/₃ cup finely chopped carrots
²/₃ cup finely chopped celery
¹/₄ cup butter or margarine
1 teaspoon minced garlic
  Lemon peel, cut in strips
2 veal shanks, sawed into 8 pieces about 2 inches long
³/₄ cup flour
¹/₂ cup oil
1 cup dry white wine

1¹/₂ cups beef broth
1 (1-pound) can Italian tomatoes, cut up, with juice
¹/₄ teaspoon thyme
¹/₂ teaspoon basil
2 bay leaves
2 sprigs parsley
  Salt
  Freshly ground black pepper

COMBINE onion, carrots, celery, butter, and garlic in large heavy casserole or Dutch oven. Cook over medium heat 8 to 10 minutes. Add 2 strips lemon peel and remove from heat. Dredge veal pieces in flour, shaking off any excess. Heat oil in skillet over medium high heat. Brown veal on all sides. Arrange on top of vegetables in casserole. Tip skillet and draw off nearly all fat with a spoon. Add wine and boil briskly for about 3 minutes, scraping up any brown bits stuck to the pan. Pour over veal. Add broth, tomatoes and juice, thyme, basil, bay leaves, and parsley. Season to taste with salt and pepper. The broth should come up to the top of veal pieces. If it does not, add more. Bring to gentle boil. Cover tightly and bake at 350 degrees about 2 hours, carefully turning and basting veal every 20 minutes. Garnish top with more strips of lemon peel.

Makes 4 servings.

Veal Piccata

18 slices veal round, about 2
    pounds
    Flour
    Cottonseed oil
 2 tablespoons butter or
    margarine

Juice of 2 lemons
$^1/_2$ cup dry white wine
    Chopped parsley
    Salt, pepper
    Lemon wedges

Valentino, a fine Italian restaurant in Santa Monica, serves this simple, yet elegant, lemony veal dish.

POUND veal paper-thin between 2 sheets of wax paper. Dip in flour and sauté, a few slices at a time, in a small amount of oil. Cook until browned, about 30 seconds on each side, turning once. Remove from pan and keep warm. Continue cooking veal, adding oil as needed, until all slices are browned. Drain oil from pan and add butter and lemon juice. Add wine and reduce sauce by one-third. Add chopped parsley and season to taste with salt and pepper. Return veal to pan and heat through. Serve with lemon wedges.

Makes 6 servings.

IME was when huge quantities of meat in the form of great barons of beef and sixteen-ounce steaks headlined almost every restaurant menu in the country. No longer. Although there is still an abundance of steak houses and prime rib specialty restaurants to satisfy big beef eaters, for the most part the trend in restaurants and at home is to smaller portions of America's favorite red meat, served in more imaginative ways.

Undoubtedly one reason for this trend is cost. However, a surging interest in good nutrition and the awareness that the average American does not require as much protein as he consumes also have a bearing on the changing attitude toward red meats of all types.

Many of the varied ethnic cuisines that have become so popular in the West illustrate well how smaller amounts and less-expensive cuts of beef can be used to advantage. Chinese beef stir-fry dishes, Korean barbecue, and ground beef seasoned in the style of a multitude of countries all fit into California menus. And no barbecue fan would dream of passing up the opportunity to enjoy a batch of meaty beef bones prepared in any of several exciting ways. As for that great American favorite, chili, no book on western cooking could possibly be considered complete without one or two chili recipes. We offer five. All different and all good.

Hamburger Loaf, page 204

203

Hamburger Loaf

This meat loaf recipe is an updated version of one we found in a cookbook published in Los Angeles in 1881.

$1/2$ pound ground beef
$1/2$ pound ground veal
$1/2$ pound ground pork
$1/4$ teaspoon thyme
$1/8$ teaspoon nutmeg
   Salt, pepper

Grated peel and juice of 1
  lemon
1 egg, beaten
$1/3$ cup fine dry bread crumbs
  Flour

MIX beef, veal, pork, thyme, nutmeg, and season to taste with salt and pepper. Add lemon peel and juice, egg, and bread crumbs. Blend well. Shape mixture into an oblong, coat thickly with flour, and place in baking pan. Bake at 375 degrees 45 to 55 minutes, basting often.

Makes 6 servings.

Marian Manners's Favorite Meat Loaf

This meat loaf won a seal of approval from Marian Manners (a pseudonym for The Times *food editor in years gone by).*

1 pound lean ground beef
$1/2$ pound lean ground pork
$1/2$ pound ground veal or
  turkey
$1^1/4$ teaspoons salt

$1/4$ teaspoon poultry seasoning
$1/8$ teaspoon hot pepper sauce
1 cup milk or water, or half
  water and half dry red wine
1 cup fine dry bread crumbs

COMBINE meats with salt, poultry seasoning, and hot pepper sauce and mix thoroughly. Add milk to crumbs and let stand 5 minutes. Add to meat mixture and mix thoroughly. Beat with spoon. Pack mixture into 8 × 4-inch loaf pan and bake at 325 degrees $1^1/4$ hours.

Makes 6 servings.

Beef Loaf

This is a homey, economical, wonderful-tasting meat loaf from Blair's, one of the few remaining luncheonettes in Los Angeles.

$1/2$ cup fine dry bread crumbs
$1/2$ cup half and half
2 pounds lean ground beef
4 eggs, beaten
$1/2$ cup minced onion
$1/4$ cup minced celery

$1/2$ cup chopped green pepper
1 clove garlic, minced
2 tablespoons Worcestershire
  sauce
  Salt, pepper
1 cup water

SOAK bread crumbs in half and half and mix with beef, eggs, onion, celery, green pepper, garlic, and Worcestershire. Season to taste with salt and pepper. Completely wrap loaf in well-greased heavy butcher's paper and place in large baking pan. Add water and bake at 350 degrees 2 hours. Serve with mushroom or onion gravy or tomato sauce, if desired. Or serve cold on a cold meat platter. (Meat loaf will not have the usual browned crust of a baked meat loaf because it has been steam-cooked in the paper.)

Makes 6 servings.

Guacamole Burgers

*³/₄ cup mashed ripe
  avocado*
³/₄ cup chopped tomato
*1 tablespoon finely
  chopped onion*
1 teaspoon salt
*¹/₂ to ³/₄ teaspoon chili powder
  Generous dash red
  pepper*

1 small clove garlic, crushed
2 teaspoons lemon juice
1 pound ground beef
*4 English muffins, split and
  toasted*
Corn chips

This open-faced hamburger sandwich has a spicy guacamole topping which reflects the Mexican influence on many Southern California dishes.

COMBINE avocado, tomato, onion, salt, chili powder, red pepper, garlic, and lemon juice to make guacamole. Mix well. Set aside. Shape beef into 4 patties. Grill about 4 inches from medium hot coals about 5 minutes on each side for medium rare or to desired degree of doneness. Place each patty on a muffin half. Top patty with some guacamole mixture and other half of muffin. Serve with corn chips and remaining guacamole on the side.

Makes 4 servings.

Albanian Burger Steaks

1¹/₂ pounds ground beef
2 cloves garlic, minced
1 egg
*2 slices bread, soaked in
  water and squeezed dry*

¹/₄ cup minced onion
2 teaspoons salt
¹/₂ teaspoon black pepper
*3 to 4 tablespoons minced mint
  leaves*

Rose Dosti's mother adapted Albanian flavor preferences to American hamburger with these results.

COMBINE beef, garlic, egg, bread, onion, salt, pepper, and mint. Shape into 4 oblong patties and fry 8 to 10 minutes on each side in lightly greased skillet. Serve on hot plates and garnish with additional mint leaves, if desired.

Makes 4 servings.

Just Plain Good Chili

Jay Pennington won the 1977 International Chili Society's World Championship Cookoff in Rosamond, California, with this recipe.

Oil
3 medium onions, finely chopped
2 medium green peppers, finely chopped
3 stalks celery, finely chopped
8 pounds coarsely ground beef
1 (6-ounce) can tomato paste
2 (1 pound 12-ounce) cans stewed tomatoes
2 (16-ounce) cans tomato sauce

3 cloves garlic, finely chopped
2 (3-ounce) jars chili powder
2 tablespoons salt
Oregano
1 (7-ounce) can chile salsa
1 medium jalapeño chile, seeded and chopped
Garlic salt
Coarsely ground black pepper

BRUSH bottom of heavy 2-gallon pot with oil. Sauté onions, green peppers, and celery for 10 minutes. Add meat and cook for another 10 to 15 minutes, or until meat loses pink color. Stir in tomato paste, stewed tomatoes, and tomato sauce. Add chopped garlic, chili powder, salt, a sprinkling of oregano, chile salsa, and jalapeño chile. Simmer for 30 minutes. Season to taste with garlic salt and pepper, then simmer 2½ hours, stirring every 10 to 15 minutes. Skim off fat occasionally.

Makes 2 gallons, about 32 servings.

Chili with Kidney Beans

Actress Polly Bergen's chili is almost as famous as she is!

3 cloves garlic, minced
2 tablespoons oil
4 pounds lean ground beef
6 onions, chopped
4 green peppers, chopped
6 (1-pound) cans whole tomatoes
4 (1-pound) cans red kidney beans, drained

2 (6-ounce) cans tomato paste
¼ cup chili powder
1 teaspoon white vinegar
3 dashes red pepper
3 whole cloves
1 bay leaf
Salt, pepper

SAUTÉ garlic in oil in large heavy kettle until golden. Crumble in beef and cook 10 minutes, or until evenly browned. Pour some of oil and drippings into a skillet. Add onions and green peppers and cook until tender. Add to cooked meat with tomatoes, kidney beans, tomato paste, chili powder, vinegar, red pepper, cloves, and bay leaf, and season to taste with salt and pepper. Cook, covered, over low heat 1 hour. If too dry, add additional tomatoes. If too liquid, uncover and simmer longer. Serve with rice, if desired.

Makes 10 to 12 servings.

Chili Colorado Con Carne
(Red Chili with Meat)

$1/2$ pound suet, coarsely
   ground
2 cups chopped onions
3 pounds coarsely ground
   lean meat (combination of
   beef, veal, and pork or any
   one of these)
6 cloves garlic

2 teaspoons salt
6 tablespoons chili powder
1 tablespoon ground cumin
1 tablespoon oregano,
   crumbled
$1^1/2$ quarts water
$1/4$ cup roasted flour or fried
   tortillas (optional)

The Acapulco chain of restaurants serves an interesting variety of Mexican dishes, including this version of chili.

COOK suet and onion in heavy kettle until onion is tender but not browned. Add meat and brown. Mash garlic in the salt and stir into meat along with chili powder, cumin, and oregano. Add water. Cover and simmer 1 hour. To thicken, blend roasted flour with $1/2$ cup water and stir into mixture. Simmer another half hour. Or soak fried tortillas in water, blend until smooth, and add.

Makes 10 servings.

Note: Chili Colorado can be served with pinto beans, rice, macaroni, or over tamales.

Chasing Chili

$1/2$ pound dry pinto beans
5 cups chopped tomatoes
1 pound green peppers,
   chopped
$1^1/2$ tablespoons oil
$1^1/2$ pounds onions, peeled and
   chopped
2 cloves garlic, minced
$1/2$ cup chopped parsley

$1/2$ cup butter or margarine
$2^1/2$ pounds ground beef
   (preferably chuck)
1 pound lean ground pork
$1/3$ cup chili powder
2 tablespoons salt
$1^1/2$ teaspoons black pepper
$1^1/2$ teaspoons cumin seeds
$1^1/2$ teaspoons MSG (optional)

For years we've been after the recipe for the real Chasen's chili made famous by the Beverly Hills restaurant's celebrated clientele. We finally caught up with one version that is allegedly authentic, but no one at Chasen's will admit that it's their recipe. Hence the name.

SOAK beans in water to cover overnight. Drain, cover with cold water, and simmer until beans are tender, about 1 hour. Add tomatoes and simmer 5 minutes longer. Sauté green peppers in hot oil until tender. Add onions and cook until tender, stirring frequently. Add garlic and parsley. In another skillet melt butter and add beef and pork. Cook and stir 15 minutes, or until crumbly and brown. Add meat to onion mixture and stir in chili powder. Cook 10 minutes. Add meat mixture to beans along with salt, pepper, cumin seeds, and MSG. Simmer, covered, 1 hour. Remove cover and simmer 30 minutes longer. Skim fat from top.

Makes 8 to 10 servings.

Coney Island Chili

In the midwestern amusement park, where it originated, this rich meat sauce is served over spaghetti. In the West, however, it's more likely to turn up as a topping for hot dogs.

2 pounds ground beef
2 medium onions, chopped
1 (6-ounce) can tomato paste
3 cups water
2 teaspoons vinegar
2 teaspoons Worcestershire sauce

2 teaspoons salt
1/4 teaspoon cinnamon
2 tablespoons chili powder
1 clove garlic, minced
1 tablespoon black pepper

BROWN beef and onions in large heavy pot or skillet. Place a portion at a time in blender container and blend a few seconds. Combine meat mixture with tomato paste, water, vinegar, Worcestershire, salt, cinnamon, chili powder, garlic, and pepper and simmer 1 to 2 hours until thick. Serve over spaghetti or hot dogs.

Makes 8 servings.

Sloppy Joes

Youngsters everywhere like Sloppy Joes. For variety we've added some international flavorings to the basic recipe.

2 pounds ground beef
1 large onion, minced
2 teaspoons salt
1/4 teaspoon black pepper
1/4 cup flour
3 cups water

1 teaspoon Worcestershire sauce
1 1/2 cups catsup
1 to 2 teaspoons chili powder
16 hamburger buns

COOK beef, onion, salt, and pepper in large skillet, stirring until beef loses its red color. Stir in flour, water, Worcestershire, catsup, and chili powder. Simmer, uncovered, 20 minutes, stirring occasionally. Split and toast buns. Spoon mixture over toasted buns.

Makes 16 servings.

Sloppy Josés

Prepare Sloppy Joe mixture but increase chili powder to 3 or 4 teaspoons. Just before serving stir in a can of undrained kidney or pinto beans. Serve over tortillas, which have been crisped in oil, or toasted bun halves.

Sloppy Giovannis

Prepare Sloppy Joe mixture but omit chili powder and season with garlic, a bay leaf, and 1/2 teaspoon basil. Stir in canned or cooked sliced mushrooms just before serving on toasted Italian rolls.

Sloppy Josefs

Prepare Sloppy Joe mixture but omit catsup and chili powder. Use half beef broth and half dry red wine for liquid. Stir in cooked or canned sliced mushrooms and small whole onions sautéed in butter just before serving. Serve on Kaiser rolls.

Meatballs and Spaghetti Sauce

1 pound ground beef
1/2 pound ground pork
1/2 pound ground veal
1 cup chopped onions
1 clove garlic, minced
1/3 cup grated Parmesan
  cheese
1 cup fine dry bread crumbs

4 eggs
1/4 cup chopped parsley
  Dash oregano
1 teaspoon salt
1/2 teaspoon black pepper
1/4 cup oil
  Spaghetti Sauce

Little Joe's, a popular downtown Italian restaurant, shared their excellent recipe for meatballs in a rich spaghetti sauce. This dish tastes better when made in quantity, and leftovers freeze well.

COMBINE beef, pork, veal, onions, garlic, cheese, crumbs, eggs, parsley, oregano, salt, and pepper. Mix well. Form into 1¹/₂-inch balls. Heat oil in skillet and add meatballs. Cook until browned, then drain. Add meatballs to Spaghetti Sauce during last 30 minutes of cooking.

Makes 6 to 8 servings.

Spaghetti Sauce

1 medium onion, minced
2 tablespoons minced green
  pepper
1 stalk celery, minced
1 clove garlic, minced
3 tablespoons oil
1 (1-pound 12-ounce) can
  whole tomatoes, chopped
1 (1-pound 12-ounce) can
  tomato puree

1 tablespoon crushed basil
1 teaspoon crushed oregano
1 bay leaf
1/2 cup dry red wine
1 cup water
2 teaspoons salt
1/2 teaspoon black pepper
2 tablespoons grated
  Parmesan cheese

Cook onion, green pepper, celery, and garlic in oil until vegetables are tender. Add tomatoes and liquid, tomato puree, basil, oregano, and bay leaf and simmer 1 hour, stirring often. Add wine, water, salt, and pepper and simmer 1 hour longer. If sauce is too thick, add more water. When sauce is cooked, add cheese and mix well.

Makes 5 to 6 cups.

Firehouse Casserole

1½ pounds ground beef
1 small onion, diced
1 tablespoon oil
2 (10¾-ounce) cans
   condensed cream of
   mushroom soup

1 soup can milk
1 (4-ounce) can diced green
   chiles
2 dozen corn tortillas
1 pound cheddar cheese,
   shredded

BROWN beef and onion in oil, stirring to crumble meat. Combine soup and milk in saucepan and cook, stirring, over medium heat until smooth. Then add chiles. Cut tortillas in 1-inch squares and place a layer in a baking dish. Spread with a layer of half the cooked meat, then with half the soup mixture, and half the cheese. Repeat layers. Bake at 325 degrees 20 to 30 minutes.

Makes 6 servings.

Morcon
(Braised Stuffed Meat Roll)

In the Philippines this savory meat roll is served on special occasions. Its origins can be traced back to early Spanish explorers.

1½ pounds sirloin or flank
   steak, ¼-inch thick
¼ cup vinegar
2 cloves garlic, minced
1½ teaspoons freshly ground
   black pepper
½ pound ham, cut julienne
2 Spanish-style chorizos, cut
   in strips
2 hard-cooked eggs, sliced
   lengthwise in eighths

½ cup chopped green olives
1 cup oil
1 onion, chopped
2 bay leaves
2 cups water
1 (8-ounce) can tomato sauce
2 teaspoons salt
2 tomatoes, diced

POUND steak as thin as possible with side of meat cleaver or mallet between 2 sheets of wax paper. Combine vinegar and garlic in large bowl. Marinate steak in this mixture 30 minutes. Remove steak, reserving marinade. Place steak on cutting board. Sprinkle with pepper. Lay successive rows of ham, chorizo strips, and hard-cooked eggs on meat. Sprinkle with olives. Roll up steak, tying securely with string. Heat oil in skillet and brown meat roll on all sides. Pour off oil. Add chopped onion, bay leaves, water, tomato sauce, salt, tomatoes, and marinade. Cover and cook over low heat 1½ hours. Remove meat and slice into serving portions. Arrange on platter and pour sauce from skillet over meat.

Makes 8 to 10 servings.

Steak Picado

1/4 cup oil
3 pounds boneless round
   steak, cut into 1/2-inch
   cubes
2 cloves garlic, minced
1 large bay leaf, crumbled
   Salt
2 medium green peppers, cut
   into 1/2-inch squares

1 or 2 hot yellow chiles,
   minced
1 onion, halved and
   sliced
4 medium tomatoes, cut
   into 6 wedges each
   Pepper

Sal Ramos cooked this one-skillet steak dish for food brokers at the wholesale produce market in Los Angeles.

HEAT oil in large skillet. Add meat, garlic, bay leaf, and season to taste with salt. Cook until meat is browned. Add green peppers and chiles and cook 4 to 5 minutes. Add onion and cook 3 minutes. Add tomatoes and season to taste with pepper. Cook 2 to 3 minutes. Serve as a main dish with rice and refried beans or spoon onto flour tortillas and wrap as burritos.

Makes 8 to 10 servings.

Hobo Steak

1 large New York steak, cut 3
   inches thick
   Freshly ground black pepper
1 (1/4-inch thick) strip fat, 3
   inches wide or several
   smaller pieces of fat

1 cup salt
2 tablespoons water
1/4 pound unsalted butter
   Sourdough French bread,
   sliced 1/4-inch thick and
   toasted

The late Dave Chasen, founder of the famous Beverly Hills restaurant that bears his name, developed this unusual treatment for New York steak which produces a rich, tender, and memorable main dish.

SEASON steak with pepper. Wrap fat around sides of steak, covering them completely but leaving top and bottom exposed. Tie fat to steak with string near the top and also near the bottom. Fat must be securely anchored to steak. Combine salt and water to make a paste. Mound about 3/4 of mixture over top of steak, covering meat completely. Place steak under broiler and broil 8 to 10 minutes, depending on size of steak. Carefully remove salt crust, keeping it in one piece. Turn steak over and place salt crust on other side. If necessary, patch crust with remaining salt mixture. Broil steak another 8 to 10 minutes. Remove steak from broiler and discard crust and fat. Slice meat, cutting slightly on the diagonal. Heat butter in chafing dish or large skillet until foaming and lightly browned. Place a few slices of meat at a time in butter and cook to desired degree of doneness. (Allow about 1 minute on each side for rare meat.) Place each slice of meat on a slice of toast and spoon some of the hot butter over.

Makes 2 servings.

Greek Steak

5 pounds coarsely ground
   lean chuck
1 onion, minced
$^1/_3$ cup soy sauce

$^1/_2$ bunch parsley, minced
1 egg
Oil

COMBINE chuck, onion, soy sauce, parsley, and egg. Mix well and form into large (8- or 12-ounce) patties. Barely coat griddle or skillet with small amount of oil and add patties. Cook on one side until firm, then turn and finish cooking to desired degree of doneness.

Makes 10 servings.

Note: Uncooked patties freeze well if carefully wrapped.

Sticky Bones

1 cup vinegar
$^1/_2$ cup honey
2 tablespoons Worcestershire
   sauce
$^1/_2$ cup catsup
1 teaspoon salt

1 teaspoon dry mustard
1 teaspoon paprika
$^1/_4$ teaspoon black pepper
1 clove garlic, minced
4 pounds beef ribs

COMBINE vinegar, honey, Worcestershire, catsup, salt, mustard, paprika, pepper, and garlic in saucepan. Cover, bring to boil, reduce heat, and simmer 15 minutes. Place ribs in a single layer in baking pan, cover with hot marinade, and let stand 1 hour. Drain off marinade, then bake ribs at 325 degrees 1 hour, turning and basting often with marinade.

Makes 6 servings.

Barbecued Beef Ribs

8 pounds beef ribs from
   standing rib roast
1 cup chopped onion
1 teaspoon instant minced
   garlic
$^1/_4$ cup oil
2 teaspoons prepared mustard
1 cup tomato puree

2 cups sugar
2 tablespoons soy sauce
1 cup white vinegar
2 bay leaves
1 teaspoon hot pepper sauce
1 teaspoon barbecue spice
   (optional)
2 teaspoons salt

ARRANGE beef ribs on a rack in baking pan. Sauté onion and garlic in oil until golden. Add mustard, tomato puree, sugar, soy sauce, vinegar, bay leaves, hot pepper sauce, barbecue spice, and salt and simmer about 15 minutes. Strain. Brush barbecue sauce generously over beef ribs, covering them thoroughly. Bake at 375 to 400 degrees 45 minutes, basting frequently with sauce until beef ribs are tender and well done. Store any remaining sauce, covered, in the refrigerator.

Makes 8 servings.

Deviled Beef Bones with Mustard Sauce

Meaty bones from cooked
beef rib roast
Prepared brown mustard
Fine dry bread crumbs
1/2 cup tomato puree

1/2 cup chicken broth
1 teaspoon salt
1 teaspoon sugar
Dash MSG (optional)

The Biltmore Hotel in downtown Los Angeles has long been famous for its twice-cooked meaty beef bones served in a rich mustard sauce.

ALLOW 3 bones per serving. Spread bones generously with brown mustard, then roll in bread crumbs to coat thoroughly. Place bones in shallow pan in single layer and bake at 300 degrees 15 minutes. Meanwhile combine tomato puree, chicken broth, 4 teaspoons brown mustard, salt, sugar, and MSG in saucepan. Bring to boil, then remove from heat. Cool slightly and pour over bones while warm.

Makes 4 servings.

Bul Kogi
(Korean Barbecue)

4 to 5 pounds beef short ribs
    2 cloves garlic, crushed
  1/4 cup sesame seeds,
        toasted and crushed
    1 cup finely chopped
        green onions

1 teaspoon pepper
1 teaspoon sesame oil
2 cups soy sauce
1 cup sugar
1/4 cup oil

This recipe came from the Wailea Steak House in Hawaii, but Los Angeles has many Korean restaurants where zesty barbecued meat dishes are served.

PLACE short ribs in bowl. Add garlic, sesame seeds, green onions, pepper, sesame oil, soy sauce, sugar, and oil and toss to coat meat well. Cover and let stand at room temperature 2 hours. Barbecue over coals or under broiler, turning and basting often with marinade until meat is tender.

Makes 4 to 6 servings.

Braised Short Ribs

The Musso & Frank Grill, one of Hollywood's oldest and best-loved restaurants, has been serving this dish to stars since Hollywood's heyday.

6 pounds beef short ribs
  Oil
  Salt, pepper
  Flour

1 large onion, chopped
1 large carrot, sliced
2 stalks celery, chopped
1 (8-ounce) can tomato sauce

BROWN ribs in small amount of oil in Dutch oven. Sprinkle with salt, pepper, and small amount of flour and continue to cook until browned on all sides. Add onion, carrot, celery, and tomato sauce. Pour boiling water over ribs to cover. Cover and cook until tender, about 1¹/₂ to 2 hours, or until meat is tender.

Makes 4 to 6 servings.

Barbecued Beef

A Knights of Columbus barbecue at Rancho San Antonio in Chatsworth featured this barbecued beef recipe with a green-chile-laden barbecue sauce.

4 to 5 pounds boneless beef
  shoulder roast
1 cup white vinegar
5 cups tomato juice
1 cup brown sugar,
  packed
1¹/₂ tablespoons
  Worcestershire sauce

1 teaspoon salt
¹/₂ teaspoon black pepper
1 teaspoon ground cumin
¹/₂ teaspoon red pepper
¹/₂ cup water
  Liquid smoke
  Rancho Barbecue Sauce

PLACE beef in a shallow pan. Combine vinegar, tomato juice, brown sugar, Worcestershire, salt, pepper, cumin, red pepper, and water. Marinate in refrigerator 3 to 4 hours, turning occasionally to coat meat with marinade. Remove meat from marinade. Do not shake off liquid clinging to meat. Place meat in Dutch oven. Do not add water. Cover tightly and bake at 325 degrees 4 to 5 hours. Add 1 or 2 drops of liquid smoke 1 hour before end of cooking time for smokey flavor. Beef should be very tender and stringy. Serve with Rancho Barbecue Sauce.

Makes 8 to 10 servings.

Rancho Barbecue Sauce

1 large onion
1 (4-ounce) can green chiles
2 cups finely diced celery

1 cup diced tomatoes
1 teaspoon salt
¹/₄ cup water

Put onion and drained green chiles through meat grinder, using a fine blade. Combine with celery, tomatoes, salt, and water, blending well. Chill.

Makes about 2 cups.

Oriental-Style Broccoli-Beef

1/2 pound flank steak	1/2 teaspoon salt
1 1/2 pounds broccoli	1/2 teaspoon sugar
2 teaspoons sherry	3/4 cup water
1/8 teaspoon black pepper	1/4 cup oil
2 teaspoons soy sauce	2 teaspoons cornstarch

Broccoli flowerets present a pleasant contrast to strips of flank steak in this delicious and easy Chinese dish.

PUT meat in freezer for a few minutes to firm before starting preparation. Cut cold meat across grain into thin slices. Wash broccoli. Cut flowerets from stalks. Cut stalks diagonally into 1/4-inch slices. Combine sherry, pepper, soy sauce, salt, sugar, and 1/2 cup water. Heat 2 tablespoons of oil in heavy skillet or electric fry pan set at 360 degrees. Add broccoli stalk slices. Cover skillet and shake. Cook for 2 minutes. Add flowerets. Cover and shake another 2 minutes. Check tenderness with fork. Broccoli should be crisp-tender. Place broccoli on hot platter. Place remaining 2 tablespoons oil in hot skillet. Add sliced meat. Brown quickly on both sides. Pour in soy sauce mixture. Cook 2 minutes, covered. Add cooked broccoli. Dissolve cornstarch in 1/4 cup water. Add to broccoli-meat mixture. Stir. Bring to boil.

Makes 6 servings.

Stir-Fried Beef with Oyster Sauce

8 ounces lean tender beef	4 cups oil for deep frying
1/2 teaspoon soda	2 cloves garlic, diced
1/4 teaspoon salt	6 slices carrot
1/8 teaspoon sugar	5 slices gingerroot
1 teaspoon cornstarch	5 green onions, cut in 1/2-inch
1 tablespoon beaten egg	slivers
3 tablespoons water	Sauce
1 tablespoon oil	1/2 teaspoon shao hsing wine

This Cantonese dish is a Chinese classic that came from a cooking teacher in Hong Kong.

CUT beef into thin slices and place in bowl. Add soda, salt, sugar, and cornstarch and mix. Add egg, water, and 1 tablespoon oil and mix again. Let stand 15 to 20 minutes. Heat wok. Add 4 cups oil to wok and heat until just hot. Add beef and fry until it changes color, about 1 minute. Remove from oil and drain. Drain off all but 1/2 tablespoon oil from wok. Add garlic, carrot, gingerroot, and green onions and stir-fry a few seconds. Return beef to wok and toss to heat through. Immediately add Sauce and stir-fry until beef is coated with a light glaze. Pour wine down sides of wok, stir, and turn mixture onto serving platter.

Makes 4 to 6 servings.

(continued on overleaf)

Sauce

1/4 teaspoon salt
1/4 teaspoon sugar
1/2 teaspoon MSG (optional)
    Dash black pepper
1/4 teaspoon cornstarch

1 1/2 teaspoons oyster sauce
2 tablespoons water
1/4 teaspoon dark soy sauce
    Dash sesame oil

Combine salt, sugar, MSG, pepper, and cornstarch. Blend in oyster sauce, water, soy sauce, and sesame oil. Stir before adding to beef mixture.

Mongolian Beef

Mongolian Beef made its debut in Los Angeles with the influx of immigrants from the Far East. The Sichuan peppercorn powder called for in this recipe from Wang Kung restaurant in Los Angeles's Chinatown can be found in Chinese markets.

1 pound lean beef
  Soy sauce
1/2 teaspoon salt
1 tablespoon sweet white
  wine
1/2 teaspoon Sichuan
  peppercorn powder

Oil
1 pound green onions
1 tablespoon sesame oil
3 tablespoons sliced garlic

SLICE beef very thin. (Meat will slice easily if partially frozen.) Place in bowl and add 1 tablespoon soy sauce, salt, wine, peppercorn powder, and 2 tablespoons oil. Cut green onions lengthwise, then in diagonal strips. Mix 1 tablespoon soy sauce and sesame oil in small bowl. Heat 1/2 cup oil in frying pan or wok until very hot. Add garlic and cook 3 seconds. Add beef and stir-fry over high heat 10 seconds. Add onion and sesame oil mixture and continue to stir-fry until thoroughly heated. Serve at once.

Makes 6 to 8 servings.

Oven Beef Burgundy

A slow-cooked oven version of beef stew seasoned with soy sauce and wine has been a reader favorite for years.

2 tablespoons soy sauce
2 tablespoons flour
2 pounds beef stew meat, cut
  in 1 1/2-inch cubes
4 medium carrots, peeled and
  cut into chunks
2 large onions, sliced

1 cup thinly sliced celery
1 clove garlic, minced
1/4 teaspoon black pepper
1/4 teaspoon marjoram
1/4 teaspoon thyme
1 cup dry red wine
1 cup sliced mushrooms

BLEND soy sauce with flour in a 2 1/2- to 3-quart Dutch oven. Add beef to soy sauce mixture and toss to coat meat. Add carrots, onions, celery, garlic, pepper, marjoram, thyme, and wine to meat. Stir gently to mix. Cover tightly and bake at 325 degrees 1 hour. Add mushrooms, stir gently, cover, and bake 1½ to 2 hours longer, or until meat and vegetables are tender. Serve with rice, noodles, or potatoes, if desired.

Makes 6 to 8 servings.

Argentinian Stew in a Pumpkin Shell

2 pounds beef stew meat, cut in 1½-inch cubes
1 large onion, chopped
2 cloves garlic, minced
3 tablespoons oil
2 large tomatoes, chopped
1 large green pepper, chopped
Salt, pepper
1 teaspoon sugar
1 cup dried apricots
3 white potatoes, peeled and diced
3 sweet potatoes, peeled and diced
2 cups beef broth
1 medium pumpkin
Melted butter or margarine
¼ cup dry sherry
1 (1-pound) can whole kernel corn, drained

Serve a rich and filling stew in a pumpkin shell. It's a wonderful conversation piece.

TRIM any excess fat from beef and cook with onion and garlic in oil until meat is browned. Add tomatoes, green pepper, 1 tablespoon salt, ½ teaspoon pepper, sugar, apricots, white potatoes, sweet potatoes, and broth. Cover and simmer 1 hour. Meanwhile, cut top off pumpkin and discard. Scoop out seeds and stringy membrane. Brush inside of pumpkin with butter and sprinkle lightly with salt and pepper. Stir sherry and corn into stew and spoon into pumpkin shell. Place shell in a shallow pan and bake at 325 degrees 1 hour, or until pumpkin meat is tender. Place pumpkin in large bowl and ladle out stew, scooping out some of the pumpkin with each stew serving.

Makes 6 servings.

Beef Stew

This stew, created by comedian Paul Lynde, relies entirely on canned vegetables. It is an ideal recipe for a slow cooker pot.

2 pounds beef stew meat, cut in 1-inch cubes
1 (1-pound) can diced carrots, drained
1 (1-pound) can small whole onions, drained
1 (1-pound) can whole tomatoes
1 (1-pound) can peas, drained
1 (1-pound) can cut green beans, drained
1 (1-pound) can small whole potatoes, drained
1/2 can beef consommé
1/4 cup quick-cooking tapioca
1 tablespoon brown sugar
1/2 cup fine dry bread crumbs
1 bay leaf
1/2 cup dry white wine
Salt, pepper

COMBINE meat, carrots, onions, tomatoes, peas, green beans, potatoes, consommé, tapioca, brown sugar, bread crumbs, bay leaf, and wine in large casserole. Season to taste with salt and pepper. Cover and bake at 250 degrees 6 to 7 hours.

Makes 8 to 10 servings.

Beef Jerky

Once found exclusively in hikers' backpacks or as free lunch snacks in taverns, beef jerky is riding a surge of popularity. Commercially made jerky is expensive but there's no need to buy it when it can be made so easily at home.

4 pounds flank steak
1/2 onion, diced
1/4 teaspoon thyme
2 bay leaves
2 tablespoons salt
2 cloves garlic, crushed
2 teaspoons black pepper
2 whole cloves
1/2 cup vinegar
1 cup dry red wine
1 cup Worcestershire sauce
1 cup soy sauce

TRIM fat and gristle, if any, from flank steak. Cut meat with grain into very thin slices. (Partially freeze first to make slicing easier.) Combine onion, thyme, bay leaves, salt, garlic, pepper, cloves, vinegar, wine, Worcestershire, and soy sauce. Pour marinade over steak strips to cover and marinate in refrigerator about 15 hours. Squeeze marinade from meat by rolling strips with rolling pin. Place meat on baking sheets or oven rack and dry in 175 degree oven 9 hours, turning once. If using rack, place foil under it to catch drippings.

Makes 40 to 50 strips.

ODAY'S leaner pork fits nicely into the lighter cuisine now favored by discriminating diners. Chinese, Japanese, and Mexican-style pork dishes which call for small amounts of pork serve the budget-conscious cook well, while traditional pork dishes such as baked pork chops and ham also have staunch supporters in the West. The latter is true undoubtedly because so many Californians are originally from elsewhere in this country. Once transplanted to the Golden State, however, few cooks can resist adding a touch of wine or some distinctive spices to their favorite old pork recipes.

The California life-style—informal, casual, with outdoor activities predominating—has had a major influence on the foods we prepare, serve, and enjoy. In our climate we can count on balmy weather for cookouts and our penchant for barbecue grilling has followed naturally. Some time-honored recipes from *The Times* pork collection, as might be expected, are those prepared on a charcoal grill. Favorite pork cuts for barbecuing—indoors or out—are thick, meaty country-style ribs or chops. Adept outdoor cooks who have learned the secret to keeping these cuts moist and juicy during the grilling like to baste them with highly seasoned barbecue sauces. Leftovers, if there are any, are served cold for breakfast or lunch the next day.

Baked Ham in Champagne, page 222

Baked Ham in Champagne

What could be more festive for the holidays than a ham baked in champagne? The recipe comes from Edward Norcio, resident host and executive chef at the Paul Masson Vineyards in Saratoga.

1 (9-pound) boneless ham
1 (1-pound) box light brown sugar
2 (⁴/₅ quart) bottles extra dry champagne

3 tablespoons honey
1¹/₂ teaspoons ground ginger
1¹/₂ teaspoons dry mustard

SCORE ham and place on rack in baking pan. Cover top with 1 cup brown sugar and pour over 1 bottle champagne. Bake at 325 degrees 2 hours. Combine remaining bottle champagne, remaining brown sugar, honey, ginger, and mustard and bring to rolling boil in saucepan. Lower heat and simmer while basting ham every 15 minutes until done. Garnish with pineapple slices and spiced apples, if desired.

Makes 15 to 20 servings.

Jelly-Glazed Ham

1 (8-pound) ready-to-eat boneless ham
1¹/₂ cups grape jelly

¹/₂ teaspoon dry mustard
1 tablespoon prepared horseradish

HEAT ham as directed on the label or at 325 degrees 1¹/₂ hours. Remove from oven and score, cutting diagonal lines ¹/₂-inch deep and 1 inch apart. Cut across lines to form diamond shapes. Combine jelly, mustard, and horseradish. Spoon mixture, small amounts at a time, at intervals, over ham throughout remainder of baking. Increase temperature to 425 degrees and bake until ham is browned and glazed, about 30 to 45 minutes.

Makes about 15 to 20 servings.

Graham-Crusted Baked Ham

A pretty ham platter for a holiday buffet—the sweet, tangy crumb coating adds a touch of extra flavor.

¹/₂ or 1 whole cooked ham
1¹/₃ cups brown sugar, packed
³/₄ cup Dijon-style mustard

³/₄ cup graham cracker crumbs
Cloves (optional)
Kiwi, figs, and grape clusters

BAKE ham on rack, uncovered. Allow 30 minuters per pound for half ham or 25 minutes per pound for whole ham. Ham should register

160 degrees when done. About 1 hour before ham is done, cut diagonal gashes across fat side to form diamonds. Combine brown sugar, mustard, and crumbs. Glaze ham with mixture, then stud with cloves. Return to oven 45 minutes. Increase heat to 425 degrees and bake 15 minutes longer. Serve hot or cold. Garnish with sliced kiwi, sliced figs, and grape clusters.

Makes 8 to 10 servings.

Barbecued Pork Chops

2¹/₂ cups water	1 teaspoon red pepper
1 tablespoon sugar	2 teaspoons chili powder
1 tablespoon black pepper	1 teaspoon hot pepper sauce
2 tablespoons butter or margarine	1 teaspoon dry mustard
¹/₄ cup vinegar	3 tablespoons Worcestershire sauce
1 tablespoon salt	6 pork loin chops, cut 1- to
¹/₄ cup chopped onion	1¹/₄-inches thick
1 clove garlic, minced	

COMBINE water, sugar, pepper, butter, vinegar, salt, onion, garlic, red pepper, chili powder, hot pepper sauce, mustard, and Worcestershire in 1-quart saucepan. Bring to boil, reduce heat, and simmer 5 minutes. Refrigerate overnight to blend flavors. Warm sauce before using. Place chops on grill over slow coals and grill 12 to 15 minutes on each side, turning and brushing frequently with sauce.

Makes 6 servings.

Barbecued Country-Style Pork Ribs

4 to 5 pounds country-style pork ribs	1 lemon, thinly sliced
1 teaspoon salt	1 onion, thinly sliced
	Barbecue Sauce

PLACE ribs in large Dutch oven or kettle with enough boiling water to cover. Add salt, lemon, and onion and cook 45 to 60 minutes. Drain ribs thoroughly, discarding lemon and onion slices. Brush ribs well with Barbecue Sauce and place over slow coals. Turn every 10 minutes, brushing frequently with sauce. Cook from 35 to 45 minutes, or until done and well coated with sauce. Serve with extra sauce.

Makes 8 servings.

Thick and meaty country-style ribs are favorites with barbecue experts. Parboiling them before grilling solves two problems: first, it eliminates much of their excess fat, and second, it reduces the amount of time needed to finish them off over the coals, leaving them moist and succulent.

(continued on overleaf)

Barbecue Sauce

2 tablespoons brown sugar
1 tablespoon salt
$1/4$ teaspoon black pepper
$2^1/4$ teaspoons chili powder
1 small clove garlic, mashed
1 tablespoon grated lemon peel

6 tablespoons lemon juice
6 tablespoons Worcestershire sauce
$2^1/4$ cups catsup
$3^3/4$ cups water

COMBINE brown sugar, salt, pepper, chili powder, garlic, lemon peel, lemon juice, Worcestershire, catsup, and water in saucepan. Bring to boil, reduce heat, and simmer for about 20 minutes, or until sauce is reduced to about 4 cups.

Baked Pork Chops

These pork chops get an old-fashioned flavor treatment that makes them extra tender and juicy.

$1/2$ teaspoon prepared mustard
1 tablespoon flour
1 tablespoon sugar
1 teaspoon salt
1 tablespoon vinegar

1 cup water
1 cup catsup
6 pork chops, cut $1^1/4$-inches thick

COMBINE mustard, flour, sugar, and salt. Add vinegar, water, and catsup and mix thoroughly. Pour mixture over chops in baking dish. Bake, covered, at 350 degrees $1^1/2$ to 2 hours.

Makes 6 servings.

Carne de Puerco en Chile Verde
(Pork with Green Chile)

One of the most popular Mexican dishes in Los Angeles, chile verde, as it is usually called, can be made with beef as well as pork.

1 pound pork or beef
Oil or lard
4 green chiles, toasted, peeled, and chopped
2 cloves garlic, crushed

1 medium onion, chopped
1 medium tomato, chopped
1 cup boiling water
Salt, pepper

CUT pork into small cubes. Sauté in oil until well browned. Drain off all but 1 tablespoon fat. Add chopped chiles, garlic, onion, tomato, and water and season to taste with salt and pepper. Cover tightly and simmer 1 hour.

Makes 4 servings.

Chorizo

2 pounds coarsely ground
    lean pork
1/4 pound pork fat, finely
    chopped (optional)
2 tablespoons paprika
2 tablespoons pasilla chili
    powder
1 teaspoon coarsely ground
    black pepper

1/2 teaspoon cinnamon
1/2 teaspoon ground cloves
1/4 teaspoon coriander seeds
1/4 teaspoon ground ginger
1 teaspoon oregano, crushed
1 teaspoon cumin
6 cloves garlic, crushed
1/2 cup white vinegar
1/2 cup sherry or brandy

George York, a food technologist at the University of California at Davis, gave us his recipe for the spicy Mexican sausage called chorizo.

COMBINE pork meat and fat thoroughly. Add paprika, chili powder, pepper, cinnamon, cloves, coriander, ginger, oregano, cumin, garlic, vinegar, and sherry. Mix well with hands. Place in earthenware crock or glass jar in a cool place (50 to 60 degrees) for at least 24 hours, or preferably 2 to 3 days. Freeze for longer storage. To serve, crumble and sauté for use in casseroles or form into thin patties and fry until done.

Makes about 2³/₄ pounds.

Note: Pasilla chili powder can be found in Mexican or Latin American specialty food stores. If unavailable, substitute any good, mild to medium hot chili powder.

Chinese Roast Pork

1/4 teaspoon salt
1/4 cup sugar
1 1/2 tablespoons thin soy sauce
1 1/2 teaspoons oyster sauce
1/4 teaspoon sesame oil
1/2 teaspoon MSG (optional)
1 tablespoon white or rosé
    wine
1 (1-inch) piece gingerroot,
    peeled and minced

1 1/2 teaspoons canned hoisin
    sauce
1 tablespoon bottled Chinese
    bean paste
1 clove garlic, minced
2 shallots, diced
1 1/4 pounds pork tenderloin
2 tablespoons honey
2 drops red food color

Chinese roast pork enjoys a great following among Los Angeles hosts and hostesses.

COMBINE salt, sugar, soy sauce, oyster sauce, sesame oil, MSG, wine, gingerroot, hoisin sauce, bean paste, garlic, and shallots in large bowl. Add pork, baste thoroughly, and marinate for 1¹/₂ to 2 hours. Place pork on rack in roasting pan. Bake at 425 degrees 15 minutes. Turn meat and bake 7 minutes longer. Remove pork and brush with honey mixed with food color. Return to oven for 10 minutes, or until done. Cut meat crosswise into thin slices and serve hot or cold.

Makes 4 to 6 servings.

Shredded Pork with Yu Shon Sauce

Sichuan-born chef P. C. Lee showed The Times *food staff how remarkably simple it is to prepare what looks like a complicated Chinese dish.*

1/4 cup wood ears (dried black fungus)
1/2 pound boneless pork, trimmed of fat
7 water chestnuts
Soy sauce
2 1/2 teaspoons cornstarch
1/2 beaten egg
1/2 teaspoon cornstarch mixed with 1 tablespoon water
1 teaspoon mixed minced garlic and ginger

2 tablespoons sugar
2 tablespoons chicken broth or water
1 1/2 tablespoons vinegar
4 cups oil
1 teaspoon hot bean paste
1 tablespoon chopped green onion
1/2 teaspoon sesame oil

SOAK wood ears in warm water until softened, about 1/2 hour. Rinse well, then shred. Cut pork in paper-thin slices and shred. Crush water chestnuts with heavy cleaver and shred. Combine pork, 2 teaspoons soy sauce, cornstarch, and egg and mix well. Meat mixture should be moist. If needed, add a little of the cornstarch-water solution. Combine 2 tablespoons soy sauce, garlic and ginger, sugar, broth, and vinegar. Heat oil in wok or large skillet. Add pork mixture, wood ears, and water chestnuts and cook, stirring gently, just until meat changes color. Immediately pour meat and vegetables into a large strainer set in a bowl to drain off oil. Return 1 to 2 tablespoons oil to pan. Mix hot bean paste with oil in pan. Add meat mixture and stir-fry. Add soy sauce mixture and continue cooking. Stir in green onion. Add remaining cornstarch solution and stir. Mix in sesame oil and turn out on serving plate.

Makes 4 servings.

Pork Spareribs with Potatoes

Oriental seasonings add a new flavor dimension to an old-fashioned meat-and-potatoes dish that won a spot in our ''My Best Recipe'' column for Ruth Leong.

1 pound pork spareribs, cut into 1 1/2-inch pieces
2 tablespoons oil, butter, or margarine
2 potatoes, peeled and cut into 1-inch cubes

1/2 cup onion slices
1 tablespoon sherry
3 tablespoons oyster sauce
2 tablespoons soy sauce
1/2 teaspoon sugar

LIGHTLY brown spareribs in hot skillet. Add oil, potatoes, onion, and sherry and cook 5 to 10 minutes, or until potatoes and onion are lightly browned. Mix in oyster sauce, soy sauce, and sugar and simmer 20 to 30 minutes.

Makes 2 to 3 servings.

Ribs Diablo

7 pounds pork spareribs or
  10 pounds beef back ribs
1 medium onion, minced
2 cloves garlic, minced
1 tablespoon butter or
  margarine
1¹/₂ cups catsup
 ¹/₃ cup bottled steak sauce

³/₄ cup honey
1 tablespoon Worcestershire
  sauce
8 ounces beer
1 tablespoon seasoned salt
1 tablespoon hot pepper
  sauce

The Biltmore Hotel in down-town Los Angeles roasts pork or beef ribs in a spicy sauce that has a real bite to it.

BOIL ribs in water to cover 1 hour. Meanwhile sauté onion and garlic lightly in butter. Add catsup, steak sauce, honey, Worcestershire, beer, seasoned salt, and hot pepper sauce. Bring to boil, reduce heat, and simmer 30 minutes. Drain ribs and bake at 350 degrees 30 to 40 minutes or until brown, basting often with sauce during the last 15 minutes of cooking until glazed.

Makes 6 to 8 servings.

Corn Dogs

1 cup flour
2 tablespoons sugar
1¹/₂ teaspoons baking powder
1 teaspoon salt
²/₃ cup cornmeal
2 tablespoons shortening

1 egg, lightly beaten
³/₄ cup milk
1 pound frankfurters
  Oil for deep frying
  Catsup
  Prepared mustard

Beachfront stands along California's southern coast sell these cornmeal-coated hot dogs on a stick. Kids love 'em.

SIFT together flour, sugar, baking powder, and salt. Stir in cornmeal. Cut in shortening until mixture resembles coarse meal. Mix egg and milk and stir into cornmeal mixture until blended. Insert wooden skewer into end of each frank. Coat evenly with batter. Fry in deep oil heated to 375 degrees until brown. Drain on paper towels and serve with catsup and mustard.

Makes 10 servings.

Katsu Donburi
(Pork-Topped Rice)

Donburi refers to food served on top of rice in a bowl. This version comes from the Yamato, a Japanese restaurant in Century City, near Beverly Hills.

6 center-cut pork loin chops,
  $^1/_2$-inch thick
  Salt, pepper
2 egg yolks, beaten
2 tablespoons water
$^3/_4$ cup fine dry bread crumbs
1 cup oil
$^1/_2$ pound mushrooms, chopped

1 large onion, chopped
2 tablespoons butter or
  margarine
$^1/_2$ cup soy sauce
$1^1/_2$ cups chicken broth
6 eggs
  Japanese-Style Rice

SEASON chops to taste with salt and pepper. Dip chops in egg yolks mixed with water, then in bread crumbs. Heat oil, add chops, and fry 4 to 5 minutes on each side. Cut meat from chops in strips and set aside. Melt butter in large skillet. Add mushrooms and onion and sauté until tender. Add meat and blend in soy sauce and broth. Bring to boil. Beat eggs and add to mixture. Cook until eggs are firm. Place meat and egg mixture over Japanese-Style Rice.

Makes 6 servings.

Japanese-Style Rice

3 cups rice
$1^3/_4$ cups water

Wash and drain rice. Bring rice and water to boil. Reduce heat and simmer 15 minutes. Remove from heat and let stand 7 minutes.

Makes 6 servings.

VEGETABLES

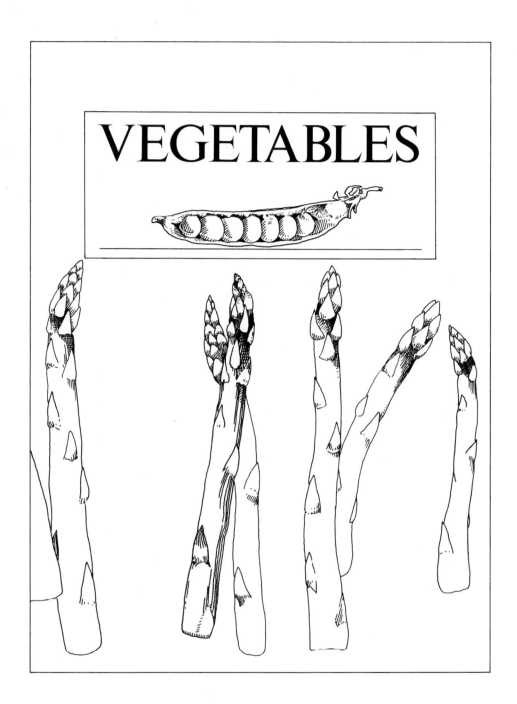

PRODUCE sections in Los Angeles area markets abound with an almost opulent abundance of vegetables. And westerners probably do more—and less—with them than cooks elsewhere.

The health-food movement, which began in California, spotlighted vegetables as main dishes and brought increased attention to their many nutritional virtues. Thus it is that they turn up in all sorts of unexpected places now, from appetizers to vegetable loaves that are the centerpiece of a meatless meal, to desserts like the zucchini and carrot cakes that have an almost fanatic following.

In their traditional supporting role, complementing a main dish, genuinely fresh vegetables are treated with the respect they deserve. Simple sautés and steamed vegetables arc probably our favorites, but we also are enthralled with preparations like stuffed zucchini and other vegetarian concoctions that take more time than most, but are too much fun to overlook.

It must be noted, however, that in spite of our predilection for the fresh product, we still include dried beans and peas on our menus frequently. A western cookout without a pot of barbecued beans simply would not be complete.

A quick look through the recipes that follow will make it easy to see that in this part of the country, certainly, vegetables are shedding their supporting character status in favor of equal, if not top, billing with meats.

Artichokes, page 232

Artichokes

6 artichokes
2 tablespoons lemon juice

1¹/₂ teaspoons salt
1 clove garlic (optional)

WASH artichokes thoroughly and trim stems to 1 inch. Remove tough bottom leaves. Trim ¹/₂-inch from spiked leaf tips with sharp knife or scissors. Stand artichokes upright in 1 inch boiling water to which lemon juice and salt have been added. Mash garlic and add to liquid. Cover tightly and cook about 45 minutes or until stems easily can be pierced with fork. Add water as needed. Remove artichokes from water and invert to drain thoroughly. Serve hot or chilled with a dip, or stuff. To stuff, gently spread center leaves apart and with a spoon scrape out and discard center thistle portion or choke. Fill center of artichoke loosely with desired stuffing. Spoon additional stuffing between leaves.

Makes 6 servings.

Stuffed Artichokes

This stuffed artichoke recipe came from a family of artichoke packers and shippers in Castroville, the artichoke capital of the world.

6 large artichokes
Olive oil
Salt
2 cups dry French bread
crumbs
1 clove garlic, crushed
1 tablespoon grated Parmesan
cheese

2 tablespoons chopped parsley
6 slices bacon
6 slices tomato
Basil

RINSE artichokes. With sharp knife, remove stems and cut 1 inch straight across tops. Place artichokes upside down on work surface, then firmly press end of each to spread leaves apart. With a sharp spoon, dig out center leaves and fuzzy portion. Drizzle with olive oil and salt, getting oil and salt between each leaf layer. Mix bread crumbs, garlic, cheese, parsley, and ¹/₂ teaspoon salt and stuff into centers and between leaf layers. Set artichokes in baking pan with about 1 inch hot water and 1 tablespoon olive oil. Place 1 slice bacon and 1 slice tomato on each artichoke. Sprinkle with basil. Cover and steam in 350-degree oven for 45 to 60 minutes, or until artichoke hearts are tender when pierced with fork. Drain any remaining liquid and continue to cook until leaves are dried and crispy, about 30 minutes more with cover removed.

Makes 6 servings.

Artichoke Heart Fritters

4 medium artichokes
1 tablespoon lemon juice
³/₄ teaspoon salt
1 egg, beaten
¹/₃ cup beer or milk

Dash black pepper
³/₄ cup prepared buttermilk
  biscuit mix
Oil for deep frying

TRIM hearts from artichokes. Quarter hearts and add to 1 inch boiling water seasoned with lemon juice and ¹/₂ teaspoon salt. Cover and cook about 20 minutes, or until just tender. Drain. Combine egg, beer, ¹/₄ teaspoon salt, and pepper. Stir in biscuit mix. Dip artichokes in batter and fry until browned in oil heated to 350 degrees, turning fritters once. Drain on paper towels. Serve hot as meat accompaniment.

Makes 16.

Fried Baby Artichokes

12 baby artichokes (2 to 3
   inches long)
2 eggs, beaten
³/₄ cup fine dry bread crumbs
2 tablespoons grated
   Parmesan cheese

¹/₄ teaspoon salt
¹/₈ teaspoon black pepper
¹/₄ teaspoon oregano
   Oil for deep frying

BABY artichokes are so tender the choke can be eaten. Cook in ¹/₂-inch boiling salted water 20 to 30 minutes, or until tender. Drain. Test underside of artichokes for tenderness with fork. Dip well-drained whole artichokes in beaten eggs, then roll in mixture of bread crumbs, Parmesan cheese, salt, pepper, and oregano. Fry until golden brown in oil heated to 360 degrees.

Makes 4 to 6 servings.

Stir-Fried Asparagus

1 whole chicken breast
1 pound asparagus
2 tablespoons oil
2 cloves garlic, minced
1/2 cup chicken broth
1 tablespoon sherry
2 tablespoons soy sauce
2 teaspoons cornstarch

2 teaspoons cold water
1/2 teaspoon MSG (optional)
1/4 teaspoon sugar
1/2 teaspoon salt
1/8 teaspoon black pepper
2 tablespoons toasted sesame
 seeds

SKIN, bone, and cut chicken breast into thin strips. Snap off lower portions of asparagus. Wash spears and slice diagonally in 2-inch pieces, leaving tips whole. Heat skillet or wok and add 1 tablespoon oil and garlic. Add asparagus and stir-fry 30 seconds. Remove asparagus from skillet and keep warm. Reheat skillet and add remaining oil. Add chicken and stir-fry 30 seconds. Add chicken broth, sherry, and soy sauce and cook 2 to 3 minutes, or until chicken turns white. Add asparagus and stir with chicken 1 minute. Blend cornstarch and water. Stir into asparagus mixture and cook, stirring, until thickened. Sprinkle with MSG, sugar, salt, pepper, and sesame seeds.

Makes 4 servings.

Asparagus and Beef

General Lee's, a Los Angeles Chinatown restaurant, serves asparagus with thinly sliced steak in this easy stir-fry dish. The dow see (fermented black beans) the recipe calls for is available in most Chinese markets.

1 tablespoon dow see
 (fermented black beans)
1 clove garlic
1 1/2 pounds asparagus, sliced
 diagonally in 1/2-inch
 pieces
2 cups boiling water
1/4 cup oil

1/2 pound flank steak, thinly
 sliced
1 1/2 teaspoons salt
1/2 cup chicken stock
1 tablespoon cornstarch
1/2 teaspoon sugar
1 tablespoon water

SOAK black beans in warm water a few minutes. Drain and mash beans with garlic. Drop asparagus in boiling water and boil 2 minutes. Drain immediately. Heat 2 tablespoons oil in skillet or wok until very hot. Add beef, stir quickly, then remove from pan. Add remaining oil to skillet and heat. Add bean mixture and stir over high heat for a few seconds. Add salt and asparagus. Stir-fry 1 minute. Add chicken stock, cover, and cook 2 minutes. Mix cornstarch, sugar, and water and stir into meat mixture. Stir until sauce is thick and smooth. Add beef and blend quickly.

Makes 4 to 6 servings.

Asparagus Maltaise

2 pounds asparagus
3 egg yolks
2 tablespoons lemon juice
1/4 teaspoon salt

1/2 cup butter or margarine
1 teaspoon grated orange
  peel
3 tablespoons orange juice

SNAP tough ends from asparagus and discard. Place asparagus in 1 inch water in large skillet, bring to boil, reduce heat, cover, and simmer until tender, 5 to 8 minutes. Blend together egg yolks, lemon juice, and salt in saucepan or top of double boiler. Add half of butter and stir constantly over low heat or boiling water until butter melts. Add remaining butter and continue stirring until it melts and sauce thickens. Stir in orange peel and juice. Drain asparagus and serve topped with sauce.

Makes 4 servings.

Asparagus with Browned Butter

1/4 cup butter or margarine
1 tablespoon lemon juice

2 1/2 pounds asparagus, cooked
  Chopped parsley

The simple treatment is best for crisp, fresh asparagus.

HEAT butter in saucepan until pale brown. Add lemon juice and mix well. Serve over hot asparagus. Sprinkle with parsley.

Makes 6 servings.

Asparagus Cantonese

2 tablespoons oil
1 clove garlic, crushed
2 pounds asparagus, sliced
  diagonally

Salt, pepper

HEAT oil in skillet over high heat almost to smoking point. Stir in garlic, then add asparagus. Cover and shake pan vigorously for 3 to 5 minutes. Asparagus should be crisp-tender. Season to taste with salt and pepper.

Makes 8 servings.

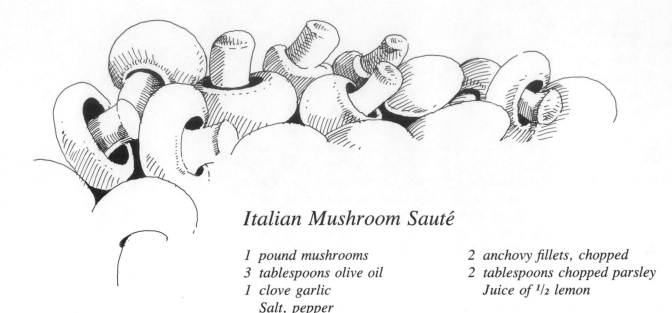

Italian Mushroom Sauté

1 pound mushrooms
3 tablespoons olive oil
1 clove garlic
   Salt, pepper
1 tablespoon butter or
   margarine

2 anchovy fillets, chopped
2 tablespoons chopped parsley
   Juice of ¹/₂ lemon

WASH mushrooms, dry, and slice thinly. Heat oil in large skillet, add garlic, and brown lightly. Remove garlic. Add mushrooms and season to taste with salt and pepper. Cook over high heat until liquid evaporates. Add butter, anchovies, and parsley. Cook over medium heat 5 minutes. Remove from heat, stir in lemon juice, and serve.

Makes 4 servings.

Stuffed Mushrooms

Robaire's, a very old Los Angeles restaurant specializing in French cuisine, shared this excellent recipe for chicken-stuffed mushrooms.

1 whole chicken breast
2 dozen medium mushrooms
   Juice of ¹/₂ lemon
2 tablespoons butter or
   margarine

1 clove garlic, crushed
1 teaspoon chopped parsley
   Salt, pepper
1 egg yolk, lightly beaten
   Fine dry bread crumbs

COOK chicken in boiling salted water until tender. Drain, reserving broth. Remove skin and bones and dice meat finely. Wash and dry mushrooms. Remove, finely chop, and reserve stems. Sprinkle mushroom caps with lemon juice. Melt butter and add stems and garlic and cook 10 minutes, stirring now and then. Add 2 or 3 tablespoons reserved chicken broth and parsley. Season to taste with salt and pepper. Add chicken and egg yolk and mix well. Spoon stuffing into mushroom cavities. Arrange on lightly greased baking sheet and sprinkle with bread crumbs. Bake at 350 degrees 15 to 20 minutes. Serve hot.

Makes 6 servings.

Stuffed Mushrooms Parmigiana

12 large mushrooms
2 tablespoons butter or
  margarine
1 medium onion, finely
  chopped
2 ounces pepperoni, finely
  diced
1/4 cup finely chopped green
  pepper
1 small clove garlic, minced

1/2 cup finely crushed cracker
  crumbs
3 tablespoons grated
  Parmesan cheese
1 tablespoon minced parsley
1/4 teaspoon oregano
  Seasoned salt
  Pepper
1/3 cup chicken broth

WASH and dry mushrooms. Remove, finely chop, and reserve stems. Melt butter in skillet. Add onion, pepperoni, green pepper, garlic, and chopped mushroom stems. Cook until all vegetables are tender but not brown. Add crumbs, cheese, parsley, and oregano and season to taste with seasoned salt and pepper. Mix well. Stir in chicken broth. Spoon filling into mushroom caps, rounding tops. Place caps in shallow baking pan with about 1/4 inch of water. Bake, uncovered, at 325 degrees 25 minutes, or until heated through.

Makes 12 stuffed mushrooms.

Stir-Fried Mushrooms and Broccoli

1 pound mushrooms
1 pound broccoli
1/4 cup butter or margarine
1/2 cup chopped onion
3 tablespoons oil
1 clove garlic, minced
1/3 cup sliced canned water
  chestnuts

1 tablespoon cornstarch
1 teaspoon sugar
1/2 teaspoon salt
1/4 teaspoon ginger
1 tablespoon soy sauce
1 chicken bouillon cube
3/4 cup boiling water

WASH, pat dry, and halve mushrooms. Wash and trim broccoli. Cut stems into 1/2-inch pieces and separate tops into flowerets. Melt butter in wok or large skillet and add onion. Sauté for 2 minutes. Add mushrooms and sauté for 5 minutes. Remove from wok and set aside. In same wok heat oil and add broccoli and garlic. Stir-fry 3 minutes. Add water chestnuts and stir-fry 2 minutes longer. Blend cornstarch, sugar, salt, and ginger with soy sauce. Dissolve bouillon cube in boiling water. Stir into cornstarch mixture. Pour into wok. Cook and stir until mixture boils and thickens. Reduce heat and simmer, covered, until broccoli is just crisp-tender, about 5 minutes. Return sautéed mushrooms to wok. Heat until hot. Served with Chinese noodles, if desired.

Makes 8 servings.

French-Fried Mushrooms

These delectable mushrooms go well with steak or poultry.

1½ pounds large mushrooms
1 cup flour
4 eggs, beaten

1 cup seasoned bread crumbs
Oil for deep frying

WASH mushrooms, pat dry, and remove stems. Coat mushrooms with flour, dip into eggs, then into bread crumbs. Deep-fry in hot oil about 3 minutes, until golden brown.

Makes 6 to 8 servings.

Santa Maria Beans

In Santa Maria, California, a spot famous for its barbecue, teams of cooks prepare a menu that includes these beans. Traditionally small pink beans grown locally would be used, but small red beans or pintos can be substituted.

1 pound dry small pink, red, or pinto beans
1 slice bacon, diced
¼ cup diced cooked ham
1 small clove garlic, minced
¾ cup tomato puree

¼ cup canned red chile sauce
1 tablespoon sugar
1 teaspoon dry mustard
1 teaspoon salt
Dash MSG (optional)

COVER beans with water and soak overnight. Drain and cover with fresh cold water and simmer 2 hours, or until tender. Meanwhile, sauté bacon and ham until lightly browned. Add garlic and sauté 1 or 2 minutes, then add tomato puree, chile sauce, sugar, mustard, salt, and MSG. Drain most of the liquid off the beans and stir in sauce. Keep warm over very low heat, or in low oven until ready to serve.

Makes 6 to 8 servings.

Cleopatra Smith's Chili Beans

Writer Mary Loos supplied this zesty bean recipe that was handed down from her great-grandmother, who sailed around Cape Horn to settle in Northern California.

2 pounds dry pinto beans
1 large ham bone and scraps from baked ham or 1 pound cooked ham, cubed
2 chorizos or 3 hot Italian sausages
3 tablespoons oil
1 (8-ounce) can tomato sauce
1 large onion
4 whole cloves

1 green pepper, quartered and seeded
2 cloves garlic
Salt, pepper
1 tablespoon chili powder
1 teaspoon ground ginger
1 teaspoon oregano
1 chile pequin, crushed
Shredded Monterey Jack cheese

WASH beans and drain. Place in Dutch oven and cover with cold water. Let soak several hours or overnight. Do not drain. Add ham bone and scraps to beans. Remove casings from chorizos, cut up, and fry in oil until browned and crumbly. Stir in tomato sauce and add to beans. Quarter onion and stick each quarter with 1 clove. Add to beans along with green pepper and garlic. Bring beans to boil, reduce heat, and simmer, covered, for 1 hour, stirring occasionally. Season to taste with salt and pepper. Add chili powder, ginger, oregano, and chile pequin. Cover and cook 3 hours longer, stirring occasionally. Add water as needed to keep beans covered. Cut into beans with spoon to break up green pepper and onion. Uncover during last hour of cooking time so beans will thicken. If beans are to be served in bowls like soup, add more water. Otherwise, turn into casserole, cover with cheese, and bake at 350 degrees until cheese is melted and beans are heated through. If desired, served chopped onion and cilantro on the side.

Makes about 8 servings.

Note: A chile pequin is a tiny, very hot chile. If not available, substitute any other small hot chile.

Frijoles Negros
(Black Beans)

1 pound dry black beans	1 bay leaf
2 onions	1/2 cup canned tomato sauce
2 green peppers	Salt
Oil or lard	1 tablespoon wine vinegar
3 cloves garlic, crushed	Olive oil
1/2 teaspoon ground cumin	Chopped onion

Try Cuban-style black beans, sparked with vinegar and cumin, in place of the usual baked beans at your next cookout.

WASH beans and soak overnight in heavy saucepan with enough water to come 2 inches over beans. Cut 1 onion and 1 green pepper in halves and add to beans. Bring beans and soaking water to boil, cover, and simmer 1 1/2 hours, or until beans are tender. Heat 5 tablespoons oil in skillet. Chop remaining onion and green pepper and add with garlic to skillet. Cook until onion is translucent and golden. Add cumin and bay leaf and cook, stirring, 5 minutes. Add tomato sauce and cook 5 minutes longer. Remove bay leaf and place mixture in blender container. Blend until smooth and add to beans. If sauce is too thick, add more water. Season to taste with salt. Remove and discard onion and green pepper halves and simmer until flavors blend and sauce thickens slightly. Add wine vinegar and stir. Float a little olive oil on surface of beans and let stand awhile before serving. Accompany beans with chopped onion, if desired.

Makes 8 servings.

Note: If black beans, sometimes known as turtle beans, are not available in your supermarket, they can be found in Latin American and Mexican food stores.

Burgundy Beans

Garlicky burgundy beans can be served at a party buffet or as a family supper dish.

4 pounds dry pinto beans
2 pounds salt pork, cut in $^1/_2$-inch cubes
$^1/_4$ cup chili powder
1 head garlic, separated into cloves and crushed
1 medium onion, chopped
Salt
3 cups burgundy

WASH beans and cover with several inches of water. Add salt pork and simmer, adding water as it evaporates. After 1 hour add 1 tablespoon chili powder. After 2 hours add garlic, onion, and another 1 tablespoon chili powder. After 4 hours season to taste with salt and add burgundy and remaining chili powder. Simmer, uncovered, about 15 minutes longer to blend spices.

Makes 14 to 18 servings.

Spicy Refried Beans

$1^1/_2$ cups dry pinto beans
$4^1/_2$ cups water
5 slices bacon, diced
$^3/_4$ cup chopped onion
1 tablespoon chili powder
Salt, pepper
Shredded Monterey Jack or cheddar cheese

COVER beans with hot water and soak overnight. Drain off water, add fresh hot water, bring to boil, and boil gently until tender, about 4 hours. Brown bacon in skillet. Add onion and cook until tender. Add beans and cooking liquid. Stir and mash beans. Add chili powder, season to taste with salt and pepper, and stir until mixture is thick. Turn into a serving bowl and sprinkle with cheese to taste.

Makes 6 servings.

Green Beans with Almonds

$2^1/_2$ pounds green beans
$^1/_2$ pound butter or margarine
$^1/_2$ pound bacon, cooked and crumbled
$^1/_4$ cup sliced blanched almonds
1 teaspoon MSG (optional)
$^1/_4$ teaspoon garlic powder
$^1/_4$ teaspoon salt

SNAP off tough ends and remove strings from beans. Cut in halves and cook, covered, in 1 inch boiling water 20 minutes or until tender.

Drain. Melt butter in saucepan and add bacon, almonds, MSG, garlic powder, and salt. Pour over green beans, toss, and serve at once.

Makes 8 servings.

Haricots Verts à la Grecque
(Marinated Green Beans)

1 pound haricots verts
1/2 cup olive oil
1/3 cup vinegar
1/3 cup dry white wine
1 teaspoon salt
1/2 teaspoon black pepper

1 bay leaf
1 or 2 cloves garlic, minced
Dash hot pepper sauce
1 teaspoon tarragon, oregano, or basil, crushed
Chopped parsley

Haricots verts, thin, delicate French green beans, are served marinated and chilled as a salad at some elegant Los Angeles restaurants.

RINSE and snap off ends of beans. Combine oil, vinegar, wine, salt, pepper, bay leaf, garlic, hot pepper sauce, and tarragon in large saucepan. Add beans and water barely to cover. Bring to boil very slowly, then reduce heat and simmer, covered, until beans are crisp-tender, about 12 to 14 minutes. Remove from heat, taste liquid for seasoning, and add more salt, if needed. Refrigerate beans in liquid. To serve, drain beans and sprinkle with chopped parsley.

Makes 4 to 6 servings.

Julie's Bean Dish

1 (10-ounce) package frozen baby lima beans
1 medium onion, minced
3 tablespoons bacon drippings
3 or 4 bacon slices, cooked and crumbled
1 (1-pound) can pork and beans

1 (1-pound) can kidney beans
1/2 cup catsup
3 tablespoons vinegar
1 tablespoon brown sugar
1 teaspoon dry mustard
1 teaspoon salt
1/4 teaspoon black pepper

Julie Byrne, a former Times *writer, shared her favorite buffet bean dish with the Food Section staff one Christmas many years ago.*

COOK limas 10 minutes as directed on package. Place onion, bacon drippings, bacon, pork and beans, undrained limas, and kidney beans in 2 1/2-quart casserole. Combine catsup, vinegar, brown sugar, mustard, salt, and pepper and gently stir into bean mixture. Cover and bake at 350 degrees 1 hour.

Makes 6 servings.

Lima Bean Health Loaf

Vegetarians and non-vegetarians alike find this sturdy, meatless loaf a good main dish.

1 cup dry lima beans
¹/₄ cup butter or margarine
1 small onion, chopped
1 cup thinly sliced celery
¹/₃ cup flour
1 cup skim milk
1 egg, beaten

1 cup soft, fine whole wheat
   bread crumbs
1¹/₂ cups chopped carrots
1 teaspoon salt
¹/₄ teaspoon black pepper
¹/₂ cup chopped peanuts
   American cheese slices

SOAK beans overnight in cold water. Drain, rinse, and cook in water to cover until tender, about 1¹/₂ hours. Drain beans and mash. Melt butter in saucepan, add onion, and sauté about 3 minutes. Add celery, cover, and cook until tender. Stir in flour and cook 2 minutes. Add milk, stirring until thickened. Remove from heat and stir in beaten egg. Add crumbs, carrots, salt, pepper, and peanuts. Spoon mixture into greased 8 x 4-inch loaf pan and bake at 375 degrees 35 to 45 minutes. Arrange cheese slices over loaf and bake until cheese melts.

Makes 6 servings.

Zucchini Lasagna

This noodleless cheese-rich lasagna was developed by a vegetarian for a school potluck supper.

6 to 8 large zucchini
   1 quart bottled thick
      marinara sauce
   1 pound ricotta cheese
   1 large onion, sliced
   ¹/₄ pound mushrooms,
      sliced
   1 tablespoon oregano,
      crushed

1 tablespoon basil, crushed
   Salt, pepper
1 pound mozzarella cheese,
   sliced
¹/₂ cup grated Parmesan
   cheese
   Toasted sunflower seeds
   (optional)

SLICE zucchini ¹/₂-inch thick. Spread a thick layer of marinara sauce in 13 x 9-inch baking dish. Add a layer of zucchini slices, then a layer of ricotta. Top with onion and mushrooms, then sprinkle with oregano and basil. Season to taste with salt and pepper. Top with a layer of mozzarella cheese slices. Cover with a second layer of sauce and repeat layering process, ending with mozzarella cheese. Sprinkle with Parmesan cheese and garnish with sunflower seeds and a few slices of zucchini or mushrooms, if desired. Bake at 350 degrees 45 minutes, or until zucchini is cooked but not mushy.

Makes 6 to 8 servings.

Note: For a non-vegetarian dish, use meat sauce or add sausage or pepperoni to marinara sauce.

Vegetarian Stuffed Zucchini

8 evenly shaped zucchini
1 large onion, diced
1 large green pepper, diced
³/4 cup butter or margarine
1 (10-ounce) package frozen
   chopped spinach, thawed
   and well drained
1 (4-ounce) can mushroom
   stems and pieces, drained
2 tablespoons diced canned
   pimiento
2 large eggs
1¹/3 cups fine dry bread
   crumbs

1¹/2 tablespoons thyme
   Salt
   Garlic powder
   Onion powder
   Nutmeg
3 (8-ounce) cans tomato
   sauce
   Oregano
¹/3 cup burgundy
¹/2 pound Swiss cheese,
   shredded

In a perfect example of the way recipes circulate, the Broadway department stores adapted one of our recipes for this vegetarian-style stuffed zucchini dish.

CUT zucchini in halves lengthwise and scoop out seeds, being careful to leave enough flesh intact. Steam zucchini shells 3 to 4 minutes or until crisp-tender. Cool. Sauté onion and green pepper in butter. Add spinach and stir to combine and coat well. Cool, then add mushrooms, pimiento, eggs, bread crumbs, and thyme. Season to taste with salt, garlic powder, onion powder, and nutmeg. Mix well. Fill each zucchini shell with about 2 or 3 tablespoons filling. Season tomato sauce to taste with salt, garlic powder, onion powder, and oregano. Add burgundy. Place zucchini in large baking pan and cover with seasoned tomato sauce. Sprinkle with Swiss cheese and bake at 325 degrees 20 minutes, or until cheese is bubbly and zucchini is tender. Serve over rice, if desired.

Makes 8 servings.

Zucchini Sauté

3 tablespoons butter or
   margarine
1 small clove garlic, crushed
4 to 6 zucchini, sliced

   Salt, pepper
2 tablespoons grated
   Parmesan cheese

There are few side dishes that provide so much satisfaction for so little work as this easy sautéed zucchini.

MELT butter in large skillet, add garlic and zucchini, and sauté 2 to 3 minutes. Season to taste with salt and pepper. Cover and cook over low heat for 10 to 12 minutes, or until zucchini is tender. Sprinkle with cheese just before serving.

Makes 4 to 6 servings.

Zucchini Monterey

Clifton's Silver Spoon cafeteria in downtown Los Angeles came up with this California-style zucchini dish which won the hearts and taste buds of their customers.

1¹/2 pounds zucchini, cubed
4 eggs, lightly beaten
¹/2 cup milk
¹/2 teaspoon MSG (optional)
1 teaspoon salt
    Dash red pepper
2 teaspoons baking powder
3 tablespoons flour
¹/4 cup chopped parsley
1 (4-ounce) can diced green chiles
2 tablespoons diced pimiento
1 pound Monterey Jack cheese, shredded
1¹/2 teaspoons oil
¹/3 cup fine dry bread crumbs
1 tablespoon butter or margarine

STEAM zucchini over a small amount of salted water until crisp-tender. Combine eggs, milk, MSG, salt, red pepper, baking powder, flour, and parsley. Mix well to remove lumps. Add chiles, pimiento, and cheese and stir thoroughly. Add steamed, well-drained zucchini and stir gently. Grease a 2-quart casserole and dust with some of the bread crumbs. Turn zucchini mixture into casserole and sprinkle with remaining crumbs. Dot with butter and bake at 350 degrees 55 minutes.

Makes 5 servings.

Spaghetti Squash with Cheese

Spaghetti squash can be served just with butter, or it can be sauced and seasoned in as many ways as the pasta for which it is named.

1 spaghetti squash, about 4 pounds
2 tablespoons butter or margarine
¹/8 cup minced onion
¹/4 cup diced green pepper
¹/4 cup diced red pepper
¹/2 teaspoon oregano
¹/4 teaspoon marjoram
¹/4 teaspoon basil
¹/4 teaspoon minced garlic
2 cups shredded Monterey Jack cheese
1 (2¹/4-ounce) can sliced black olives
    Salt, pepper

PIERCE squash with fork in several places. Place on baking sheet and bake at 350 degrees 45 minutes. Turn and bake 45 minutes longer, or until shell yields to pressure. When cool enough to handle, cut squash in half. Scoop out and discard seeds. Remove spaghetti-like strings inside squash with fork and reserve. Melt butter in skillet. Sauté onion and green and red peppers until tender. Add squash strands, oregano, marjoram, basil, garlic, cheese, and olives. Season to taste with salt and pepper. Toss until cheese is evenly distributed. Place in 1¹/2-quart casserole and return to oven until cheese is melted, about 10 to 15 minutes.

Makes about 6 servings.

Oven-Fried Eggplant

2 eggplants, about 1 pound
    each
    Flour
1 egg
1 tablespoon oil
1 teaspoon salt

$^1/_4$ teaspoon black pepper
    Seasoned fine dry bread
    crumbs
3 tomatoes, sliced
6 ounces mozzarella cheese,
    shredded

CUT eggplants into diagonal slices. Dredge in flour. Beat together egg, oil, salt, and pepper. Dip eggplant slices in egg mixture, then in seasoned bread crumbs. Place in greased baking pan and cover with foil pierced with fork to make air vents. Bake at 400 degrees 15 minutes. Unwrap, top each slice of eggplant with a slice of tomato, and sprinkle with shredded cheese. Return to oven and bake 10 minutes longer, or until cheese is bubbly.

Makes 6 servings.

Eggplant with Spicy Meat

4 Oriental eggplants (about 1
    pound)
    Oil
1 tablespoon chile oil
1 tablespoon mashed garlic
1 cup ground pork or $^1/_2$ cup
    ground beef and $^1/_2$ cup
    ground pork
    Soy sauce

$^3/_4$ cup chicken broth
2 tablespoons bottled hoisin
    sauce
1 tablespoon Chinese vinegar
2 teaspoons cornstarch
1 teaspoon water
1 tablespoon minced green
    onion (green part only)

Chang Sha restaurant in Chinatown introduced us to this superb hot and spicy northern Chinese wok dish.

REMOVE blossom ends of eggplants. Cut in halves lengthwise. Cut each half in $^1/_2$-inch-thick diagonal slices. Steam eggplants until tender or cook in 1 inch hot oil in large skillet or wok until golden brown. Drain well on paper towels. Drain all oil from skillet and add chile oil. Cook over high heat 30 seconds. Add garlic and cook, stirring, 10 seconds. Add ground pork, 1 tablespoon soy sauce, broth, and hoisin sauce, and stir-fry until pork is browned. Add vinegar and eggplants, toss lightly to blend flavors, and heat through. Season to taste with more soy sauce, if needed. Mix cornstarch with water and stir into pork mixture. Cook and stir until ingredients glisten. Add green onion and stir-fry 5 seconds. Serve at once.

Makes 6 servings.

Note: Chile oil is available in Chinese markets and specialty food shops.

Seafood-Stuffed Eggplant

The Egg & Eye restaurant has a distinctive way with food. This seafood-stuffed eggplant recipe is one of their most unusual dishes.

1 large eggplant
2 tablespoons oil
3 tablespoons butter or margarine
1/2 medium onion, chopped
8 mushrooms, sliced
Medium white sauce
2 teaspoons sherry
2 ounces cooked crabmeat
2 ounces cooked shrimp
Salt, pepper
1/4 cup hollandaise sauce
2 to 4 tablespoons grated Parmesan cheese

CUT eggplant in half lengthwise. Heat oil in skillet, place eggplant flat side down, and brown. Place on baking sheet flat side up, cover with foil, and bake at 400 degrees 45 minutes. Scoop out pulp and chop. Reserve eggplant shells. Melt butter in small skillet, add onion, and sauté until tender. Remove onion and set aside. Add mushrooms to skillet and sauté until tender. Drain any excess liquid. Combine eggplant pulp, onion, mushrooms, 1/4 to 1/3 cup white sauce (just enough to make mixture creamy but not runny), sherry, crabmeat, and shrimp. Season to taste with salt and pepper. Fill eggplant shells with creamed mixture. Combine hollandaise sauce and 1 tablespoon white sauce and spoon over eggplants. Sprinkle with cheese. Brown under broiler.

Makes 2 servings.

Cheese-Stuffed Eggplant

Guido Dimicco, a hairdresser from Beverly Hills, entertains guests royally when he serves this Italian eggplant specialty.

1 large eggplant
4 eggs
1/2 cup half and half
2 tablespoons chopped parsley
1/2 teaspoon garlic powder
Salt, pepper
1/4 cup grated Romano or Parmesan cheese
1 cup seasoned fine dry bread crumbs
Olive oil
1/4 pound mozzarella cheese
1 pound ricotta cheese
Simple Tomato Sauce

SLICE eggplant lengthwise, as thin as possible. Mix 2 eggs, half and half, 1 tablespoon parsley, and garlic powder in wide shallow bowl. Season to taste with salt and pepper. Mix Romano cheese and bread crumbs in another wide shallow bowl. Dip eggplant slices in bread crumb mixture, then in egg mixture, and finally in bread crumb mixture again. Sauté in 1 inch hot olive oil until golden brown. Drain on paper towels. Chop or shred mozzarella and ricotta cheeses. Beat together in electric mixer bowl with remaining eggs and remaining parsley and season to taste with salt and pepper. Place small amount of this mixture on each eggplant slice. Fold over like an omelet.

Arrange filled slices in bottom of greased large baking dish and cover with Simple Tomato Sauce. Bake, uncovered, at 350 degrees 30 to 35 minutes. Garnish with parsley sprigs.

Makes 4 to 6 servings.

Simple Tomato Sauce

1 small onion, chopped
1 clove garlic, minced
　Olive oil
1 tablespoon chopped fresh
　basil

1 (1-pound 12-ounce) can
　whole tomatoes
　Salt, pepper

Sauté onion and garlic in 1 to 2 tablespoons olive oil. Add basil and tomatoes. Season to taste with salt and pepper. Simmer, uncovered, 30 minutes, stirring occasionally. For a smoother sauce, blend in food processor bowl.

Makes about 2$\frac{1}{2}$ cups.

Eggplant Teriyaki

4 Oriental eggplants (about 1
　pound)
　Sesame oil
$\frac{1}{4}$ cup soy sauce
$\frac{1}{4}$ cup sake or mirin

$\frac{1}{4}$ cup sugar
1 tablespoon grated
　gingerroot
　Dash MSG (optional)
　Toasted sesame seeds

SLICE eggplants 1 inch thick. Soak in water 10 to 15 minutes. Drain and dry on paper towels. Heat heavy skillet and add about $\frac{1}{8}$ inch oil. Cook eggplant slices on both sides until tender. Remove from heat. Mix soy sauce, sake, sugar, gingerroot, MSG, and few drops sesame oil. Add to eggplant, stir, and let marinate 10 to 20 minutes before serving. Sprinkle with sesame seeds.

Makes 6 servings.

Vegetable Nut Roast

This vegetarian loaf makes a fine, nutrition-packed main dish.

1/3 cup butter or margarine
1 cup chopped mushrooms
2 large onions, finely chopped
1/4 cup chopped green pepper
3 cups grated carrots
1 1/2 cups chopped celery
1/2 cup sunflower seeds

3/4 cup coarsely chopped walnuts
5 eggs, beaten
3 cups soft whole wheat bread crumbs
Dash basil
Dash oregano
Salt, pepper

MELT butter in skillet, add mushrooms, onions, and green pepper and cook until tender but not browned. Combine mushroom mixture in bowl with carrots, celery, sunflower seeds, walnuts, eggs, bread crumbs, basil, and oregano. Mix well. Season to taste with salt and pepper. Line a 9 x 5-inch loaf pan on bottom with wax paper, then grease paper and sides of pan generously. Turn mixture into pan and bake at 325 degrees 1 hour.

Makes 8 servings.

Vegetable Tempura

Crisp Japanese vegetable tempura is a wonderful way to use up odds and ends in the vegetable bin.

2 eggs
1/2 teaspoon salt
1/4 teaspoon sugar
1 cup ice water
3/4 cup flour
Oil for deep frying
2 zucchini, cut in 1/8-inch-thick slices
1/2 pound green beans, tips trimmed
1 green pepper, cored, seeded, and cut in squares

1 sweet potato, peeled and thinly sliced
1 cucumber, peeled and thinly sliced
Parsley sprigs
Green onion frills
2 canned or fresh lotus roots, sliced
Tempura Dip

BEAT eggs with salt and sugar until frothy in small bowl. Beat in ice water until well blended. Add flour and mix gently but thoroughly. Do not overbeat. Keep batter cold by placing over a bowl of ice. Pour 2 to 3 inches oil into a heavy skillet or tempura pan and heat to 400 degrees. Dip zucchini, green beans, green pepper, sweet potato, cucumber, parsley, green onions, and lotus root, a few pieces at a time, into batter and add to hot oil. Cook until lightly browned, then drain on paper towels. Skim any crumbs of cooked batter from oil before adding next batch of vegetables. Serve with Tempura Sauce.

Makes 6 to 8 servings.

Tempura Dip

¹/₄ cup dashi or chicken stock
1 tablespoon soy sauce
1 tablespoon mirin or cream
  sherry
¹/₄ teaspoon MSG (optional)

1 tablespoon grated daikon
1 tablespoon grated fresh
  gingerroot

Combine dashi, soy sauce, mirin, and MSG. Just before serving, stir in daikon and gingerroot. Serve as dip for tempura.

Makes ¹/₂ cup.

Soybean Burgers

¹/₂ cup dry soybeans
1 eggplant
1 onion, diced
3 to 4 cloves garlic, minced
1 cup oats

1¹/₂ cups wheat germ
¹/₂ teaspoon salt
  Oil
  Mushroom Gravy

The Golden Temple Conscious Cookery restaurant in Los Angeles is a vegetarian natural-foods place that does some very interesting things with soybeans.

COOK soybeans in 3 cups water until tender, about 2¹/₂ hours. Drain, cool, and grind or blend to make 1 cup. Peel eggplant and cube. Combine with onion and garlic in saucepan and cook in enough oil to cover bottom of pan until onion is tender. Add oats, wheat germ, soybean mixture, and salt. Stir in 2 tablespoons water. Dough should have consistency of a thick paste. Press into patties and fry in ¹/₄ inch oil until done on both sides. Serve with Mushroom Gravy.

Makes 6 servings.

Mushroom Gravy

1 cup chopped onions
2 cloves garlic, minced
1 cup chopped mushrooms
3 tablespoons butter or
  margarine

1 tablespoon arrowroot
¹/₂ cup water
1 tablespoon tamari

Sauté onions, garlic, and mushrooms in butter until mushrooms are tender. Dissolve arrowroot in water and add to mushroom mixture. Cook and stir until thickened. Add tamari.

Makes about 2 cups.

Note: Tamari, a soy-based flavoring, can be found at many health-food stores.

Vegetarian Chili

This delicious chili makes a meatless meal that does not sacrifice good protein value.

1 medium onion, thinly sliced
1/2 green pepper, diced
2 tablespoons butter or margarine
1 clove garlic, minced
2 tablespoons chili powder
1 (28-ounce) can whole tomatoes, crushed

3 cups cooked or canned kidney beans
Salt, pepper
1 1/2 cups shredded cheddar cheese
3 cups cooked brown rice
1/2 cup chopped green onions

SAUTÉ onion and green pepper in butter until tender but not brown. Stir in garlic and chili powder. Add tomatoes and beans and season to taste with salt and pepper. Simmer 10 minutes. Add cheese. Cook until cheese melts, stirring constantly. Spoon mixture into individual mounds of hot rice. Garnish with green onions.

Makes 6 servings.

Creamed Corn

Diners at Gulliver's, a local chain of restaurants, find this creamed corn with its light topping of Parmesan cheese much to their liking.

8 ears corn
1 cup whipping cream
2 teaspoons salt
1 teaspoon sugar

1/2 teaspoon MSG (optional)
Butter or margarine
2 teaspoons flour
Grated Parmesan cheese

CUT corn from cob and place in saucepan with whipping cream. Bring to boil, reduce heat, and simmer 5 minutes. Stir in salt, sugar, and MSG. Melt 2 teaspoons butter in small pan and stir in flour. Do not brown. Stir butter-flour roux into corn and cook until slightly thickened. Turn corn into ovenproof dish, sprinkle with cheese, and dot with butter. Brown under broiler.

Makes 8 to 10 servings.

Magic Carrots

No sleight-of-hand cooking is required for these simple carrots from the Magic Castle, a private club for magicians and magic fans in Hollywood.

1 (1-pound) can baby carrots
2 tablespoons butter or margarine

3 tablespoons sugar
1 teaspoon rum flavoring

DRAIN carrots. Melt butter in saucepan and add sugar, rum flavoring, and carrots. Simmer until sauce just begins to thicken and carrots are glazed.

Makes 4 servings.

Carrot Ring

4 cups mashed cooked carrots
1/3 cup chopped onion
2/3 cup fine dry bread or
    cracker crumbs

4 eggs, lightly beaten
1 1/4 teaspoons salt
1/2 teaspoon black pepper

Mix carrots, onion, and crumbs in a large bowl. Add eggs, salt, and pepper and mix well. Turn into a well-greased 5-cup ring mold and bake at 350 degrees 30 to 35 minutes. Cool a few minutes, loosen edges carefully with a sharp knife, and turn out onto plate. Fill center with hot buttered green peas or other vegetables, if desired.

Makes 6 servings.

Sparkling Carrots

1 small onion, chopped
2 tablespoons butter or
    margarine
1 1/2 pounds carrots, sliced 1/8-
    inch thick

1 cup lemon-lime carbonated
    beverage
Salt, pepper
1 tablespoon sugar

This unusual method of cooking carrots in a carbonated beverage came from the Arbor restaurant in Upland.

Sauté onion in butter in large saucepan. Add carrots and carbonated beverage. Season to taste with salt and pepper. Add sugar and cook over high heat until liquid is absorbed and carrots are slightly glazed, about 8 to 10 minutes.

Makes 6 servings.

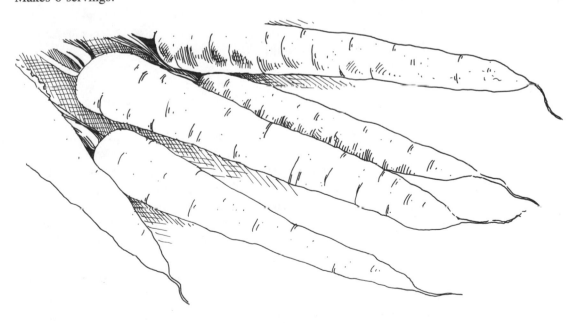

Sweet-Sour Red Cabbage

Sweet-sour red cabbage side dishes are very popular in Southern California. This recipe from the Alpine Village Inn restaurant in Torrance is typical of those relished by residents and visitors alike.

1 onion, chopped
1/4 pound bacon, chopped
1 head red cabbage, coarsely shredded
2 apples, quartered
3 cloves
2 bay leaves

Salt, pepper
1 teaspoon sugar
2 tablespoons wine vinegar
1/4 cup red wine
Few drops lemon juice
1 tablespoon cornstarch

COMBINE onion and bacon in saucepan. Cook 2 to 3 minutes. Cover bottom of pan with 1 inch water. Add cabbage and top with apples. Tie cloves and bay leaves in cheesecloth bag and add to pan. Season to taste with salt and pepper. Add sugar and wine vinegar. Cover and simmer 30 to 40 minutes. Just before serving, remove spice bag and add wine and lemon juice to pan. Mix cornstarch with enough water to make a paste. Stir into pan liquid and heat until smooth and thickened.

Makes 4 to 5 servings.

Broccoli Supreme

2 (10-ounce) packages frozen chopped broccoli
3 cups cottage cheese
3 eggs
6 tablespoons butter or margarine, softened
1/3 cup flour
1/4 cup finely minced onion
1 (8-ounce) can whole kernel corn, drained

1/2 pound cheddar or Swiss cheese, diced
1/2 teaspoon salt
1/4 teaspoon black pepper
Few drops hot pepper sauce
2 slices white bread
1/2 cup crumbled, cooked bacon

COOK broccoli according to package directions and drain. Combine cottage cheese, eggs, 4 tablespoons butter, and flour in blender container or mixer bowl. Blend or beat until cottage cheese mixture is smooth and creamy. Fold in broccoli, onion, corn, cheddar cheese, salt, pepper, and hot pepper sauce. Pour cottage cheese mixture into a greased, deep 2 1/2-quart casserole. Make soft bread crumbs by tearing 1 bread slice into blender container and blending on low speed until soft crumbs have formed. Repeat with remaining bread slice. Melt remaining 2 tablespoons butter in skillet. Add soft crumbs and sauté until golden brown. Sprinkle buttered bread crumbs and bacon over cottage cheese mixture. Bake at 350 degrees 1 hour, or until mixture is set.

Makes 8 to 12 servings.

Broccoli Mushroom Casserole

1 to 1¹/₂ pounds broccoli
6 tablespoons butter or margarine
¹/₄ cup flour
¹/₂ teaspoon salt
¹/₄ teaspoon black pepper
2 cups milk

1 cup shredded cheddar cheese
¹/₂ pound small mushrooms
2 tablespoons chopped green pepper
Paprika

SEPARATE broccoli stalks and cook in 1 inch boiling salted water 3 to 5 minutes. Drain. Arrange broccoli in a greased 9-inch square pan. Melt 5 tablespoons butter and blend in flour, salt, and pepper. Cook and stir until smooth. Remove from heat and stir in milk. Bring to a boil and boil 1 minute, stirring constantly. Add cheese and remove from heat. Sauté mushrooms in remaining 1 tablespoon butter until tender and add to sauce. Add green pepper and cook 1 minute. Pour sauce over broccoli. Sprinkle with additional cheese and paprika, if desired. Bake at 350 degrees 15 to 20 minutes.

Makes 4 servings.

Citrus Broccoli Bake

2 egg whites
¹/₂ cup mayonnaise
¹/₃ cup grated Parmesan cheese
¹/₄ cup chopped parsley
2 tablespoons grated grapefruit or orange peel
1¹/₂ pounds broccoli, cut in 2-inch pieces or 2 (10-ounce) packages frozen broccoli, cooked and drained

1 grapefruit or large orange, peeled and sectioned
2 tablespoons butter or margarine, melted

BEAT egg whites until soft peaks form in small bowl. Fold in mayonnaise. Stir in cheese, parsley, and grapefruit peel. Arrange cooked broccoli and grapefruit sections in 1¹/₂-quart ovenproof dish. Pour melted butter over broccoli and grapefruit. Top with egg white mixture. Bake at 450 degrees 5 minutes, or until puffy and lightly browned.

Makes 4 to 6 servings.

Broccoli Strascicati
(Stir-Fried Broccoli)

This is a nearly effortless way to prepare broccoli.

1 pound broccoli
5 tablespoons olive oil
1 large clove garlic

Salt, pepper
Dash crushed dried chiles

REMOVE large tough stems from broccoli and discard. Cut remaining broccoli into 1½-inch pieces. Heat oil in heatproof casserole, preferably terra-cotta, and add whole peeled garlic clove. Sauté the garlic lightly 2 minutes, then discard. Immediately add the broccoli pieces. Season to taste with salt, pepper, and chiles. Stir to coat broccoli with seasoning and oil, then cover. Cook over low heat, stirring occasionally. If needed, add a small amount of cold water. Cook 20 minutes.

Makes 4 servings.

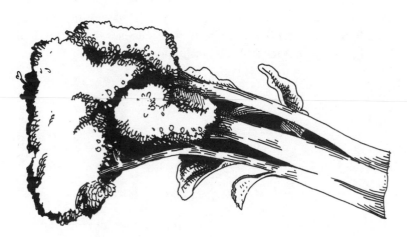

Lemon Broccoli

1½ pounds broccoli
1 large clove garlic, split
2 tablespoons oil
½ teaspoon salt
¼ teaspoon black pepper

2 tablespoons warm water
1 tablespoon slivered lemon peel
½ lemon, sliced

TRIM tough stem ends from broccoli. Cut into spears, splitting thick stems almost to heads. Cook in a small amount of boiling salted water about 8 minutes or until tender. Drain well and keep warm. Sauté garlic in oil until browned, then discard. Add drained broccoli, salt, pepper, and warm water to garlic oil. Bring to boil and add lemon peel and half the lemon slices. Simmer about 3 minutes. Turn out onto hot platter and arrange remaining lemon slices at edges of dish.

Makes 4 to 6 servings.

Broccoli Chantilly

1¹/₂ pounds broccoli
²/₃ cup whipping cream
¹/₃ cup sour cream
 1 teaspoon dry mustard

1 tablespoon lemon juice
1 teaspoon grated onion
 Salt, pepper
 Paprika (optional)

A simple broccoli dish becomes special when topped with a mustard-flavored chantilly sauce.

CUT tough stem ends from broccoli and split stems if large. Cook in 1 inch boiling salted water until tender, 10 to 15 minutes. Drain carefully and place in warm broilerproof casserole. Beat whipping cream until stiff. Fold in sour cream, mustard, lemon juice, and onion. Season to taste with salt and pepper. Spoon dollops of whipping cream over broccoli and sprinkle with paprika. Place under broiler until lightly browned, watching to prevent scorching.

Makes 6 servings.

Creamed Spinach

2 (10-ounce) packages frozen
　 leaf spinach or 2 (12-ounce)
　 bunches fresh spinach
3 slices bacon
1 small onion
3 tablespoons flour

1¹/₄ cups milk
 1 teaspoon salt
¹/₂ teaspoon coarsely ground
　 black pepper
¹/₂ teaspoon MSG (optional)

This famous dish from Gulliver's restaurants can be made with fresh as well as frozen spinach.

THAW spinach and squeeze completely dry. Grind bacon and onion very fine and place in saucepan. Sauté bacon and onion until bacon is cooked. Stir in flour to make a smooth paste. Gradually add milk, bring to boil, and simmer 10 minutes over low heat until thickened. Add salt, pepper, and MSG. Grind spinach fine and add to cream sauce. Heat through.

Makes 6 servings.

Cauliflower con Queso

1 head cauliflower
Water
Salt
2 tablespoons butter or
margarine
1/4 cup chopped onion
2 tablespoons flour
1 (1-pound) can whole
tomatoes

1 bay leaf
1 (4-ounce) can diced green
chiles, drained
1/4 teaspoon hot pepper sauce
1 cup shredded Monterey
Jack or mild cheddar
cheese

WASH cauliflower and remove leaves. Place in 1 inch boiling salted
water in large saucepan. Cook, uncovered, 5 minutes, then cover and
cook 15 to 25 minutes or until crisp-tender. Meanwhile, melt butter
in saucepan. Add onion and cook until tender, about 5 minutes.
Blend in flour. Stir in tomatoes with liquid. Cook, stirring, until mixture thickens and comes to boil. Add bay leaf, green chiles, 1 teaspoon salt, and hot pepper sauce. Cook 5 minutes. Add cheese and
stir until melted. Drain cauliflower and serve topped with sauce.

Makes 6 servings.

Curried Cauliflower

3 tablespoons butter or
margarine
1/2 teaspoon ground cumin
1/4 teaspoon black pepper
4 teaspoons ground coriander
1 teaspoon turmeric
1 large head cauliflower,
separated into flowerets

1 small onion, diced
1 (10-ounce) package frozen
green peas
1/4 cup water
1 bay leaf
Salt

HEAT butter until bubbling, then stir in cumin, pepper, coriander, and
turmeric. Add cauliflowerets, onion, peas, water, and bay leaf. Cover
and simmer 10 to 15 minutes, turning with fork or spatula now and
then to prevent scorching. Season to taste with salt. Remove bay leaf
and serve.

Makes 8 servings.

Au Gratin Potatoes

2¹/₂ pounds potatoes
    Salt
1 tablespoon flour
    Nutmeg
    MSG (optional)
2 tablespoons sherry
2 tablespoons evaporated
    milk

    Grated Parmesan cheese
¹/₂ cup shredded American
    cheese
4 cups milk
    Paprika
    Melted butter or margarine

Tom Bergin's Horseshoe Tavern on Fairfax in Los Angeles claims to be the "Home of Irish Coffee" but they also serve this interesting potato casserole.

COOK potatoes until tender. Cool, peel, then chop. Season to taste with salt. Add flour and season to taste with nutmeg and MSG. Add sherry, evaporated milk, ¹/₂ cup Parmesan cheese, and American cheese. Stir well. Turn into greased shallow pan and pour in milk, stirring lightly to blend. Sprinkle with additional Parmesan cheese and paprika. Drizzle top with melted butter. Bake at 350 degrees 30 minutes, adding more milk if necessary.

Makes 6 to 8 servings.

Twice-Baked Cheese Potatoes

4 medium potatoes
1 tablespoon shortening
1¹/₂ teaspoons minced onion
³/₄ cup evaporated milk
2 tablespoons butter or
    margarine

¹/₂ teaspoon salt
1 tablespoon parsley
1 cup shredded cheddar
    cheese

SCRUB potatoes well. Rub skins with shortening and pierce in several places to allow steam to escape. Bake at 400 degrees about 1 hour or until done. Add onion to evaporated milk and let stand while potatoes are baking. When potatoes are done, cut in halves lengthwise. Scoop out insides, reserving shells. Mash potatoes and beat in butter, milk-onion mixture, salt, and parsley. Blend in cheese. Spoon mixture back into shells. Return to oven about 10 minutes.

Makes 8 servings.

Potato Pancakes

The recipe for these crisp potato pancakes came from the Alpine Village Inn restaurant in Torrance.

2¹/₂ pounds potatoes,
    preferably russets
1 cup flour
2 eggs

Salt, pepper
2 tablespoons chopped chives
Oil or shortening

PEEL potatoes and grate or grind very fine into bowl. Add flour and eggs and blend well. Season to taste with salt and pepper and add chives. Heat grill or large skillet and grease generously. Drop pancake mixture by heaping tablespoon on grill, flattening out to form pancakes. Fry until golden on both sides, adding oil as needed.

Makes 8 servings.

Pommes Boulanger
(Potatoes Baker's-Style)

Potatoes are arranged in a fan-like pattern over onions in this attractive vegetable dish from The Cove restaurant in Los Angeles.

  4 potatoes, peeled
1¹/₂ onions, sliced
    Chicken broth
    Salt, pepper

Crushed thyme
3 bay leaves
  Dash MSG (optional)

CUT potatoes into ¹/₄-inch-thick slices. Press slices together to re-form potato. Sprinkle onion slices in bottom of greased 5-inch-deep casserole. Place re-formed potatoes on top of onions. They will fan out slightly. Cover with chicken broth. Season to taste with salt, pepper, and thyme. Add bay leaves and MSG. Bake at 350 degrees 45 minutes, or until fork-tender.

Makes 8 servings.

Potato Fritters

2 cups mashed cooked
  potatoes
1/3 cup flour
1/3 cup shredded cheddar
  cheese

2 eggs
1/4 cup milk
1 to 1 1/2 cups oil

COMBINE potatoes, flour, cheese, eggs, and milk and beat until light. Heat oil in deep heavy skillet until very hot. Drop potato mixture by tablespoons into hot oil and cook until golden brown. Drain on paper towels.

Makes 12.

Fried Okra

1 pound okra
3/4 cup cornmeal

Salt, pepper
Bacon drippings

Try this with pork chops or a thick slice of broiled ham.

CHOOSE small, tender okra. Wash thoroughly, cut off ends, and cut in 1/2-inch-thick slices. Combine cornmeal and salt and pepper to taste in plastic bag. Dampen okra and shake in cornmeal mixture. Brown on both sides in bacon drippings in skillet.

Makes 4 to 6 servings.

Brantley Peppers

2 slices bacon, chopped
2 tablespoons butter or
  margarine
2 cloves garlic, crushed

2 green peppers, cut in strips
1/4 cup rice vinegar
1/4 teaspoon chicken stock base

Garlic and bacon complement tangy green peppers in an appetizing side dish for meats. It was developed by John Holly, who was the subject of a "Guys & Galleys" column in The Times *Sunday Home magazine.*

COOK bacon in skillet until crisp. Remove bacon bits and reserve. Add butter to drippings and heat over medium heat. Add garlic and sauté a few minutes. Stir in green peppers and sauté about 7 minutes. Reduce heat and add vinegar and stock base. Stir. Cover and simmer 7 minutes. Drain. Serve topped with reserved bacon. Serve as an accompaniment to meat dishes.

Makes about 4 servings.

Curried Peas

The Golden Temple Conscious Cookery combines peas with curry spices and mushrooms.

2 teaspoons oil
2 teaspoons butter or
  margarine
1 cup minced onions
1 clove garlic
1 (¹/₂-inch-thick) slice
  gingerroot, peeled
  Dash caraway seeds
¹/₂ teaspoon salt

Dash black pepper
Dash turmeric
¹/₄ cup tomato puree
1 (10-ounce) package frozen
  peas or 1 pound fresh
  Dash ground coriander
¹/₈ teaspoon ground cumin
¹/₈ teaspoon red pepper
1¹/₄ cups sliced mushrooms

HEAT oil and butter in large heavy skillet. Add onions and sauté until tender. Puree garlic and ginger in blender container with a small amount of water and add to onions. Add caraway seeds, salt, pepper, and turmeric. Cook 8 minutes, stirring often to prevent sticking and scorching. Add tomato puree and heat through. Add peas and simmer 5 minutes. Add coriander, cumin, and red pepper and cook 10 minutes. Add mushrooms, cover, and cook 10 minutes longer, or until mushrooms are tender. Serve with yogurt and sweet chutney, if desired.

Makes 4 servings.

Note: If curry is too hot, add yogurt a little at a time until it is less fiery.

Chinese Peas

¹/₂ pound Chinese pea pods
1 tablespoon oil
¹/₂ cup thinly sliced water
  chestnuts

1 cup chicken stock
1 tablespoon cornstarch
2 tablespoons cold water
  Salt

SNAP ends from pea pods and remove strings. Heat oil in skillet. Add peas, water chestnuts, and stock. Cover and cook over high heat 3 minutes. Combine cornstarch and cold water. Push vegetables to one side and add cornstarch mixture to liquid. Cook, stirring, until slightly thickened. Season to taste with salt. Serve with soy sauce, if desired.

Makes 4 servings.

Crunchy Onion Rings

4 onions
   Milk or buttermilk
2 cups cornmeal

1 teaspoon salt
  Dash black pepper
  Oil for deep frying

Onion rings are as popular as French fries, the crunchier the better. These cornmeal-coated ones are among the best.

SLICE onions ¼-inch thick. Separate into rings. Soak in milk 30 minutes. Drain. Mix cornmeal, salt, and pepper. Coat onion rings in cornmeal mixture and drop into deep oil heated to 375 degrees. Fry until golden, then drain on paper towels. Serve immediately.

Makes 4 to 6 servings.

RELISHES &
PRESERVES

ICKLES and preserves are very much a part of western dining, but they often have unique and unexpected flavor accents that reflect the tastes and products of the region. Kumquats and mangoes find their way into chutneys. Spicy jalapeño jelly is served as a meat accompaniment, an appetizer with cheese and crackers, or is put up in pretty glasses to give as gifts. And peaches, strawberries, cantaloupes, and other summer fruits are transformed into jewel-like sweets designed to enhance winter menus.

As often as not, the ingredients for preserving are homegrown, for Southern California boasts a long growing season, an incentive to avid year-round home gardening. But the beautiful fruits and vegetables available in local markets also inspire the home canner. Summer brings an abundance of tomatoes, squash, and other traditional vegetable crops while autumn provides persimmons, all of which are carefully preserved for future use. At harvest time, the Food Section receives an avalanche of requests for pickling and canning recipes.

Visitors from other parts of the country and from overseas are always impressed by the quality and profusion of produce in supermarket displays. And though Southern Californians may grow a bit blasé about this abundance, they never fail to put it to good use.

Clockwise from bottom: *Onion Confetti Relish, Corn Relish, Spiced Tomato and Pineapple Jam, Apple Chutney, Chow-Chow Relish, Hawaiian Papaya Chutney,* pages 266–68

Onion Confetti Relish

2 cups chopped onions
$^1/_2$ cup diced green pepper
3 tablespoons diced pimiento
$^1/_2$ cup vinegar
$^1/_4$ cup water

$^1/_4$ cup sugar
1 teaspoon caraway seeds
$^3/_4$ teaspoon salt
$^1/_8$ teaspoon hot pepper sauce

COMBINE onions, green pepper, and pimiento and set aside. Combine vinegar, water, sugar, caraway seeds, salt, and hot pepper sauce in a saucepan. Bring to a boil and simmer 5 minutes. Pour over onion mixture. Refrigerate several hours before serving.

Makes $2^3/_4$ cups.

Corn Relish

16 to 20 ears tender corn or $2^1/_2$ quarts frozen whole kernel corn, thawed
$1^1/_4$ cups chopped onions
1 cup chopped green peppers
1 cup chopped sweet red peppers

1 cup chopped celery
$2^2/_3$ cups white vinegar
2 cups water
$1^1/_2$ cups sugar
$4^1/_2$ teaspoons mustard seeds
1 tablespoon salt
1 teaspoon celery seeds
$^1/_2$ teaspoon turmeric

PEEL husks and silks from corn and trim blemishes. Boil corn 5 minutes, then quickly dip in cold water. Cut kernels from cob. Measure $2^1/_2$ quarts cut corn. Combine corn with onions, green peppers, red peppers, celery, white vinegar, water, sugar, mustard seeds, salt, celery seeds, and turmeric in large kettle. Simmer, uncovered, 20 minutes. Pack into hot sterilized jars, leaving $^1/_4$-inch head space. Make sure vinegar solution covers vegetables. Adjust lids and process in boiling water bath 15 minutes.

Makes 6 to 7 pints.

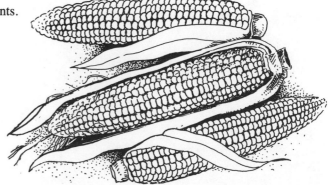

Spiced Tomato and Pineapple Jam

1³/₄ pounds tomatoes (about),
    scalded, peeled, and
    chopped
1 (1³/₄-ounce) box powdered
    fruit pectin
1 (13¹/₂-ounce) can crushed
    pineapple

2 tablespoons vinegar
2 teaspoons Worcestershire
    sauce
¹/₂ teaspoon cinnamon
¹/₂ teaspoon ground allspice
¹/₄ teaspoon ground cloves
5¹/₂ cups sugar

BRING tomatoes to boil. Reduce heat and simmer 10 minutes, stirring occasionally. Remove from heat. Measure 2 cups into large saucepan. Thoroughly mix fruit pectin, undrained pineapple, vinegar, Worcestershire, cinnamon, allspice, and cloves into tomatoes in saucepan. Place over high heat and stir until mixture comes to hard boil. Immediately add all sugar. Bring to full rolling boil and boil hard 1 minute, stirring constantly. Remove from heat and skim off foam with metal spoon. Stir and skim 5 minutes to cool slightly and prevent fruit from floating. Ladle quickly into hot sterilized glasses and seal at once with ¹/₈-inch hot paraffin or canning lids.

Makes about 8 6-ounce glasses.

Apple Chutney

8 cups peeled, cored, and
    chopped tart apples (about
    16)
1 cup chopped onions
1 clove garlic, crushed
1 cup chopped green peppers
2 pounds raisins
4 cups brown sugar, packed

4 cups vinegar
2 small hot red chiles
3 tablespoons mustard seeds
2 tablespoons minced
    gingerroot
2 teaspoons salt
2 teaspoons whole allspice

COMBINE apples, onions, garlic, green peppers, raisins, brown sugar, vinegar, red chiles, mustard seeds, gingerroot, salt, and allspice in large saucepan. Simmer 2 hours or until thick, stirring occasionally to prevent sticking. Pour, boiling hot, into hot sterilized jars, leaving ¹/₄-inch head space. Adjust lids. Process 10 minutes in boiling water bath.

Makes about 5 quarts.

Chow-Chow Relish

4 cups chopped cabbage
3 cups chopped cauliflower
2 cups chopped onions
2 cups chopped green
   tomatoes
2 cups chopped green
   peppers
3 tablespoons salt

$2^1/_2$ cups vinegar
$1^1/_2$ cups sugar
2 teaspoons dry mustard
1 teaspoon turmeric
$^1/_2$ teaspoon ground ginger
2 teaspoons celery seeds
1 teaspoon mustard seeds

COMBINE cabbage, cauliflower, onions, green tomatoes, and green peppers. Sprinkle with salt. Let mixture stand 4 to 6 hours in a cool place. Drain well. Combine vinegar, sugar, mustard, turmeric, ginger, celery seeds, and mustard seeds in large saucepan. Simmer 10 minutes. Add vegetable mixture and simmer 10 minutes longer. Bring to boil. Pack, boiling hot, into hot sterilized jars, leaving $^1/_4$-inch head space. Adjust lids and process 10 minutes in boiling water bath.

Makes 4 pints.

Hawaiian Papaya Chutney

1 cup white vinegar
$1^3/_4$ cups brown sugar, packed
1 medium onion, chopped
2 limes or lemons, unpeeled
   and thinly sliced
1 clove garlic, crushed
1 cup golden raisins
2 large tomatoes, peeled
   and coarsely chopped
1 green pepper, chopped
$^1/_2$ cup preserved ginger, cut
   in strips

$^1/_2$ cup whole blanched
   almonds
$^1/_4$ teaspoon red pepper
$1^1/_2$ teaspoons salt
1 cup dry white wine
3 very firm papayas, peeled,
   seeded, and cut up
2 cups peeled, cored, and
   chopped fresh pineapple

COMBINE vinegar, brown sugar, onion, limes, garlic, raisins, tomatoes, green pepper, ginger, almonds, red pepper, salt, and white wine in large heavy kettle. Cook gently 1 hour, stirring frequently, until liquid is clear and syrupy. Add more wine or water, if needed, to prevent sticking. Add papayas and pineapple. Continue cooking about 15 minutes or until fruit is tender. Cool and refrigerate, or fill hot sterilized jars, leaving $^1/_2$-inch head space. Seal.

Makes about 4 pints.

Rumtopf

1 (⁴/₅-quart) bottle rum,
  bourbon, or brandy
  Peel of 1 orange, cut in a
  spiral
1 tablespoon whole cloves
1 stick cinnamon
1 teaspoon whole allspice
1 pound cherries, pitted
8 cups sugar
1 pound peaches, peeled and
  pitted

1 pound apricots, peeled and
  pitted
1 pound plums, pitted
1 pound seedless grapes
1 pint strawberries
1 pint raspberries
1 pound pineapple, peeled,
  cored, and cut in chunks

Spirit-soaked fruit can be enjoyed year round as a dessert alone, as a sauce over pudding or ice cream, or as a topping for pound cake. Be sure to read the recipe through carefully before starting it, as fruits are added over a period of weeks.

SCALD a 6-quart stone crock with boiling water and dry it. (A very large glass jar will work equally well.) Pour rum into crock and add orange peel, cloves, cinnamon stick, and allspice. Add cherries and 1 cup sugar. Stir gently, cover crock with foil, and set aside in a cool spot. Continue adding layers of fruit and sugar as fruits come in season. Add at intervals of not less than one week. For each pound or pint of fruit added, add 1 cup sugar. Stir gently each time fruits and sugar are added. Keep crock covered with foil, held in place with a small plate if necessary. Add more rum if fruit absorbs the initial amount. After sufficient fruits are added, put crock in cool, dark place to ripen 2 to 3 months or as long as possible. It develops richer flavor with time. If only a small amount of Rumtopf mixture is used at a time, a pound of fruit and 1 cup of sugar may be added to replenish the supply. Be sure all fruit is ripe, free of blemishes, and well cleaned before using. If desired, after all fruits have been added and stirred, the mixture can be spooned into hot sterilized jars and processed in boiling water bath 15 minutes.

Champagne Jelly

1 (1³/₄-ounce) package
  powdered pectin
³/₄ cup water

3 cups champagne or dry
  white wine
4 cups sugar

Champagne jelly is not only a gala treat with holiday meals; it makes a wonderful gift from your own kitchen.

THOROUGHLY mix pectin and water in large saucepan. Bring to boil over high heat and boil 1 minute, stirring constantly. Reduce heat to medium and immediately add champagne and sugar. Keep mixture just below boiling and stir until sugar is dissolved, about 5 minutes. Remove from heat. Skim off foam with metal spoon if necessary. Pour quickly into hot sterilized half-pint jars. Seal at once with ¹/₈-inch hot paraffin or canning lids. Serve with poultry or meat.

Makes about 6 half-pints.

Jalapeño Jelly

Californians serve jalapeño jelly as a condiment with different meats. Its sweet but spicy-hot flavor is especially good on hamburgers.

3/4 cup seeded and ground
   green peppers
1/2 cup seeded and ground
   jalapeño chiles
6 cups sugar

1 1/2 cups cider vinegar
1 (6-ounce) bottle liquid
   pectin
   Green food color

MIX green peppers, chiles, sugar, and vinegar and bring to rolling boil. Boil 1 minute. Remove from heat and allow to cool slightly. Add pectin and 4 or 5 drops food color. Mix well. Strain into hot sterilized jars and seal.

Makes about 6 half-pints.

Note: If your skin is sensitive, wear protective gloves when handling chiles.

Peach-Cantaloupe Jam

6 peaches, peeled, pitted, and
   sliced
1/2 cantaloupe, peeled, seeded,
   and sliced

2 small oranges, sectioned and
   seeded
   Sugar

COMBINE fruit and measure. Add enough sugar to equal quantity of fruit and let stand overnight. Cook, stirring frequently, until fruit is clear and tender and syrup is thick. Ladle at once into hot sterilized jars. Seal with 1/8-inch hot paraffin or canning lids.

Makes about 5 half-pints.

Persimmon Jam

When the large, bright orange Japanese persimmons appear in the fall, this recipe is put to good use by our readers. It's important that the fruit be very ripe.

8 medium to large ripe
   persimmons
1/4 cup lemon juice

1 (1 3/4-ounce) package
   powdered pectin
6 cups sugar

WASH persimmons, cut stem ends, and force fruit through food mill or coarse strainer. Measure 4 cups pulp into deep saucepan. Add lemon juice and pectin to persimmon pulp and mix well. Heat to boiling, stirring constantly. Add sugar and mix well. Bring to full rolling boil, stirring constantly. Boil without stirring 4 minutes. Remove from heat and alternately stir and skim for 5 minutes to cool. Spoon into hot sterilized jars and seal.

Makes about 8 half-pints.

Spiced Strawberry Preserves

6 cups firm ripe strawberries,
  stems removed
5 cups sugar

2 whole allspice
¹/₃ cup lemon juice

COMBINE strawberries and sugar in large bowl. Let stand 4 to 5 hours, stirring occasionally. Turn strawberry mixture into large saucepan, add allspice, and bring to boil over modcratcly high heat, stirring occasionally. Boil 10 to 12 minutes. Add lemon juice and boil 5 minutes longer. Remove from heat and ladle into hot sterilized jars. Seal with ¹/₈-inch paraffin or canning lids.

Makes 5 half-pint jars.

Lemon-Lime Marmalade

3 cups thinly sliced unpeeled
  limes
1 cup thinly sliced, seeded,
  unpeeled lemons

3 quarts water
9 cups sugar

COMBINE lime and lemon slices and water in large kettle. Bring to boil and boil 20 minutes, or until peels are tender. Drain and measure liquid. Add enough water to make 3 quarts liquid, then combine liquid, fruit, and sugar in kettle. Bring to boil and cook rapidly until mixture sheets off spoon or to 221 degrees on candy thermometer. Pour boiling hot into hot sterilized jars and seal.

Makes 6 to 8 half-pints.

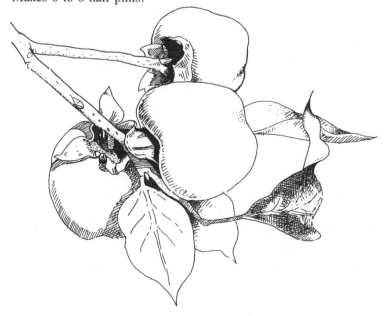

Kumquat Chutney

Kumquats all seem to ripen at the same time, leaving those with loaded trees in their yards frantic for ways to use the glut. This unusual recipe is a favorite solution.

2 cups whole kumquats
3/4 cup granulated sugar
3 cups dark brown sugar, packed
1/2 cup water
3/4 cup white vinegar
1/2 cup raisins
1 pound rhubarb, cut in 1-inch pieces
1 cup chopped celery
1 large onion, chopped
1 green pepper, chopped
2 cloves garlic, crushed
1/4 cup slivered citron
Juice and grated peel of 1 large orange

1 cup peeled and chopped gingerroot
1 tablespoon Worcestershire sauce
2 teaspoons salt
1 teaspoon curry powder
1 teaspoon ground allspice
1 teaspoon cinnamon
1 teaspoon ground ginger (optional)
1 teaspoon black pepper or 1/2 teaspoon red pepper (optional)

WASH kumquats in hot water. Slice kumquats lengthwise and remove seeds. Place in large heavy pan with sugars and water. Mix well and simmer slowly, uncovered, 30 minutes. Add vinegar, raisins, rhubarb, celery, onion, green pepper, garlic, citron, orange juice and peel, gingerroot, Worcestershire, salt, curry powder, allspice, and cinnamon. Mix well. Simmer slowly, uncovered, until mixture is dark in color, about 4 to 5 hours, stirring occasionally. Taste and add ground ginger and pepper, if needed. Pour into hot sterilized jars and seal immediately.

Makes about 4 1/2 pints.

Mango Chutney

2 1/4 cups cider vinegar
3 1/2 cups sugar
2 tablespoons chopped gingerroot
2 small dried red chiles, seeded and chopped (optional)

1 clove garlic, minced
1 1/4 teaspoons salt
14 cups peeled and coarsely chopped half-ripe, firm mangoes
3 cups raisins

BOIL vinegar and sugar for 5 minutes. Add gingerroot, chiles, garlic, and salt. Cook 10 minutes longer. Add mangoes and raisins. Cook over low heat until mixture thickens to desired consistency. Pour into hot sterilized jars and seal.

Makes 3 pints.

Kimchi
(Korean Cabbage Relish)

1 head Chinese cabbage	1/2 teaspoon crushed dried
3 tablespoons salt	hot red chile
3 to 6 green onions, chopped	1 teaspoon chopped
1 to 3 cloves garlic, minced	gingerroot

CUT cabbage in 1¹/₂-inch strips. Soak in salted water to cover 5 to 10 hours. Drain. Combine cabbage with salt, green onions, garlic, chile, and gingerroot. Mix well and spoon into large jar. Cover and refrigerate 1 to 2 days before using. Keeps well several weeks. Use as relish or salad.

Makes about 1 quart.

Korean kimchi is not for the uninitiated. It is decidedly redolent and possesses a genuine bite. Once tried, however, this spicy fermented cabbage relish quickly develops devotees.

Pineapple Cranberry Relish

1 (1-pound 4-ounce) can	3 thin lemon slices
pineapple chunks	3 thin orange slices
¹/₂ cup syrup from pineapple	1 stick cinnamon
¹/₄ cup sugar	1 cup fresh cranberries

DRAIN pineapple chunks and reserve. Pour syrup into small saucepan. Add sugar, lemon and orange slices, and cinnamon. Bring to simmer and cook 5 minutes. Add cranberries and simmer until they begin to burst. Stir in drained pineapple chunks. Serve warm or cold.

Makes about 2¹/₂ cups.

Sweet Pickled Carrots

2 pounds carrots, peeled	1 teaspoon salt
1 cup sugar	1 stick cinnamon
2 cups vinegar	1 tablespoon mixed pickling
1¹/₂ cups water	spice

COOK carrots in boiling water until crisp-tender. Drain. Cut carrots into 3-inch-long sticks and pack upright in small hot sterilized jars. Combine sugar, vinegar, water, and salt in a saucepan. Tie cinnamon stick and pickling spice in cheesecloth bag and add to vinegar mixture. Boil 5 to 8 minutes. Fill jars with boiling syrup, leaving ¹/₂-inch head space. Adjust lids and process in boiling water bath 30 minutes.

Makes about 3 pints.

Our Best Zucchini Pickles

4 pounds zucchini
1 pound small onions, peeled
  and thinly sliced
1/2 cup salt
4 cups vinegar

2 cups sugar
2 teaspoons celery seeds
2 teaspoons turmeric
2 teaspoons mustard seeds
1 teaspoon dry mustard

TRIM ends from zucchini and cut in very thin slices. Combine zucchini and onions, mix well, cover with water, and add salt. Let stand 1 hour. Drain. Combine vinegar, sugar, celery seeds, turmeric, mustard seeds, and dry mustard. Bring to boil and pour over vegetables. Let stand 1 hour. Bring to boil and cook 3 minutes. Pack hot in hot sterilized jars, leaving 1/4-inch head space. Adjust lids. Process 15 minutes in boiling water bath.

Makes about 8 pints.

Re-Pickled Pickles

A reader who likes dill pickles a bit sweeter turns ordinary dills into flavorful homemades this way.

1 (2-quart) jar dill pickles,
  drained
3 medium onions, sliced
2 1/2 cups sugar

1 1/2 cups apple cider vinegar
1/2 cup water
2 large sticks cinnamon

SLICE pickles 1/2-inch thick. Place pickle slices in jars alternately with onion slices. Dissolve sugar in vinegar and water. Pour vinegar mixture over pickles. Add cinnamon sticks. Refrigerate two days before using.

Makes 2 1/2 to 3 quarts.

Watermelon Pickles

4 quarts prepared watermelon
  rind
2 tablespoons salt
4 cups white vinegar
8 cups sugar

2 or 3 sticks cinnamon, broken
1 tablespoon whole cloves
1 (1-inch) piece
  gingerroot (optional)

To prepare watermelon rind, cut rind into 2 × 1-inch pieces. Trim green skin and pink flesh from rind. Place rind in large kettle and add salt and enough boiling water to cover. Simmer until tender. Drain and chill rind in very cold water at least 1 hour or overnight in refrigerator. Combine vinegar, sugar, and a mixture of cinnamon, cloves, and gingerroot tied in a bag. Bring to boil and boil 5 minutes. Drain watermelon rind and add to syrup. Simmer until rind becomes translucent, about 10 minutes. Remove and discard spice bag. Pack rind and syrup into hot sterilized quart jars, leaving 1/4-inch head space. Adjust lids and process in boiling water bath 20 minutes.

Makes 4 to 5 quarts.

Champagne Mustard

2/3 cup champagne vinegar
2/3 cup dry mustard

3 eggs
3/4 cup sugar

Sheila Ricci, an accomplished Los Angeles hostess, introduced us to this glamorous homemade mustard which she also gives as Christmas gifts.

COMBINE vinegar and mustard. Beat eggs and sugar. Add egg and sugar mixture to mustard mixture in top of double boiler over boiling water, stirring until thick. Refrigerate. Serve with baked ham.

Makes 1 1/2 cups.

Mustard Ring Mold

1 envelope unflavored gelatin
3/4 cup water
4 eggs
3/4 cup sugar
1 tablespoon dry mustard

1/2 cup vinegar
1 1/2 teaspoons salt
1 cup whipping cream, whipped, or mayonnaise

Serve this mustard-flavored mold with cold meats at a summer buffet.

SOFTEN gelatin in 1/4 cup water. Beat eggs in top of double boiler. Add remaining 1/2 cup water, sugar, mustard, vinegar, salt, and softened gelatin. Cook, stirring, until slightly thickened. Cool. Fold in whipped cream. Turn into 4-cup ring mold and chill. Unmold onto lettuce-lined plate and garnish with tiny beets, if desired.

Makes 6 servings.

Note: Any 4-cup mold or bowl may be used in place of a ring.

Low-Calorie Maple-Flavored Syrup

This maple-flavored syrup, made with cornstarch and only 5 tablespoons of sugar, boasts just 14 calories per tablespoon compared with 48 calories per tablespoon for regular maple syrup.

1 tablespoon cornstarch
5 tablespoons sugar
   Dash salt

1 cup cold water
2 teaspoons maple extract

COMBINE cornstarch, sugar, salt, and water in small saucepan. Mix well. Cook, stirring, over medium heat, until syrup thickens and bubbles. Reduce heat and simmer 1 minute. Remove from heat and stir in maple extract. Cool.

Makes 1 cup.

Low-Calorie Mayonnaise

Calorie-counters find this gelatin-based mayonnaise a boon at only about 20 calories per tablespoon compared to 100 calories per tablespoon for regular mayonnaise.

1 teaspoon unflavored gelatin
$3/4$ cup milk
1 egg yolk
1 tablespoon vinegar

$1/2$ teaspoon salt
$1/4$ teaspoon dry mustard
   Dash hot pepper sauce

SOAK gelatin in $1/4$ cup milk. Heat remaining $1/2$ cup milk until hot and add to gelatin mixture. Stir until gelatin is dissolved. Beat egg yolk slightly with vinegar, salt, mustard, and hot pepper sauce and stir into milk mixture. Chill until mixture begins to thicken, then whip until fluffy. Store in refrigerator.

Makes about 1 cup.

Garlic Olives

A few herbs and spices can do wonders for ordinary canned olives.

2 cups canned green
   olives, drained
1 or 2 cloves garlic, slivered
3 thin slices lemon
1 teaspoon black
   peppercorns

3 bay leaves
   Whole sprigs dried thyme,
   basil, or oregano (optional)
$1/4$ cup sherry or vinegar
   Olive oil

COMBINE olives, garlic, lemon slices, peppercorns, bay leaves, sprigs of thyme, and sherry in jar. Add oil to cover. Marinate at least 24 hours or overnight to blend flavors.

Makes 2 cups.

SANDWICHES

THAT trusty mainstay of the brown-bag lunch, the sandwich, takes on new character in the West. Although peanut butter and jelly has its devotees, California-style sandwiches tend to be more inventive. Even ordinary hamburgers develop new dimensions when made the western way with cheese and vegetables mixed into the meat before it is shaped into patties and broiled.

The breads chosen as the bases for sandwiches are of great importance. Sturdy whole grain breads of all types, sourdough breads, and hard French rolls are always popular. Pita breads, the handy little pocket breads of Middle Eastern origin, are filled with everything from Sloppy Joe mixtures to falafel.

Informal parties are frequently planned around sandwiches. Some, in the form of ''super hero'' suppers, require specially ordered three- to four-foot-long loaves of French or Italian bread. Cut in halves lengthwise and topped with an assortment of cold cuts and crisp fresh vegetables, these super sandwiches are especially popular with teenagers.

Vegetarian sandwiches built around lentil burgers, bean and alfalfa sprouts, cheeses, avocados, tomatoes, and other fresh vegetables often turn into masterpieces that would delight Dagwood. Even the ubiquitous Mexican burrito, although technically not a sandwich, is treated as such by hungry diners on the run.

California Open-Face Sandwich, page 280

California Open-Face Sandwich

12 slices dark pumpernickel
  Butter or margarine,
  softened
12 lettuce leaves
 3 cups bean sprouts
 2 cups sliced mushrooms
1/2 teaspoon salt
1/4 teaspoon pepper

6 large slices cooked turkey
  breast
3 tablespoons chopped chives
  Tomato slices
  Hard-cooked eggs, sliced
1 (8-ounce) bottle Thousand
  Island Dressing

SPREAD bread with butter. Place 1 lettuce leaf on each slice of bread. Mix bean sprouts, mushrooms, salt, and pepper. Sprinkle about 1/3 cup of the bean sprout mixture over bread. Top with turkey slices. Sprinkle another 1/3 cup of bean sprout mixture on each sandwich. Sprinkle chives over sprouts. Top sandwiches with sliced tomatoes and eggs. Pour about 2 tablespoons Thousand Island Dressing over each sandwich. Garnish with black olive and parsley sprig, if desired.

Makes 6 sandwiches.

Rotisseried French Dip Sandwiches

1 (3 1/2- to 4-pound) rib eye
  roast
  Salt, pepper
1 teaspoon rosemary
1 (10 1/2-ounce) can beef
  consommé

Beef drippings, strained
Dash Worcestershire sauce
1 clove garlic, split
1 tablespoon prepared
  horseradish
6 French rolls, split

RUB beef on all sides with salt, pepper, and rosemary. Place on spit rod and push spit forks firmly into ends of meat. Make sure meat is balanced on rod. Insert meat thermometer into meat so tip is near center, but not touching spit rod or fat and so that face of thermometer clears grill as meat turns. Start spit motor and cook meat until thermometer registers 140 degrees for rare or 160 degrees for medium. Remove meat from spit to warm platter and let rest 15 minutes before carving. Carve into thin slices. Combine consommé, beef drippings, Worcestershire, garlic, and horseradish in skillet and simmer 5 minutes. Remove garlic and discard. Arrange 2 or 3 warm beef slices on bottom half of each roll, folding beef to fit. Dip cut sides of top halves of rolls into sauce and use to close sandwiches. Serve at once.

Makes 6.

Note: If preferred, meat may be roasted in a 325-degree oven. Allow 15 to 25 minutes per pound, depending upon the degree of doneness desired.

Vienna Dip Sandwiches

1 cup bouillon
1 teaspoon beef extract
1 tablespoon sherry
  Cooked pastrami slices

French rolls, split
Pickle slices
Prepared mustard (optional)

This is a pastrami version of the French dip roast beef sandwiches sold at many fast-food stands in Southern California.

HEAT bouillon and stir in beef extract and sherry. Stir until extract dissolves. Dip pastrami slices into bouillon mixture and layer generously over bottom halves of rolls. Place pickle slices on top of meat in each sandwich and spread with mustard. Dip top halves of rolls cut sides down into bouillon mixture and use to close sandwiches.

Sauce is enough for 6 sandwiches.

Pork and Chile Burritos

3 pounds boneless lean
  pork, cut in ½-inch cubes
1½ pounds onions, diced
½ pound green peppers,
  diced
½ bunch cilantro, chopped
2 tomatoes, chopped
1 teaspoon garlic powder
1 tablespoon salt
½ teaspoon ground cumin
¼ teaspoon ground cloves

¼ teaspoon black pepper
2 bay leaves
1 jalapeño chile, chopped
1 pound tomatillos
  Juice of ½ lemon
½ cup cornstarch blended
  with 1 cup water
12 (12-inch) flour tortillas
  Shredded Monterey Jack
  and cheddar cheeses

Burritos call for flour tortillas rather than corn. Here is a somewhat fancy version of this handy snack from the Jailhouse, a Mexican restaurant in Studio City.

PLACE meat in Dutch oven. Add 1 gallon water and bring to boil. Reduce heat and simmer, covered, until meat is half-cooked, about 35 minutes. Drain off water. Add onions, green peppers, cilantro, tomatoes, garlic powder, salt, cumin, cloves, pepper, bay leaves, and chile to meat and simmer. Remove husks from tomatillos and boil in saucepan in 1 quart water until tender, about 15 minutes. Drain off water. Mash tomatillos, add to meat mixture, and simmer, stirring constantly for 15 minutes. Add lemon juice. Blend cornstarch with 1 cup water, stir into meat mixture, and simmer 15 minutes longer, stirring constantly. Heat tortillas gently until softened (heat 1 at a time directly on burner of range, or wrap in foil and place in 350-degree oven for a few minutes). To make burritos, place a heaping ½ cup of meat mixture on tortilla. Fold sides in, then roll up from one end. Sprinkle burritos generously with cheese and place under broiler just until cheese melts.

Makes 12.

Monte Cristo Sandwich

This batter-dipped deep-fried sandwich comes from the Blue Bayou, a New Orleans-style restaurant in Disneyland.

6 slices cooked turkey
6 slices Swiss cheese
6 slices cooked ham
12 slices white bread

Batter
Oil for deep frying
Powdered sugar

PLACE 1 slice turkey on each of 6 slices bread, top turkey with a layer of cheese and a layer of ham. Top sandwiches with remaining slices of bread. Cut each sandwich into quarters, using wood picks to hold quarters together. Dip each sandwich quarter into Batter and fry in oil heated to 360 degrees until golden brown. Remove picks and sprinkle with powdered sugar. Serve with jelly, if desired.

Makes 6.

Batter

1¹/₂ cups flour
1 tablespoon baking powder
¹/₄ teaspoon salt

1¹/₃ cups water
1 egg

Sift flour, baking powder, and salt. Add water to beaten egg and add to flour mixture. Mix well.

Makes about 3 cups.

Pocket Sandwiches

Mel Hokanson, a Los Angeles fireman, created these sausage-filled pita sandwiches.

¹/₂ pound hot Italian sausage, sliced
1 onion, chopped
1 clove garlic, minced
1 cup sliced mushrooms
1 cup diced green pepper

¹/₂ cup diced celery
Pepper
6 pita breads
1 cup shredded Monterey Jack cheese

SAUTÉ sausage in large skillet until browned. Drain off all but 2 tablespoons fat and add onion, garlic, mushrooms, green pepper, and celery. Sauté until vegetables are tender and sausage is done. Season to taste with pepper. Cut pita breads in halves crosswise. Open pockets and stuff with sausage filling. Sprinkle filling with cheese. Fit sandwiches snugly upright in baking pan and bake at 400 degrees 10 minutes, or until cheese begins to melt. Serve at once.

Makes 6.

Note: Instead of sausage, use diced cooked chicken, turkey, shellfish, or any leftover cooked meat and sauté in 2 tablespoons of oil instead of sausage fat.

Avocado Pocket Sandwiches

1 avocado, halved and peeled
$1/2$ cup chopped cucumber
$1/2$ cup chopped carrot
$1/2$ cup chopped cauliflower
$1/2$ cup sliced mushrooms

$1/2$ cup cubed Monterey Jack
   cheese
$1/4$ cup bottled Italian dressing
4 pita breads
1 teaspoon lemon juice
$1/2$ cup chopped tomato

DICE half the avocado. Reserve other half. Gently toss diced avocado, cucumber, carrot, cauliflower, mushrooms, and cheese with Italian dressing. Slit pita breads and separate halfway around by pulling edges apart to form a pocket. Fill each with ¼ of the mixture. Mash remaining avocado with fork and stir in lemon juice and tomato. Spoon inside each sandwich.

Makes 4.

Falafel Sandwiches

$1/2$ cup dry split green peas
$1/2$ teaspoon salt
1 teaspoon black pepper
$1/2$ cup garbanzo bean flour
$1/4$ teaspoon onion powder
1 teaspoon chopped parsley
$1/2$ cup water

$1/2$ teaspoon ground cumin
2 cups oil
6 small pita breads
   Sliced tomatoes, onions,
   and dill pickle slices
   Humus Dip or Tahini Dip

Vegetarians find this type of pita bread sandwich appealing. The garbanzo bean flour needed is available in Middle Eastern markets.

SOAK split peas in water overnight. Then drain and mash. Add salt, pepper, garbanzo bean flour, onion powder, parsley, water, and cumin and mix well. Shape into small balls. Fry in hot oil and drain on paper towels. Slit pita bread to form pockets. Fill pockets with split pea balls and tomato, onion, and pickle slices. Top with Humus or Tahini Dip.

Makes 6.

Humus Dip

$1/2$ cup mashed, cooked
   garbanzo beans
2 tablespoons oil
2 tablespoons lemon juice
1 teaspoon salt

$1/4$ cup tahini (sesame seed
   paste)
$1/4$ teaspoon garlic powder
1 teaspoon sugar

Combine beans, oil, lemon juice, salt, tahini, garlic powder, and sugar. Mix well.

Makes about 1 cup.

(continued on overleaf)

Tahini Dip

1 cup tahini (sesame seed
  paste)
¹/₄ cup oil
¹/₄ teaspoon garlic powder

¹/₂ teaspoon salt
1 tablespoon lemon juice
¹/₄ teaspoon sugar
¹/₄ teaspoon ground ginger

Combine tahini, oil, garlic powder, salt, lemon juice, sugar, and ginger. Blend well.

Makes about 1¹/₄ cups.

Lentil Burgers

Lentil burgers are excellent
high-protein sandwiches for
those who prefer meatless
meals. These can be served on
any kind of bread, but they're
particularly good when tucked
into pita bread pockets.

2 cups cooked lentils
1 cup soft whole wheat bread
  crumbs
¹/₂ cup wheat germ
¹/₂ cup finely chopped onion

1¹/₄ teaspoons salt
2 eggs, lightly beaten
1 tablespoon Worcestershire
  sauce
3 tablespoons oil

MASH lentils slightly. Stir in bread crumbs, wheat germ, onion, salt, eggs, and Worcestershire. Form into 6 3¹/₂-inch patties, using ¹/₂ cup lentil mixture for each. Heat oil in large skillet. Cook patties until golden brown on both sides, about 5 minutes. Serve in whole wheat pita breads, if desired.

Makes 6.

Tacos

The taco is classified as a
sandwich too. Elva Medina
served these to Times staffers
who doted on the little Mexican
restaurant she ran for years
near the paper.

1 pound lean ground beef
  Salt
¹/₂ teaspoon ground cumin
  Dash black pepper
¹/₂ cup lard
10 corn tortillas

¹/₂ onion, sliced
  Shredded lettuce
1 tomato, cut in thin wedges
  Shredded Monterey Jack
  cheese

COOK meat until browned, stirring to crumble. Season to taste with salt and add cumin and pepper. Heat lard in skillet. Fry each tortilla until softened, then fold it in half and cook on each side until crisp. Drain. Fill each taco shell with heaping tablespoon of meat. Add few slices onion, generous amount of lettuce, a little tomato, and then cheese. Serve with green chile salsa on the side, if desired.

Makes 10.

Soft Tacos

1 pound lean pork butt or
  shoulder, cut in $1/2$-inch
  cubes
1 tablespoon lard or
  shortening
2 tablespoons chopped onion

3 sprigs cilantro,
  chopped
9 to 12 corn tortillas
  East L.A. Guacamole
  Lemon wedges

COOK meat in lard 20 minutes. Reduce heat, cover, and cook 30 minutes longer. Drain meat and shred. (There should be about $1^1/2$ cups shredded meat.) Combine onion and cilantro. Heat each tortilla on griddle or in skillet until pliable. Spread with guacamole, then top with some of pork mixture. Top meat with some onion mixture and sprinkle with juice from a lemon wedge. Roll up and serve with additional lemon wedges.

Makes 9 to 12.

Most Americans think that tacos always have crisp, fried shells. But Mexicans often prefer to wrap the filling in soft, hot tortillas as in these tacos, served at Las Carnitas restaurant in East Los Angeles.

East L.A. Guacamole

1 small avocado, halved and
  peeled
2 teaspoons minced onion
  Dash garlic powder

$1/2$ teaspoon salt
$1/4$ teaspoon black pepper
1 teaspoon lemon juice
1 small tomato, chopped

Mash avocado and blend in onion, garlic powder, salt, pepper, and lemon juice. Fold in tomato.

Makes about $1^1/4$ cups.

Steak Rolls

8 cube steaks
  Bottled steak sauce
$1/4$ cup fine dry bread crumbs
2 tablespoons minced onion
$1/2$ teaspoon salt
$1/8$ teaspoon lemon pepper

$1/4$ cup butter or margarine,
  melted
1 tablespoon vinegar
1 tablespoon catsup
  Dash oregano
8 long French rolls

SPREAD steak flat and brush with steak sauce. Combine crumbs, onion, salt, and pepper and sprinkle over steaks. Roll up tightly and secure with thread or wood picks. Skewer for grilling. Mix butter, vinegar, catsup, and oregano and heat. Use as baste while steak rolls are cooking. Grill steak from 9 to 15 minutes, depending on degree of rareness desired. Serve on rolls.

Makes 8 servings.

Mexican Heroes

In Mexico, sandwiches like
these are called tortas. Lee
Anderson sent this recipe to
our "My Best Recipe" column.

6 French rolls (about 8 inches
 long), split
1 cup sour cream
1 medium head iceberg
 lettuce, finely shredded
1 pound rare roast beef, thinly
 sliced
 Salt
1 onion, thinly sliced and
 separated into rings

Cilantro, coarsely chopped
2 avocados, peeled and thinly
 sliced
2 tablespoons chili powder
1 (10-ounce) can red chile
 sauce or enchilada sauce
1 cup shredded Monterey Jack
 cheese

REMOVE some bread from inside surfaces of rolls. Spread bottom half
of each roll thickly with sour cream and add some lettuce. Spread
with another layer of sour cream, then roast beef. Season to taste
with salt and top with onion rings, chopped cilantro, avocado slices,
and more sour cream. Sprinkle with about 1 teaspoon chili powder,
then top with more lettuce and drizzle with chile sauce. Top with
Jack cheese. Spread cut surface of top half of roll with chile sauce.
Place on top of cheese.

Makes 6.

Swinger Sandwiches

Swingers, hamburgers with
vegetables mixed into the meat
patties, became popular when
the health-food movement
moved into the restaurant
scene.

2 pounds lean ground beef
1 1/2 cups minced onions
1 1/2 cups finely diced green
 peppers
1 1/2 cups chopped peeled
 tomatoes

1/4 cup minced stuffed olives
2 cups shredded cheddar
 cheese
1 teaspoon salt
 Hot hamburger buns

THOROUGHLY mix ground beef, onions, green peppers, tomatoes, olives, cheese, and salt. Shape into 6 to 8 thick patties, place on a
platter or tray, and refrigerate 2 or 3 hours. When ready to cook,
press each meat patty firmly to prevent crumbling while cooking.
Grease a hot grill or heavy skillet, add patties, and brown on each
side. Turn heat low and cook until done as desired, about 10 minutes
on each side for medium rare. Serve on hot buns.

Makes 6 to 8.

BREADS

WHILE there's little doubt that Southern California's bakeries and restaurants have been treasure troves of outstanding bread recipes, we also have our readers to thank for their creative contributions. Homemade breads of all types are popular with area residents. Ethnic breads such as pita and lavash, the Armenian cracker bread, are served with almost as great a frequency as muffins and popovers.

Commercial bakeries and other professional bread makers have willingly shared some of their more interesting recipes with us. Fortunately, so have our readers, who have no qualms about experimenting within the confines of their own kitchens. An overabundance of backyard fruit trees or a garden zucchini patch that has gone wild will often bring us an exciting new quick-bread recipe. Still other dedicated home cooks, frustrated because neither we nor they can get a specific recipe from an uncooperative source, will spend days working out a facsimile that closely resembles the sought-after bread. That's how a popular squaw bread recipe that had eluded our files finally found a home there.

Many of the more popular bread recipes are quick breads or breads that have high drama yet take little time or effort to make. East Indian naan, the two L.A. corn breads, monkey bread, pumpkin bread, and brown bread included in this chapter are fine examples of the varieties of breads that have wide appeal in the West.

Clockwise from bottom: *Papaya Bread and Banana Bread, sliced; Pineapple-Macadamia Nut Bread, sliced; Banana Bread; Papaya Bread,* pages 290, 291.

Papaya Bread

1 cup sugar
$^1/_2$ cup butter or margarine
2 eggs
1 cup mashed ripe papaya
$^1/_4$ cup chopped walnuts
$^1/_2$ cup raisins
1$^1/_2$ cups flour

$^1/_4$ teaspoon baking powder
1 teaspoon soda
$^1/_2$ teaspoon salt
$^1/_2$ teaspoon ground cinnamon
$^1/_2$ teaspoon ground allspice
$^1/_2$ teaspoon ground ginger

CREAM together sugar and butter until light. Add eggs and beat until fluffy. Add papaya, nuts, and raisins and mix. Sift together flour, baking powder, soda, salt, cinnamon, allspice, and ginger. Add to butter mixture. Pour batter into greased wax-paper-lined 9 x 5-inch loaf pan. Bake at 325 degrees about 1 hour 5 minutes. Or fill greased muffin pans $^3/_4$ full and bake at 325 degrees 25 minutes.

Makes 1 loaf or 16 muffins.

Banana Bread

2 cups mashed banana
3 eggs
1 cup oil
1 teaspoon vanilla

2 cups flour
1 cup sugar
1 teaspoon soda
$^1/_4$ teaspoon salt

COMBINE banana, eggs, oil, and vanilla and mix well. Sift together flour, sugar, soda, and salt and add to banana mixture. Pour batter into greased and wax-paper-lined 9 x 5-inch loaf pan. Bake at 350 degrees 50 minutes or until done. Or fill greased muffin pans $^3/_4$ full and bake at 350 degrees 25 minutes.

Makes 1 loaf or 16 muffins.

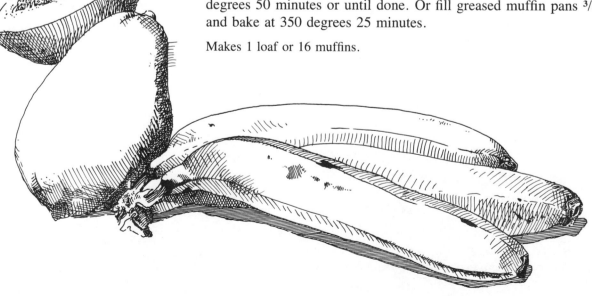

Pineapple-Macadamia Nut Bread

4 eggs
1 cup sugar
1/2 cup oil
3/4 cup pineapple juice
1/2 cup canned crushed
  pineapple, with juice

1 tablespoon baking powder
3 cups flour
1/2 cup chopped macadamia
  nuts

COMBINE eggs, sugar, oil, juice, and pineapple and mix well. Sift together baking powder and flour and mix into pineapple mixture. Fold in nuts. Pour into greased wax-paper-lined 9 x 5-inch loaf pan and bake at 350 degrees about 50 minutes. Or fill greased muffin pans 3/4 full. Bake at 350 degrees 25 minutes.

Makes 1 loaf or 18 muffins.

Tropical fruit breads have long appealed to Southern Californians. Recipes for this rich pineapple-macadamia nut creation and the papaya and banana breads that precede came from Hawaii's Coco Palms Resort on Kauai.

Pão Doce
(Sweet Bread)

1 pound potatoes, peeled
  Sugar
2 packages dry yeast
1/8 teaspoon ground ginger
3/4 cup milk

2 teaspoons salt
6 eggs
1/2 cup butter or margarine,
  melted and cooled
8 cups flour

BOIL potatoes in water to barely cover until tender. Drain, reserving 1/2 cup potato water. Mash potatoes to make 1 cup. Combine 3 tablespoons sugar, yeast, and 1/2 cup lukewarm potato water and stir until dissolved. Blend in potatoes and ginger. Set aside to rise until doubled in bulk. Scald milk, add salt, and cool to lukewarm. Beat eggs. Add 1 3/4 cups sugar gradually while continuing to beat. Stir in cooled butter. Combine yeast and egg mixtures. Blend thoroughly. Stir in 2 cups flour, add milk, and beat until thoroughly blended. Add 2 more cups flour. Beat 5 minutes. Add remaining 4 cups flour gradually, kneading when dough becomes too stiff to beat. Turn out on floured board and knead 10 minutes, adding only enough extra flour to prevent sticking. Place dough in greased bowl, turn to grease top, cover, and let rise until doubled in bulk. Divide dough into 4 portions, shape into round loaves on greased baking sheets or place in greased loaf pans. Allow to rise until doubled in bulk. Brush loaves with additional beaten egg, if desired. Bake at 350 degrees 20 minutes, then lower heat to 325 degrees and bake about 20 minutes longer, or until brown.

Makes 4 loaves.

The Portuguese took the formula for pão doce, or sweet bread, to Hawaii years ago, and Southern Californians visiting the islands liked it so much, they begged for the recipe.

Whole Wheat Bread

Hotel del Coronado on
beautiful Coronado Island off
San Diego was once a retreat
for film stars. Today it still puts
on a good table, and this bread
is among the many hotel
recipes requested by our
readers.

2 packages dry yeast
2 cups lukewarm water
3¼ cups all-purpose flour
1 teaspoon salt
⅓ cup plus 1 tablespoon
   sugar

3 eggs
¼ cup molasses
⅓ cup plus 1 tablespoon
   shortening
3½ cups whole wheat flour
   Oil

DISSOLVE yeast in warm water. Add 2 to 3 tablespoons all-purpose flour, salt, and sugar to yeast mixture and let stand until yeast mixture begins to bubble. Add eggs, molasses, and shortening and mix well. Add half the remaining all-purpose flour and beat in mixer with dough hook or by hand until smooth. Gradually add remaining all-purpose and whole wheat flours and mix well. Knead until a soft, smooth dough is formed. (Dough will be very soft and sticky.) Place dough in a warm oiled bowl and turn to grease surface. Let stand until doubled in bulk. Beat again, using dough hook. Place dough into 2 well-greased 9 x 5-inch loaf pans, turning to grease all surfaces. Let rise until dough reaches rim of pan. Bake at 400 degrees 10 minutes. Reduce heat to 350 degrees and bake 45 minutes longer, or until bread is done.

Makes 2 loaves.

Monkey Bread

No one we know really knows
the origin of monkey bread, but
it's been a Southern California
favorite for years. Mahalia
Jackson's is one of the best
home recipes.

2 cups milk
2 tablespoons sugar
2 to 3 teaspoons salt
1 tablespoon shortening

2 packages dry yeast
½ cup lukewarm water
6 to 7 cups flour, about
   Butter or margarine

SCALD milk and add sugar, salt, and shortening. Cool mixture to lukewarm. Sprinkle or crumble yeast into lukewarm water and stir until dissolved. Stir yeast into cooled milk mixture. Gradually add flour to milk mixture, mixing well. Add enough flour to make dough stiff enough to be handled easily. Turn dough onto floured surface and knead until smooth and satiny. Shape dough into 18 x 3-inch long loaf. Brush surface lightly with a little melted butter. Cover and let rise in warm place free from draft until doubled in bulk, 1 to 1½ hours. Cut loaf crosswise into 32 slices and dip slices in 1 cup melted butter. Place 8 slices each in bottoms of 2 9-inch tube pans. Top bottom layer, covering cracks, with 8 more slices each. Let rise again until doubled, about 1 hour. Bake at 350 degrees 50 to 60 minutes, or until golden and crusty.

Makes 2 loaves.

Roman Bread

1 tablespoon sugar
1 package dry yeast
1¹/₂ cups lukewarm water
4 cups flour

Salt
¹/₂ cup chopped onion
Oil
1 tablespoon rosemary

ADD sugar and yeast to lukewarm water in large bowl and stir until dissolved. Add flour, 2 teaspoons salt, and onion. Turn out on floured board and knead until smooth. Place dough in greased bowl and let rise until doubled in bulk. Punch down. Flatten dough on greased baking sheet to round shape about 2 inches thick. Brush top of dough with oil. Let rise until doubled in bulk. Sprinkle with salt and rosemary. Bake at 400 degrees 30 to 35 minutes. Serve hot.

Makes 1 loaf.

One of the charms of homemade bread is the fragrance that permeates the house while it's baking. Onion and rosemary give a special aroma to this loaf from Monti's La Casa Vieja in Tempe, Arizona.

Squaw Bread

2 cups water
¹/₃ cup oil
¹/₄ cup honey
¹/₄ cup raisins
5 tablespoons brown sugar
2 packages dry yeast
¹/₄ cup warm water
2¹/₂ cups unbleached all-purpose flour, about

3 cups whole wheat flour
1¹/₂ cups rye flour
¹/₂ cup instant nonfat milk powder
2¹/₂ teaspoons salt
Cornmeal
Melted butter

Our years-long search for an authentic squaw bread similar to that sold by bakeries and served in restaurants throughout Southern California ended when Marilyn Martell, a schoolteacher and frequent county fair blue-ribbon winner, developed her own recipe.

COMBINE water, oil, honey, raisins, and 4 tablespoons brown sugar in blender container. Blend to liquefy. Soften yeast in warm water with remaining 1 tablespoon brown sugar. Sift together 1 cup unbleached flour, 2 cups whole wheat flour, 1 cup rye flour, nonfat milk powder, and salt in large bowl. Add honey mixture and yeast. Beat with mixer at medium speed until smooth, about 2 minutes. Gradually stir in enough of the remaining flours to make a soft dough that leaves sides of bowl. Turn out onto floured surface and knead until smooth and satiny, about 10 to 12 minutes. Place dough in lightly greased bowl and turn to grease other side. Cover and let rise until doubled, about 1¹/₂ hours. Punch down and let rest 10 minutes. Shape into 4 round loaves. Place 2 loaves on each of 2 lightly greased baking sheets sprinkled with cornmeal. Cover and let rise in warm place until light and doubled in size, about 1 hour. Bake at 375 degrees 30 to 35 minutes. Cool on racks. While still hot, brush with melted butter.

Makes 4 loaves.

Pita Bread

Sandwiches made with pita bread have become great fast-food favorites on the West Coast. Clever hosts surround baskets of the breads with a variety of fillings and let their guests make their own sandwiches at informal poolside parties.

5 to 6	cups bread flour	2	cups water
3	tablespoons sugar	1/4	cup oil or shortening
2	teaspoons salt		Cornmeal
2	packages dry yeast		

COMBINE 2 cups flour, sugar, salt, and yeast in large bowl and blend well. Heat water and oil in small saucepan until very warm (120 to 130 degrees). Add warm liquid to flour mixture. Blend at low speed until moistened. Beat 3 minutes at medium speed. By hand stir in 2½ to 3 cups flour until dough pulls cleanly away from sides of bowl. On floured surface knead in ½ to 1 cup flour until dough is smooth and elastic with blisters under the surface, about 10 minutes. Place dough in greased bowl, cover loosely with plastic wrap and cloth towel. Let rise in warm place until light and doubled in bulk, about 1½ hours. Punch down dough, divide in 2 parts, then mold into balls. Allow to rest on counter, covered with inverted bowl, 15 minutes. Divide dough in 14 equal pieces and shape into balls. On lightly floured surface, roll each ball into a 7-inch circle about ⅛-inch thick. Place circles about 2 inches apart on cornmeal-sprinkled baking sheets. Cover and let rise in warm place about 30 minutes. Bake at 450 degrees 8 to 10 minutes, or until edges turn a light golden brown.

Makes 14 pocket breads.

Hungarian Loaf

Visitors to the Lake Arrowhead area of the San Bernardino Mountains find the bakery at Jensen's Market in Blue Jay difficult to resist. This bread with a sweet nutty top is a good example of their wares.

1	cup water	3¾	cups all-purpose flour
2	small eggs	1½	cups pastry flour
2	packages dry yeast	⅓	cup brown sugar, packed
1½	teaspoons salt	1	tablespoon cinnamon
⅓	cup plus 1 tablespoon granulated sugar		Honey Smear
½	cup plus 2 tablespoons instant nonfat milk powder	½ to 1	cup whole pecans or walnuts
½	cup shortening		

COMBINE water, eggs, yeast, salt, granulated sugar, nonfat milk powder, shortening, and flours in mixing bowl. Mix for 6 minutes on medium speed. Cover and let stand 1½ hours until doubled in bulk. Add brown sugar and cinnamon and mix ½ minute. Divide Honey Smear in half. Pour each half into well-greased 8 x 4-inch loaf pan. Sprinkle bottom of each pan with half the pecans. Divide dough in halves and place each half in pans over Honey Smear. Bake at 350 degrees 35 minutes, or until bread sounds hollow when tapped.

Makes 2 loaves.

Honey Smear

  6 tablespoons brown sugar
5¹/₂ tablespoons granulated
   sugar
  1 tablespoon butter
 ¹/₄ cup margarine

  2 tablespoons honey
1¹/₂ teaspoons vanilla
1¹/₂ teaspoons cinnamon
1¹/₂ teaspoons hot water

Combine sugars, butter, margarine, honey, vanilla, cinnamon, and hot water in mixing bowl. Cream until light and well blended.

Makes about 1¹/₄ cups.

Lavash
(Armenian Cracker Bread)

  1 package dry yeast
1¹/₂ cups warm water
  1 teaspoon salt

  2 cups all-purpose flour
  2 cups whole wheat flour
    Toasted sesame seeds

SPRINKLE yeast into warm water in large bowl and stir until dissolved. Add salt. Combine all-purpose and whole wheat flours and add enough to yeast mixture to make a stiff dough. Turn out on floured surface and knead until smooth and elastic, 8 to 10 minutes. Shape into a ball. Place in greased bowl and turn to grease top. Cover and let rise until doubled in bulk, about 1¹/₂ hours. Punch down and let rise again until doubled, about 30 minutes. Divide dough into 8 pieces and roll each out on lightly floured surface to very thin circle about 9 inches in diameter. Place 1 at a time on baking sheet and sprinkle with sesame seeds. Bake at 400 degrees 5 to 6 minutes, or until bread appears dry, lightly browned, and blistered. Place palest side under broiler until lightly browned. Cool and store in dry place.

Makes 8 breads.

An ancient Middle Eastern unleavened cracker, often baked in crisp rounds the size of a dinner plate, has become a popular novelty bread on Los Angeles tables.

Garlic Bread

¹/₂ cup butter or margarine
  2 cloves garlic, ground
  1 (1-pound) loaf French
    bread, cut in 15 slices

  2 cups shredded process
    American cheese

MELT butter, add garlic, and let mixture stand several hours or overnight to blend flavors. Strain off garlic. Brush bread slices with butter mixture, then sprinkle with cheese. Place under broiler until heated and golden brown.

Makes 15 slices.

A great novelty bread to serve with barbecued ribs or roast originated in a popular Los Angeles barbecue restaurant, the Smoke House.

Sopaipillas

Puffy sopaipillas are native to New Mexico and southern Arizona but are very popular in Los Angeles. Usually served with honey, they can also be stuffed with beans or meat.

2 cups flour
2 teaspoons baking powder
1/2 teaspoon salt
1/4 cup shortening

1/2 cup cold water
Oil for deep frying
Honey

COMBINE flour, baking powder, and salt in bowl. Cut in shortening with pastry blender or 2 knives. Add water gradually to make a stiff dough, adding more water if necessary. Knead dough on lightly floured board. Cover with cloth and let rest 15 minutes. Roll dough out on floured board until very thin. Cut into 2- or 3-inch circles or squares. Drop into deep hot oil and fry until browned, turning several times. Dough will puff as it fries. Serve with honey.

Makes about 2 dozen.

L.A. Sweet Corn Bread

In Los Angeles the sweet, cake-like corn bread similar to that served at family restaurants is preferred. No one would share the recipe so we developed our own in The Times test kitchen with extraordinarily good results.

1 (18.5-ounce) package yellow
  cake mix
1 (15-ounce) package corn
  bread mix

MIX cake and corn bread batters according to package directions. Blend together and turn into 2 greased 9-inch square baking pans. Bake at 350 degrees 30 to 35 minutes, or until corn bread springs back when lightly touched.

Makes about 32 servings.

L.A. Savory Corn Bread

Substituting packaged biscuit mix for the cake mix in a similar recipe resulted in a fine savory alternative to the sweeter corn bread.

1 (20-ounce) package
  buttermilk biscuit mix
1 (15-ounce) package corn
  bread mix

PREPARE biscuit batter according to package directions for muffins. Prepare corn bread batter according to package directions. Blend together and turn into 2 8-inch square baking pans. Bake at 350 degrees 30 to 35 minutes, or until bread tests done in center and is lightly browned.

Makes about 32 servings.

Spoon Bread

1 (1-pound) can cream-style
  corn
³/₄ cup milk
¹/₃ cup shortening
2 eggs, lightly beaten
1 cup cornmeal
¹/₂ teaspoon soda

1 teaspoon baking powder
1 teaspoon salt
1 (4-ounce) can diced green
  chiles, drained
1¹/₂ cups shredded cheddar
  cheese

Ken Curtis, who played the
marshall's sidekick, Festus, in
the old ''Gunsmoke'' TV series,
is also a very good cook. He
gave us this recipe for spoon
bread, which he serves with
cornmeal-coated sand dabs.

COMBINE corn, milk, shortening, eggs, cornmeal, soda, baking powder, salt, drained chiles, and cheese and mix well. Pour into greased 9-inch square pan. Bake at 400 degrees 45 minutes until golden. Serve hot.

Makes 6 servings.

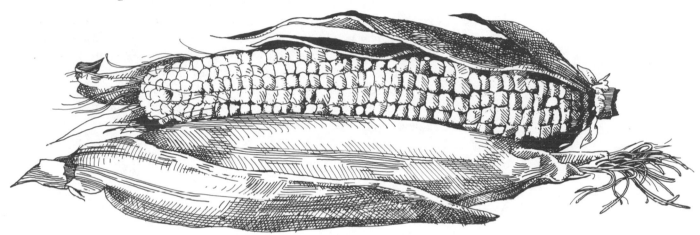

Scones

1¹/₃ cups shortening
1¹/₂ cups powdered sugar
4 eggs
¹/₄ teaspoon salt
10 cups flour
3 tablespoons cream of
  tartar

4 teaspoons soda
3¹/₂ cups cold milk
1 cup currants
1 egg, lightly beaten
  (optional)

The Park Pantry, a family
restaurant and bakery in
Torrance, California, provided
the recipe for these outstanding
scones.

CREAM shortening with powdered sugar until light. Stir in eggs until thoroughly blended. Sift together salt, flour, and cream of tartar. Mix soda and milk. Combine creamed mixture with flour mixture. Add milk mixture to remaining batter and mix thoroughly. Fold in currants. Roll out dough to 1¹/₂-inch thickness. Cut scones with 3-inch cutter dipped in flour. Place on greased baking sheets 2 inches apart. Brush with lightly beaten egg and bake at 400 degrees 15 to 25 minutes.

Makes 4 dozen.

Brown Bread

Nuns at the Monastery of the Angels in Hollywood developed this bread to sell at fund-raising events. It sells out very quickly.

2 cups water
3 tablespoons brown or raw sugar
2 tablespoons shortening
1 tablespoon salt
3 tablespoons carob powder

2¹/₂ tablespoons sesame seeds
1 package dry yeast
5¹/₃ cups whole wheat flour
¹/₃ cup plus 1¹/₂ teaspoons instant nonfat milk powder

COMBINE half the water with brown sugar, shortening, salt, carob powder, and sesame seeds in mixing bowl. Stir with spoon or whip until mixture is just blended. Place yeast in remaining 1 cup water and let stand to dissolve. Mix flour with instant milk powder. Reserve 1 cup. Combine rest of flour mixture with sugar mixture and add yeast mixture. Mix at low speed until ingredients are well incorporated, then turn speed to medium and beat 4 to 5 minutes. If necessary, add reserved flour gradually. Flour mixture should leave sides of bowl. Cover bowl with clean cloth, then cover with plastic film to speed rising. Let rise 1¹/₂ hours until doubled in bulk. Punch dough down and let rise again, 20 to 30 minutes. Divide dough in halves, shape into loaves, and place in greased 8 x 4-inch loaf pans, or shape into rounds on greased baking sheets. Let rest 15 minutes. Bake at 375 degrees 40 minutes.

Makes 2 loaves.

Pumpkin Bread

Another creation from the Monastery of the Angels in Hollywood, this bread has become a reader favorite throughout the years.

3¹/₂ cups sifted flour
3 cups sugar
2 teaspoons soda
1 teaspoon cinnamon
1 teaspoon nutmeg
1¹/₂ teaspoons salt

4 eggs, beaten
1 cup oil
²/₃ cup water
2 cups mashed cooked pumpkin
Walnut halves

SIFT together flour, sugar, soda, cinnamon, nutmeg, and salt. Combine eggs, oil, water, and pumpkin and mix well. Stir into dry ingredients. Turn into 3 greased 8 x 4-inch loaf pans and top with a few walnut halves. Bake at 350 degrees 1 hour, or until wood pick inserted in center comes out clean. Cool before slicing. (Tastes best slightly warm, spread with butter.)

Makes 3 loaves.

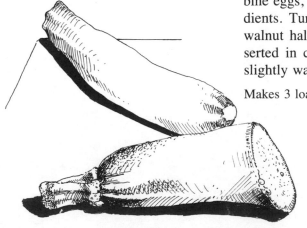

Zucchini Bread

½ cup oil
1 cup sugar
2 eggs
1 cup grated unpeeled
    zucchini

1½ cups flour
1½ teaspoons cinnamon
¾ teaspoon soda
¼ teaspoon baking powder

*The Broadway department
store's zucchini bread is lovely
as a gift or to serve at teas.*

BLEND oil and sugar together. Beat eggs into mixture one at a time.
Place grated zucchini in separate bowl. Fold egg mixture into zucchini. Sift together flour, cinnamon, soda, and baking powder. Gradually add flour mixture to zucchini mixture. Mix well. Pour batter
into 2 greased 8 x 4-inch loaf pans. Bake at 325 degrees 1 hour.

Makes 2 loaves.

Beer Bread

3 cups self-rising flour
2 tablespoons sugar
1 (12-ounce) can beer

½ cup butter or margarine,
    melted

*It's the beer that gives this
simple quick bread its unique
flavor and texture, but for best
results the self-rising flour used
in this recipe must be strictly
fresh.*

MIX flour and sugar with wooden spoon. Blend in beer one-third at
a time. Turn batter into 3 (6 x 3-inch) loaf pans and drizzle butter
over tops. Bake at 350 degrees 50 minutes.

Makes 3 loaves.

Indian Fry Bread

4 cups flour
2 tablespoons baking powder
1 teaspoon salt
½ cup lard or shortening

1 cup warm water, about
Oil for deep frying
Honey

MIX flour, baking powder, and salt. Cut in lard until mixture is about
the texture of cornmeal. Gradually add warm water, using only
enough to make dough stick together. Divide dough into 6 balls the
size of a fist. Cover with towel and let stand 10 minutes. Pat each
ball out to size of large pancake. Fry in deep hot oil until golden
brown on both sides. Serve with honey.

Makes 6 breads.

Naan Bread

The Third Floor restaurant at Honolulu's Hawaiian Regent Hotel serves warm East Indian naan bread baked in a tandoori oven, the huge clay high-heat oven of India. This recipe, created for home ovens, closely resembles the real thing.

4 cups flour	2 eggs
1 tablespoon sugar	3/4 cup milk
1/4 teaspoon soda	1/4 cup plain yogurt
1 tablespoon baking powder	2 tablespoons oil
1/2 teaspoon salt	

COMBINE flour, sugar, soda, baking powder, and salt in deep bowl and mix well. Make well in center and add eggs, milk, yogurt, and oil. Mix until dough is somewhat sticky. Add warm water sparingly, if necessary. Cover bowl with towel and let dough rise for about 1 hour. Moisten hands with a little oil and divide dough into 8 portions. Flatten and form each portion into a triangle 3/4-inch thick. Arrange bread on ungreased baking sheets and bake at 450 degrees for about 10 minutes. Serve hot.

Makes 8 breads.

Carob-Whole Wheat Doughnuts

Lower in calories and sodium, carob powder has been gaining popularity as a replacement for cocoa or chocolate.

1 cup all-purpose flour	2/3 cup sugar
3 tablespoons carob powder	2 tablespoons melted
2 teaspoons baking powder	shortening
1/8 teaspoon soda	1 teaspoon vanilla
1/4 teaspoon salt	1/3 cup buttermilk
1 teaspoon cinnamon	Oil for deep frying
1 cup whole wheat flour	Powdered sugar
1 egg	

SIFT together all-purpose flour, carob powder, baking powder, soda, salt, and cinnamon. Mix in whole wheat flour. Beat egg until light in large bowl. Gradually add sugar. Stir in shortening and vanilla. Add flour mixture alternately with buttermilk, stirring lightly until mixed. Roll out dough, half at a time, about 1/2-inch thick on floured surface. Keep rest of dough chilled. Cut with floured doughnut cutter. Drop, a few at a time, into deep oil heated to 375 degrees and cook 2 to 3 minutes, turning once or twice. Drain on paper towels. Sprinkle with powdered sugar.

Makes 10 to 12.

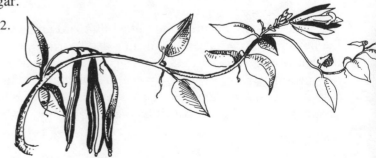

Ranch Wedgies

2 cups boiling water
1¹/₄ cups bulgur
¹/₂ cup brown sugar, packed
1 teaspoon salt
2 tablespoons butter or
  margarine

2 packages dry yeast
²/₃ cup warm water
4¹/₂ cups flour, about

POUR boiling water over bulgur, then stir in brown sugar, salt, and butter. Cool to lukewarm. Sprinkle yeast into warm water and stir until dissolved. Beat the yeast mixture into bulgur mixture. Stir in enough flour to make a sticky dough. Turn onto floured surface and knead until smooth and elastic, about 10 minutes. Dough is sticky, so keep hands well floured while kneading. Place in greased bowl and turn to grease top. Cover and let rise until doubled in bulk, about 1 hour. Punch down and let rise again 30 minutes. Punch down and turn out onto a floured surface. Divide dough in halves and pat each half into a well-greased 8-inch round pan. Cover and let rise until puffed slightly above rims of pans. Bake at 350 degrees about 1 hour, or until done. Turn out of pans and cool on wire racks. Cut in wedges and serve with butter; or split wedges, toast, and butter.

Makes 2 loaves.

Merk's Coffee Cake

¹/₂ cup shortening
³/₄ cup sugar
1 teaspoon vanilla
3 eggs
2 cups sifted flour
1 teaspoon baking powder
1 teaspoon soda

1 cup sour cream
6 tablespoons butter or
  margarine, softened
1 cup brown sugar, packed
2 teaspoons cinnamon
1 cup chopped nuts

Merk's coffee cake has been a sought-after recipe as long as anyone in The Times *Food Section can remember.*

CREAM shortening, sugar, and vanilla thoroughly. Add eggs one at a time, beating well after each addition. Sift together flour, baking powder, and soda. Add to creamed mixture alternately with sour cream, blending after each addition. Grease a 10-inch tube pan and line bottom with wax paper. Turn half the batter into pan. Cream softened butter with brown sugar and cinnamon. Add nuts and toss to make crumbly. Place half of mixture over first layer. Spread with remaining cake batter and top with remaining nut mixture. Bake at 350 degrees 30 to 40 minutes, or until cake springs back when lightly touched.

Makes 8 servings.

Bruschetta
(Heart-Shaped Garlic Rolls)

Mauro's, a North Italian restaurant in Glendale, serves these delicate and fragrant heart-shaped rolls hot and fresh.

1 cup water	2 tablespoons olive oil
1 cup milk	5 to 6 cups flour
2 eggs	Salt
2 packages dry yeast	1 or 2 cloves garlic, crushed
2 teaspoons sugar	1/4 cup vegetable oil

COMBINE water, milk, eggs, yeast, sugar, and olive oil in large bowl. Mix well and add half the flour and 2 teaspoons salt. Knead in remaining flour and 1 teaspoon salt. Knead until dough forms a ball. Place in greased bowl and turn to grease top. Cover and let stand 30 minutes to 1 hour until doubled. Punch down, turn, and let stand again 30 minutes to 1 hour. Punch down. Roll out dough on floured surface. Cut into heart or other desired shapes using cookie cutter. Place rolls on generously greased baking sheet. Combine garlic, vegetable oil, and salt and brush over rolls. Bake at 400 degrees 12 to 15 minutes or until golden.

Makes about 2 dozen.

Conchas
(Coiled Sweet Rolls)

These coiled rolls are only one of many forms of Mexican pan dulce (sweet bread).

3 1/2 to 4 cups flour	2/3 cup very warm water
1/4 cup sugar	2 eggs, at room temperature
1 teaspoon salt	1/2 cup honey
1 package dry yeast	3/4 cup chopped almonds
Softened butter or margarine	

MIX 3/4 cup flour, sugar, salt, and undissolved yeast in large bowl. Add softened butter. Gradually add water and beat 2 minutes at medium speed of electric mixer, scraping bowl occasionally. Add eggs and 1/2 cup flour. Beat at high speed 2 minutes, scraping bowl occasionally. Stir in enough additional flour to make a stiff dough. Turn out onto lightly floured board and knead until smooth and elastic, 5 to 10 minutes. Place in greased bowl, turning to grease top. Cover and let rise in warm place until doubled in bulk. Punch dough down. Divide in halves. On a lightly floured board, roll half of dough to a 15 x 12-inch rectangle. Spread with 2 tablespoons softened butter. Fold in half. Roll out again to a 15 x 12-inch rectangle. Spread with 2 tablespoons more butter. Fold in half and roll out to an 18 x 6-inch rectangle. Cut dough lengthwise into 6 (1-inch) strips. Fold each strip in half lengthwise so that it is 1/2-inch wide. Gently roll to round and lengthen each strip to a rope $1/4$ to $1/2$ inch in diameter. Hold one end of each rope firmly and wind dough loosely around to form a coil. Tuck end underneath. Place on greased baking sheets about 2 inches apart. Repeat with remaining dough. Cover and let rise in warm place until doubled in bulk. Heat honey until thin. Gently brush rolls with half of honey and sprinkle with almonds. Bake at 400 degrees 15 minutes or until browned. Remove at once from baking sheets and cool on wire racks. Drizzle while hot with remaining honey.

Makes 12 rolls.

Orange-Nut Muffins

2 cups flour	Grated peel of 1 orange
1 tablespoon baking powder	2 eggs
1 teaspoon cinnamon	1 cup milk
$1/4$ teaspoon salt	$1/2$ cup oil
1 cup chopped walnuts	1 cup brown sugar, packed

SIFT together flour, baking powder, cinnamon, and salt. Add nuts and orange peel and mix lightly. Beat eggs and stir in milk, oil, and brown sugar. Make a well in the flour mixture and add egg mixture all at once. Mix very quickly, just until dry ingredients are moistened. Spoon into greased muffin cups, filling about $2/3$ full. Bake at 375 degrees 12 to 15 minutes.

Makes 12 to 14.

The orange-nut muffins served in the tearooms of the Buffum's department store chain in the Los Angeles area are a delicious treat.

Dark Moist Bran Muffins

2 cups whole wheat flour	2 cups buttermilk
$1^1/2$ cups bran flakes	1 egg
2 tablespoons sugar	$1/2$ cup dark molasses
$1/4$ teaspoon salt	2 tablespoons melted butter
$1^1/4$ teaspoons soda	or margarine

COMBINE flour, bran, sugar, salt, and soda and mix well. Combine buttermilk, egg, molasses, and butter and add all at once to dry ingredients. Stir just enough to moisten flour mixture. Fill greased muffin cups $2/3$ full and bake at 350 degrees 20 to 25 minutes.

Makes about 24.

Note: Bran flakes are available in health-food stores.

Bran muffins, especially the dark, moist type found in many coffee shops, have a tremendous following in the Los Angeles area.

Bran Muffins

One of the most frequently requested bran muffin recipes comes from Griswold's, a family restaurant in Claremont, California.

1/4 cup butter or margarine
6 tablespoons brown sugar, packed
1 cup granulated sugar
6 tablespoons honey
1 tablespoon water
1/2 cup whole wheat flour
1/2 cup plus 2 tablespoons cake flour
1 teaspoon salt
1/2 teaspoon soda
1/2 teaspoon cinnamon
1/2 cup raisins
2 eggs
1/4 cup oil
1/4 cup well-drained canned crushed pineapple
3 cups whole bran cereal
1 1/2 cups buttermilk

CREAM butter until light and fluffy. Gradually beat in brown sugar and 6 tablespoons granulated sugar. Blend in 2 tablespoons honey and water and whip until fluffy. Coat 18 large muffin cups liberally and evenly with mixture, using about 2 teaspoons per cup. Combine whole wheat flour and cake flour, remaining 10 tablespoons granulated sugar, salt, soda, and cinnamon. Stir in raisins. Add eggs, remaining 1/4 cup honey, oil, and pineapple and blend. Stir in bran and buttermilk and mix until batter is smooth. Fill coated muffin cups 3/4 full. Bake at 400 degrees 18 to 20 minutes. Remove muffins from cups immediately by turning upside down on racks.

Makes 18.

Note: Honey glaze may be reduced, if desired.

Buttermilk Biscuits

Buttery home-style biscuits are among the many attractions at Clifton's, one of Los Angeles's oldest cafeterias.

3 cups white pastry flour
4 1/4 teaspoons baking powder
1 1/2 teaspoons salt
1/2 cup shortening
1/8 teaspoon soda
1 cup plus 2 tablespoons buttermilk
1/4 cup flour
1 egg white

SIFT together flour, baking powder, and salt. Add shortening and mix at low speed of electric mixer (using dough cutter attachment or mixing paddle attachment) until shortening is well broken up. Combine soda and buttermilk and add to flour mixture. Mix until all ingredients are well blended. Place dough on floured board and roll out in rectangle about 3/4-inch thick. Cut with 2-inch biscuit cutter dipped in flour. Place cut biscuits, touching each other, on lightly greased baking sheet. Brush tops of biscuits with egg white mixed with 1 teaspoon water. Bake at 375 degrees 15 to 18 minutes.

Makes 1 1/4 dozen.

PIES

SOMETIMES we think that if we did nothing but print recipes for chocolate desserts our readers would be happy. And when we really want to please, we provide recipes for chocolate pies. Not just ordinary chocolate pies, of course, but sinfully rich and spectacularly elegant chocolate pies like Justice Mildred Lillie's chocolate mousse pie that calls for two kinds of chocolate in the filling and a chocolate cookie crust.

Still other pies that have caught the fancy of *Times* readers are fruit pies—strawberry, apple, and lemon rate high—and pumpkin and coconut pies. Oddly enough, although Southern Californians tend to prefer meats, vegetables, and fruits prepared in the simplest fashion, they want their pies to be both showy and a dieter's downfall. Dedicated calorie-counters have been known to cheerfully destroy a full week's progress when confronted with a slice of another favorite, the ice-cream-based mud pie.

Chocolate Mousse Pie, page 308

Chocolate Mousse Pie

Justice Mildred Lillie of the Court of Appeals in Los Angeles is one of the city's finest hostess-cooks. Tired of having to go to a restaurant to enjoy a spectacular chocolate mousse pie, she decided to develop a recipe for it. The pie was and is a local favorite.

8 eggs, separated
  Sugar
2 teaspoons vanilla
1/4 teaspoon salt
1/2 cup brandy
10 ounces unsweetened
  chocolate

2 ounces semisweet
  chocolate
3/4 cup butter, softened
1/2 cup coffee
1 1/2 cups whipping cream
  Chocolate Crust
  Cherry Cordials

COMBINE egg yolks, 1 1/2 cups sugar, vanilla, salt, and brandy in top of double boiler. Place over simmering water and beat until pale yellow and thick, about 8 to 10 minutes. Remove from water and set aside. Melt both types of chocolate in top of double boiler over hot water. When melted, remove from water and beat in butter, a bit at a time. Gradually beat chocolate into egg yolk mixture until smooth. Chocolate mixture will congeal and become very stiff. Beat in coffee. Beat egg whites (at room temperature) into soft peaks. Gradually beat in 3 tablespoons sugar until stiff peaks form. Beat 1 cup of the beaten egg whites into chocolate mixture to thin it, then carefully fold in remaining beaten egg whites until thoroughly incorporated. Whip the cream until stiff and gently fold into chocolate mixture. Pour into prepared crust and chill overnight in refrigerator. Garnish with Cherry Cordials.

Makes 6 to 8 servings.

Chocolate Crust

2/3 (8 1/2-ounce) package dark
  chocolate wafers
2 tablespoons butter, melted

Grind wafers in blender container until crumbs are very fine. Combine butter with crumbs and pat onto sides and bottom of buttered 9-inch springform pan. Bake at 325 degrees 10 minutes. Remove from oven and cool completely.

Cherry Cordials

13 maraschino cherries with
  stems, drained
1/2 cup brandy
5 ounces semisweet chocolate

Soak cherries in brandy and place in freezer. Melt chocolate over hot water. When cherries are frozen, dry on paper towel and quickly dip, one at a time, into chocolate, swirling around by the stem until completely covered. The chocolate will harden almost immediately. Place on wax-paper-lined rack in refrigerator until ready to use.

Davos Torte

2¹/₂ cups sugar
  1 cup whipping cream
  1 cup chopped walnuts

1 cup butter or margarine
1 egg
1³/₄ cups flour

A reader acquired the recipe for this fabulous nut torte at a ski hut in Davos, Switzerland.

MELT 2 cups sugar in skillet over medium heat until golden. Quickly add whipping cream, stirring briskly with long-handled wooden spoon until smooth and creamy. Remove from heat. Add walnuts and cool. Cream butter with remaining ¹/₂ cup sugar until light. Beat in egg until smooth. Sir in flour to make a soft dough. Gather dough and chill a few minutes. Press ³/₄ of dough in bottom and on sides of 9-inch tart pan with removable bottom. Pour in nut mixture. Roll out remaining pastry dough in 10-inch circle between 2 sheets of wax paper. Chill filled pastry and pastry circle 1 hour. Remove sheet of paper from circle and carefully invert dough on top of pie. Remove top sheet of paper. Flute edges around pan with fingers or tines of fork. Pierce top pastry with fork tines or cut vent holes. Bake at 325 degrees about 1¹/₂ hours, or until pastry is golden. Cool in pan before loosening. Will keep well in the refrigerator for several weeks.

Makes 8 to 10 servings.

Macadamia Nut Cream Pie

1¹/₃ cups milk
 ³/₄ cup sugar
    Chopped toasted
    macadamia nuts
    Dash salt

1 teaspoon vanilla
3 eggs, separated
1 tablespoon cornstarch
1 (8-inch) baked pastry shell
   Whipped cream

Visitors to Hawaii returned with a liking for macadamia nuts and a wonderful way to use them in this delicate cloudlike pie that melts in the mouth.

COMBINE 1 cup milk, ¹/₄ cup sugar, ¹/₄ cup nuts, salt, and vanilla in top of double boiler. Place over boiling water and scald. Combine remaining ¹/₃ cup milk, egg yolks, and cornstarch and add to hot milk mixture. Cook, stirring, until thickened. Remove from heat and cool slightly. Beat egg whites with remaining ¹/₂ cup sugar until stiff. Carefully fold into milk mixture and turn into pastry shell. When cool, top with whipped cream and sprinkle with additional chopped nuts, if desired.

Makes 6 servings.

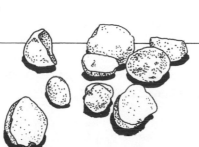
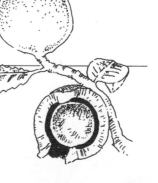

Mud Pie

²/₃ (8 ¹/₂-ounce) package dark chocolate wafers
¹/₄ cup butter or margarine, softened

¹/₂ gallon coffee ice cream
Chocolate Fudge Sauce
Whipped cream
Toasted sliced almonds

CRUSH wafers and mix with butter. Press into 9-inch pie pan to form a crust. Chill thoroughly or bake at 350 degrees 7 minutes, then chill. Pack ice cream into chilled crust, smoothing surface. Freeze until firm. (Freezing before adding Chocolate Fudge Sauce is essential to keep fudge from slipping off.) Pour ³/₄ cup Chocolate Fudge Sauce evenly over pie and freeze until ready to serve. To serve, top with dollops of whipped cream and sprinkle with almond slices.

Makes 6 to 8 servings.

Note: Canned fudge sauce is used by restaurants, but you may use your own recipe or the one given here.

Chocolate Fudge Sauce

5 ounces unsweetened Swiss chocolate
¹/₂ cup butter or margarine

²/₃ cup evaporated milk
3 cups powdered sugar
1¹/₄ teaspoons vanilla

Melt chocolate and butter together. Remove from heat and blend in milk alternately with powdered sugar. Bring to boil over medium heat, stirring constantly. Cook, stirring, 8 minutes or until thickened and creamy. Remove from heat and stir in vanilla. Store in refrigerator and use as needed.

Makes 3 cups.

Glazed Fresh Strawberry Pie

5 to 6 cups strawberries, washed and hulled
1 cup sugar
3¹/₂ tablespoons cornstarch

¹/₂ cup water
1 (9-inch) baked pastry shell
Whipped cream

MASH 2 cups strawberries. Mix sugar and cornstarch in 3-quart saucepan. Stir in water and mashed berries. Cook over medium heat, stirring constantly, until mixture comes to a boil and boil 2 minutes. Remove from heat. Cool. Fold remaining berries into cooled mixture. Pile into pastry shell. Chill. Serve with whipped cream.

Makes 6 servings.

Purple Prune Plum Pie

20 to 21 purple prune plums
1 cup sugar
1/4 cup flour
1 to 2 tablespoons cinnamon

1 (9-inch) unbaked pastry shell
2 tablespoons butter or
margarine

Prune plums, sometimes called Italian plums, give brilliant, deep color and good tart flavor to this pie. This variety of plum is available for only a few weeks in August and September.

WASH and dry plums. Cut in halves and remove pits. Combine sugar, flour, and cinnamon. Sprinkle 1/4 of this mixture over bottom of pastry shell. Overlap plums in circles over sugar mixture. Sprinkle remaining mixture over and dot with butter. Bake at 425 degrees 10 minutes. Reduce heat to 350 degrees and bake 30 to 35 minutes longer.

Makes 6 to 8 servings.

Apple Pie with Port

2 cups sifted flour
1 teaspoon salt
2/3 cup shortening
3/4 cup shredded sharp
cheddar cheese

5 to 6 tablespoons cold water
Apple Filling

MIX flour, salt, and shortening with pastry blender until mixture resembles coarse meal. Stir in cheese. Add water gradually and mix lightly with fork to form a dough. Divide pastry in half and roll out one half to fit a 9-inch pie pan. Roll second half of pastry and cut into 10 1/2-inch strips. Spoon Apple Filling into pastry-lined pan. Weave pastry strips across filling to make lattice top. Bake at 375 degrees 30 to 45 minutes, or until done. Serve warm.

Makes 6 to 8 servings.

Apple Filling

1 1/2 cups sugar
1/4 cup cornstarch
2/3 cup apple juice
2/3 cup port
2 tablespoons butter or
margarine

Grated peel of 1 lemon
8 medium cooking apples,
peeled and sliced (about 7 to
8 cups)

Combine sugar and cornstarch in large saucepan. Stir in apple juice, port, butter, and lemon peel. Cook over medium heat until mixture boils. Add apples and cook gently until barely tender.

Heavenly Lemon Pie

Department store tearooms are frequently good sources for excellent recipes. This one for lemon pie with a meringue crust came from Bullock's.

4 eggs, separated
1/2 cup sugar
  Grated peel and juice of 1
  large lemon

2 cups whipping cream,
  whipped
  Meringue Crust
1 tablespoon powdered sugar

BEAT the egg yolks with sugar, lemon peel, and juice until light. Cook, stirring, in top of double boiler over boiling water until thickened. Remove from heat and cool thoroughly. Fold in half the whipped cream. Turn into Meringue Crust and refrigerate at least 2 hours to set. Fold powdered sugar into remaining whipped cream and spread over chilled pie.

Makes 6 to 8 servings.

Meringue Crust

4 egg whites
1 cup sugar
1 teaspoon lemon juice

Beat egg whites until soft peaks form. Gradually add sugar, beating until stiff but not dry. Blend in juice. Grease a 9-inch pie pan generously. Spoon meringue mixture into pan and with a tablespoon push mixture up around edges to form pie shell. Bake at 200 degrees 2 hours. Cool.

Margarita Pie

The Mexican cocktail tastes very good in pie form too.

1 envelope unflavored gelatin
1 cup sugar
1/4 teaspoon salt
4 eggs, separated
1/2 cup lime juice

1 teaspoon grated lime peel
1/3 cup tequila
3 tablespoons cointreau or
  triple-sec liqueur
1 (9-inch) baked pastry shell

MIX gelatin, 1/2 cup sugar, and salt in saucepan. Beat egg yolks and lime juice together and add to gelatin mixture. Cook, stirring, over low heat until gelatin is dissolved, 5 to 7 minutes. Remove from heat and stir in lime peel, tequila, and liqueur. Chill over ice water or in refrigerator until mixture mounds slightly when dropped from a spoon. Beat egg whites and remaining 1/2 cup sugar until stiff. Fold whites into gelatin mixture. Turn filling into pastry shell and chill until firm. Garnish with lime twists and whipped cream dollops, if desired. For best results, serve pie same day.

Makes 6 to 8 servings.

Sweet Potato Pie

1½ cups mashed cooked sweet
   potatoes
½ cup butter or margarine,
   softened
4 eggs
1 cup granulated or brown
   sugar

1½ teaspoons nutmeg
1½ teaspoons vanilla
   Dash cinnamon
½ cup milk
1 (9-inch) unbaked pastry
   shell

Odessa Shaw of Los Angeles grew her own sweet potatoes to make this outstanding pie. The filling should be refrigerated overnight before baking.

BLEND sweet potatoes with butter. Add eggs, sugar, nutmeg, vanilla, and cinnamon. Stir in milk. Let stand overnight in refrigerator to set slightly. Turn into pastry shell and bake at 350 degrees 1½ hours. Cool.

Makes about 6 servings.

Fresh Coconut Cream Pie

2 cups milk
½ cup sugar
   Dash salt
   Grated fresh coconut
4 egg yolks
3 tablespoons cornstarch

3 tablespoons water
1 tablespoon butter or
   margarine
1 teaspoon vanilla
1 (9-inch) baked pastry shell
   Meringue

The fresh coconut cream pie served at The Willows restaurant in Honolulu has generated hundreds of requests for the recipe throughout the years.

COMBINE milk, sugar, salt, and ¼ cup grated coconut in medium saucepan. Cook until mixture is very hot. Beat egg yolks, then blend in cornstarch and water. Add egg yolk mixture to milk mixture. Cook, stirring, until thickened, about 1 minute. Add butter and vanilla. Cool filling and pour into pastry shell. Swirl Meringue over filling, making sure it is sealed to edge of pie shell. Sprinkle with grated coconut. Bake at 400 degrees until golden brown, about 10 minutes. Cool completely.

Makes 6 to 8 servings.

Meringue

4 to 6 egg whites
¼ teaspoon cream of
   tartar
   Sugar

Beat egg whites with cream of tartar until soft peaks form. Gradually add 1 tablespoon sugar for each egg white used and continue beating until stiff peaks form.

Guava Chiffon Pie

The crust of this light and fruity chiffon pie from Coco Palms Resort on Kauai in Hawaii is a bit tricky to handle, but it's delicate, flaky, and worth the trouble.

1 envelope unflavored gelatin
1 tablespoon lemon juice
4 eggs, separated
1 cup guava juice
³/₄ cup sugar
   Few drops red food color

¹/₈ teaspoon cream of tartar
1 (9-inch) baked Flaky Pastry
   Shell
   Sweetened whipped cream
   Guava slices

SOFTEN gelatin in lemon juice. Set aside. Combine egg yolks, guava juice, and ¹/₂ cup sugar. Add a few drops red food color. Cook and stir over medium heat until mixture thickens. Add gelatin mixture and stir until melted. Cool mixture until it reaches consistency of unbeaten egg whites. Beat egg whites and cream of tartar together until soft peaks form. Gradually add ¹/₄ cup sugar and beat until stiff peaks form. Fold in gelatin mixture and pour into baked pastry shell. Chill. Top with sweetened whipped cream and garnish with extra guava slices.

Makes 6 to 8 servings.

Note: To make Orange Chiffon Pie, substitute 1 cup orange juice for guava juice, add a few drops yellow and red food colors, and garnish with orange slices.

Flaky Pastry Shell

1 cup flour
¹/₄ teaspoon salt
¹/₄ cup shortening

¹/₄ cup butter
2 tablespoons cold water

Combine flour and salt. Cut in shortening and butter until lumps are pea-size. Add water and stir until mixture is moistened. Press into a ball and chill 45 minutes. Roll out on floured board with well-floured or stockinette-covered rolling pin. Carefully transfer pastry to 9-inch pie plate. Pierce all over with a fork. Bake at 400 degrees 15 minutes.

Makes one 9-inch pastry shell.

Double-Crust Lemon Pie

Pastry for 1 (8-inch)
double-crust pie
Sugar
2 tablespoons flour
Dash salt
1/4 cup butter or margarine,
softened

3 eggs
1 teaspoon grated lemon peel
1 unpeeled medium lemon,
thinly sliced
1/2 cup water
1/2 teaspoon cinnamon

The advent of spring and burgeoning backyard lemon trees bring on nostalgic requests for the double-crust lemon pie readers remember from their youth.

ROLL out half the pastry and fit into 8-inch pie pan. Mix 1¼ cups sugar, flour, and salt. Blend in butter. Reserve about 1 teaspoon egg white and beat remaining eggs well. Add eggs to sugar mixture, then mix in lemon peel, lemon slices, and water. Mix well and turn into pastry shell. Roll out remaining pastry and fit over pie. Cut slits in top and seal and flute edges of pastry. Brush top of pie with reserved egg white. Mix 2 teaspoons sugar and cinnamon and sprinkle over pie. Bake at 400 degrees 30 to 35 minutes. Serve warm.

Ribbon Pumpkin Pie

1 envelope unflavored
gelatin
1/4 cup cold water
3 eggs, separated
Sugar
1¼ cups cooked or canned
pumpkin
1/2 cup sour cream
1/2 teaspoon salt

1½ teaspoons pumpkin pie
spice
1 tablespoon chopped
candied ginger
Crunchy Praline Pastry
Shell
1 cup whipping cream
Lace Cookies

One of our writers introduced this pie to readers many years ago and it has become a holiday issue standby ever since. We have printed the recipe with and without the lace cookies garnish, which definitely adds a sprightly touch and taste to the pie.

SOFTEN gelatin in cold water. Beat egg yolks well with 1/3 cup sugar. Add pumpkin, sour cream, salt, pumpkin pie spice, and ginger to egg yolk mixture. Cook, stirring, over medium heat until mixture comes to boil. Reduce heat and simmer 2 minutes, stirring constantly. Remove from heat and stir in gelatin until dissolved. Cool. Beat egg whites until frothy. Gradually add 1/4 cup sugar and continue to beat until stiff peaks form. Fold whites into pumpkin mixture. Spoon half the filling into Crunchy Praline Pastry Shell. Chill until almost set. Whip the cream and spread half over pumpkin filling in pie shell. Top with remaining pumpkin mixture. Chill until almost set and garnish with remaining whipped cream and Lace Cookies, rolled into cornucopias.

Makes 6 to 8 servings.

(continued on overleaf)

Crunchy Praline Pastry Shell

¹/₃ cup butter or margarine
¹/₃ cup brown sugar, packed
¹/₂ cup chopped pecans

1 (9-inch) lightly baked
pastry shell

Combine butter and brown sugar in saucepan. Cook, stirring, until sugar melts and mixture bubbles vigorously. Remove from heat, stir in pecans, and spread over bottom of pastry shell. Bake at 425 degrees 5 minutes or until bubbly. Remove from oven and cool thoroughly.

Lace Cookies

¹/₃ cup butter or margarine,
softened
²/₃ cup brown sugar, packed
¹/₄ teaspoon salt
¹/₂ teaspoon baking powder

1 cup oats
¹/₂ cup chopped pecans
1 tablespoon milk
¹/₄ teaspoon lemon extract

Cream together butter and sugar until light and fluffy. Stir in salt, baking powder, oats, pecans, milk, and lemon extract, blending well. Drop by teaspoons about 2 inches apart on ungreased baking sheets. Bake at 350 degrees about 8 minutes. Cool 2 to 3 minutes, then remove from baking sheet. If cookies harden before removal from sheet, reheat in oven a few minutes to soften. Cookies will be very thin and lacy. Cookies must be very warm to roll into cornucopias. Roll cookies one by one to form a cornucopia shape, pinching points slightly.

Makes 2¹/₂ dozen.

Note: Use only as many cookies as are needed for pie and reserve remaining ones for later use.

Impossible Pumpkin Pie

One of our readers came up with this variation on the popular impossible pie, a pie that develops its own crust as it bakes.

1¹/₃ cups milk
3 tablespoons butter or margarine, softened
4 eggs

¹/₂ cup sugar
¹/₂ cup buttermilk biscuit mix
1 cup canned pumpkin
Pumpkin pie spice

COMBINE milk, butter, eggs, sugar, biscuit mix, pumpkin, and pumpkin pie spice to taste in blender container. Blend until thoroughly mixed. Turn into greased 9-inch pie pan and bake at 400 degrees 25 to 35 minutes, or until a knife inserted halfway between center and rim comes out clean. Cool and serve with whipped cream, if desired.

Makes 6 to 8 servings.

Four-Minute Brownie Pie

2 eggs
1 cup sugar
1/2 cup butter or
    margarine, softened
1/2 cup flour
3 to 4 tablespoons cocoa

1 teaspoon vanilla
Dash salt
1/2 cup chopped walnuts
Whipped cream or ice
cream

This old-timer is a Food Section classic going back to its first printing in 1965. It's a moist and fudgy brownie in the shape of a pie.

PLACE eggs, sugar, butter, flour, cocoa, vanilla, and salt in small mixer bowl. Beat 4 minutes. Stir in nuts and pour into greased 8-inch pie pan. Bake at 325 degrees 30 minutes, or until done. Pie will settle like a meringue when cool. Cut in wedges and serve with whipped cream.

Makes 8 servings.

Fudge Satin Pie

1 1/2 cups graham cracker
    crumbs
1 cup ground toasted
    almonds
    Powdered sugar
1/2 cup butter, melted
4 eggs
1 1/2 cups granulated sugar
1 teaspoon vanilla

2 teaspoons coffee liqueur
1 (8-ounce) package
    semisweet chocolate
    pieces, melted
1 1/2 pounds unsalted butter,
    softened
2 cups whipping cream
2 tablespoons powdered
    coffee

The satiny-smooth texture of this fudgy pie from Hemingways in Corona del Mar is due to the huge amount of butter in the recipe.

MIX crumbs, almonds, 1/3 cup powdered sugar, and melted butter and press into 10-inch glass pie pan. Chill. Beat eggs with mixer and add granulated sugar. Beat until light and custardy. Add vanilla and coffee liqueur. Mix well and add melted chocolate. Continue beating and add unsalted butter, a stick at a time, until smooth and satiny. Turn into prepared pie crust and chill until set. Whip cream with 1/2 cup powdered sugar and powdered coffee. Pipe through pastry tube onto pie using rose tip. Chill.

Makes 8 servings.

Chocolate Chess Pie

The pie from Angus Barn restaurant in Raleigh, North Carolina, made such a big hit with our test kitchen panel and readers that we decided to include it among our favorite recipes here.

³/₄ cup butter
1¹/₂ squares unsweetened chocolate
1¹/₄ cups sugar
¹/₄ cup light corn syrup

3 eggs, lightly beaten
¹/₈ teaspoon salt
¹/₂ teaspoon vanilla
1 (9-inch) unbaked pastry shell

COMBINE butter and chocolate in top of double boiler. Melt over boiling water. Combine sugar, syrup, eggs, salt, and vanilla. Blend sugar mixture into butter mixture and turn into pastry shell. Bake at 375 degrees 35 minutes, or until set.

Makes 6 to 8 servings.

Granola Pie Crust

Even a beginner can make a perfect pie crust with this never-fail recipe.

¹/₂ cup butter or margarine, melted
1¹/₂ cups granola

¹/₃ cup chopped nuts
3 tablespoons brown sugar

MIX together butter, granola, nuts, and brown sugar. Press in an 8-inch pie pan and chill until set.

Makes 1 (8-inch) pastry shell.

Vinegar Pie Crust

3 cups flour
1 teaspoon salt
1¹/₄ cups shortening

1 egg
5 tablespoons water
1 teaspoon white vinegar

COMBINE flour and salt. Work in shortening until mixture is consistency of cornmeal. Beat egg lightly. Add water and stir, then add vinegar. Blend into flour mixture to form soft dough. Gather dough into a ball. Cut in halves. Flour board well and roll each half into circle 1 inch larger than pie pan. Fit into pan and flute edges.

Makes enough pastry for 2 (9-inch) pastry shells.

DESSERTS

CHEESECAKE, carrot cake, and chocolate mousse in any form are runaway best sellers in our part of the country. They are rich and caloric, but even ardent dieters find themselves giving in to the overpowering urge to have ''just one small piece'' when these dessert favorites are offered.

Oddly enough, some of the other desserts that rate high with *Times* readers are the old-fashioned bread puddings, rice puddings, and other homey sweets that evoke a certain nostalgia. They always make a hit when they appear on a menu. Fruitcake recipe requests mount during the holidays, while requests for flans, whether the real thing or an adapted recipe, appear steadily throughout the year.

Cookies that appeal to westerners the most seem to be the sturdy oatmeal or other cereal-based types. When dried fruits and nuts are added, so much the better. The appeal of ''good'' ingredients probably can be attributed to the impact of the health-food movement in the sixties and early seventies. Brownies and chocolate chip cookies also are local favorites, as they are elsewhere. In fact, it must be admitted that any chocolate sweet—whether a cookie, candy, cake, or soufflé—will have strong following in the West.

Cold Pumpkin Soufflé, page 322

Cold Pumpkin Soufflé

Flavored with spices and spiked with rum, this airy pumpkin dessert makes a delightful change from the usual holiday pie.

2 envelopes unflavored gelatin
1/4 cup water
4 eggs
2/3 cup sugar
1 (1-pound) can pumpkin
1/4 cup rum

1/2 teaspoon cinnamon
1/2 teaspoon ginger
1/4 teaspoon mace
1/4 teaspoon ground cloves
1 cup whipping cream, whipped
Candied kumquats

SPRINKLE gelatin over water to soften. Heat over low heat to dissolve gelatin. Beat eggs thoroughly in bowl. Gradually add sugar and continue to beat until mixture is smooth and very thick. Stir in pumpkin, rum, cinnamon, ginger, mace, and cloves. Blend in the gelatin well and fold in whipped cream. Oil a 6-inch band of foil and place around outside edges of an oiled 1½-quart soufflé dish, oiled side in, to form a standing collar. (Or use an oiled 2-quart fluted ring mold and do not add collar.) Fill dish with pumpkin mixture and chill until set. Carefully remove foil collar and decorate the top of the soufflé with candied kumquats. Or dip fluted mold in hot water very quickly and turn out onto serving platter. Serve with additional whipped cream, if desired.

Makes 6 to 8 servings.

Chocolate Soufflé

The Bistro restaurant in Beverly Hills is almost as famous for these soufflés as for its celebrity clientele.

5 egg yolks
3/4 cup sugar
4 drops vanilla
1 cup flour
2 cups milk

2 ounces unsweetened chocolate, melted
8 egg whites
Powdered sugar
Sweetened whipped cream

BEAT egg yolks with 1/2 cup sugar and vanilla until light and fluffy. Gradually beat in flour until a paste is formed. Meanwhile bring milk to a boil. Add egg mixture all at once to milk, bring again to a boil, and with a heavy wire whisk quickly and vigorously beat until paste is well incorporated into milk and is smooth. Continue to stir with a wooden spoon until mixture is thick as a light choux paste or pastry cream. Add melted chocolate and stir until blended. Cool. Beat 3 egg whites with 1/3 of remaining sugar until light and frothy. Add 3 more egg whites and half of remaining sugar. Continue beating until sugar is incorporated. Add remaining 2 egg whites and remaining sugar and beat until whites are stiff and shiny but not dry. Egg whites should not slide if bowl is tipped. Fold egg whites into soufflé batter. Pipe or spoon into 12 greased and sugared 2-inch soufflé dishes or custard cups or 2 (5-inch) soufflé dishes and bake at 350 degrees 30 minutes for individual soufflés or 1 hour or longer for large soufflés. Dust with powdered sugar and serve topped with sweetened whipped cream.

Makes 12 servings.

Lemon Soufflé

Omit chocolate from recipe and add grated peel and juice of 1 lemon to soufflé batter before cooling.

Vanilla Soufflé

Omit chocolate from recipe and increase vanilla to 2 teaspoons.

Grand Marnier Soufflé

Omit chocolate from recipe and add 1 ounce Grand Marnier to soufflé batter before cooling.

Club Cheesecake

1 cup sugar
$^1/_4$ cup whipping cream or
   evaporated milk
4 cups cottage cheese
$^1/_4$ teaspoon salt

4 eggs, separated
$^1/_2$ cup sifted flour
1 teaspoon vanilla
1 teaspoon grated lemon peel
   Zwieback Crumb Crust

Members of the Los Angeles Athletic Club have an advantage over others who sample the club's rich cheesecake. They have readily accessible facilities for working off the calories it adds.

COMBINE sugar and cream and stir until sugar is dissolved. Add cottage cheese, salt, well-beaten egg yolks, flour, vanilla, and grated lemon peel. Beat thoroughly until well blended and smooth. Beat egg whites until stiff and fold into cheese mixture. Turn into chilled Zwieback Crumb Crust and sprinkle with reserved crumbs. Bake at 350 degrees 1 hour 20 minutes. Let cake cool in baking pan.

Zwieback Crumb Crust

1 (6-ounce) package zwieback
$^1/_2$ cup sugar
$^1/_8$ teaspoon salt

$^1/_2$ cup butter or margarine,
   melted

Crush zwieback and roll to fine crumbs. Combine half the crumbs with sugar, salt, and melted butter and mix until well blended. Press onto bottom and sides of 9-inch cake pan with removable bottom. Reserve rest of crumbs for top of cake. Cover crust with wax paper and chill.

Classic Cheesecake

Attorney R. Roy Finkle laces his rich cheesecake with just a hint of Grand Marnier.

1¹/₂ cups graham cracker crumbs, about
³/₄ cup sugar
1 teaspoon cinnamon
¹/₃ cup butter, melted
2 eggs

2 (8-ounce) packages cream cheese, softened
1 teaspoon vanilla
1 teaspoon Grand Marnier
Sour Cream Topping

PLACE crumbs in mixing bowl and add ¹/₄ cup sugar and cinnamon, then stir in butter. More butter, up to ³/₄ cup, may be added if needed. Butter an 8-inch springform pan on bottom and sides. Sprinkle a thin layer of crumbs on bottom of pan and press down with a metal ¹/₄-cup measure. Pat crumbs on sides and press into position with side of measuring cup. Work around sides with fingers to make crumbs of even height. Any remaining crumbs may be added to bottom crust. Bake crust at 350 degrees 5 minutes. To make filling, beat eggs until light, then add ¹/₂ cup sugar and beat 5 minutes. Add cream cheese, vanilla, and Grand Marnier and mix well. Turn into prepared crust and bake at 375 degrees 20 minutes. Cool 15 minutes, then pour Sour Cream Topping over filling and bake at 475 degrees 5 minutes. Cool cake and chill overnight before serving.

Sour Cream Topping

1 pint sour cream
6 tablespoons sugar

1 teaspoon vanilla
1 teaspoon Grand Marnier

Blend sour cream, sugar, vanilla, and Grand Marnier well, then pour over filling and bake as directed above.

Strawberry Cheesecake

Beaten egg whites folded into the cream cheese mixture make this no-bake cheesecake from San Diego's Hotel del Coronado especially light and delicate.

2 (8-ounce) packages cream cheese
1 cup sugar
1 cup whipping cream
4 egg whites
1 teaspoon vanilla

¹/₂ envelope unflavored gelatin
1 cup water
Graham Cracker Crumb Crust
Strawberry Sauce

BEAT cream cheese with ¹/₂ cup sugar until light. Add cream and beat until smooth. Beat egg whites until frothy. Gradually add remaining sugar and vanilla and continue beating until egg whites are stiff but not dry. Fold into cheese mixture. Soften gelatin in a small amount of the water, about 5 minutes. Dissolve over low heat, then add remaining cold water. Chill until syrupy, then fold into cheese mixture. Turn into prepared pan and chill 2 hours. Spoon Strawberry Sauce evenly over cake.

Graham Cracker Crumb Crust

1¹/₄ cups graham cracker crumbs
3 tablespoons sugar

6 tablespoons butter or margarine, melted

Combine crumbs with sugar. Work in butter. Line a 9-inch springform pan with crumb mixture. Bake at 350 degrees 10 minutes, then cool thoroughly before adding filling.

Strawberry Sauce

2 (10-ounce) packages frozen strawberries

1¹/₂ tablespoons cornstarch

Thaw strawberries and drain juice into saucepan. Heat juice with cornstarch. Cook, stirring, until slightly thickened. Cool and add strawberries. Use as topping for cheesecake.

Chocolate Cheesecake

1 tablespoon butter or margarine
3 ounces unsweetened chocolate
9 ounces semisweet chocolate
4 (3-ounce) packages cream cheese, softened

2 tablespoons vanilla
1 cup whipping cream
6 eggs
¹/₂ to 1 cup sugar
Chocolate Wafer Crust

This chocolate cheesecake from La Belle Helene in St. Helena, California, can be prepared two ways: increase the amount of sugar for a sweeter, less chocolatey creation, or use a smaller amount of sugar and the flavor will have more of a bitter chocolate emphasis.

MELT butter in top of double boiler over hot water. Add chocolates and stir until melted. Beat cheese until creamy. Add vanilla and whipping cream. Stir in chocolate mixture. Beat eggs with sugar and slowly beat into chocolate mixture. Turn into Chocolate Wafer Crust and bake at 350 degrees 40 to 45 minutes, or until cake puffs slightly in center. Cool and chill thoroughly before unmolding. Serve with whipped cream, if desired.

Makes 14 to 16 servings.

(continued on overleaf)

Chocolate Wafer Crust

1 (8¹/₂-ounce) package chocolate wafers	*2 tablespoons unsalted butter, melted*

Crush wafers. Add melted butter to make a crumbly dough. Press into bottom of 9-inch springform pan.

Double Cheese Cheesecake

The Broadway department store created a gelatin-based cheesecake our readers seem to like.

1 (3-ounce) package lemon gelatin	*¹/₂ cup cottage cheese*
1¹/₄ cups boiling water	*¹/₂ cup lemon juice*
¹/₂ cup evaporated milk, chilled	*¹/₄ teaspoon vanilla*
1¹/₂ cups whipping cream	*¹/₄ teaspoon salt*
2 (8-ounce) packages cream cheese, softened	*¹/₂ cup sugar*
	Graham Cracker Crust

DISSOLVE gelatin in boiling water and set aside until syrupy. Combine evaporated milk and whipping cream and beat until mixture is quite thick. Mix cream cheese, cottage cheese, lemon juice, vanilla, salt, and sugar in separate bowl. Add cheese mixture to cream mixture. Add partially set gelatin. Mix thoroughly. Pour into prepared crust and chill 4 hours.

Graham Cracker Crust

1¹/₄ cups graham cracker crumbs	*6 tablespoons butter or margarine, melted*
3 tablespoons sugar	

Using fingers, work crumbs and sugar into melted butter. Divide mixture, using ²/₃ to cover bottom and sides of 9-inch springform pan and remaining ¹/₃ as topping to sprinkle over filling.

Chocolate Mousse

1/4 cup sugar
1/4 cup water
2 egg whites, at room temperature

1 cup semisweet chocolate pieces
1/4 cup rum
3 cups whipping cream

The Sanglier restaurant in the San Fernando Valley provided the recipe for this rum-touched chocolate mousse.

COOK sugar in saucepan with water to point where syrup turns a pale golden color (just before it starts to caramelize). Beat egg whites and gradually add syrup, beating constantly. Melt chocolate with rum over hot water and fold into sugar mixture. Cool 2 hours in refrigerator. Whip cream and fold into chocolate mixture. Spoon into serving dishes, demitasses, or stemmed glasses.

Makes 8 servings.

Pavlova

4 egg whites
1 1/4 cups sugar
1/4 teaspoon salt
1 tablespoon cornstarch
1 teaspoon vanilla

1 teaspoon white vinegar
1 cup whipping cream, whipped
Kiwis, strawberries, or other fresh fruit, sliced

The secrets of making this popular meringue dessert from Down Under were revealed to The Times *food staff by Tui Flower, a newspaper food editor from New Zealand.*

CUT circle of wax paper to fit bottom of 8-inch springform pan. Cut strip of wax paper 2 inches wider than pan is deep. Grease one side of strip and line pan with greased side toward pan. Grease exposed surfaces of wax paper well. Dip fingers in cold water and sprinkle over prepared pan. Beat egg whites in large bowl of electric mixer until soft peaks form. Add sugar and salt and continue beating until sugar is thoroughly incorporated. Add 3 tablespoons cold water and beat in well. Add cornstarch and continue beating. Add vanilla and vinegar and beat until whites are glossy and stiff peaks form when beater is lifted. Turn meringue into pan and spread it evenly over bottom with a spatula. Top should be fairly even. Bake at 350 degrees 15 minutes. Check Pavlova to see if it has begun to rise. If so, turn oven off and let Pavlova sit for 1 hour if oven retains heat well. Or bake for another 10 to 15 minutes at 350 degrees and then turn oven off for 1 hour. If oven does not retain heat well, reduce heat to 175 degrees after first 15 minutes and bake 1 hour longer. When cool, remove from pan. To serve, top with whipped cream and kiwis.

Makes 6 to 8 servings.

Note: If free-form Pavlova is preferred, line a baking sheet with greased wax paper and turn stiffly beaten meringue into center. With a spatula shape into an 8- or 9-inch circle. Bake and serve as directed for springform pan.

Yugoslav Carrot Cake

Helen Stefanac, who over the years has tested thousands of recipes that flow through The Times test kitchen, is an inspired cook in her own right. She brought this version of carrot cake from her native Yugoslavia.

4 eggs, separated
1¹/₂ cups sugar
1 cup grated carrots
1 cup minced walnuts
1¹/₂ cups flour
1 teaspoon baking powder
¹/₄ teaspoon nutmeg
¹/₂ teaspoon cinnamon
1 teaspoon vanilla
¹/₈ teaspoon salt

1 cup oil
2¹/₂ tablespoons hot water
¹/₂ teaspoon soda
Cream Cheese Filling
¹/₂ cup strawberry, apricot, or raspberry jam
1 cup whipping cream, whipped
Powdered sugar

CREAM together egg yolks and 1 cup sugar until light. Stir in carrots, nuts, flour, baking powder, nutmeg, cinnamon, vanilla, salt, and oil. Mix together hot water and soda and stir into flour mixture. Beat egg whites until foamy and gradually add remaining sugar. Beat until stiff and glossy. Fold egg white mixture into flour mixture. Turn into greased 13 x 9-inch pan lined with greased wax paper and bake at 350 degrees 45 minutes, or until cake tests done. Cool. Remove from pan, pull off paper, and slice cake in halves horizontally. Cover one half with Cream Cheese Filling, then cover cream cheese with jam. Top with remaining half and frost entire cake with whipped cream sweetened to taste with powdered sugar.

Cream Cheese Filling

1 (8-ounce) package cream cheese
¹/₂ cup sugar

Soften cream cheese and gradually beat in sugar until smooth and fluffy.

14-Carat Cake

If there is such a thing as a classic Los Angeles-style carrot cake, this is it.

2 cups flour
2 teaspoons baking powder
1¹/₂ teaspoons soda
1 teaspoon salt
2 teaspoons cinnamon
4 eggs
2 cups sugar

1¹/₂ cups oil
2 cups grated raw carrots
1 (8¹/₂-ounce) can crushed pineapple, drained
¹/₂ cup chopped nuts
Vanilla Cream Cheese Frosting

SIFT together flour, baking powder, soda, salt, and cinnamon. Beat eggs and add sugar. Let stand until sugar dissolves, about 10 minutes. Stir in oil, carrots, drained pineapple, and nuts. Turn into 3 greased and floured 9-inch round cake pans or a 13 x 9-inch pan and bake at 350 degrees 35 to 40 minutes for layer pans and about 55 minutes for 13 x 9-inch pan, or until cake springs back when lightly touched. Cool in pans about 10 minutes, then turn onto wire racks to cool completely. Frost between layers, top, and sides of layer cake. Frost top and sides of sheet cake.

Vanilla Cream Cheese Frosting

$^1/_2$ cup butter or margarine	1 teaspoon vanilla
1 (8-ounce) package cream cheese, softened	1 pound powdered sugar, sifted

Combine butter, cream cheese, and vanilla in large bowl and beat until well blended. Add sugar gradually, beating vigorously. If too thick, thin with milk to spreading consistency.

Vanilla Ice Cream

3 tablespoons cornstarch	1 (13-ounce) can evaporated milk
6 cups milk	
$2^2/_3$ cups sugar	2 cups whipping cream
4 eggs	$3^1/_2$ tablespoons vanilla
$^3/_4$ teaspoon salt	

MIX cornstarch with $^1/_2$ cup milk until smooth. Add an additional $1^1/_2$ cups milk and cook in double boiler until thick and smooth, beating constantly to avoid lumps. Blend sugar, eggs, salt, and evaporated milk in electric mixer bowl. Add hot cornstarch mixture and beat well. Add whipping cream, remaining 4 cups milk, and vanilla. Pour into gallon electric or hand-crank freezer. Churn and freeze according to manufacturer's directions until firm, then carefully remove paddle. Seal ice cream container well. Fill freezer with crushed ice and ice cream salt. Cover freezer tightly and set aside several hours to let ice cream season. Or spoon ice cream into another container which has been chilled and store in home freezer to season.

Makes about 1 gallon.

Berry Ice Cream

Add 2 cups crushed fresh berries and omit half the vanilla. (It may be necessary to increase the amount of sugar slightly.)

(continued on overleaf)

Chocolate Ice Cream

Add 2 ounces melted semisweet chocolate and omit half the vanilla.

Peach Ice Cream

Add 2 cups crushed ripe peaches. Use only 1 tablespoon vanilla and add ¹/₂ teaspoon almond extract.

Coffee Liqueur Ice Cream

Coffee powder and coffee liqueur combine to provide the rich, dark flavor coffee lovers seek in this easy ice cream.

2 eggs	1 to 2 tablespoons instant
¹/₂ cup sugar	coffee powder
4 cups evaporated milk	¹/₂ cup coffee liqueur

BEAT eggs and sugar in large mixing bowl until well blended. Scald evaporated milk and coffee powder over medium heat until bubbles appear along edge. Gradually stir about 2 cups hot evaporated milk mixture into egg mixture. Then blend egg mixture into remaining hot milk mixture. Cook, stirring, over low heat until mixture thickens slightly. Remove from heat. Refrigerate until well chilled. Stir in coffee liqueur. Pour into ice cream freezer container. Churn and freeze according to manufacturer's directions.

Makes 2 quarts.

Fried Mexican Ice Cream

If you like conversation-piece desserts, this one is for you. A thick coating of cornflake crumbs around these ice cream balls insures the success of this tricky recipe.

1 pint vanilla or other flavor	2 teaspoons sugar
ice cream	1 egg
¹/₂ cup crushed cornflake or	Oil for deep frying
cookie crumbs	Honey
1 teaspoon cinnamon	Whipped cream

SCOOP out 4 or 5 balls of ice cream. Return to freezer. Mix cornflake crumbs, cinnamon, and sugar. Roll frozen ice cream balls in half the crumb mixture and freeze again. Beat egg and dip coated balls in egg, then roll again in remaining crumbs. Freeze until ready to use. (For thicker coating, repeat dipping in egg and rolling in crumbs.) When ready to serve, heat oil to 350 degrees. Place a frozen ice cream ball in fryer basket or on a perforated spoon and lower into hot oil 1 minute. Immediately remove and place in dessert compote. Drizzle with honey and top with a dollop of whipped cream. Continue to fry balls one at a time. Balls will be crunchy on the outside and just beginning to melt inside.

Makes 4 to 5 servings.

Strawberry Ice

2 cups sugar
1 cup water
8 cups strawberries

¹/₄ cup lemon juice
¹/₃ cup orange juice

COMBINE sugar and water in medium saucepan. Heat, stirring, until sugar dissolves, then boil 5 minutes. Cool. Force berries through food mill or blend in blender container or food processor bowl. Strain to remove seeds, if desired. Blend strawberry puree and lemon and orange juices into syrup. Pour into freezer trays and freeze. Remove from freezer 20 minutes before serving.

Makes 8 to 12 servings.

Kiwi Ice

1 teaspoon unflavored gela-
    tin
1¹/₂ cups water

³/₄ cup sugar
3 kiwis
¹/₂ teaspoon lime juice

A tart-sweet kiwi ice makes a light dessert or a delightful mid-meal palate cleanser at a multi-course dinner party.

SOFTEN gelatin in ¹/₂ cup water. Combine remaining water with ¹/₂ cup plus 2 tablespoons sugar in small saucepan. Bring to boil over high heat, stirring. Lower heat and cook 5 minutes longer without stirring. Remove from heat and add gelatin, stirring until dissolved. Set aside to cool in refrigerator. Peel and cut kiwis into small pieces. Put through food mill or puree in blender container or food processor bowl. Pour into bowl. Add lime juice and remaining sugar to puree. Stir in cooled syrup. Cover bowl and place in freezer 2 hours, then beat with chilled rotary beater until velvety. Pour into plastic freezer container, cover, and freeze until firm. Let stand in refrigerator 2 hours before serving.

Makes 4 servings.

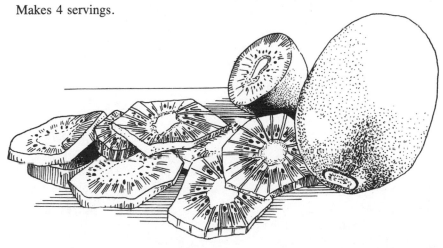

Spoom

*When Rockresorts first opened
Mauna Kea in Hawaii some
years ago, executive food director Walter Blum won diners'
hearts with this delicate champagne ice. Vacationing Southern Californians continue to request the recipe.*

1 cup sugar
1/2 cup water
4 egg whites
1 quart lemon sherbet,
   softened

1 1/2 cups champagne, rosé, or
   white wine

COMBINE sugar and water in saucepan. Cook over medium heat just
until temperature reaches 238 degrees on candy thermometer. Meanwhile, beat egg whites until soft peaks form. Continue beating, pouring hot syrup in a thin thread into whites. Stir in sherbet. Spoon
mixture into individual serving dishes. Cover and freeze. Before
serving, pour 2 tablespoons champagne over each serving.

Makes 12 servings.

Lemon Snow

*This light-as-a-cloud dessert
was served molded in a spiral
shape to suggest a frothy snow-
capped mountain at the now
nonexistent Curtain Call restaurant in the Music Center.*

1 envelope unflavored gelatin
1/4 cup water
8 egg whites
1/2 cup sugar

Juice and grated peel of 1
lemon
Sherried Vanilla Sauce

SOFTEN gelatin in water, then dissolve over hot water. Cool slightly.
Beat egg whites in large bowl of electric mixer until foamy. Continue
to beat, gradually adding sugar, until stiff. Fold gelatin into egg
whites along with lemon juice and peel. Place mixture in a large
pastry bag and pipe into individual spiral-shaped cones. Or spoon
into individual pyramid molds and chill until firm, about 1 hour.
Serve with Sherried Vanilla Sauce.

Makes 6 servings.

Sherried Vanilla Sauce

1 (3 1/4-ounce) package vanilla
   pudding mix
3/4 cup whipping cream
1/4 cup sherry

Prepare pudding according to package directions. Thin pudding to
make sauce by adding cream and sherry, blending well. Sauce should
be consistency of pancake batter.

Makes about 3 cups.

Frozen Mocha Toffee Dessert

12 ladyfingers, split
2 tablespoons instant coffee
  powder
1 tablespoon boiling water
1 quart vanilla ice cream,
  softened

4 chocolate-covered toffee
  bars, frozen and crushed
1/2 cup whipping cream
2 tablespoons coffee liqueur

LINE bottom and 2 inches up sides of an 8-inch springform pan with split ladyfingers, cutting to fit. Dissolve coffee powder in boiling water. Cool. Blend coffee, ice cream, and crushed candy. Spoon into prepared pan. Cover and freeze until firm. Just before serving, whip cream with coffee liqueur until stiff. Spread over or pipe onto frozen ice cream. Garnish with additional pieces of broken toffee bars or with shaved chocolate, if desired.

Makes 8 to 10 servings.

Heirloom Fruitcake

2 pounds candied cherries
2 pounds candied pineapple
1/2 pound citron
1/2 pound candied orange peel
1/2 pound candied lemon peel
2 pounds pitted dates
2 pounds golden raisins
1 pound dark raisins
1 pound currants
11 ounces shelled pecans
  Flour
1 pound butter or margarine

1 pound brown sugar
1 dozen eggs
1 tablespoon vanilla
  Juice of 1 large lemon
  Juice of 1 large orange
2 teaspoons baking powder
2 teaspoons soda
1 teaspoon nutmeg
1 teaspoon allspice
1 tablespoon cinnamon
1 1/2 cups grape juice or wine

This tried-and-true fruitcake recipe has been in our files for many years. It's far from inexpensive to make, yet as Christmas approaches requests from readers for still another printing pour in.

CUT fruit into small pieces and chop nuts. Mix fruit and nuts with flour to coat well. Cream butter and sugar until light. Add eggs, one at a time, beating well after each addition. Add vanilla and lemon and orange juices. Resift 4 cups sifted flour with baking powder, soda, nutmeg, allspice, and cinnamon. Add alternately with grape juice to egg mixture. Stir in fruit and nut mixture. Grease 2 (9 x 5-inch) loaf pans and 1 (10-inch) tube pan. Line with brown paper and grease the paper. Turn batter into pans, filling 3/4 full. Bake at 200 degrees. Loaf pans will require about 4 1/2 hours; tube pan about 6 1/2 hours. About 30 minutes before cake is done, brush light corn syrup over top and decorate with nuts and fruits. Cool in pans. Pour a little additional wine over top of cooled cake, if desired, wrap, and put away in a cool place a month before using.

Makes 2 loaves and 1 tube cake.

Bourbon Nut Cake

This is another do-ahead fruit-cake. It is at its best when cake and bourbon have mellowed together for a week or more.

4 cups sifted flour
1 teaspoon baking powder
4 teaspoons nutmeg
1 cup butter or margarine
2 cups sugar
6 eggs
4 ounces bourbon, about

4 cups coarsely chopped pecans
1 pound dark raisins
$1/2$ pound candied cherries, sliced or chopped
Powdered sugar

SIFT together flour, baking powder, and nutmeg. Cream butter well, then gradually add sugar and continue to cream until fluffy. Beat in eggs, one at a time. Add sifted dry ingredients alternately with bourbon. Stir in nuts, raisins, and cherries. Turn batter into well-greased 10-inch tube pan lined on bottom with wax paper. Bake at 300 degrees 2 hours, or until cake tester inserted near center comes out clean. If top of cake begins to brown before it is done, cover loosely with foil. Remove cake from oven and let stand 10 to 15 minutes, then turn out onto rack to cool completely. When cool, sprinkle with additional bourbon and wrap. Use more bourbon if a fragrant cake is desired. Let cake mellow a week or longer for best flavor. Sprinkle with sifted powdered sugar before slicing.

Evie's Fruitcake

Mollie and Dollie of Jacksboro, Texas, who mail-order Evie's fruitcake throughout the country, sent us this recipe, and it's a winner every year.

$4^1/2$ cups chopped pecans
$3^1/2$ cups chopped walnuts
2 pounds dates, chopped
1 pound candied cherries, cut up
1 pound candied pineapple, cut up

2 (14-ounce) cans sweetened condensed milk
2 (4-ounce) cans shredded coconut

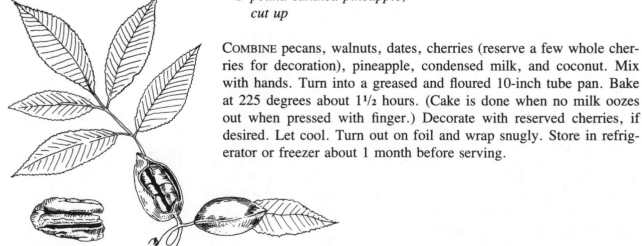

COMBINE pecans, walnuts, dates, cherries (reserve a few whole cherries for decoration), pineapple, condensed milk, and coconut. Mix with hands. Turn into a greased and floured 10-inch tube pan. Bake at 225 degrees about $1^1/2$ hours. (Cake is done when no milk oozes out when pressed with finger.) Decorate with reserved cherries, if desired. Let cool. Turn out on foil and wrap snugly. Store in refrigerator or freezer about 1 month before serving.

Coconut Cake

6 eggs
1/2 cup oil
1/2 cup water
1 teaspoon vanilla
1/2 teaspoon salt
1 1/2 teaspoons baking powder
1 cup cake flour

Sugar
Milk
1 tablespoon cornstarch
1 1/2 cups whipping cream
3 cups freshly grated coconut

Freshly grated coconut in the frosting is the secret in this light white cake that's a favorite on the menu of the restaurants in Hawaii's Kahala Hilton Hotel.

SEPARATE 4 eggs. Mix egg yolks, oil, water, and 1/2 teaspoon vanilla. Add salt, baking powder, cake flour, and 3/4 cup sugar and mix until smooth. Beat 4 egg whites until stiff and carefully fold into batter. Pour into a 10-inch springform pan that has been greased and floured or wax paper lined. Bake at 325 degrees about 50 minutes, or until cake tests done. Cool. Cut cake into 4 very thin or 3 thicker layers. Prepare filling by combining 2 cups milk, 3/4 cup sugar, and 1/2 teaspoon vanilla in saucepan. Bring to boil. Mix cornstarch with 2 tablespoons cold milk and 2 beaten eggs. Blend cornstarch mixture into sugar mixture and cook, stirring, until thickened. Cool. Spread custard between cake layers. Whip cream with 3 tablespoons sugar until stiff. Frost top and sides of cake with whipped cream. Sprinkle top and sides generously with coconut. Chill thoroughly.

Coffee Crunch Cake

1 1/2 cups sugar
1/4 cup strong coffee
1/4 cup light corn syrup
1 tablespoon soda, sifted

1 (10-inch) angel food cake
2 cups whipping cream
2 tablespoons sugar
2 teaspoons vanilla

When Blum's tearoom in Beverly Hills closed a number of years ago, they left behind a legacy in the form of this outstanding cake with a spectacular crunchy coffee-flavored topping.

COMBINE sugar, coffee, and corn syrup in a saucepan at least 5 inches deep. Bring mixture to boil and cook to 310 degrees on candy thermometer or hard-crack stage (a small amount of mixture dropped into cold water will break with a brittle snap). Remove syrup from heat, immediately add soda, and stir vigorously just until mixture thickens and pulls away from sides of pan. (Mixture will foam rapidly when soda is added. Do not destroy foam by excessive beating.) Immediately pour foamy mass into ungreased 9-inch square metal pan (do not spread or stir). Let stand without moving until cool. When ready to garnish cake, knock hardened mixture out of pan and crush between sheets of wax paper with rolling pin to form coarse crumbs. Split cake into 4 equal layers. Combine cream, sugar, and vanilla in chilled bowl and beat until cream holds its shape. Spread about 1/2 of cream between layers and remainder over top and sides. Sprinkle cake generously and thoroughly with crushed topping. Refrigerate until ready to serve.

Zucchini Cake

Clifton's cafeterias serve a delicious zucchini cake that has quite a following among their customers.

2 cups sugar
1 cup oil
3 eggs
2 cups flour
1 teaspoon soda
1 teaspoon salt

1 tablespoon cinnamon
2 cups shredded, unpeeled zucchini, packed
1 cup finely chopped nuts
1 tablespoon vanilla
Cream Cheese Frosting I

BEAT sugar, oil, and eggs at medium speed in electric mixer bowl 4 minutes. Sift together flour, soda, salt, and cinnamon. Fold zucchini and nuts into sugar mixture. Fold in flour mixture and vanilla, blending thoroughly. Turn batter into a well-greased 10-inch tube pan. Bake at 350 degrees about 60 to 65 minutes. Cool in pan on rack 15 minutes or longer. Remove pan and cool cake thoroughly on rack before frosting with Cream Cheese Frosting I.

Cream Cheese Frosting I

3 cups powdered sugar, sifted
2 (3-ounce) packages cream cheese, softened

5 tablespoons butter or margarine
1 teaspoon lemon extract

Beat powdered sugar, cream cheese, margarine, and lemon extract until thoroughly blended.

Grapefruit Cake

The historic Brown Derby at Hollywood and Vine numbers among its many legends a grapefruit cake recipe that has been circulating in Los Angeles for years.

1$^1/_2$ cups sifted cake flour
$^3/_4$ cup sugar
1$^1/_2$ teaspoons baking powder
1 teaspoon salt
$^1/_4$ cup water
$^1/_4$ cup oil
3 eggs, separated
3 tablespoons grapefruit juice

$^1/_2$ teaspoon grated lemon peel
$^1/_4$ teaspoon cream of tartar
Cream Cheese Frosting II
1 grapefruit, peeled and sectioned or 1 (1-pound) can grapefruit sections

SIFT together flour, sugar, baking powder, and salt into bowl. Make well in center and add water, oil, egg yolks, grapefruit juice, and lemon peel. Beat until very smooth. Beat egg whites with cream of tartar until stiff but not dry. Gradually pour egg yolk mixture over egg whites and fold in gently until just blended. Do not stir. Turn batter into an ungreased 9-inch springform pan and bake at 350 degrees 30 minutes, or until top springs back when touched lightly with finger. Invert onto rack and cool thoroughly. Loosen edges of cake carefully and remove cake from pan. With a serrated knife cut cake crosswise to make two layers. Reserve a few fruit sections for frosting. Fill with part of the Cream Cheese Frosting II and grapefruit sections. Spread top and sides of cake with frosting and decorate with additional fruit sections.

Cream Cheese Frosting II

2 (3-ounce) packages cream cheese
2 teaspoons lemon juice
1 teaspoon grated lemon peel
3/4 cup sifted powdered sugar

6 to 8 drops yellow food color (optional)
Reserved grapefruit sections

Soften cream cheese at room temperature. Beat until fluffy. Add lemon juice and peel. Gradually blend in sugar and beat until well blended. Stir in food color. Crush enough grapefruit sections to measure 2 teaspoons and blend into frosting.

Scandinavian Apple Cake

5 pounds apples
Sugar
Lemon juice
Melted butter or margarine
1½ cups toasted cake crumbs

½ cup currant jelly
3 ounces mixed nuts, ground
12 macaroons
3 ounces sliced blanched almonds
1 cup whipping cream

Scandia restaurant responded willingly to our request for their wonderful apple cake recipe.

CORE, peel, and slice apples. Season to taste with sugar and lemon juice and cook in a small amount of water until apples are tender. Drain in a large strainer and press to extract water. Pour melted butter into a 2-inch-deep 10-inch layer cake pan, spreading evenly in pan. Sprinkle ½ cup cake crumbs over bottom of pan. Spread half the apples over crumbs. Top with jelly, then nuts, then ½ cup more crumbs. Place macaroons in a layer over crumbs. Top with remaining apples and cover with remaining ½ cup cake crumbs. Bake at 450 degrees 30 minutes. Cool in refrigerator. Sprinkle almonds lightly with water, then sprinkle with sugar and toast at 350 degrees 15 to 20 minutes or until golden. Shake pan after 10 minutes to keep almonds from sticking together. Whip cream and frost cake. Sprinkle with almonds.

Butter Pound Cake

2 cups butter
1 pound powdered sugar

6 eggs
3 cups cake flour

CREAM butter with sugar until light. Add eggs one at a time, beating after each addition. Add flour, mixing only until smooth. Turn into 10-inch fluted tube pan. Bake at 325 degrees 1 hour 15 minutes. Cool before turning out on wire rack.

Snow White Cake

If you're looking for a snowy white, light, satiny-textured white cake, Schaber's cafeteria in Los Angeles has the answer.

3 tablespoons shortening
2 tablespoons butter
2/3 cup sugar
1/2 teaspoon vanilla
1 cup flour

1 1/2 teaspoons baking powder
1/2 teaspoon salt
1/3 cup milk
4 egg whites, stiffly beaten

CREAM shortening, butter, and sugar until light. Add vanilla and mix well. Sift together flour, baking powder, and salt. Add to creamed mixture alternately with milk, beating after each addition. Gently fold in egg whites. Turn into a greased and lightly floured 9-inch round layer cake pan and bake at 375 degrees 18 to 20 minutes, or until cake springs back when lightly touched. Frost with favorite boiled white frosting, caramel frosting, or any desired frosting.

Fudge Cake

1/4 cup shortening
2 cups sugar
2 eggs, separated
1 1/2 cups milk
4 ounces unsweetened chocolate, melted

2 cups sifted cake flour
2 teaspoons baking powder
1 teaspoon salt
1 teaspoon vanilla
1 cup chopped nuts
Sea Foam Frosting

CREAM shortening, 1 1/2 cups sugar, and egg yolks until light. Add a few drops of milk if needed to cream sugar. Add chocolate and blend thoroughly. Sift together flour, baking powder, and salt. Add dry ingredients alternately with milk to chocolate mixture, blending well after each addition. Stir in vanilla and chopped nuts. Beat egg whites until frothy. Gradually add remaining 1/2 cup sugar, beating until whites are stiff. Fold into batter. Turn into 2 greased and floured 9-inch layer cake pans. Bake at 350 degrees 30 to 40 minutes, or until cake springs back when lightly touched with finger in center of cake. Remove layers from pans onto cake rack and cool. Frost with Sea Foam Frosting.

Sea Foam Frosting

3/4 cup granulated sugar
3/4 cup brown sugar, packed
1/3 cup hot water

1/2 teaspoon cream of tartar
3 egg whites

Combine sugars in heavy saucepan. Add hot water and cream of tartar and stir to blend. Cover pan and slowly bring to simmer. Uncover pan and cook until syrup spins a long thin thread. Remove from heat. Beat egg whites until stiff. When syrup stops bubbling, pour over beaten whites in a thin stream, beating constantly until fluffy.

Makes enough frosting for 2 (9-inch) layers.

Note: If desired, melt 1 ounce semisweet chocolate with 1/4 teaspoon butter and drizzle over Sea Foam Frosting. Carefully swirl it over the frosting with a thin spatula to give a marbled effect.

Chocolate Prune Cake

1/4 cup boiling water
3/4 cup pitted prunes
2/3 cup oil
1 cup sugar
2 tablespoons cocoa
2 teaspoons cinnamon
1 teaspoon salt

1 teaspoon vanilla
2 eggs
1 cup buttermilk
2 1/2 cups flour
1 1/2 teaspoons soda
2 teaspoons baking powder
Chocolate Fudge Icing

This interesting cake has a surprisingly light texture and a great taste.

POUR boiling water over prunes and let soak 30 minutes. Combine oil, sugar, cocoa, cinnamon, salt, and vanilla in bowl. Add eggs and beat well for 2 minutes. Combine soaked prunes and buttermilk in blender container or food processor bowl and chop finely. Add to creamed mixture with flour, soda, and baking powder. Beat well and turn into well-greased and floured 13 x 9-inch baking pan or 2 (8-inch) round pans. Bake at 350 degrees 30 minutes, or until a wood pick inserted near center comes out clean. Cool and frost with Chocolate Fudge Icing.

(continued on overleaf)

Chocolate Fudge Icing

1/4 cup water	1/2 cup cocoa
1/4 cup shortening	1/4 teaspoon salt
1/4 cup light corn syrup	1/2 teaspoon vanilla
2 cups sifted powdered sugar	

Bring water to boil. Remove from heat and beat in shortening and corn syrup. Add powdered sugar, cocoa, salt, and vanilla and cream well to spreading consistency.

German Chocolate Cake

Traditionally hospitals are not considered prime sources of good food. The Los Angeles area seems to have a number of exceptions to that rule, however, as this elegant German chocolate cake from St. John's Hospital in Santa Monica proves.

1 (4-ounce) bar sweet chocolate	1 teaspoon vanilla
1/2 cup boiling water	1/2 teaspoon salt
1 cup butter or margarine	1 teaspoon soda
2 cups sugar	2 1/2 cups sifted cake flour
4 eggs, separated	1 cup buttermilk
	Coconut Pecan Frosting

MELT chocolate in boiling water. Cream butter and sugar until mixture is light and fluffy. Add egg yolks, one at a time, beating well after each addition. Add chocolate mixture and vanilla. Sift together salt, soda, and cake flour. Add alternately with buttermilk to chocolate mixture until batter is smooth. Beat egg whites until stiff. Fold into batter. Pour into 3 greased wax-paper-lined 8- or 9-inch layer cake pans. Bake at 350 degrees 30 to 40 minutes. Cool on racks. Frost tops with Coconut Pecan Frosting and stack.

Coconut Pecan Frosting

1 cup evaporated milk	1 teaspoon vanilla
1 cup sugar	1 1/3 cups flake coconut
3 egg yolks	1 cup chopped pecans
1/2 cup butter or margarine	

Combine evaporated milk, sugar, egg yolks, butter, and vanilla in saucepan. Cook, stirring, over medium heat until mixture thickens, about 12 minutes. Add coconut and pecans and beat until thick enough to spread. Spread between layers and on top of cake.

Chocolate Damnation

12 ounces semisweet chocolate
   squares or pieces
¹/₄ cup strong coffee
2 eggs, separated
¹/₄ cup coffee liqueur

3 tablespoons sugar
¹/₄ cup whipping cream
   Brownie Shell
   Chocolate Glaze
   Chocolate curls (optional)

This incredibly rich dessert sends chocolate lovers into a state of complete bliss. Its originator, Lee Srednick, won a local contest with it.

COMBINE chocolate and coffee in top of double boiler and melt over hot water. Remove from heat. Beat egg yolks until pale yellow in color and stir in some of the chocolate mixture. Return to chocolate in pan, stirring until smooth. Gradually stir in liqueur and cool. Beat egg whites until foamy. Gradually add sugar and beat until stiff. Whip cream until stiff. Fold cream into cooled chocolate mixture, then fold in egg whites. Line bottom and sides of a greased 9-inch square baking dish with Brownie Shell, cutting strips for sides and a 9-inch square for bottom of mold. Turn filling into cake-lined mold and cover with plastic wrap. Chill 3 to 4 hours or until firm. Invert onto serving platter. Glaze with Chocolate Glaze. Let glaze set and decorate with chocolate curls. Cut in very thin slices to serve.

Makes 20 to 30 servings.

Note: To make chocolate curls, bring 1 ounce square of semisweet chocolate to room temperature. With vegetable peeler, scrape thin curls of chocolate from sides of square onto wax paper.

Brownie Shell

²/₃ cup butter or margarine
4 ounces semisweet chocolate
2 cups sugar
4 eggs, well-beaten

1¹/₂ cups flour
1 teaspoon baking powder
¹/₂ teaspoon salt
1 tablespoon vanilla

Melt butter with chocolate in saucepan over low heat. Remove from heat and add sugar and eggs. Combine flour, baking powder, and salt and beat into chocolate mixture. Add vanilla. Line a greased 15 x 10-inch jelly-roll pan with wax paper. Pour in batter and spread evenly. Bake at 350 degrees 12 to 15 minutes, or until cake springs back when lightly touched. Cake should be soft, not crisp. Turn out on rack and cool. Invert on towel and peel off paper.

Chocolate Glaze

4 ounces semisweet chocolate
3 tablespoons strong coffee

Combine chocolate and coffee in top of double boiler and melt over hot water.

Trifle

Here is the classic trifle. If you're in a hurry, a pound cake from the freezer or a bakery can be substituted for the suggested basic sponge cake. This is a dessert to serve in an elegant glass bowl so the colored layers will show to best advantage.

1 Sponge Cake or pound cake
1 (1-pound) jar raspberry jam
4 cups strawberries, washed and hulled
Sugar

6 tablespoons sweet sherry
Boiled Custard
1 cup whipping cream, whipped
Slivered almonds

SLICE Sponge Cake in half horizontally. Spread each half with jam. Cut in 1-inch cubes. Reserve a few strawberries for garnish and slice the rest. Place ¹/₃ of the berries in 2-quart bowl and sprinkle lightly with sugar. Top with ¹/₃ of the cake cubes. Sprinkle with 2 tablespoons sherry, then pour ¹/₃ of Boiled Custard over cake. Continue layering until berries, sherry, cake, and custard are used up. Cover and refrigerate overnight. Before serving, top with whipped cream and reserved whole berries. Sprinkle with almonds.

Makes about 10 to 12 servings.

Sponge Cake

2 eggs, separated
1 cup sugar
6 tablespoons hot water
¹/₄ teaspoon lemon extract

1 cup flour
1¹/₂ teaspoons baking powder
¹/₄ teaspoon salt

Beat egg yolks until thick and lemon-colored. Add ¹/₂ cup sugar gradually and continue beating. Slowly add water, then add remaining ¹/₂ cup sugar and lemon extract. Beat egg whites until stiff and fold in. Sift flour with baking powder and salt and add. Turn batter into an ungreased 9-inch square cake pan and bake at 350 degrees 25 minutes. Invert pan on rack and let stand until cake is cold. Loosen with spatula and carefully remove cake from pan.

Boiled Custard

3 eggs
¹/₄ cup sugar
¹/₈ teaspoon salt

2 cups milk, scalded
¹/₂ teaspoon vanilla

Beat eggs lightly. Add sugar and salt. Add milk, stirring constantly. Cook, stirring, in top of double boiler over hot, not boiling, water until mixture coats a spoon, about 7 to 10 minutes. Add vanilla and cool.

Short-Cut Trifle

1 (3¹/₄-ounce) package vanilla pudding mix
2 cups half and half
2 tablespoons dark rum
2¹/₄ cups whipping cream
3 tablespoons sugar
2 tablespoons red raspberry
  preserves

1 (10-inch) round
  sponge cake layer,
  2 inches thick
¹/₄ cup brandy
¹/₄ cup sherry
30 to 38 whole strawberries

*The Five Crowns restaurant in
Corona del Mar serves a trifle
that is about as short-cut a version and as pretty as a trifle
can be.*

COMBINE pudding mix and half and half in saucepan. Cook over low
heat until mixture comes to boil and partially thickens. Stir in rum,
then chill pudding thoroughly. Combine 1¹/₄ cups whipping cream
and 1 tablespoon sugar and whip until cream is stiff. Fold into chilled
pudding mixture. Using a brush, coat a deep 10-inch bowl with raspberry preserves to within 1 inch of top of bowl. Slice sponge cake
horizontally into fourths. Place top slice, crust side up, in bottom of
coated bowl. Cut remaining slices into fingers about 2 inches wide
and stand against sides of bowl, pressing so fingers adhere to coating.
Combine brandy and sherry and sprinkle over cake in bottom and on
sides. Spoon custard into bowl. Beat remaining 1 cup whipping
cream with remaining 2 tablespoons sugar until stiff. Fill pastry bag
with whipped cream mixture. Pipe whipped cream around rim of
bowl and in mounds around center. Decorate whipped cream with
strawberries. Refrigerate at least 2 hours. To serve, spoon onto
chilled dessert plates.

Makes 6 to 8 servings.

Fudge Pudding Cake

1 cup sifted flour
2 teaspoons baking powder
¹/₂ teaspoon salt
¹/₂ cup granulated sugar
³/₄ cup chopped walnuts
¹/₂ cup milk
1 teaspoon vanilla

2 tablespoons melted shortening
1 ounce unsweetened chocolate, melted
¹/₄ cup cocoa
³/₄ cup brown sugar, packed
1³/₄ cups hot water

SIFT together flour, baking powder, salt, and granulated sugar into
bowl. Add nuts, then stir in milk, vanilla, shortening, and chocolate.
Spread batter in greased 8-inch square pan. Mix cocoa with brown
sugar, stir in hot water, and pour over batter. Bake at 375 degrees 40
minutes. As pudding bakes, cake layer forms on top and rich sauce
on the bottom. Spoon warm pudding into dessert dishes and top with
whipped cream or ice cream, if desired.

Makes 8 servings.

Hot Fig Pudding

A "Guys & Galleys" column cook, James Green, makes this wonderful, rich holiday dessert. Double the hot wine sauce recipe for more generous servings.

1/2 cup butter or margarine
2 eggs
1 cup molasses
2 cups finely chopped dried
  figs
1/2 teaspoon grated lemon peel
1 cup buttermilk

2 1/2 cups sifted flour
1/2 teaspoon soda
2 teaspoons baking powder
1 teaspoon ground ginger
1 teaspoon salt
Hot Wine Sauce

CREAM butter until soft. Beat in eggs and molasses until fluffy. Stir in figs, lemon peel, and buttermilk. Resift flour with soda, baking powder, ginger, and salt. Stir dry ingredients into pudding mixture. Pour into greased 9-inch tube pan and bake at 325 degrees 1 hour or until done. Serve with Hot Wine Sauce.

Makes about 10 servings.

Hot Wine Sauce

1/2 cup butter or margarine
1 cup sugar
1 or 2 eggs

3/4 cup dry sherry
1 teaspoon grated lemon peel
1/4 teaspoon nutmeg

Cream butter and sugar until light. Beat in eggs. Stir in sherry, lemon peel, and nutmeg. Shortly before serving, beat the sauce over hot water in double boiler. Heat thoroughly.

Makes about 1 1/2 cups.

Almond Persimmon Pudding

1 1/2 cups sifted flour
1 1/2 teaspoons soda
1/2 teaspoon salt
1/2 teaspoon cinnamon
2 eggs
1 1/4 cups sugar
1 1/2 cups sieved persimmon
  pulp

1/4 cup butter or margarine,
  melted
3/4 cup milk
1 cup raisins
1/2 cup chopped almonds
Hard sauce or whipped
cream

RESIFT flour with soda, salt, and cinnamon. Beat eggs until light. Beat in sugar. Stir in persimmon pulp and melted butter. Add flour mixture alternately with milk and beat until smooth. Fold in raisins and almonds. Pour batter into well-greased 9 x 5-inch loaf pan and set in pan of hot water. Bake at 325 degrees 1 1/2 to 2 hours or until done. Serve warm with hard sauce or cold with whipped cream.

Makes 8 servings.

Double-Boiler Bread Pudding

1 cup brown sugar, packed
3 slices buttered white bread,
    cut into ³/₄-inch cubes
2 eggs

2 cups milk
¹/₂ teaspoon salt
1 teaspoon vanilla

A Times *reader sent in the recipe for this delicious bread pudding, which forms its own caramel sauce as it cooks.*

PLACE brown sugar in top of double boiler. Place bread cubes on top of sugar. Beat eggs with milk, salt, and vanilla and pour over bread. Place over simmering water, cover, and cook 1¹/₂ hours. Do not stir. The brown sugar forms a sauce in bottom of pan. Turn pudding into serving dish.

Makes 6 servings.

Note: Raisins may be added, if desired.

Bread Pudding

6 eggs
1 quart milk
1 teaspoon vanilla
³/₄ cup sugar

¹/₂ teaspoon nutmeg
6 thick slices egg bread,
    diced, or 12 regular size
    slices egg bread, diced

The famous old Ambassador Hotel in Los Angeles makes a bread pudding that is one of the best of the firm, custardy, homey types.

BEAT eggs. Beat in milk, vanilla, sugar, and nutmeg. Mix in bread cubes. Turn into a greased 2-quart baking dish and sprinkle with cinnamon and coconut, if desired. Bake at 325 degrees 45 minutes, or until set. If desired, jam or jelly may be swirled through mixture, or add cherries, raisins, or other fruit.

Makes 8 servings.

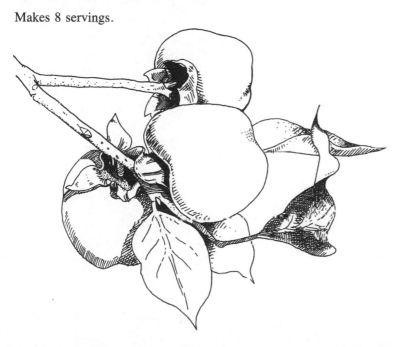

Arroz Dulce
(Sweet Rice)

A nostalgic reader who remembered how her mother used to make her very special rice pudding won a "My Best Recipe" award for this.

1 cup uncooked rice
1/2 cup raisins
1 1/2 sticks cinnamon
1 cup sugar
1 tablespoon grated gingerroot

1 cup canned coconut cream
2 cups milk
1/2 teaspoon vanilla
1/4 cup unsalted butter
Ground cinnamon

LET rice and raisins soak in water to cover for 1/2 hour. Bring 2 cups water to boil in large saucepan. Drain rice and raisins and add to boiling water with cinnamon sticks and 1/4 cup sugar. Cook over low heat until rice is tender. Boil gingerroot in 1/2 cup water 5 minutes, strain, and blend liquid with remaining 3/4 cup sugar, coconut cream, milk, and vanilla. Add this mixture with butter to rice. Cover and continue cooking over low heat until milk is absorbed, stirring every 5 to 10 minutes. Spoon into serving dish or individual custard cups, sprinkle with ground cinnamon, and chill.

Makes 8 to 10 servings.

Rum Flan Cake

1 cup sugar
3 egg yolks
2 eggs
1 tall can evaporated milk

1 teaspoon grated orange peel
2 tablespoons rum
Chiffon Cake Batter
Whipped cream

CARAMELIZE 1/2 cup sugar in 9-inch (about 3 1/2 to 4 inches deep) heart-shaped or round pan. Beat together egg yolks, eggs, remaining 1/2 cup sugar, evaporated milk, orange peel, and rum. Set aside. Prepare Chiffon Cake Batter. Pour custard mixture into caramel-lined pan. Gently spoon cake batter over flan mixture. Place pan in larger pan and pour in hot (not boiling) water until it reaches half the depth of the pan. Bake at 325 degrees 50 to 60 minutes, or until cake is done. Cool on rack or chill until ready to serve. Invert onto serving platter and garnish top edges of flan with whipped cream rosettes.

Makes 8 servings.

Chiffon Cake Batter

3/4 cup sifted cake flour
1/2 cup sugar
1 teaspoon baking powder
1/4 teaspoon salt
2 egg yolks

3 tablespoons oil
1 tablespoon rum
3 tablespoons orange juice
3 egg whites
1/4 teaspoon cream of tartar

Sift together flour, ¼ cup sugar, baking powder, and salt. Place in small bowl and make a well in the center. Place yolks, oil, rum, and orange juice in well. Stir until blended, starting from center. Beat egg whites with cream of tartar until foamy. Gradually add remaining ¼ cup sugar, beating until stiff but not dry. Gently fold batter into whites.

9-Point Flan

1¼ cups sugar
8 to 10 egg yolks
  1 (13-ounce) can evaporated milk

2 to 4 tablespoons rum

A thin sliver of this ultra-rich and creamy flan goes a long way. It was developed in The Times *test kitchen when there were a lot of leftover egg yolks.*

HEAT ¾ cup sugar until melted and caramel-colored. Pour into 5-cup baking dish and swirl to line dish with caramel. Set aside. Beat egg yolks with ½ cup sugar. Add evaporated milk and rum to taste and beat well. Turn custard into prepared baking dish. Place dish in pan of hot water and bake at 350 degrees about 1 hour, or until knife inserted in center comes out clean. Cool thoroughly at room temperature, then unmold on serving plate.

Makes 8 servings.

California Flan

¾ cup sugar
 4 eggs
 1 (14-ounce) can sweetened condensed milk

1 cup water
2 teaspoons vanilla

This typically Mexican-style flan has been reprinted many times in response to reader requests. It was sent to our ''Border Line'' column by Judi Powers of Nipomo.

PLACE sugar in skillet and cook, stirring, over moderate heat until melted and golden brown. Pour into 1-quart casserole and swirl to coat sides and bottom evenly with the caramel. Beat eggs. Add milk and beat until blended. Beat in water and vanilla. Turn into prepared baking dish and place in a pan containing 1 inch hot water. Bake at 325 degrees 1 hour 40 minutes, or until knife inserted in center comes out clean. Cool completely, then turn out on a serving plate.

Makes 6 to 8 servings.

Note: Recipe may be doubled, if desired.

Rum Balls

1 (12-ounce) package vanilla
   wafers
   Powdered sugar
2 tablespoons cocoa

1 cup finely chopped nuts
1/2 cup light corn syrup
2 to 4 ounces dark rum

CRUSH vanilla wafers very fine. Blend in 1 cup powdered sugar, cocoa, and nuts. Mix syrup and rum. Add to wafer mixture and let stand 30 minutes. Form into small balls and roll in additional powdered sugar. Store in airtight containers.

Makes about 6 dozen.

Chocolate Chip Butter Cookies

Chocolate chip cookie fans rave over these rich, buttery creations from the Pioneer Boulangerie in Santa Monica.

1 pound butter or margarine
   Powdered sugar
1/2 teaspoon salt
2 teaspoons vanilla

4 1/2 cups flour
1 (12-ounce) package semisweet chocolate pieces

CREAM together butter and 2 cups powdered sugar. Add salt, vanilla, and flour and mix until blended. Mixture will be stiff. Stir in chocolate pieces. Pinch off pieces of dough. Roll into 1-inch balls and flatten with a fork on baking sheet. Bake at 350 degrees 15 minutes. Sprinkle with additional powdered sugar while hot.

Makes 64.

Haystacks

These fruit and nut cookies laced with coconut are a specialty of Griswold's, a popular restaurant and bakery in Claremont, California.

13 egg whites, lightly beaten
 2 cups sugar
6 1/2 cups flake coconut
1 1/2 cups chopped dates

1 cup chopped walnuts
1/2 teaspoon salt
1 1/2 teaspoons vanilla

COMBINE egg whites and sugar. Cook in top of double boiler over simmering water until mixture reaches 120 degrees or feels hot to the touch. Combine coconut, dates, walnuts, salt, and vanilla in mixing bowl. Add hot sugar mixture and blend well. Mixture will be fairly stiff. Using small ice cream scoop, form into balls and place on lightly greased baking sheet. Bake at 350 degrees 20 minutes, or until golden brown. Allow to cool and remove from pan.

Makes about 3 dozen.

Turtle Cookies

$1^1/_2$ cups sifted flour
$^1/_4$ teaspoon soda
$^1/_2$ teaspoon salt
$^1/_2$ cup butter or margarine
$^1/_2$ cup brown sugar, packed

2 eggs
$^1/_4$ teaspoon vanilla
Pecan halves
Chocolate Frosting I

RESIFT together flour with soda and salt. Cream butter and brown sugar together thoroughly. Add 1 whole egg and 1 egg yolk and beat well. Stir in vanilla. Add dry ingredients and mix well. Arrange pecan halves in groups of 3 or 5 on greased baking sheets to resemble head and legs of turtle. Roll rounded teaspoons of dough into balls. Dip bottom of each into remaining unbeaten egg white and press lightly onto nuts so tips of nuts show. Bake at 350 degrees 10 to 13 minutes. Cool and frost tops with Chocolate Frosting I.

Makes $2^1/_2$ dozen.

Chocolate Frosting I

2 ounces unsweetened chocolate
$^1/_4$ cup milk

1 tablespoon butter or margarine
1 cup sifted powdered sugar

Combine chocolate, milk, and butter in top of double boiler. Cook over boiling water, stirring until smooth. Remove from heat and beat in sugar until smooth and glossy, adding more sugar if needed.

Chinese Almond Cookies

2 cups flour
$^1/_2$ teaspoon soda
$^3/_4$ teaspoon baking powder
1 egg
$^1/_2$ pound lard
$^1/_2$ cup brown sugar, packed

$^1/_2$ cup granulated sugar
$^1/_2$ teaspoon almond extract
Blanched whole almonds
1 or 2 egg yolks

The secret behind these just-like-the-real-ones Chinese almond cookies is the lard.

SIFT flour with soda and baking powder. Beat egg and lard together. Add sugars and almond extract. Gradually mix in dry ingredients until well blended. For each cookie, roll 1 tablespoon dough into a ball. Place on ungreased baking sheets and press an almond in the middle of each. Brush with beaten egg yolk and bake at 350 degrees 15 to 20 minutes.

Makes about 3 dozen.

Finska Pinnar
(Finnish Fingers)

Los Angeles has many residents of Scandinavian descent. They like rich, buttery cookies like sugar-coated Finska Pinnar and jam-filled Syltkakor. Both recipes were translated from old Swedish cookbooks.

1/2 pound butter or margarine	1/2 teaspoon vanilla
1/2 cup sugar	2 1/4 cups flour
1 egg, separated	Pearl sugar

BEAT butter until creamy, then beat in sugar and egg yolk. Add vanilla. Gradually work in flour to form a dough. Chill. Roll dough out into long ropes about 1/2 inch in diameter. Brush ropes with lightly beaten egg white, then cut into 2 1/2-inch lengths. Dip each in pearl sugar to coat. Place on greased baking sheets and bake at 350 degrees 15 to 20 minutes.

Makes about 4 dozen.

Note: Pearl sugar is usually available in stores that specialize in Scandinavian foods. Any coarsely ground sugar can be substituted, but the effect will be different.

Syltkakor
(Jam-Filled Cookies)

1/2 pound butter or margarine, at room temperature	7 tablespoons powdered sugar
1/3 cup plus 1 tablespoon sugar	1 tablespoon water
1/2 beaten egg	Finely chopped blanched almonds
2 1/3 cups flour	Jelly or jam
1/2 teaspoon almond extract	

CREAM butter until light, then beat in sugar. Add egg. Gradually work in flour, then add almond extract. On a floured board, roll dough out 1/8-inch thick. Cut with scalloped circular cutter about 2 inches in diameter. With a thimble or other small round cutter, cut a hole in center of half the cookies. Place on greased baking sheets and bake at 350 degrees until lightly browned, 10 to 15 minutes. Beat powdered sugar and water together to make a glaze. Glaze cookies with hole in the center with this mixture and sprinkle with chopped nuts. Spread remaining cookies with favorite jelly. Sandwich cookies together with glazed cookies on top.

Makes about 2 dozen.

Persimmon Cookies

1 teaspoon soda
1 cup sieved persimmon pulp
1/2 cup butter or margarine
1 cup sugar
1 egg
2 cups flour

1 teaspoon baking powder
1/2 teaspoon salt
1/2 teaspoon cinnamon
1/2 teaspoon cloves
1/2 teaspoon nutmeg
1 cup raisins and/or nuts

The Christmas season always brings a demand for this sweet spice cookie recipe.

STIR soda into persimmon pulp and set aside. Cream butter and sugar together. Beat in egg, then persimmon mixture. Sift flour with baking powder, salt, cinnamon, cloves, and nutmeg. Add to creamed mixture along with raisins or nuts. Mix thoroughly. Drop by teaspoons onto greased baking sheets and bake at 350 degrees 8 to 10 minutes.

Makes 4 dozen.

Mexican Wedding Cakes

1 cup butter or margarine
  Powdered sugar
1/8 teaspoon salt

2 teaspoons vanilla
2 cups flour
1/2 cup chopped nuts

These rich sugar-dusted cookies literally melt in your mouth. They are very popular in Southern California, particularly around Christmas.

CREAM together butter and 1/4 cup powdered sugar. Add salt, vanilla, flour, and nuts and mix well. Roll dough into small balls and place on greased baking sheets. Bake at 325 degrees 15 minutes. Roll in additional powdered sugar while warm.

Makes about 4 dozen.

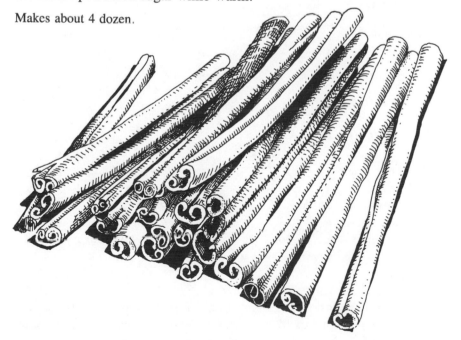

Potato Chip Cookies

After a potato chip cookie recipe was printed in the "Culinary SOS" column, reader Frances Dewar sent us hers, which she thought was better.

1 cup butter or margarine
1/2 cup sugar
1 teaspoon vanilla

1/2 cup crushed potato chips
1/2 cup chopped nuts
2 cups flour

CREAM butter and sugar. Add vanilla, potato chips, nuts, and flour and mix well. Form into small balls and place on ungreased baking sheets. Dip bottom of a glass in sugar and flatten cookies. Bake at 350 degrees 16 to 18 minutes.

Makes about 6 dozen.

Zucchini Oatmeal Cookies

A USC Medical Center dietetic department trainee, Leigh Hinkleman, won first prize for these spicy morsels during a nutrition-week event.

1/2 cup margarine
3/4 cup honey
1 egg
2 cups whole wheat flour
1 teaspoon soda
1 teaspoon cinnamon
1/4 teaspoon ground cloves

1/2 teaspoon nutmeg
1/4 teaspoon salt
1 cup grated zucchini
1 cup rolled oats
1 cup chopped dates or raisins

CREAM margarine with honey. Add egg and beat well. Sift together flour, soda, cinnamon, cloves, nutmeg, and salt. Add flour mixture alternately with zucchini to egg mixture. Stir in oats and dates. Drop by teaspoons onto greased baking sheets. Bake at 375 degrees 10 to 12 minutes.

Makes 5 dozen.

Great Oatmeal Cookies

The giant moist oatmeal cookies served at Martin Luther King Hospital in Los Angeles are among the best you'll ever eat.

1 1/2 cups raisins
2 eggs
1 1/2 teaspoons vanilla
1 cup shortening
3/4 cup plus 2 tablespoons granulated sugar

1 1/3 cups brown sugar, packed
2 cups flour
1 1/8 teaspoons salt
1/2 teaspoon soda
2 1/8 teaspoons baking powder
3 3/4 cups rolled oats

COVER raisins with warm water and soak 10 minutes. Drain thoroughly and set aside. Combine eggs, 2 tablespoons water, vanilla, shortening, and sugars in mixer bowl. Sift together flour, salt, soda, and baking powder. Add to egg mixture and beat at low speed 2 to 3 minutes or until smooth. Add oats and raisins and mix until blended. Form into 2-inch-thick rolls. Wrap in wax paper and chill until firm. Slice rolls into 1/2-inch-thick slices and place on baking sheets. Flatten to 1/4-inch thickness and bake at 375 degrees 10 to 12 minutes.

Makes about 32.

Mother's Sugar Cookies

1 cup butter or margarine
  Sugar
3/4 teaspoon soda
1/2 teaspoon salt

1 teaspoon vanilla
3 eggs, beaten
3 2/3 cups sifted flour
2 teaspoons baking powder

Thanks to the request from a reader, we are lucky to have this old-fashioned and delicious cookie recipe from the Valley Hunt Club of Pasadena in our files.

CREAM butter and 2 cups sugar with soda, salt, and vanilla. Add beaten eggs and beat until smooth. Sift together flour and baking powder and add to creamed mixture, mixing until smooth. Chill dough until firm enough to roll out on floured pastry cloth. Sprinkle with sugar and cut into fancy cookie shapes with cookie cutters. Place on greased baking sheets and bake at 450 degrees 8 minutes, or until cookies are golden.

Makes 10 dozen medium-size cookies.

Beatles

3/4 cup butter or margarine
  Sugar
3 eggs
5 1/4 cups flour
3/4 teaspoon salt
3/4 teaspoon soda

1 tablespoon baking powder
1 1/2 cups sour cream
1 1/2 teaspoons vanilla
1/2 cup semisweet chocolate
  pieces
1 tablespoon cinnamon

John Adams Junior High School in Santa Monica first offered these sour cream chocolate chip cookies to students at the peak of the Beatles craze, hence the name.

CREAM butter and 2 1/4 cups sugar. Add eggs and mix well. Sift together flour, salt, soda, and baking powder. Alternately add to egg mixture with sour cream. Add vanilla and fold in chocolate. Drop by heaping teaspoons onto greased baking sheets. Combine 2/3 cup sugar and cinnamon and sprinkle some on each cookie. Bake at 375 degrees 12 minutes.

Makes 8 to 10 dozen.

Granola Cookies

1 cup shortening
3/4 cup brown sugar, packed
2 eggs
2 tablespoons vanilla
3 cups flour

1 1/2 teaspoons cream of tartar
1 teaspoon baking powder
1 teaspoon salt
3 cups granola with raisins
1 cup milk

CREAM together shortening, sugar, eggs, and vanilla. Sift together flour, cream of tartar, baking powder, and salt. Add granola to creamed mixture. Add flour mixture alternately with milk. Drop by heaping teaspoons onto greased baking sheets and bake at 350 degrees 12 to 15 minutes.

Makes 5 dozen.

Peanut Butter Bars

Don't use a blender or food processor to make the crumbs for this recipe. Crush the crackers with a rolling pin or they'll be too fine and the end result will be too crumbly to handle.

1 (18-ounce) jar peanut butter, at room temperature
3/4 cup butter or margarine, softened
1 (1-pound) package powdered sugar

1 (1-pound) box graham crackers, crushed coarsely
1 (12-ounce) package semi-sweet chocolate pieces

USING an electric mixer, cream together peanut butter and butter until very soft and smooth. Beat in powdered sugar until smooth, then beat in half of crumbs. Beat until well blended and moist. Mix in remaining crumbs with hands. Spread mixture in 13 × 9-inch baking pan, patting evenly. Melt chocolate in top of double boiler over hot water or in microwave oven and pour over cracker mixture. Mark off desired size squares or bars and refrigerate 3 to 4 hours or overnight.

Makes about 5 dozen.

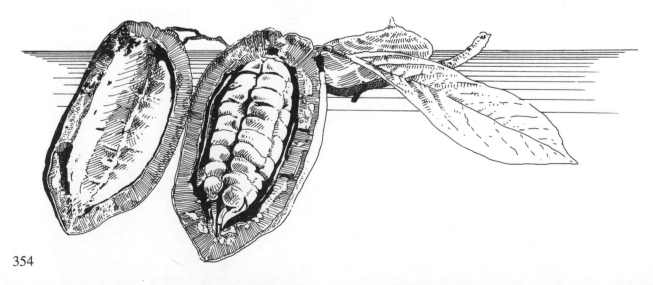

Brownies

10 ounces unsweetened chocolate
2¹/₂ cups butter or margarine
10 eggs
5 cups sugar

2 teaspoons salt
4 teaspoons vanilla
4 cups sifted flour
1¹/₃ cups coarsely chopped walnuts

MELT chocolate with butter in top of double boiler over hot water. Beat eggs, sugar, salt, and vanilla in large mixer bowl. Add melted chocolate mixture. Mix until blended. Add flour gradually while beating on low speed. Mix in nuts. Turn into 2 greased 18 x 12-inch baking pans, spreading mixture evenly in pans. Bake at 350 degrees 20 to 25 minutes, being careful not to overbake. While still warm, cut into squares.

Makes about 40.

Mannings is the food service company that runs the employees' cafeteria at The Times. On the days they make brownies the news travels fast, and these chocolate bar cookies disappear quickly.

Fudgy Wudgy Brownies

4 ounces unsweetened chocolate
¹/₂ cup butter or margarine
2 cups sugar
4 eggs, beaten
1 cup sifted flour

1 teaspoon vanilla
1 cup coarsely chopped walnuts
1 (6-ounce) package semisweet chocolate pieces

MELT the unsweetened chocolate and butter in top of double boiler over hot water. Cool slightly. Gradually add sugar to eggs, beating thoroughly after each addition. Blend in chocolate mixture. Stir in flour. Add vanilla, half the nuts, and half the semisweet chocolate pieces. Spread in greased 9-inch square pan. Sprinkle remaining chocolate pieces and nuts over batter. Bake at 325 degrees 30 minutes. Remove and cool in pan. Cut in squares.

Makes 16.

Songwriter Carol Connors made these for a Bastille Day picnic. They're the fudgiest brownies you'll ever eat.

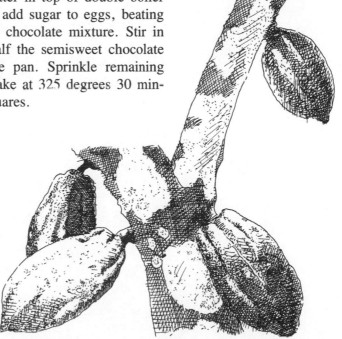

Chocolate Mayonnaise Cupcakes

Mayonnaise substitutes for the shortening in these moist and delicious lunchbox cupcakes.

3 cups sifted flour
1¹/₂ cups sugar
¹/₃ cup cocoa
2¹/₄ teaspoons baking powder
1¹/₄ teaspoons soda

1¹/₂ cups mayonnaise
1¹/₂ cups water
1¹/₂ teaspoons vanilla
Chocolate Frosting II

RESIFT together flour with sugar, cocoa, baking powder, and soda into bowl. Gradually stir in mayonnaise. Stir in water and vanilla. Fill 2 dozen greased or paper-lined muffin pans ¹/₂ full with batter. Bake at 350 degrees 25 to 30 minutes. Cool in pans 5 minutes. Remove from pans and cool on rack. Frost with Chocolate Frosting II. Garnish tops with nuts, if desired.

Makes 2 dozen.

Chocolate Frosting II

3 tablespoons butter or margarine
2 ounces semisweet chocolate
2 cups powdered sugar

¹/₈ teaspoon salt
2 to 4 tablespoons hot milk
¹/₂ teaspoon vanilla

Melt butter and chocolate in top of double boiler over hot water. Sift together powdered sugar and salt. Add chocolate mixture and blend. Beat in enough milk to make a spreadable consistency. Beat in vanilla.

Oxy Fudge

This rich fudge recipe has been printed numerous times since it won a "My Best Recipe" column award in 1973.

4¹/₂ cups sugar
1 (13-ounce) can evaporated milk
Salt
¹/₂ pound butter or margarine

3 cups semisweet chocolate pieces
2 cups chopped nuts
1 tablespoon vanilla

COMBINE sugar, evaporated milk, and dash of salt in large saucepan. Boil over medium heat 14 minutes, timing after mixture comes to full boil. Stir occasionally. While syrup is cooking, place butter, chocolate pieces, and dash of salt in large mixer bowl. After syrup is cooked, pour it over the chocolate-butter mixture in bowl and blend at low speed first, then beat at high speed 10 minutes. Add nuts and vanilla and stir to blend. Pour fudge into greased 13 × 9-inch pan and chill until firm.

Makes about 4 pounds.

Can't-Fail Fudge

4 cups miniature
   marshmallows
²/₃ cup evaporated milk
¹/₄ cup butter or margarine
1¹/₂ cups sugar

¹/₄ teaspoon salt
1 (12-ounce) package
   semisweet chocolate pieces
1 teaspoon vanilla
¹/₂ cup chopped nuts

To keep this never-fail fudge glossy and smooth-looking, do not overbeat and don't touch after pouring into the pan until it's completely set.

COMBINE marshmallows, milk, butter, sugar, and salt in saucepan. Cook and stir until mixture comes to full boil. Boil 5 minutes over medium heat, stirring constantly. Remove from heat and add chocolate pieces, beating until melted. Do not overbeat. Fold in vanilla and nuts. Pour into greased 9-inch square pan. Chill until firm.

Makes 2¹/₂ pounds.

Chocolate-Dipped Strawberries

1 (12-ounce) package
   semisweet chocolate pieces
6 tablespoons butter or
   margarine

¹/₂ teaspoon vanilla
Strawberries with stems

Chocolate-covered strawberries are served as a finale to dinner at some fine Los Angeles restaurants. They also make attractive decorations for cakes and pies.

MELT chocolate pieces in top of double boiler. Add butter and vanilla. Dip strawberries in chocolate, swirling to coat evenly. Place on wax paper and set in cool dry place.

Makes about 1¹/₃ cups dip.

Note: Cherries or other fruit may be substituted for strawberries.

Frozen Chocolate Banana Pops

Chocolate banana pops can be made by the batch to serve as a nutritious after-school snack.

6 firm ripe bananas
  Chocolate Topping
  Colored sprinkles, grated
  coconut, or coarsely ground
  nuts

CUT peeled bananas in halves crosswise. Impale each half on a wooden skewer and place in freezer for 1 hour or until frozen. (Coatings will run off if fruit is at room temperature.) Remove bananas from freezer a few at a time. Dip and roll bananas in melted Chocolate Topping, making sure all banana surfaces are completely covered. Shake or twirl banana before removing from pan to remove excess coating. While coating is still soft, roll the covered banana in colored sprinkles, coconut, or nuts. If coating becomes too hard to hold decorations, apply a little warm coating to the pop. When covering sets, place pops on squares of foil, wrap securely, and store in freezer until ready to eat.

Makes 12.

Chocolate Topping

1 (12-ounce) package
  semisweet chocolate pieces
6 tablespoons oil

Melt chocolate in top of double boiler over hot, not boiling, water. Add oil and stir until smooth. Keep warm over hot water while dipping.

Makes enough topping to cover 12 pops.

Peach Leather

Sun-dried fruit leathers make wonderful natural snacks for the after-school crowd. If you run into a cloudy day, the leathers can be dried in the oven.

10 large fully ripe peaches
 1 cup sugar

PEEL and slice peaches to measure 10 cups. Put peaches into large saucepan. Add sugar and bring mixture to boil, stirring until sugar is dissolved. Pour mixture into blender container and puree. Cool to lukewarm. Meanwhile, prepare a smooth, level drying surface in full sunlight. Cover baking sheets, jelly-roll pans, or other flat surfaces with plastic wrap. Pour peach puree onto prepared surface, spread to $1/8$-inch thickness, and let dry in sunlight. Cover with screen to avoid insects. Drying may take 20 to 24 hours. Bring puree inside at end of day and finish drying a second day. Or set sheets of fruit in baking pans in oven at 150 degrees and leave door open. Fruit is dry when puree can be peeled off plastic easily. For storing, roll up leather with plastic wrap. Wrap in more plastic wrap and seal tightly. Leather will keep at room temperature about 1 month, in refrigerator about 4 months, or 1 year in freezer. Tear or cut into strips to eat.

Makes about 3 (15 × 10-inch) sheets.

Note: Other fresh fruits in season, such as strawberries, plums, apricots, and pears, may be substituted for the peaches. Compatible combinations of fruits also may be substituted for a single fruit.

BEVERAGES

RINKS in Southern California are probably more colorful and experimental than in any other place in the United States. The warm climate and casual way of life inspire a taste for fruit-flavored daiquiris, Hawaiian cocktails, and Mexican drinks made with tequila. In Los Angeles, people are as likely to relax with an unusual kind of margarita as a conventional martini. And they like their margaritas big, served in enormous bowl-shaped glasses over lots of ice and flavored in a variety of ways.

Wine—and California's wines are now recognized worldwide—is popular not only with meals but as an aperitif, replacing stronger alcoholic drinks. Wine spritzers, combining red or white wine with sparkling water or a soft drink, are also well liked. And the mimosa cocktail, which blends two California products, champagne-like sparkling wine and orange juice, is lovely for brunches.

After dinner, Californians may take their coffee Irish-style, laced with Irish whiskey and topped with whipped cream, or Mexican-style, with tequila and coffee liqueur. And the influx of Thai restaurants has brought a taste for Thai tea, a milky, sweet, nonalcoholic drink that is served cold.

Nonalcoholic drinks include a wide range of vitamin-rich, high-energy beverages developed as part of California's continuing health-food craze and as sustenance for exercise devotees. Diet drinks, light in flavor and calories, are also basic to the California scene.

In this section we begin with drinks that include alcohol and finish with a group of nonalcoholic beverages. This is a refreshing selection that ranges from hot to cold and from mild to anything but.

Left to right: *Scorpion, Pink Palace, Vanda Daiquiri, Sundowner*, pages 364, 365

Scorpion

1 cup crushed ice
2 ounces light rum
1 ounce brandy

2 tablespoons Sweet-Sour Mix
¹/₄ cup orange juice

COMBINE ice, rum, brandy, Sweet-Sour Mix, and orange juice in a blender container and blend. Serve in a 14-ounce old-fashioned glass.

Makes 1 serving.

Note: Recipe for Sweet-Sour Mix is on page 367.

Pink Palace

1 to 2 cups crushed ice
1 ounce light rum
1 ounce Grand Marnier
4 teaspoons grenadine syrup

2 tablespoons whipping cream
2 tablespoons coconut cream
4 teaspoons lemon juice
2 tablespoons pineapple juice

COMBINE ice, rum, Grand Marnier, grenadine syrup, whipping cream, coconut cream, lemon juice, and pineapple juice in blender container and blend. Serve in a tall soda glass.

Makes 1 serving.

Vanda Daiquiri

³/₄ cup crushed ice
¹/₂ ounce dark rum
1 ounce light rum

2 tablespoons Sweet-Sour Mix
¹/₄ cup pineapple juice

COMBINE ice, dark and light rums, Sweet-Sour Mix, and pineapple juice in blender container and blend. Serve in a 14-ounce coupette.

Makes 1 serving.

Note: Recipe for Sweet-Sour Mix is on page 367.

Sundowner

Ice cubes
1¹/₂ ounces cognac
¹/₂ ounce Galliano

¹/₂ ounce orange liqueur
Sweet-Sour Mix
Dash grenadine syrup

FILL an 8-ounce highball glass with ice cubes. Add cognac, Galliano, and orange liqueur. Add enough Sweet-Sour Mix to almost fill glass, then add grenadine syrup.

Makes 1 serving.

Note: Recipe for Sweet-Sour Mix is on page 367.

Strawberry Daiquiri

1 cup strawberries, stemmed
3 ounces dark rum
3 ounces orange liqueur

1 tablespoon lime juice
2 teaspoons superfine sugar
6 ice cubes

Tangy citrus-based daiquiris are wonderful poolside refreshers. They are even better when other fruits are added.

PLACE strawberries, rum, orange liqueur, lime juice, sugar, and ice cubes in blender container. Process until fruit and ice are crushed. Pour into stemmed glasses. Garnish each with a whole strawberry, if desired.

Makes 2 servings.

Peach Daiquiri

¹/₂ cup cracked ice
1¹/₂ ounces light rum
¹/₂ peach, unpeeled

1 tablespoon lime juice
¹/₂ to 1 teaspoon sugar

COMBINE ice, rum, peach, lime juice, and sugar in blender container. Cover and blend until smooth. Serve, unstrained, in large cocktail glass.

Makes 1 serving.

Banana Daiquiri

1 whole banana, cut-up
1¹/₂ ounces light rum
1¹/₂ ounces banana liqueur
1 tablespoon lemon juice

2 teaspoons superfine sugar
6 ice cubes
Banana slices

PLACE banana, rum, banana liqueur, lemon juice, sugar, and ice cubes in food processor bowl or blender container. Process until ice is crushed and banana is smooth. Pour into 2 stemmed glasses. Garnish each with a banana slice.

Makes 2 servings.

Mai Tai

With Hawaii so accessible as a vacation spot, it's not at all surprising that Californians have adopted an island tradition, the Mai Tai, as a special-occasion drink.

Crushed ice
1¹/₂ ounces light rum
¹/₂ ounce orange Curaçao

Dash orgeat syrup
1 tablespoon lime juice
1 ounce dark rum

FILL double old-fashioned glass or brandy snifter with crushed ice. Pour light rum, orange Curaçao, orgeat syrup, and lime juice over and mix well. Add dark rum and mix lightly but not thoroughly. Add garnish of pineapple chunk, mint sprig, and maraschino cherry, if desired.

Makes 1 serving.

Pink Butterfly

The Kapalua Bay Hotel on Maui serves this frothy pink drink in a large brandy snifter.

3 cups crushed ice
¹/₄ cup unsweetened
   pineapple juice
¹/₄ cup orange juice
1¹/₄ ounces Sweet-Sour Mix

2 tablespoons coconut cream
2 ounces dark rum
1 tablespoon grenadine syrup
Ice cubes

COMBINE ice, pineapple juice, orange juice, Sweet-Sour Mix, coconut cream, dark rum, and grenadine syrup in blender container. Blend until frothy and well mixed. Pour over a few ice cubes in large brandy snifter.

Makes 1 serving.

Sweet-Sour Mix

2 cups lemon juice
1 cup sugar

Combine lemon juice and sugar. Stir until sugar dissolves.

Makes about 2^1/$_2$ cups.

Piña Colada

^{1}/$_2$ cup coconut milk
1 cup pineapple juice
6 ounces light rum

16 ice cubes, crushed
Fresh pineapple wedges
Maraschino cherries

PLACE coconut milk, pineapple juice, rum, and ice in blender container. Blend until frothy. Pour into 4 tall glasses. Garnish each drink with pineapple wedge and maraschino cherry.

Makes 4 drinks.

Peach Smash

1 (6-ounce) can frozen orange juice concentrate
4 to 6 ounces rum, vodka, or gin
1 large peach, peeled and sliced, or ^{1}/$_2$ (10-ounce) package frozen sliced peaches

^{1}/$_2$ ounce orange liqueur
4 or 5 ice cubes
Mint sprigs dipped in powdered sugar

PLACE orange juice concentrate, rum, peach slices, orange liqueur, and ice in blender container and blend at high speed until smooth and slushy. Pour immediately into champagne or old-fashioned glasses. Garnish with sugared mint sprigs.

Makes 4 to 6 drinks.

Note: This drink must be blended just before serving. Dust mint sprigs with powdered sugar just before use.

Margarita

Classic Mexican margaritas are never made with a mix. But they are well worth the small effort involved.

Lime wedge
Salt
1¹/₂ ounces tequila

³/₄ ounce orange liqueur
1¹/₂ tablespoons lime juice
Crushed ice

RUB lime wedge around rim of cocktail glass. Swirl glass rim in mound of salt to coat edge. Combine tequila, orange liqueur, and lime juice in cocktail shaker. Add ice and shake well. Pour into prepared glass and serve at once.

Makes 1 serving.

Frothy Margarita

Americans are apt to like their margaritas somewhat less austere than the classic version. Here is a frothy variation that is also a little sweeter.

Lime juice
Salt
1¹/₂ ounces tequila
¹/₂ ounce orange liqueur

3 tablespoons bottled sweet and sour mix
Crushed ice

MOISTEN rim of glass with lime juice and swirl glass rim in mound of salt to coat edge. Combine tequila, orange liqueur, and sweet and sour mix with crushed ice in blender container. Blend until frothy and pour into prepared glass.

Makes 1 serving.

Margaritas de Toronja
(Grapefruit Margaritas)

A grapefruit-flavored margarita is especially refreshing on a hot summer day.

Grapefruit slices, cut in quarters
Salt
³/₄ cup grapefruit juice

6 ounces tequila
2 ounces triple sec
2 cups cracked ice

MOISTEN rims of cocktail glasses with cut grapefruit. Swirl in mound of salt to coat edges. Combine grapefruit juice, tequila, triple sec, and cracked ice in blender container. Blend until smooth. Pour into prepared glasses. Place a grapefruit wedge on each rim.

Makes 6 to 8 servings.

Tequila Sunrise

$1^1/_2$ ounces tequila   Crushed ice
$^1/_2$ cup orange juice $1^1/_2$ teaspoons grenadine syrup

POUR tequila and orange juice over ice in tall glass. Add grenadine, which will form a layer at bottom of glass.

Makes 1 serving.

Havana Banana

$^3/_4$ ounce light rum   Ice cubes
$^3/_4$ ounce banana liqueur   Maraschino cherry
$^1/_2$ cup pineapple-coconut   Orange slice
     drink

COMBINE rum and banana liqueur. Add pineapple-coconut drink and stir to blend. Pour over ice cubes in large or small brandy snifter. Garnish with maraschino cherry and orange slice.

Makes 1 serving.

Pineapple, coconut, and banana flavors are combined in Havana Banana, a special drink at the Warehouse, a waterfront Marina del Rey restaurant.

Mimosa Cocktail

Orange juice, chilled   Melon balls
Champagne, chilled   Mint sprigs

COMBINE equal parts orange juice and champagne. Pour into chilled wineglasses and garnish with melon balls and mint sprigs.

The sparkling mimosa cocktail appears often at brunches and summery outdoor parties.

Bloody Mary

$1^1/_2$ ounces vodka   Dash salt
     Ice cubes   Dash celery salt
$^3/_4$ cup tomato juice   Dash hot pepper sauce
$^1/_2$ teaspoon Worcestershire   1 celery stick
     sauce

POUR vodka over ice cubes in 10- or 12-ounce glass. Add tomato juice, Worcestershire, salt, celery salt, and hot pepper sauce. Stir and garnish with celery stick.

Makes 1 serving.

Galliano-Type Liqueur

4 cups sugar
2 cups water
16 ounces 100-proof vodka

1 (1/2-ounce) bottle Strega extract
Dash yellow food color

COMBINE sugar and water in saucepan. Bring to boil, reduce heat, and simmer about 10 minutes or until syrupy. Cool. Add vodka, Strega extract, and food color and mix well. Store in glass containers or bottles and let stand 30 days before using.

Makes about 1¹/2 quarts.

Note: Strega extract is generally available at Italian import grocery stores.

California Sangria

This Sangria owes its sunny flavor to fresh pineapple.

1 (750 ml) bottle dry, red wine, chilled
2 ounces brandy
2 tablespoons sugar
1 lemon, sliced

1 orange, sliced
1 cup fresh pineapple chunks, sliced peaches, pears, or any other seasonal fruit

COMBINE wine, brandy, and sugar in pitcher. Add lemon, orange, and pineapple chunks. Let stand 30 minutes in the refrigerator before serving. Serve with or without ice.

Makes 4 to 6 servings.

Sangria Blanca
(White Sangria)

Although the classic Sangria is made with red wine, this white-wine-based version makes a nice change.

1 (750 ml) bottle dry white wine
1/2 cup apple juice
1¹/2 ounces orange liqueur
2 tablespoons sugar
1 orange, thinly sliced

1/2 lemon, thinly sliced
1 lime, thinly sliced
1 cup fresh or frozen raspberries (optional)
Ice cubes

MIX wine, apple juice, liqueur, sugar, orange, lemon slices, lime slices, and raspberries in large pitcher. With wooden spoon, press fruit against sides and bottom of pitcher. Add ice cubes and stir to chill.

Makes about 6 servings.

Mock Champagne

²/₃ cup sugar
²/₃ cup water
1 cup grapefruit juice
¹/₂ cup orange juice

3 tablespoons grenadine syrup
1 (28-ounce) bottle ginger ale, chilled

When a nonalcoholic punch is needed, this is an excellent not-too-sweet champagne substitute.

COMBINE sugar and water in saucepan over low heat. Stir until sugar is dissolved. Bring to boil and boil 10 minutes. Cool. Add sugar syrup to grapefruit and orange juices. Chill thoroughly. Add grenadine and ginger ale just before serving.

Makes about 1¹/₂ quarts.

Liquid Lunch

³/₄ cup plain yogurt
³/₄ cup raspberry juice
¹/₂ cup crushed ice
1 banana, peeled and cut into pieces

8 strawberries, hulled
2 teaspoons lecithin
2 teaspoons bee pollen
1 teaspoon honey

COMBINE yogurt, raspberry juice, ice, banana, strawberries, lecithin, bee pollen, and honey in blender container. Blend at high speed until thick. Serve in chilled glasses.

Makes 2 servings.

Orange Eggnog

2 quarts milk
12 egg yolks
1 cup sugar
2 teaspoons vanilla

1 (6-ounce) can frozen orange
    juice concentrate, thawed
Meringue
Orange sections

HEAT milk in large heavy saucepan. Beat egg yolks with sugar. Stir in about 1 cup hot milk. Quickly stir into remaining hot milk and cook, stirring constantly, over very low heat until mixture thickens and coats a metal spoon. Remove from heat and add vanilla. Chill. Stir in undiluted orange concentrate. Pour into punch bowl. Float heaping tablespoons of Meringue on top of eggnog. Garnish with orange sections. To serve, include one portion of Meringue with each serving.

Makes 16 servings.

Meringue

12 egg whites
1/2 cup sugar

Beat egg whites until foamy. Add sugar, 2 tablespoons at a time, and continue beating until mixture stands in stiff peaks.

Holiday Eggnog

6 eggs, separated
1/2 cup sugar
4 cups milk
1/4 teaspoon salt

2 cups whipping cream
2 teaspoons vanilla
Nutmeg

BEAT egg yolks until light, add 1/4 cup sugar, and beat thoroughly. Scald milk and stir slowly into yolks. Cook slowly over low heat until mixture coats a metal spoon, stirring constantly. Chill. Several hours before serving, add salt to egg whites and beat until stiff, gradually adding remaining 1/4 cup sugar. Fold into custard mixture. Whip cream and fold into eggnog. Add vanilla. Chill several hours. To serve, ladle into punch cups and sprinkle lightly with nutmeg.

Makes about 24 servings.

Serenity Cocktail

1 tablespoon brewers' yeast
2 tablespoons powdered raw liver
2 teaspoons bone powder
2 teaspoons calcium gluconate
1/4 teaspoon magnesium oxide powder
1 teaspoon kelp granules
1 tablespoon wheat germ oil
1/4 cup soya lecithin

12 (250 to 500 mg) vitamin C tablets
2 tablespoons black strap molasses
1 banana, peeled and cut in pieces
1 apple, cored and chopped
1 (6-ounce) can frozen orange juice concentrate
Raw milk

Gladys Lindberg, well-known in the Los Angeles area for her health-food stores, has touted the virtues of the serenity cocktail to customers for years. Most health-food stores should be able to supply the ingredients.

COMBINE yeast, liver, bone powder, calcium, magnesium, kelp, wheat germ oil, lecithin, vitamin C, and molasses in blender container. Blend until thoroughly mixed. Add banana, apple, and orange juice and blend until smooth. Store in refrigerator. To make 1 drink, pour 1/6 of mixture in blender container. With blender running, add enough raw milk to reach desired consistency.

Makes 6 servings.

Tahn

2 cups plain yogurt
2 cups cold water

Dash salt
Ice cubes

Tahn, an unsweetened yogurt drink of Armenian origin, makes a refreshing contrast to the usual fruit and yogurt concoctions.

COMBINE yogurt, water, salt, and ice cubes and stir vigorously. Serve very cold.

Makes 4 servings.

Hi-Potency Drink

2 cups orange juice
1 ripe banana, peeled and cut in chunks
2 egg yolks

2 tablespoons honey
1 1/2 tablespoons raw wheat germ

Healthy drinks like this one from The Source restaurant in Hollywood are sought after by joggers and others who follow regular physical-fitness routines.

COMBINE orange juice, banana, yolks, honey, and wheat germ in blender container. Blend at high speed until smooth.

Makes 3 to 4 cups.

High-Protein Drink

1 cup vanilla honey ice milk
1 cup raw milk
1 banana, peeled and cut in
    chunks

3 pecans, broken
2 tablespoons raw wheat germ
2 tablespoons protein powder

COMBINE ice milk, raw milk, banana, pecans, wheat germ, and protein powder in blender container. Blend until smooth but still thick. Pour into chilled glass.

Makes 1 serving.

Hot Carob Cereal Drink

^{1}/$_3$ cup nonfat dry milk powder
 1 cup granola cereal
 1 tablespoon carob powder
^{1}/$_4$ teaspoon vanilla or 1
    teaspoon instant coffee
    powder

1 cup hot water
1 tablespoon honey

COMBINE milk powder, cereal, carob powder, and vanilla in blender container. Add hot water and honey and blend. Pour into 2 cups. Top with whipped cream sprinkled with additional granola, if desired.

Makes 2 servings.

Hot Spiced Cider

 1 gallon apple cider
1^1/$_2$ teaspoons whole allspice
1^1/$_2$ teaspoons cinnamon

^{1}/$_2$ teaspoon ground cloves
^{3}/$_4$ cup brown sugar, packed

COMBINE apple cider, allspice, cinnamon, cloves, and brown sugar. Bring to boil and simmer 5 minutes. Serve warm or chilled.

Makes 25 servings.

Orange Juliana

1 cup orange juice
1 cup crushed ice
2 tablespoons nonfat dry milk
    powder

1 egg white

A staff member's attempt to duplicate a popular fast-food orange drink resulted in Orange Juliana.

COMBINE orange juice, ice, nonfat dry milk, and egg white in blender container and blend until frothy. Pour into tall chilled glass.

Makes 1 serving.

Russian Tea Mix

2 cups orange drink mix
1 (3-ounce) package dry
    lemonade mix
3/4 cup instant tea powder

1¹/₃ cups sugar
1 teaspoon cinnamon
¹/₄ teaspoon ground cloves

A homemade spicy tea mix is a fine kitchen gift for tea lovers.

COMBINE orange drink mix, lemonade mix, instant tea powder, sugar, cinnamon, and cloves and mix well. Store in an airtight container. To make tea, use 2 to 3 tablespoons per cup boiling water.

Makes about 4¹/₂ cups mix.

Thai Tea

8 cups water
6 tablespoons Thai tea
    Sugar

Ice cubes
Half and half or sweetened
    condensed milk

Thai immigrants who opened restaurants in Southern California during the mid-1970s introduced a refreshing, delicious, thirst-quenching cold tea drink to West Coasters. This recipe came from the Krung Tep Thai restaurant in Tarzana.

BRING water to boil. Add tea and steep 5 minutes. Strain and season to taste with sugar. Cool, then chill in refrigerator. When ready to serve, place ice cubes in each of 6 tall glasses. Pour tea over ice, leaving room to add half and half to taste.

Makes 6 servings.

Note: Thai tea is available in Oriental and some specialty food markets.

Mexican Coffee

Coffee liqueur and tequila pep up this version of Mexican coffee, served at La Golondrina, a restaurant on Olvera Street in downtown Los Angeles.

5 ounces coffee liqueur
5 ounces tequila
2¼ cups hot black coffee

4 lemon wedges
Whipped cream
Maraschino cherries

COMBINE coffee liqueur, tequila, and hot coffee. Pour about 7 ounces each of the coffee mixture into 4 (9-ounce) stemmed glasses. Squeeze juice from a lemon wedge into each glass and mix. Drop wedge into glass. Top with a dollop of whipped cream and garnish with cherry.

Makes 4 servings.

Coffee Liqueur

When the holiday season rolls around, the requests for this coffee liqueur recipe multiply. It makes an unusual gift.

2 cups instant coffee powder
7 cups sugar
4 cups boiling water

1 quart vodka
1 vanilla bean

MIX coffee powder and sugar. Pour boiling water over coffee mixture and stir to dissolve. Cool. Stir in vodka. Drop vanilla bean into a ½-gallon bottle or jug and add vodka mixture. Seal and allow to stand 3 to 4 weeks.

Makes about 2½ quarts.

Café Cappuccino

1 cup water
2 tablespoons instant coffee
1 cup milk

2 teaspoons sugar
Cinnamon
Nutmeg

BRING water to a boil in small, heavy saucepan. Add instant coffee and stir until dissolved. Add milk and sugar. Heat to serving temperature. Beat until foamy. Sprinkle each serving with cinnamon and nutmeg.

Makes 2 cups.

San Francisco Irish Coffee

1¹/₄ ounces Irish whiskey
   Strong hot coffee

Sugar cubes (optional)
Whipped cream

Californians enjoy this Irish coffee as a wonderful nightcap after the theater or at the end of a day of skiing.

COMBINE whiskey and hot coffee in 6-ounce glass with holder. Season to taste with sugar cubes and stir to dissolve. Top with whipped cream.

Makes 1 serving.

When one finds a new recipe that sounds good, it often creates questions. How should it be served? What other foods will go well with it? Such questions arise more frequently where ethnic menus are concerned.

With that in mind, *The Times* food staff has put together a group of suggested menus based on recipes contained in this book. Recipes for most of the foods mentioned in these menus can be found by checking the index. A few very basic foods, such as corn on the cob, may be listed without the recipe being given.

The menus offered cover a wide range of meals—from elegant parties to do-it-yourself get-togethers for youngsters. All of these menus are typical of meals one might enjoy on occasion in Southern California.

Creating an appetizing and attractive menu is not always easy, so we hope these suggestions will help.

Chinese-Style Buffet Salad, page 90

LUNCHEON BY THE PACIFIC

Guests create their own salad by selecting from a variety of ingredients set out buffet-style.

Mai Tai

Won Ton Soup

Chinese-Style Buffet Salad

Fresh Coconut Cream Pie

White Wine   Iced Tea

BUSY-DAY SUPPER

The stew is assembled quickly, without prior browning of the meat, and simmers unattended. Brownies can be made in advance, keep well, and are an easy dessert.

Oven Beef Burgundy

Tossed Mixed Greens with Basic French Dressing

L. A. Savory Corn Bread

Fudgy Wudgy Brownies

Coffee   Milk

CHAMPAGNE BRUNCH

Whether the occasion is a wedding, a holiday gathering, or any special daytime meal for company, a brunch is an elegant, easy way to entertain.

Mimosa Cocktail

Roquefort Mousse Spread with Crackers

Baked Ham in Champagne

Cold Asparagus with Vinaigrette Dressing

Scones   Peach-Cantaloupe Jam

Fruit Basket   Fruit Juices

Finska Pinnar
(Finnish Fingers)

Coffee   Tea

ITALIAN DINNER

Marinated Squid

Minestrone

Veal Piccata

Risotto

Broccoli Strascicati

Strawberry Ice

Red Wine

Plentiful tender Pacific squid, when marinated, offers a promising start to an Italian dinner of lemony veal and stir-fried broccoli.

ELEGANT LUNCHEON ON THE TERRACE

Watercress Soup   Crackers

Chicken Fruit Salad in Pineapple Boats

Squaw Bread or Naan Bread

Davos Torte

White Wine   Iced Tea

Wedges of nutty-good Davos torte make a perfect ending to a luncheon featuring a main-dish salad beautifully presented in fresh pineapple shells.

DELUXE LOS ANGELES DINNER

Flaming Spinach Salad

Hobo Steak

Pommes Boulanger

Green Beans with Almonds

Chocolate Mousse Pie

Cabernet Sauvignon or other red wine

Despite the name "Hobo" attached to the steak, this is a luxury menu for an occasion when expense and calories are not an issue.

GOURMET POTLUCK PICNIC

With proper planning and the delegation of dishes to willing cooks, a potluck can become a no-fuss, successful picnic party. The white sangria will travel well in a vacuum bottle.

Sangria Blanca

Picnic Pâté   Cheese Crock Blend   Melba Rounds

Spicy Marinated Mushrooms

Meatballs

Cold Sliced Chicken Breasts Tarragon

Mustard Ring Mold   Creamy Coleslaw

*French Rolls   Roman Bread

Crisp Apples   Grapes

Fudge Satin Pie

Hot or Iced Tea or Coffee

CELEBRATION BARBECUE

When the season is right for outdoor dining, gather friends around and celebrate the good weather with an abundance of good food. The creamy smooth dessert is a cool finale for the succulent barbecued meat and zesty salads and vegetables.

Minted Berry Soup

Barbecued Country-Style Pork Ribs or Barbecued Beef

Santa Maria Beans

Beer Potato Salad   Tossed Mixed Greens with Creamy Mustard
Dressing

Brantley Peppers   *Corn on the Cob

Garlic Bread

*Assorted Melon Wedges   *Fresh Pineapple Fingers

Frozen Mocha Toffee Dessert

Beer   *Punch   Iced Tea

*Recipe not included in this book

384

VEGETARIAN SUPPER

Peanut Butter Soup

Zucchini Lasagna

Grapefruit and Spinach Salad

Yugoslav Carrot Cake

Thai Tea

Refreshingly cold Thai tea is a delightful finishing touch for this meatless supper of rich textures and tastes—a meal for all seasons.

SEAFOOD MENU I

Shrimp Boiled in Beer

Grilled Swordfish with Barbecue Sauce

Greek Salad

Zucchini Sauté

Kiwi Ice

White Wine

Shrimp boiled in beer offers a different way to begin a seafood dinner and teams well with the flaky texture and barbecue flavor of the grilled swordfish.

SEAFOOD MENU II

Marinated Cracked Dungeness Crab

Sand Dabs Meunière

Tossed Mixed Greens with Caesar Dressing

Asparagus with Browned Butter

Lemon Rice

Watermelon Salad Boat

Iced Tea

Dungeness crab and sand dabs are two indigenous Pacific seafood specialties that complement each other well. When paired in a meal that offers accompaniments of lightly cooked asparagus, lemon-accented rice, and a fresh fruit dessert, they can be properly appreciated.

LOW-CALORIE GOURMET SUPPER

This menu shows how flavor and originality can coexist with calorie-consciousness. Vegetables are steamed with chicken to provide extra nourishment, the salad dressing tastes rich and zesty, and the iced dessert is refreshingly tart-sweet.

Cold Cucumber Soup

Steamed Chicken and Vegetables

Tossed Greens and Mushrooms with Low-Calorie Tomato Dressing

Kiwi Ice

Coffee

JAPANESE DINNER

The popularity of Japanese cuisine is explained by its colorful presentations and use of a wide variety of ingredients, as exemplified in this dinner. Browned pork is served over fluffy white rice, complemented by crisply fried vegetables. Although westerners might not expect to find dessert on such a menu, this one suggests mouth-refreshing strawberry ice.

Wined Teriyaki Strips

Katsu Donburi

Vegetable Tempura

Crisp Lettuce with Oriental Salad Dressing

Hot Tea   Strawberry Ice   Sake

CALIFORNIA-STYLE MEXICAN DINNER

A typical combination plate at Mexican restaurants in California would include enchiladas, rice, and beans. Sopa de albóndigas, or meatball soup, is almost always on the menu, as is guacamole, which can be added as an appetizer or accompaniment.

Margarita

Sopa de Albóndigas

Chicken Enchiladas

Mexican Rice

Spicy Refried Beans

*Corn Tortillas

California Flan or Fried Mexican Ice Cream

Mexican Coffee

*Available where Mexican foods are sold

MEXICAN BRUNCH

Tequila Sunrise

Huevos Rancheros

Spicy Refried Beans

Assorted Fruits

Conchas or Sopaipillas

Coffee   Hot Chocolate

Fried eggs served on tortillas and topped with a sauce of tomatoes, onions, garlic, and green chiles are the outstanding centerpiece of this brunch. Spice the hot chocolate with cinnamon for a more typically Mexican flavor.

MIDDLE EASTERN PARTY

Cheese Triangles

Falafel Sandwiches

Taboulleh

Melon Slices, Dates, Pistachio Nuts, and Almonds

*Turkish Coffee

Place the ingredients for the sandwiches in separate serving dishes and pile freshly made pita breads in a basket. Include cubes of feta cheese along with the falafel, if desired. Turkish coffee is a rich blend available in most gourmet food sections.

DO-AHEAD PATIO PARTY

Bloody Mary

Apple-Curry Soup

Poached Salmon with Pink Mayonnaise

Molded Egg Salad

Bibb Lettuce and Sliced Kiwi Fruit with Poppy-Seed Dressing

Bruschetta (Heart-Shaped Garlic Rolls)   *Hot Dinner Rolls

Pavlova

Espresso

Everything on this menu, from the fragrant chilled soup to the spectacular meringue dessert, is prepared in advance. Only the lettuce and sliced kiwi fruit should be tossed with the dressing at the last moment.

*Recipe not included in this book

387

THANKSGIVING DINNER

The aromatic fruit-and-rice stuffing for the turkey provides a colorful change from the usual holiday menu, and the traditional pumpkin dessert appears in two out-of-the-ordinary treatments.

Consommé Madrilène

Roast Turkey with Dried Fruit-Rice Stuffing

Creamed Spinach   Magic Carrots

Mystery Tomato Mold

Corn Relish   Watermelon Pickles

Squaw Bread

Cold Pumpkin Soufflé or Ribbon Pumpkin Pie

Champagne, Sparkling Burgundy, or White Wine

Coffee

INTERNATIONAL CHRISTMAS OPEN HOUSE

This rich stew in its own fresh pumpkin tureen always provokes conversation, as will the crisp marinated chicken wings and the many-layered creamy trifle.

Orange Eggnog

Chicken Wings Pacifica

Stuffed Mushrooms, Italian-Style

Argentinian Stew in a Pumpkin Shell

Spanish Rice Salad

Curried Peas

Pineapple-Macadamia Nut Bread   Papaya Bread

Trifle

Chocolate-Dipped Strawberries

California Sangría

PASTA PARTY

Caponata with Crackers

Provolone   Mortadella   Water-Packed Mozzarella

Linguine with White Clam Sauce

Sicilian Mostaccioli

Garlic Bread

Three Bean Salad

Lemon Snow

Chianti   Café Cappuccino

For an appealing beginning to this Italian dinner, set out a heaping bowl of caponata and arrange alternate slices of provolone and mortadella around a serving platter with the mozzarella in the center. The double main course of a white and a red pasta dish turns this meal into a pasta party.

COCKTAIL BUFFET

Caviar Mold

Oaxacan Nuts

Hot Brie with Toasted Almonds

Stuffed Chinese Pea Pods

Napa Valley Chicken Wings

Indonesian Meatballs

Chipped Beef Dip   Celery Sticks or Crackers

Fresh Fruit Platter

White Wine   Mock Champagne   Mixed Drinks

Sparkling Mineral Water

Many of the dishes on this festive menu can be prepared ahead of time. When presented together, the visual effect is as impressive as the variety of tastes. White wine and mineral water with a squeeze of lime are more popular with fitness-conscious Californians than stronger drinks.

*The avocado soup may be
served from a vacuum bottle
hot or chilled. Mix the salad
just before serving and keep the
monkey bread warm. Chilled
champagne is poured over
berries in stemmed glasses.*

HOLLYWOOD BOWL PICNIC

Chilled Dry Sherry

Avocado Soup

Salad Niçoise

Monkey Bread

Strawberries in Champagne

Chinese Almond Cookies

Hot or Iced Tea or Coffee

INDEX

Asterisks (*) indicate restaurants.

Banana bread, *illus. 288,* 290
Banana daiquiri, 366
Banana pops, frozen chocolate-
    covered, 358
Barbecue:
    beans, 231
    beef:
        ribs, 212
        shoulder roast, 214
    butterflied lamb, *illus. 192,* 194
    chicken:
        with honey-mustard sauce, 173
        spicy, 173
    Korean (bul kogi), 213
    menu, 384
    pork, 221
        chops, 223
        country-style ribs, 223
    rancho sauce, 214
    sauce, 224
    swordfish, 105
Barley mushroom soup, 54
Bass, baked, with vegetables, 109
Bastilla, March of Dimes, 178
Bean noodles, 125
Bean(s):
    barbecued, 231
    black, Cuban-style, 239
    burgundy, 240
    chili:
        chasing, 207
        Cleopatra Smith's, 238
        Polly Bergen's, 206
        vegetarian, 250
    green:
        with almonds, 240
        marinated, 241
    Julie's bean dish, 241
    lima bean health loaf, 242
    refried, 17, 157
        spicy, 240
    Santa Maria, 238
    soup, 57
    three bean salad, 85
Bean threads, 12
Beatles (chocolate chip cookies), 353
Beef, 203–18
    and asparagus, 234
    barbecued shoulder roast, 214
    braised stuffed roll, 210
    chile verde, 224
    firehouse casserole, 210
    ground (*see also* Chili):
        Albanian burger steaks, 205
        guacamole burgers, 205
        Joe's Special, 159
        loaf, 204
        one pot pasta dinner, 136
        Sloppy Joes, Josés, Giovannis,
            Josefs, 208–9
        tacos, 284
    jerky, 218
    Mongolian, 216
    Oriental-style broccoli-beef, 215

Beef *(cont.)*
    rib eye roast, for French dip
        sandwich, 280
    ribs:
        barbecued, 212
        braised short ribs, 214
        deviled, with mustard sauce, 213
        Diablo, 227
        Korean barbecue, 213
        sticky bones, 212
    salad, 86
        taco salad, 84
    satay, 25
    stew:
        Argentinian, in a pumpkin shell,
            217
        burgundy, 216
        Paul Lynde's, 218
    stir-fried, with oyster sauce, 215
    wined teriyaki strips, 22
    See also Steak
Beer, shrimp boiled in, 119
Beer bread, 299
Beer potato salad, 73
*Bel-Air Hotel, 122
*Belle Helene, La, St. Helena, 325
*Benihana of Tokyo, Los Angeles, 100
Bergen, Polly, 206
Bergin, Tom, 257
*Bernard's restaurant, Los Angeles, 46
Berry ice cream, 329
Berry minted soup, 48
Beurre blanc, 115
Beverages, 363–77
    alcoholic, 364–70 (*see also*
        Cocktails; Daiquiris;
        Margaritas)
        California Sangria, 370
        coffee liqueur, 376
        Galliano-type liqueur, 370
        Sangria blanca, 370
    non-alcoholic, 363, 371–75
        high-protein drink, 374
        hi-potency drink, 373
        holiday eggnog, 372
        hot carob cereal drink, 374
        hot spiced cider, 374
        liquid lunch, 371
        mock champagne, 371
        orange eggnog, 372
        orange Juliana, 375
        Russian tea mix, 375
        serenity cocktail, 373
        tahn, 373
        Thai tea, 375
    See also Coffee
*Bicycle Shop restaurant, Santa
    Monica, 99
*Biltmore Hotel, Los Angeles, 213,
    227
Biscuits, buttermilk, 304
*Bistro, The, Beverly Hills, 322
*Blair's luncheonette, Los Angeles,
    204

Bloody Mary, 369
Bloomingdale, Mrs. Alfred, 27
*Blue Bayou restaurant, Disneyland,
    282
Blue cheese dressing, 96
    mock, 98
Blue cheese soufflé:
    herbed, 148
    yogurt, 147
Blue-cheese-stuffed eggs, 160
Blum, Walter, 332
*Blum's tearoom, Beverly Hills, 335
Bombay salad, 77
Borracho lentil soup, 57
Bouillabaisse, 104
Bourbon nut cake, 334
Braised short ribs, 214
Braised stuffed meat roll, 210
Braised turkey wings, 187
Braised veal shanks, Milan-style, 198
Bran muffins, 304
    dark moist, 303
Brantley peppers, 259
Bread, 289–304
    banana, *illus. 288,* 290
    beer, 299
    brown, 298
    cracker, Armenian (lavash), 295
    garlic, 295
    Hungarian loaf, 294
    Indian fry, 299
    monkey, 292
    naan, 300
    papaya, *illus. 288,* 290
    pineapple-macadamia nut, *illus.
        288,* 290
    pita, 294
    pumpkin, 298
    Roman, 293
    savory corn, 296
    scones, 297
    spoon, 297
    squaw, 293
    sweet, 291
    sweet corn, 296
    whole wheat, 292
    zucchini, 299
    See also Muffins; Rolls
Bread crumbs, kinds of, 10
Bread pudding, 345
    double-boiler, 345
Bresnik, Les, 54
Brie, hot, with toasted almonds, 41
*Broadway department stores, 243,
    299, 326
Broccoli:
    beef, Oriental-style, 215
    Chantilly, 255
    cheese soup, 56
    citrus bake, 253
    lemon broccoli, 254
    and mushroom casserole, 253
    stir-fried:
        with mushrooms, 237

PICTURE CREDITS

Food Stylists

Edena Sheldon: Jacket, Soups, Salad Dressings, Eggs, Sandwiches, Pies
Alfred Beck: Appetizers
Elizabeth W. James: Salads
Mary Ann Parshall: Pasta & Rice, Beef
Antonia Allegra Griffin; Fish & Shellfish
Julia Weinberg: Chicken, Relishes & Preserves
Justine Frank and Virginia Gray: Turkey & Duck, Desserts
Joan Dektar: Lamb & Veal, Menus
Carolyn Murray: Breads
Betsy Balsley: Beverages

Photographers

Jerry Fruchtman: Jacket, Appetizers, Salad Dressings, Pasta & Rice, Pies
Brian Leatart: Soups
Richard Fukuhara: Salads
Friend & Denny Productions: Fish & Shellfish
Brent Bear: Eggs
Hans Albers: Chicken, Ham & Pork
Doug Kennedy: Turkey & Duck, Beef, Desserts
Phillip Cripps: Vegetables, Lamb & Veal
Tom Engler: Relishes & Preserves
Marshal Safron: Sandwiches
Chuck O'Rear: Breads
Lawrence Bessel: Beverages
Jay Ahrend: Menus

The color photographs in this book were created for HOME, the Sunday magazine section of the *Los Angeles Times.*

The black-and-white drawings were created specially for this book by *Glenn Wolff.*